MASS

BEHAVIOR IN

BATTLE

AND

CAPTIVITY

MASS BEHAVIOR IN BATTLE AND CAPTIVITY

THE COMMUNIST SOLDIER IN THE KOREAN WAR

RESEARCH STUDIES DIRECTED BY
WILLIAM C. BRADBURY

EDITED BY
Samuel M. Meyers and Albert D. Biderman

THE UNIVERSITY OF CHICAGO PRESS

Chicago   *London*

Library of Congress Catalog Card Number: 68–16705

THE UNIVERSITY OF CHICAGO PRESS, CHICAGO 60637
The University of Chicago Press, Ltd., London, W.C.1

© *1968 by The University of Chicago*

Published 1968

Printed in the United States of America

FOREWORD

The Korean conflict and its aftermath led to widespread attention to and interest in the behavior of prisoners of war. Very different popular images developed about the presumed behavior of Americans under captivity in contrast to that of the Chinese and North Koreans. First, events such as the riots in the prisoner-of-war compounds on Koje-do Island conveyed an image of the Chinese and North Korean prisoners under United States military control as fanatically active and rebellious against their captors. Second, highly publicized "germ warfare" confessions of American personnel, the reports from sick and wounded prisoners repatriated in 1953, and subsequent writings in the mass media—all led to a picture of Americans captured by the Chinese as weak, supine, and brainwashed.

It was even claimed by some writers that the Americans failed to show the will to live and to survive which human beings normally demonstrate. The behavior of these troops was judged to be weak, both physically and morally. Because these soldiers were ideologically unprepared, they could not resist their Communist captors and therefore collaborated with the enemy in a fashion which was unprecedented for Americans. The fighting men of other United Nations were tougher and more heroic. As a result, these accounts of Americans as prisoners of war in Korea were used as a basis for criticizing American society and for denouncing its moral degeneration and lack of civic virtue.

The research efforts and publications of Albert Biderman, among others, have served to counteract such distortions, although these beliefs still persist. Americans in Communist prisoner-of-war compounds behaved very much like other human beings in terms of the amount of shock they experienced and the severity of the pressure applied. There was considerable variation in their behavior which could be linked to the battle situation, the journey to the camp sites, the conditions of the camp, and to the manner in which they were treated by Chinese authorities on a day-to-day basis.

Chinese efforts at brainwashing were rather ineffective, given their expenditure of effort. Although there was an American "style" in captivity, national differences were grossly exaggerated. Ideological indoctrination—or its absence—seems in retrospect to have been a minor factor in conditioning resistance to Chinese Communist tactics of pressure and persuasion. No doubt some of the troops captured in the initial outbreak of hostilities had not been exposed to adequate levels of training. Intensive military training supplies a basis for group solidarity after capture. To some degree, troops can be prepared for life in a prisoner-of-war compound, but the limits on such preparation are great.

There was a great deal of suffering and personal tragedy, but the actual story did not reflect unfavorably on the troops and on American society. If one is to pass moral judgment, it must relate to the observation that the ground forces, which sustained the bulk of the casualties in the field and made up most of the captives, were mainly drawn from lower socio-economic groups. This was the result of both the working of Selective Service and the system of manpower allocation within the military establishment. To some limited degree, these factors may have affected the group response in the prisoner-of-war compounds, in that a more representative force might have behaved somewhat differently. Certainly, a democratic society cannot afford to allow one social group to bear the brunt of battle and captivity.

There is also another issue in the prisoner-of-war story in the Korean War. It is necessary to explain the behavior of Communist prisoners, especially the Chinese, whose behavior was in some respects truly unprecedented. The Chinese soldiers fought well under very difficult circumstances, even though after capture many revealed that they had long-standing disaffection from the Chinese authority structure. Chinese command and control, which incorporated elaborate communication procedures, were effective and achieved their objectives. Immediately after capture these soldiers were highly docile and most cooperative to an unanticipated extent.

Subsequently, small groups of Communist and anti-Communist activists battled physically for control of individual compounds. Whichever group achieved control was able to extend its management over most of the prisoners. The controlling group could induce extreme mass behavior. The resulting demonstrations were either anti-American or anti-Communist, depending upon the political orientation of the leadership. The lack of trained American personnel and the failure of camp commanders to recognize the political nature of these intra-compound struggles contributed to the outbursts.

A similar situation had been known in prisoner-of-war camps during World War II, although perhaps not to the same extent. However, the most astounding aspect of the Chinese Communist prisoner-of-war behavior is the fact that at the time of repatriation 14,325 of the 21,014 Chinese captured refused to return home, in contrast to the 22 Americans of 4,450. Such behavior was unprecedented in the annals of modern history, but in crucial respects the Chinese Communist forces were not modern—a source of both strength and weakness. Thus, in effect,

the American image of American prisoners had an element of truth—
if it was applied to the Chinese soldier rather than to the American.

In an effort to provide an understanding of these events, this volume
presents a unique set of research studies. These studies were prepared
in response to an official request by the military authorities, seeking a
fuller understanding of the Chinese Communist indoctrination system
and its influence on prisoner-of-war behavior. These studies are, so to
speak, applied research. But this distinction can be overdrawn, for the
work was done by social scientists who had a theoretical point of view
and who strived to maintain a sense of detachment.

The field conditions for doing this research were hardly ideal, but
that was part of the setting which needed to be taken into account. The
organization for social research by the military during the Korean conflict was also most cumbersome, and hardly reflected the experiences
and knowledge gained during World War II. In addition, the work was
hampered by professional differences among the specialists themselves.

Nevertheless, data were collected which constitute the only materials
in depth on these Communist prisoners of war. In the course of these
events, William C. Bradbury was involved in the field-work phase of the
research; later, as task leader, he came to have a deep influence on the
conduct of the research, especially in the analysis phase. For this reason
we speak of these studies as being "directed" by him.

In the introduction and in the text of the volume, the reader will be
repeatedly reminded of the limitations of these data. But they are based
on direct observation by research scholars with the raw human material
on which the Chinese Communist system is based. These pages reflect
the aspirations and struggles for an objective and detached perspective
on what is one of the most difficult and emotionally tinged subjects of
the contemporary period—the Chinese indoctrination and social-control
system. In their own view, clearly the Chinese government developed an
effective control system over their troops which emphasized a continuous flow of communication and interpersonal interaction. When this
system was disrupted by defeat in battle, the individual soldier revealed
the extent to which the norms of the system had not been fully internalized. In captivity, the control system was partly reestablished.
Again, because of the underlying failure to achieve effective and extensive internalization, significant numbers of soldiers deserted when
given an opportunity to change allegiance.

The notion of citizenship as an expression of loyalty to a modern state
has been slow in developing; it took hundreds of years in the West. Despite the asset of traditional loyalties, the Chinese Communist efforts
to speed up this process can be judged as only partly successful as of
1950. The social turmoil and unrest of 1967 continue to attest to the
complexities of the task.

Therefore, these materials are more than an analysis of prisoner-of-
war behavior and the impact of captivity. They constitute an important

document about social relations and political integration in Communist China. They supply one of the few sources for understanding conflict and mass behavior in contemporary China. The reasons are twofold. First, the Chinese Communist political and social system must be studied at a distance, or by the use of a small number of highly selected refugees. This is a profound limitation, especially in the study of social control and mass behavior. By contrast, these materials, together with Alexander George's study of captured Chinese soldiers, are based on direct contact with much more representative and larger samples of the population. The special character of the present sample—namely, that they are members of the armed forces—is an advantage in that it is possible to relate personal responses to the institutional setting from which they came.

Second, and even more important, is that these studies were undertaken from a vantage point which was at variance with most research on China. Until recently, and certainly at the time of the Korean War, scholarship on China was the almost exclusive domain of a group of area and language specialists. These men stressed mastery of the details of Chinese language, with little regard for systematic conceptual analysis. They had developed an almost mystic concern with their subject matter which hindered a truly critical approach. In particular, the intellectual posture of the specialists at that time avoided an examination of socialization, social control, and mass behavior. By contrast, the men who prepared the studies in this volume had distinct advantages because of their different perspective. They were outsiders without preconceptions; they were not unduly influenced by, or in awe of, their subject matter; and, most important of all, they had commitments to academic disciplines and intellectual perspectives. They were social scientists who did not avoid a concern with social, psychological issues.

The publication of these studies is designed to make available a body of data and a set of interpretations both to those interested in the China field and to those concerned with political warfare and the consequences of captivity. It is also a posthumous recognition of the contribution of William C. Bradbury, whose life was tragically ended in 1958. The idea of the book was originally discussed in the proceedings of the Inter-University Seminar on Armed Forces and Society. The objective was to assemble materials written by William C. Bradbury and by others in the project. Funds from the Inter-University Seminar supported by the Russell Sage Foundation were used in the work of assembling and editing the documents.

Special appreciation is extended to Albert Biderman for diligently and persistently taking the necessary steps to have the publication restrictions on these materials removed. Machinery exists in the federal government to make this possible, but his was the human effort which made the machinery work.

As a posthumous document, it is particularly appropriate that this book should be published by the University of Chicago Press. From the moment of his arrival on the University of Chicago campus, William C. Bradbury was involved in its intellectual and community life. He devoted much of his professional efforts to the life of The College, with its strong emphasis on interdisciplinary social science and with its concern with social values and social policy. He also plunged into the collective efforts of the University of Chicago and its neighborhood community in pioneering efforts to reconstruct, on an inter-racial basis, the surrounding areas. He was an active community leader, who worked through a particularly bitter period and who was convinced of the moral necessity of his efforts.

It seems fitting that these research efforts should be published at a period when this reconstruction effort is finally coming to an end. Likewise, because the intellectual issues of understanding Chinese mass behavior are contemporary, the tragedy is not in the delay in the publication of these findings but in the fact that William Bradbury cannot note how central and highly relevant his efforts continue to be.

MORRIS JANOWITZ

Center for Social Organization Studies
University of Chicago

ACKNOWLEDGMENTS

This volume could not have been prepared without the help and encouragement of Meredith Crawford, Director, Human Resources Research Office, George Washington University, in whose organization the studies reported here were originally done. We appreciate also the help of Saul Lavisky, Research Information Coordinator of that organization, for handling the various administrative and coordinative details involved. We also wish to thank the Office of the Adjutant General and the Office for the Freedom of Information, Department of the Army, for granting access to the necessary documents, as well as for facilitating final clearance of this volume.

S. M. M.
A. D. B.

CONTENTS

PART III

Socio-Political Behavior of Koreans and Chinese as Prisoners of War

FIGURES

INTRODUCTION

During the Korean War (1950–53), the United Nations forces faced armies of Communist soldiers from North Korea and China for the first time in their history. The behavior of these soldiers, initially as combat fighters and then as prisoners of war, was so substantially different from what was expected that it was labeled "unprecedented" and "strange."

But, how was this behavior strange? First, in battle the Chinese troops showed good discipline and courage; few surrendered unless their combat situation was acutely unfavorable. Yet interrogation of prisoners and their subsequent behavior as prisoners suggested strongly that dissatisfaction was widespread and disaffection serious in the Chinese Communist Forces.[1] How could this be? What was there about the system of military-political control that could produce such excellent soldiers in the face of what seemed to be such widespread dissatisfaction?

Second, as prisoners of war, the behavior of both the North Koreans and the Chinese was found to be strikingly unusual in three respects. (1) The prisoners divided into militant factions—pro-Communist and anti-Communist—fighting bloody, life-and-death battles for domination of their prison compounds. While squabbles between individual prisoners or between small groups of prisoners have, of course, occurred in modern warfare, prisoners usually have tended to live peaceably under the conditions of internment. (2) The Communist-led prisoners resisted United Nations custodial authority persistently, violently, and in a highly disciplined way. Further, resistance against custodial authority is by no means unknown in modern warfare. Such resistance has, however, generally been sporadic and passive, and has been carried out more often by loosely constituted groups rather than by highly organized groups. (3) When a truce seemed likely, thousands of prisoners under anti-Communist leadership addressed urgent petitions to the United Nations begging to be allowed to remain in non-Communist ter-

[1] It was military as well as newspaper practice in the United States to use this name for the Chinese forces (and the initials CCF) rather than their proper, propagandistic label, the People's Liberation Army, and the Communists' designation of the units in Korea as Chinese Volunteers.

ritory. This aggressive loyalty to the government of the Republic of Korea or Nationalist China, as the case might be, created serious problems for the United Nations custodial authorities during the last stages of the war. This kind of mass resistance to repatriation has been almost unknown in modern warfare until very recent times.

How could one explain such behavior? To answer this central question, the Psychological Warfare Section of the Human Resources Research Office, George Washington University, was asked by the United States Army early in 1953 to undertake studies of the Chinese and North Korean prisoners of war who were then in the custody of the United Nations forces.[2] This volume is based upon reports of those studies.

This volume is in three parts. The first part, "Loyalty and Disaffection in Chinese Communist Soldiers," contains an analysis by William C. Bradbury and Jeane J. Kirkpatrick, "Determinants of Loyalty and Disaffection in Chinese Communist Soldiers during the Korean Hostilities."[3] An extensive discussion of the rationale for making broad generalizations on the basis of a select sample is drawn from the original Bradbury and Kirkpatrick report. The second part, "Chinese Responses to Communist Military-Political Control," includes three reports: "The Role of Traditional Orientations toward Social Relations in Chinese Responses to Communist Military-Political Control," by Samuel M. Meyers; "Wang-Tsun Ming, Anti-Communist: An Autobiographical Account of Chinese Communist Thought Reform"; and "Adjustment of Chinese Soldiers to the Communist Demand for Ideological Participation," by Jeane J. Kirkpatrick and Pio D. Uliassi. The third and final part deals with the "Socio-political Behavior of Koreans and Chinese as Prisoners of War," and is based on a report by Samuel M. Meyers and William C. Bradbury: "The Political Behavior of Korean and Chinese Prisoners of War in the Korean Conflict: A Historical Analysis."

All these reports were completed ten or more years ago, and one may ask why are they being published now.

First, their publication constitutes a memorial to the late William C. Bradbury, associate professor of sociology, University of Chicago, under whose direction these studies were carried out. The approximately two and a half years that he spent working for the Human Resources Research Office on a leave of absence from the University of Chicago had a profound effect upon him. This experience changed the entire course of his career. As a result of the work he undertook there, he became

---

[2] While the war was fought in the name of the United Nations, the United States Army in fact bore almost exclusively the burden of administering the prisoner-of-war population.

[3] This volume contains reports originally prepared by the Human Resources Research Office. Editorial changes and deletions of material of no significance to the general reader, have been made by the editors. The Human Resources Research Office assumes no responsibility for such changes.

deeply interested in Chinese affairs. When he returned to the university, he began to prepare himself as a specialist on the Far East through formal language and area study. He was thus engaged at the time of his death.

A second reason for publishing this material is that it illustrates the scholarly contribution that can derive from crash studies that social scientists have frequently been called upon to perform for military agencies. Sometimes, initially—as was true in these studies—national interest considerations may require that the work carry a classified label. All too often such work remains forever unpublished, despite its significance and interest to the academic community. This is one reason why scholars are reluctant to work on projects which carry security restrictions. The passage of time, however, may make the original security classification unnecessary, and it was Bradbury's intention to seek open publication of these materials for the academic community. Since his death, this effort has been too long delayed.

Still a third reason—the major one—for the publication of this work now is that the editors regard the material contained in the reports as still intrinsically and singularly valuable. At the time this study was initiated, Communist China was still consolidating its position on the Chinese mainland, and North Korea had been under Communist control for only eight years. Little competent knowledge of the techniques of political-military control was then readily available. The twenty-one thousand Chinese and the one hundred fifty thousand North Korean prisoners of war in United Nations prison camps provided excellent sources for informants about these matters. Unlike so much of our knowledge regarding Oriental Communist practices, this study was not based on the testimony of highly self-selected refugees. Persons, who by the vagaries of war happen to be captured, afford a different and, perhaps, less biased selection of informants regarding a society than the refugee. The military institution of this period of Chinese history had a particular significance. In addition to contributing specifically to the understanding of Communist authority patterns, the studies also contribute perspectives to the lively discussions among American scholars of Chinese brainwashing and prisoner-of-war behavior. The present material provides an interesting contrast to the studies of the behavior of Americans who were captured during that same year.

These studies are among the earliest which examined Chinese Communist thought-reform efforts in a disenchanted and dispassionate manner. Then, as now, brainwashing was the fashionable way to explain the kinds of extreme shifts in behavior and allegiance manifest among the Chinese prisoners. The project staff probably never completely freed itself from some of the preconceptions about brainwashing that were then universally accepted. However, its members had backgrounds which helped them avoid accepting brainwashing theories that begged more questions than they answered. Further, the political flip-flops of masses of prisoners who became violently anti-Communist in the United Nations prison camps raised serious objections to accepting some of the more extremely overdramatized conceptions of the durable potency of brainwashing.

While these reports were being prepared, and for several years afterward, both scholarly and public thinking about Chinese Communist control methods were misdirected by sensationalized accounts and theoretical formulations.[4] Biderman has traced the gradual emergence of scientifically detached discussions of these Communist practices.[5] He attributed the slowness of this development in part to the selected nature of the subjects in the studies of Chinese and Westerners released from captivity in the mid-fifties. Another factor involved the difficulties of gaining detached perspectives in the studies of released American prisoners of war. Had these studies been published earlier, they might have greatly hastened the debunking process he described and the subsequent development of scientific comprehension of thought reform.

Finally, this material is published to demonstrate some of the difficulties and accommodations that must be made in doing interdisciplinary work. The project staff was composed of sociologists, anthropologists, psychologists, and political scientists, and they experienced the frustrations that normally occur in interdisciplinary activities—those that have been written about in the literature. Moreover, divergent methodological perspectives toward doing research affected the relationships between the project staff and the Human Resources Research Office (HumRRO) organization. HumRRO was committed to a rigorous, quantitative, controlled-experiment methodology. The project staff, on the other hand, was more qualitative in orientation. They were willing to accept perhaps less rigorous, but certainly different, ideas of valid evidence and inference. These differences between permanent research officials of HumRRO and project personnel created difficult problems for the latter, since reports had to be approved by HumRRO before distribution of the reports could be made. Some of these difficulties and how they were resolved will be discussed later.

As indicated earlier, the research reported here was formally initiated in January, 1953, but not until the summer of that year was a research plan approved and the administrative arrangements made to send a research team to Korea to do the field work.[6]

   [4] Edward Hunter, *Brainwashing in Red China* and *Brainwashing: The Story of Men Who Defied It;* Joost A. H. Meerloo, "The Crime of Menticide," 107, 594–98, and "Pavlovian Strategy as a Weapon of Menticide," pp. 809–13.
   [5] Albert D. Biderman, "The Image of Brainwashing," 26, 547–63.
   [6] The major task of the team was to conduct interviews with Chinese and North Korean prisoners of war. The team included three members of HumRRO: Robert M. Beezer, Alvin G. Edgell, and Reuben Goldstein. Four others were from the University of Chicago: Joseph D. Lohman, Lloyd E. Ohlin, William C. Bradbury, and Samuel M. Meyers. Lohman, a criminologist and penologist, participated in some of the initial planning of the research, particularly in those aspects relating to prisoner-of-war behavior, since it was conjectured that there might be some similar-

The team arrived in Korea on July 28, 1953—the day after the truce was signed. The urgency to do the interviewing before the respondents —prisoners of war—would be gone was now greatly intensified. The team leader, who had arrived in Korea in advance of the research team, now concluded that it was not practical to follow the plan that had originally been prepared. He informed the team in Korea that they were to orient their interviewing toward two topics: the military and political control exercised by the Communists, and the unusual events that had occurred within the prisoner-of-war compounds. The team was told little more than that. There was no time to prepare written schedules or interviewing guides to follow. There was no explicit theoretical under-pinnings agreed upon. The team had little or no knowledge of the Far East and limited knowledge of Communist organization and doctrine. The study turned out to be prototypically a "quick and dirty" endeavor.

Since all the reports were based on substantially the same data— interviews from the field—the method for the collection of the data will be discussed here rather than repeated for each individual report.

It was apparent from the start that non-random sampling of prisoners was the only possible course. The press of time and the fact that plans were already under way momentarily to move prisoners out of the camps precluded any other alternative. The team decided that in the circumstances they should select prisoners who had had a wide range of experience in the Communist system and who had knowledge of events within the prisoner-of-war compounds. The team wanted men who were competent observers and reporters of social, especially organi-zational, phenomena. This meant that the interviews would be long and intensive, that relatively few men could be interviewed so intensively within the limited time available, that questions and answers would vary substantially from one interview to another, and that the interview data from each respondent would be complex and rich. The acceptance of these requirements for the interviews committed the analysts to the use of predominantly qualitative methods.

But how could one select such informants? No information source in the prison camps was adequate to pre-screen reliably and pinpoint the selection of desirable informants. Overt leaders in the prisoner organi-zations *could* be picked out, however, and certain prisoners had been segregated because they held high rank in the Chinese Communist Forces or in the North Korean army, because they were rejected by the dominant prisoner organizations in individual compounds, because they had changed their repatriation choices after the initial screening in

ities between civil prison rioting and the rioting that occurred in the prisoner-of-war camps. He was also appointed to lead the field team, and it was at his request that the other three members from the University of Chicago were selected to go to Korea (two of whom were also specialists in criminology and penology). These three members joined the team about two days before leaving for Korea. They had little advance idea of the problem or study plan, having had a briefing of only a few days before departing for Korea.

1952,[7] or because they had taken leading parts in prison camp riots. Beyond such ambiguous or incomplete guides as these, it was necessary to rely on the judgments of American compound officers, the interpreters, and even the prisoners themselves for the selection of appropriate informants.

With few exceptions, the interviews were conducted within the prison enclosures. Secluded areas in which to interview were almost always provided by the camp command, although on occasion informants were interviewed out in the open. The interviewers introduced themselves as American university men interested in understanding the feelings and aspirations of people in Asia. This approach gained for the questioner the prestige of the scholar and encouraged the informant to tell his own story frankly.

Usually the interviewer, the informant, and an interpreter were the only persons present. Interpreters were required because no team member could speak Chinese or Korean. The interpreters were Chinese or Koreans employed by U.S. Army agencies in Korea. All had considerable experience in interrogating and working with prisoners. Nonetheless, many had difficulty with the English language. The researchers continually had troubling questions about how accurate the translations were and whether the answers were being systematically distorted.

The interviewers sought to create a permissive atmosphere. Respondents were assured that the interviews were wholly voluntary, had no connection with the camp authority, could not affect the men's personal situation, and that the prisoner was free to decline to discuss any topic.[8]

The interviews averaged eight to ten hours in length; the shortest was two hours, the longest about twenty. The length depended occasionally on external conditions, but principally on the richness and variety of the respondent's experience and on his articulateness. It should be borne in mind that mediation by interpreters added considerably to the length of the interview.

Three general topics were covered in each interview: the respondent's personal history, especially in regard to the sources and development of his attitude toward living in a Communist-controlled country; his perception of, and adaptation to, Communist indoctrination techniques

[7] At the truce talks, which began in July, 1951, the U.N. Command took the position that prisoners of war had the right to choose whether or not they wished to be returned to their homeland at the conclusion of hostilities. With the tacit agreement of the Communist negotiators, the U.N. Command attempted in April, 1952, with varying degrees of success, to ask all prisoners what their choices were concerning repatriation. Disposition of the prisoners was one of the major stumbling blocks to an early truce, and was one of the principal factors in the prison disturbances.

[8] After the passage of time, it is apparent that the interviewers were somewhat naïve in expecting the prisoners to accept uncritically the introduction offered, considering the difficulties they had already experienced with U.N. Command. The interviewers also used interpreters who were well known to the prisoners. Further, the interviewers had no control over how interpreters used the knowledge they obtained.

and other control methods, especially as employed in the army; his experience as a U.N. prisoner of war, his perception of social and political organization in the prison compounds, and his attitudes toward U.N. prisoner-of-war administration.

In general, the respondent was invited to tell his story and express his feelings in his own way. Practice was to interrupt with probing questions only where the interviewer felt he needed clarification. On the one hand, both Chinese and Korean prisoners who had rejected repatriation responded freely and seemed eager to talk to the interviewers about their experience under the Communists and as prisoners of war. Some of the Koreans who wished to be turned over to North Korea were hostile to U.N. personnel, and regarded the interviewers as military intelligence agents. In most cases, their responses about events in the compounds, particularly when asked about the structure and activities of the Communist organization within the compounds, were guarded. On occasion. they were patently false. Such prisoners talked freely about alleged U.N. mistreatment of the prisoners, however, as well as about their feelings regarding the prisoner-of-war experience.

Chinese prisoners who had elected to return to Communist China were considerably more cooperative and gracious in manner than the Koreans who chose repatriation, although here, too, problems existed. For example, at the principal Chinese repatriate camp on Cheju Island, an attempt to talk with the leader of the prisoners was unsuccessful. He declined to be interviewed, but suggested that one of his subordinates be, instead. This, however, proved to be unsatisfactory; the respondent was hostile, and insisted that the interview be monitored by several of his fellows. He seldom departed from a rigid, though not very fluent, version of the official party line.

Authorities of this camp finally discouraged continuation of the enterprise, not only because of the hostility of the prison leaders, but because these Chinese prisoners were about to be repatriated. Consequently, eight of the nine interviews conducted by members of the team with repatriating Chinese were in the Pusan enclosures. In each of these cases, the man had been taken prisoner *after* March, 1952. The inability to question prisoners who were captured before March, 1952, and who elected to return to Communist China, left a gap in the account of the developments within the Chinese prison compounds.

The interviewers were asked to record the responses of the informants —or rather, the responses of the informants as filtered through the interpreters—as verbatim as possible. For one of the interviewers, who used a Stenotype machine, this was no problem, and he had a verbatim record of all his interviews. For the other interviewers, completeness of the recorded responses varied considerably.

In all, 118 interviews were conducted during an approximate six-week period—seventy-three with Koreans and forty-five with Chinese. Two Chinese interviews dealt almost exclusively with prisoner-of-war experience, and these were used only in the analysis of prisoner-of-war behavior. Forty of the Chinese were interviewed in Korea in July and August, 1953—thirty-eight of them in the camps where they were interned, and two escaped prisoners in a Pusan restaurant. The last three respondents were interviewed about a year later when they came to the United States as members of a delegation of former prisoners of war. These were Chinese who elected not to return to Communist China but rather to join the Nationalists on Taiwan.

While informants were selected primarily on the basis of their experience with Communism and as prisoners, the 118 persons interviewed came from a variety of social groups. They were men of various social class origins—from the highest to the lowest. They came from various areas of China and North Korea. They ranged from highly educated intellectuals to illiterates. There were Communist party members, nonmembers, and men the Communists had labeled "unreliable." Some were officers; others non-commissioned officers or common soldiers. Included were prisoner-of-war leaders, men who had been rejected by the dominant organizations (anti-Communist or Communist) in individual compounds, and ordinary prisoners of war. And finally, among the 118 informants, there were some who were captured by the U.N. early in the war (1950) and others late (1953).

Valuable supplementary data came from fifty-six interviews with non-repatriate Chinese and Korean prisoners which had been conducted by U.S. Army personnel. These interviews, conducted in late 1952 and in 1953 were given to the research staff after its field work. Of the fifty-six prisoners in this group, twelve were Chinese prison leaders and thirty-five were Koreans who had held leadership positions in the compounds. These interviews dealt principally with events in the Koje-do compounds [9] in 1951–52, and were conducted as part of an evaluation of the Civil Information and Education Program [10] which had been offered to the prisoners by military authorities.

The staff also acquired many documents produced by the prisoners of war. These included: essays by Chinese and Koreans on their experiences and reactions; petitions prepared by groups of prisoners; answers to questions used in examinations as part of the Civil Information and Education Program; newspapers, plays, and poems written by the prisoners; and tables of organization and operational directives of the Communist and anti-Communist organizations in the compounds.

The military personnel interviewed by the research team included

[9] Koje-do is an island off the coast of South Korea, not far from Pusan, where the bulk of prisoners of war were moved in 1951. See Chapter 5, below, for details concerning these events.

[10] This was an ambitious program for the prisoners which encompassed political and vocational education as well as recreational activities. See Chapter 5, below, for details about this program as well as the role it played in the behavior of the prisoners.

camp commanders, personnel of the Civil Information and Education Program, and medical officers of the prison hospitals. One such informant should be mentioned specifically because of his importance as both reporter and actor: a lieutenant whom we will here call Pak Chang-Mo, an English-speaking officer of the Republic of Korea army who was attached to United States units throughout the Korean War. Most of his duty assignments were in the prisoner-of-war camps. Because he played an active part in the events which precipitated camp-wide organization of anti-Communist Korean prisoners, and because during this early period he was more acutely aware than most Americans of what was happening in the compounds and of the growing danger to the U.N. Command, he has been relied upon as a major source of information. He wrote two detailed documents for the use of the research team and was interviewed at length on three occasions, both in Korea and in the United States.

Finally, extensive use was made of existing U.S. Army reports [11] relating to the administration and behavior of the prisoners, and of American press coverage of events in the prisoner-of-war camps.

Following the field-work phase, which lasted about six weeks, the team returned to the United States.[12]

The analysis of the data proved difficult and time-consuming. The interviews obtained in the field were particularly difficult to analyze, principally because they varied so much in both quantity and quality, and were not always comparable in terms of coverage or in degree of detail. Considering the circumstances under which the interviewing was done and the variously trained personnel, this was predictable.

Many methodological questions were raised, not only by the researchers themselves, but by other HumRRO persons, on the way the informants were selected, and by the lack of comparability of the interviews. How could one make any generalizations beyond the group

[11] Most of these sources are classified. Since such documents are unavailable for public inspection, it is pointless to identify them. However, full documentation is available in the original reports. Scholars who have a bona fide interest in this topic and who wish to do "unofficial" historical research may apply to The Adjutant General, Headquarters, Department of the Army, Washington, D.C., ATTN: AGAR-S, for permission to gain access to these classified documents. This is the procedure followed by the present editors.

[12] Some of the unrecorded knowledge and sensitization was thereupon lost. Joseph D. Lohman and Lloyd E. Ohlin had no further connection with the work—both had other professional commitments. The three HumRRO staff members participated in some of the analysis but were not involved in any of the report writing, having been assigned to other duties. William C. Bradbury, however, was so impressed and stimulated by the field work experience that he took a leave of absence from the University of Chicago to become the task leader. He became responsible for the completion of the task. Samuel M. Meyers, the remaining member of the field team, rejoined the research team the following year. Others who participated in the study in various capacities and for various times were Virginia Heyer, Pio D. Uliassi, Rita Mao Hechler, Richard Harris, and Jeane J. Kirkpatrick.

of respondents interviewed? The methodological orientations of the HumRRO staff led to particularly strong questioning of the validity of the attempts being made to order and evaluate the data.

Bradbury literally agonized over the data for months. At times he had serious misgivings as to whether anything could be done with it. He concluded that in spite of the shortcomings of the data, other available knowledge of the events under study was so meager that any information ought to be disseminated, although not of course without qualification and caution. In this view he was supported by two Far Eastern area specialists, David Rowe and Lucien Pye. They had examined the data and felt that it could be translated into acceptable, meaningful, and important reports.

The first report was written by William C. Bradbury and Jeane J. Kirkpatrick. It appears in this volume as "Determinants of Loyalty and Disaffection in Chinese Communist Soldiers during the Korean Hostilities." The report evoked the most criticism of any in the series because of the generalizations made, going beyond the immediate sample. In addition, it was labeled "literature" and "journalism." To answer these criticisms, Bradbury felt impelled to write a methodological note in which he sought to explain and to defend his use of the data and his method of analysis. The methodological note appears in the second section of Chapter 1.

The other reports which appear in Parts II and III escaped serious methodological criticism from the HumRRO staff. They were deliberately presented in an historical and descriptive-analytical style, using material not only from the interviews obtained in the field but also from the very rich supplementary data available to the staff. This methodological emphasis was deliberately employed to disarm internal criticism —the authors believing that the HumRRO reviewers were less certain regarding the standards appropriate for judging such work. The rigorous methodological climate of the HumRRO organization tended, however to constrain the report writing even when this device was adopted.

The most striking feature of the Chinese and Korean prisoners of war was the rapidity with which their behavior changed in response to changing external circumstances. This was noted in three principal ways. First, when Chinese Nationalist soldiers were captured by the Chinese People's Liberation Army (Communist), they quickly conformed to the behavior demands of their captors. It apparently made little difference in this initial conformity whether the soldiers were enlisted men or officers, rich or poor, younger or older, educated or not. Second, when Chinese and Korean soldiers were captured by the U.N. Command, substantial numbers of them were ready and willing to fight against the Communist forces if only they were asked, or to assist the U.N. Command in other ways. Third, rapid shifts in behavior of the prisoners within the camps was noted as the character of the war changed. When it appeared almost a certainty that the United Nations would win the war, the Korean prisoners were docile and cooperative. Then, when the large forces of the Chinese Communists entered the war and it appeared that a stalemate might ensue, the behavior of prisoners shifted to one of watchful waiting. And finally, when the truce talks began, with the protracted discussions concerning disposition of prisoners, the prisoners began a phase of intensive political activity and riot behavior.

The research staff had extended discussions on this characteristic of the prisoners. The data showed that some of the informants had undergone the experience of brainwashing or thought reform. It had been assumed earlier that brainwashing might be one important aspect of Communist military-political control. Consequently, the interviewing team explored in depth the various forms of brainwashing experienced by the soldiers.

As the staff studied the data and read what was then available on the subject, it became increasingly clear to them that most prisoners were describing forms of indoctrination or reeducation. These varied in degree or intensity depending upon the social class position of the soldier, and/or the previous rank he held in the Nationalist army. The techniques that were used were found to be not fundamentally esoteric, mysterious, or new. Similar practices were frequently found in the Western world.[13]

It also became clear to the researchers that the observed behavior could not be explained solely by these techniques. While the indoctrination seemed remarkably successful, what impressed the staff was how receptive the Chinese students were to the techniques. Apparently this success depended to a great degree upon the receptivity of the students. Why were they so receptive? The staff began to ask themselves if the answer might not lie in the social-psychological character of the Chinese.

The role of severe and immediate punishment as an explanatory principle was also explored in accounting for the observed rapid conformity. This was a view then commonly accepted by the general public. But some of the research staff believed that while fear of punishment was involved, it was not that decisive. The data did not show that the Communists had to use such excessive punishment to obtain the desired conformity. Genuine persuasion also played a part, but only a modest one, according to the data. Opportunists and men motivated solely by their own self-interest were also noted, but the data suggested something more fundamental. The staff began to feel more and more that it was dealing with some traditional orientations to authority and toward social relations in general.

But what were these traditional orientations? Since no member of the

---

[13] It should be noted that when these studies were being done, brainwashing was a new concept and had been portrayed as a dramatically new and diabolical technique which the Communists had developed to control men's minds.

research team was an area specialist, the team had to acquire some knowledge of the traditional ways the Oriental related to other persons and more particularly to those in authority. Through reading, as well as through contact and discussion with Far Eastern area consultants, a number of commonly asserted premises about the social behavior of the Oriental seemed salient and pertinent to the research team:[14]

The Oriental typically seeks to establish harmonious social relations.

Harmony, according to this view, will be established and maintained if each person carefully observes rules of behavior prescribed for particular situations and for specific roles. Acting properly—according to the rules—is an important moral injunction.

Shaming, or loss of face through public disapproval, is a potent sanction for enforcing group rules of conduct.

Desire for social recognition or gaining face is a strong motivating principle.

Fate is an important consideration in success. One cannot fight against the environment, nor can one manipulate external factors and relationships; one must accept them even though they seem capricious. Only by adjusting to this pattern can one hope to influence events. Thus, one cannot plan too far ahead. One should wait and act correctly in the situation hoping that by so doing one will be favored.

Following from these is the notion of personal bargaining. The Oriental assumes that he can make bargains with the representatives of power, trading his active assistance for personal security and small favors.

Obviously, these premises are likely to prove oversimple, especially in a country as large and as complex as China. It was not assumed that these were the only traditional factors involved in the understanding of this behavior, but in the opinion of the analysts these seemed the most relevant. Furthermore, these premises can also be asserted about the behavior of Westerners and others, but they seem more significant in the life of the Oriental.

The researchers also found these premises useful in understanding the behavior of the Koreans, for in spite of differences in the historical experiences of Chinese and Koreans there seem to be similarities in their approach to social relations.

Another perspective, particularly in Parts I and II, is that the emphasis given by the Chinese Communists to indoctrination and their demand for ideological participation can be considered a formal resocialization process. The Chinese soldier had to acquire, in a relatively short time, new values, new goals, new norms, and new concepts of himself

[14] See Samuel M. Meyers, Chapter 2, below, for a more detailed account of the consistency of the behavior of Chinese soldiers with these premises.

and of others. The Communist regime could not wait for a new generation to be affected by the social changes supposedly to be brought about by their new system of economic relations.

In Part III, the emphasis was upon the role of small, formally organized Communist and anti-Communist groups in controlling and manipulating large masses of prisoners of war who themselves were part of a larger organized group, the United Nations Prisoner of War Command. The task was one of analyzing the process by which these groups were formed and how they could become so significant in the life of the prisoners and to the U.N. Command. There were differences in these processes between the Communists and anti-Communists. The principal difference was that the Communists had the task of rebuilding a preexisting comprehensive and well-structured organization, shattered by their imprisonment, whereas the anti-Communists had to create a new and fresh organization.

The researchers tended to see this process as encompassing a number of mechanisms.[15] First, there was social unrest. Prisoners were uneasy, generally unhappy, frustrated, and angry. In such circumstances, they were susceptible to appeals and suggestions. Then there was agitation, which aroused them and aided in the recruitment to the group which was agitating. Agitation can induce unrest, can intensify that unrest, and can define the unrest by providing some goal, some objective set of symbols. While agitation helped in recruiting members to a specific organization, it was also necessary to tie the new members to the groups emotionally. The development of *esprit de corps* was one way this was done. The development of morale was still another mechanism in the growth and maintenance of the groups. Morale gave persistence and determination to the groups in the face of adversity. In addition, there had to be developed some group ideology—a body of doctrine, beliefs, and myths. This is what gave the groups their direction. It provided the criteria for criticism of existing situations and also provided a rationale for the defense of its policies. The role of tactics was another important mechanism in the success of these groups. Tactics, of course, varied greatly, depending upon the particular set of situational circumstances. Competent leadership was a vitally necessary ingredient in the growth of the groups. Finally—and very importantly—opportunity had to be provided to allow these mechanisms to operate. The data were analyzed with these mechanisms in mind, but they were not always discussed in precisely these terms in the written reports.

Finally, another idea was prominent—the very limited role which ideology played for most soldiers in the cohesiveness and military

---

[15] These are, in abbreviated form, ideas developed by Herbert Blumer, "Collective Behavior," *New Outline of the Principles of Sociology*, ed. Alfred McClung Lee, pp. 199–221, and in unpublished lecture notes. These ideas were developed in connection with the study of social movements, but events within the prison compounds seemed to have the character of a social movement, and these concepts proved fruitful in ordering the data.

effectiveness of the CCF as well as in the effectiveness of the organized prison groups. More decisive and crucial was the part played by organized primary groups. This was not a new thought, but it tended to substantiate what Shils and Janowitz observed in their studies of the *Wehrmacht* during World War II.[16] These groups were, however, not comprised of spontaneously interacting members as in the groups described by Shils and Janowitz and by others.[17] Rather, intragroup relations were carefully nurtured, monitored, and channeled by the Communist hierarchy through the use of a well-trained, militant cadre of activists. For these people, ideology was significant. These cadre members functioned at all levels of organization, down to platoon, squad, and even to the small work groups. Consequently, the standards of behavior which these primary groups enforced were well articulated with the requirements of the formal authority. This control of primary groups by the Communist hierarchy, coupled with the traditional way the Chinese related to those in authority, made for a highly effective and cohesive military organization. However, this cohesiveness and effectiveness could be maintained only if these groups remained both intact and embedded in the elaborately organized Communist control structure. Even during the relatively fluid conditions of battle, these groups could remain cohesive if the cadremen maintained links to the larger control system and received support from it. But when the disorganization of battle isolates the small groups from this system, the cadremen lose their support; their position of authority can deteriorate and with it their ability to influence and mobilize the group members. The control system can collapse, and the group members are then free to act according to their own personal assessment of the immediate situation.

The data clearly showed that when the Chinese and for that matter the North Koreans became captives of the United Nations forces, the Communist system of control had been seriously disrupted. This disruption of Communist control permitted elements hostile to Communism to emerge within the prison compounds. Much of the conflict that occurred within the prison camps resulted from Communist attempts to reform their shattered network and hence to regain control over the prisoners and from that of the anti-Communists to thwart that attempt and to substitute their own system of control. The efforts of the latter were based to a large extent upon what they had learned of Communist organizational techniques. Communists were successful in gaining control in some compounds, anti-Communists in others. But whatever the political coloration of the successful leadership, the prisoners were once again transformed into cohesive and effective units.[18]

S. M. M.

A. D. B.

[16] Edward A. Shils and Morris Janowitz, "Cohesion and Disintegration in the *Wehrmacht* in World War II."

[17] Morris Janowitz and Roger Little, *Sociology and the Military Establishment,* pp. 77–99.

[18] See Part III, below, for a description and analysis of these processes.

PART I

Loyalty and Disaffection in Chinese Communist Soldiers

DETERMINANTS OF LOYALTY AND DISAFFECTION IN CHINESE COMMUNIST SOLDIERS DURING THE KOREAN HOSTILITIES: AN EXPLORATORY STUDY

William C. Bradbury & Jeane J. Kirkpatrick

PROBLEM AND ASSUMPTIONS

On what bases do Chinese soldiers judge their Communist superior officers? Why are some soldiers scrupulously loyal to the Communist system of military-political authority while others hate it?

Focus of the Research

Communist Control and Chinese Soldier Motivation

The body of Western scholarship on China provides guidance on the patterns of motivation before the advent of Communist rule; party directives, cadre training materials, and the like provide a picture of the kinds of motives the new regime is trying to foster. But the ways in which the motives of the hundreds of millions of Chinese people are actually changing under the impact of Communist indoctrination and control are not known. This research is focused on the Communist army—for a generation the principal agency of revolutionary recruitment, education, and control. From this study of the army, readers who know China well will be able to draw some inferences about motivational changes in other areas of contemporary Chinese life.

Designed to study soldier reactions to Communist military-political authority, this research deals with those aspects of the soldier role in which new and old standards of behavior clash most directly and violently. The authors are not concerned with attitudes toward inherent features of military service. Instead, they have investigated the specific features that characterize life in the Chinese Communist Forces (CCF)—for example, continual indoctrination and the demand for active ideological participation, daily criticism and the requirement that one inform on one's friends as well as oneself, the special position of the party and the new requirements for advancement, and the enforcement of novel rules governing association with civilians. The objective has been to see how the new ideas and the new ways of exercising power have affected traditional Chinese motivations.

Identification, Loyalty, and Habituation

All the elements which influence a soldier's acceptance of his role operate through their effect on the degree to which he is loyal to his leaders and to the system of military authority as a whole; the degree to which he is comfortable in the everyday performance of the actions expected of him.

These factors interact to some extent. If a man feels that his leaders are evil or that the system is inherently hostile to his interests and values, his day-in, day-out emotional equilibrium in doing what is expected of him is likely to be affected. If he finds it easy to learn his job and to relate himself to his fellows in the required way, he is also likely to find it easier to give his loyalties to his superiors.

Nonetheless, there is a real distinction between the two factors. Loyalty is not the same as habituation, but both do contribute to identification with a military role and role system. Hatred is not the same as general uneasiness, but both are components of rejection of a military role and role system.

The subject is too complex for both factors to be dealt with adequately in a single report. This report will be concerned primarily with those influences on a soldier's internalization of his role which operate through his loyalties.

Definition of Terms

In speaking of motives which are common to most Chinese officers and men, and which importantly and persistently influence their loyalty or disaffection, just what do the authors have in mind?

Motives.—One must distinguish clearly between attitudes and the reasons which underlie them. If A is favorably disposed toward the government and B is hostile to it, their attitudes are contrary. The reasons behind their attitudes, however, may be similar. Perhaps A's parents have more land as a result of the government's policy of redistribution, while B's parents were killed as landlords during the same redistribution. If so, A and B are employing the same criterion—the well-being of their families.

It is motives in this broad sense—the criteria, the standards of judgment, the general valuations which underlie particular judgments—with which this report is concerned. The analysis was an effort to distill, from the careers of Chinese PW's interviewed by the research team, an orderly statement of the standards by which these men decided whether Communist authority did or did not deserve their support.

Four kinds of determinants of behavior need to be distinguished:

> One's expectations with respect to natural consequences of one's action: "I felt sure I would be killed in the artillery bombardment, so I deserted."
>
> One's expectations with respect to rewards and punishments that will result from what one does: "He fought well because he thought the cadres would praise him and he would be allowed to join the party."
>
> Goals and rules with which an individual identifies, usually because he has internalized them from his culture: "I argued with the battalion political officer because, while land reform is good, it is wrong to kill people unnecessarily."
>
> Mechanisms of adjustment and character attributes: "He began to cooperate with the Communists as soon as he was captured, because he is a passive, dependent person."

In any action, all four elements are almost invariably present; it can almost be said that they are different concepts, for purposes of scientific analysis, of the same phenomenon. Nevertheless, the distinctions among them are meaningful.

The primary interest in this report is in motives of the third type listed—the goals and rules with which individuals identify. This approach was adopted even though the Chinese soldiers interviewed had emphasized their efforts to calculate the social consequences of alternative lines of conduct open to them. It would have been relatively easy to analyze such behavior simply in terms of expectations of reward and punishment, and to relate these expectations to Communist mechanisms for manipulating the self-interest of Chinese soldiers. But there were more fundamental questions: Why do the respondents fear certain kinds of penalties more than others? Why do they want rewards of one kind but seem indifferent to others? What general values underlie their calculations? These are the values which determine Communist choices of the sanctions and incentives they use in manipulating individual soldiers, and these are the values the authors have tried to identify.

Common.—In the analysis of the interviews, the underlying standards of judgment of individual soldiers were identified and compared, and certain common premises of action were noted. Where the criteria did differ, the authors have tried to identify the elements within Chinese society and military life which permit and foster the differences.

Important and Persistent.—Any standard of judgment that is reflected continually in the behavior of an individual is *ipso facto* persistent and, other things being equal, more important than one which appears infrequently; any standard common to a group is *ipso facto* more important and more likely to persist.

This statement does not dispose of the problem, however. A standard of judgment may be crucial in shaping a man's loyalties even though it is exercised but once. For example, some soldiers were decisively alienated from Communist authority by the fate their parents suffered in the land reform, even though their personal careers were reasonably successful.

Loyalty.—A whole continuum of loyalty-disaffection is reflected in the interviews. The crucial point is how the soldier feels about his superior officers and the system of authority they represent. If he does what he is told with a sense that he is being coerced and only because he feels there is no alternative, he is not a loyal subordinate, although he may be an obedient, even an efficient, one. On the other hand, in the Chinese concept, loyalty does not necessarily imply complete identification of self with the wishes of one's superiors.

Thus, some of these soldiers obeyed orders—and, moreover, vigorously supported Communism—simply out of what we would call self-interest. They felt that the new regime was offering them a chance to make good, that its demands were reasonable and could be fulfilled. These men described themselves as having been voluntary supporters of the Communists; as such they endured personal risks, unpleasant work, and painful self-criticism without complaint. They were by no means unconditionally loyal but, in the sense with which we are here concerned, they did show a significant measure of loyalty to their Communist superiors and the whole system of military-political authority.

Assumptions

This report is thus an attempt to identify certain personality elements which are common to many individuals because they have grown up in the same society, have been reared and taught alike, and have internalized the same basic values or standards of judgment. Certain assumptions must be made in such research; the character of the assumptions made in the study has already been suggested, but a more specific statement should be made.

Standards of judgment can be isolated from accounts of individual behavior.—The concept of persistent value attitudes underlying varied behavior is familiar; everyone employs it in judging and predicting the behavior of others. In the study it was assumed that the same thing could be done more systematically. To analyze any given attitudinal response in this way, the researchers needed rich contextual information about each man interviewed:

His social situation—what others expected of him and what he expected of them, his relations with others, the rewards or punishments that entered into his thinking.

Other social-cultural ties such as his regional and class origin, his educational and occupational experience.

His particular characteristics; the ways in which his orientation and pattern of response to his life differed from those of other people of similar background and social position.

Cultures are properties of groups.—The concept of culture has a long history, but it has commonly embodied the notion of a body of valuations and beliefs shared by the members of a group. In the research an effort has been made to select representatives from the various cultures to be found in the Chinese Communist forces. It was assumed that just so far as the respondents exemplified the relevant pre-military and military groupings, the researcher would have the principal guide he needed to identify an all-Chinese soldier culture and specialized subcultures within it. Individuals were selected who were products of the various regional and social class subcommunities that comprise the military population, and who belonged to the several military and political strata of the CCF.

Culture and basic personality tend to persist.—It was assumed that the standards of judgment which the members of a group hold in common are more likely than most other characteristics of behavior to persist over time and to characterize future members of the group.

Individuals learn about and internalize group standards of judgment as they grow up, principally through daily relationships with parents and other older members of their communities. In other words, such standards are not merely functions of the social relationships in which individuals become enmeshed as adults; they are for the most part products of the basic processes of human social development.

Because these standards are shared by the group, they are elements of the basic personality of the typical member of the group. Because they underlie communication and permeate much group activity, they are part of the group's culture. Both personality and culture are wholes, the parts of which are interdependent; any single part is more resistant to change than it would be if it were an isolated fact.

The standards of judgment and styles of problem solving which determine men's choices do not change swiftly or capriciously; indeed, these are the principal elements of continuity and predictability in any rapidly changing social order. It is by no means assumed that basic personality and group cultural characteristics never change. Twenty-five years hence, in Chinese Communist armies made up of men born and reared in a Communist-controlled society, the value attitudes which determine their loyalties would almost certainly differ from those of the present generation of soldiers. What is assumed is that changing them is difficult, even when, like the Communist rulers of China, one is prepared to adopt any measures to achieve this result.

METHODOLOGICAL CONSIDERATIONS [1]

The conditions under which the data for this research were collected, as shown above, required improvisation of procedures both then and later.

[1] This section was written solely by William C. Bradbury.

At several points in their analysis the staff had to reflect at length on the justification of what they proposed to do, and out of these reflections have emerged some judgments which are recorded for those who may wish to assess thoroughly or to improve upon the methods used in this research.

Three obstacles to social-psychological research on Communist China are: the likelihood of distortion in the statements of persons who have moved from the Communist to the free world; the difficulty of translating meanings from one social, cultural, and linguistic setting to another, very different, one; and the difficulty of generalization on the basis of a nonrepresentative sample. This section deals with aspects of each of these problems. The methods by which the trustworthiness of the interview data was evaluated are described first. Then are discussed the premises underlying the procedures by which the analysts identified and interpreted hypotheses about common standards of judgment. Finally, the problem of applying the findings of this study to larger Chinese soldier populations is dealt with.

Evaluating the Trustworthiness of the Interview Data

The character of the interviews and the limited time available for interviewing made rigorous tests of the reliability of the interview responses impossible. Beyond the question of reliability, however, lay that of the accuracy of the statements made by the respondents. A variety of resources brought to bear upon the assessment of the data enabled the analysts to take account of certain sources and directions of distortion in the interviews without destroying the usefulness of the affected data.

The interview responses included two kinds of statements: information about the social and cultural context in which the respondents acted and data on their personal experiences. While the ways of testing the accuracy of both kinds of information are similar in principle, they differ in application. First, let us consider the accuracy of the statements about prevalent or institutionalized practices in Chinese Communist military life and about historical events in China.

Statements about Social Practice

This kind of information, it should be noted, was provided in the form of general statements. The respondents had a good deal to say about such matters as the way in which Communist indoctrination and other controls normally operate in military units, persistent Communist policies for the recruitment of cadres and the assessment of party members, and the general level of conformity to Communist demands exhibited by soldiers. To the extent to which they are judged to be accurate, such sociological statements are directly applicable to the larger groups about which they are made. The problem of sampling as such (and the more general problem of the relation between the respondent group and the larger population to which the statements are to be applied) does not arise with respect to such information. The question of accuracy, however, is crucial. Since a direct empirical test of accuracy was impossible, the tests of competence, internal consistency, and correspondence with other sources were applied. The sociological information passed these tests well.

Competence of the Interviewees as Observers and Informants

The respondents were selected largely on the basis of characteristics believed to be related to their competence as informants on the operation of the Communist military-political control system—that is, their knowledgeability and articulateness. The group included substantial proportions of men with long Communist service, party members, responsible officers, others who held good "observation" posts, and men whose pre-Communist backgrounds prepared them to observe intelligently and to report intelligibly.

Internal Consistency of the Data

Although the competence of the sources is not, of course, a guarantee against willful or unconscious distortion, the internal consistency of the body of information provided by these informants argues against the presence of significant distortion. To begin with, the respondents exhibited a very high degree of consensus with respect to the social structure in the context of which the behavior of individual Chinese soldiers must be interpreted. Pro-Communist and anti-Communist informants sometimes described this social structure in somewhat different terms and emphasized different elements of the whole. But almost invariably it is evident that, with or without special probing by the interviewer, they were talking about the same things and that their statements are mutually compatible. More generally, the total picture of Communist military-political organization emerging from the interviews is characterized by a very high degree of internal consistency. Apart from some local and unit variations in detail, there are no serious discrepancies within this picture.

Correspondence with Other Sources

Furthermore, the Communist practices reported by the informants correspond with those reported to other investigators, and the larger events recounted in the interviews fit in with known history.

Statements about Personal Experiences

While a great deal of the analysis depended upon the accuracy of the informants' statements about the social structure of the CCF, the heart of it concerned the personal experiences of the respondents—the ways in which they individually were treated, the course of their careers under Communist control, the adaptations they made to Communist demands, and the development of their attitudes toward Communist authority. The interviewees provided a great deal of information about these. In attempting to discover whether they told the truth, the analysts first applied the conventional tests and then examined the probable effects, so far as these could be estimated from external sources, of certain influences that were expected to distort the responses (for example, the organizational pressures to which the PW's were subjected).

Two preliminary considerations, however, need to be mentioned. First, how important is it in an investigation of this kind, which concerns a little explored field, that the respondents should give literally truthful accounts of their own attitudinal histories? Truthfulness is clearly important in descriptions of objective phenomena; there the tests described earlier can be and have been applied. With respect to attitudinal data, however, some qualification may be in order.

Let us suppose that a respondent understated the degree to which he was formerly pro-Communist or gave an incomplete account of the considerations which underlay his current attitude. He still had to give an account that seemed to him to be plausible, either in order to avoid probing questions or in response to them. That is, he had to explain why if not he, then a man like him, would do the things and take the positions he attributed to himself. Although such a response would seriously mislead a biographer, it can be relevant and useful to a study of factors that influence Chinese soldier attitudes toward the Communist regime.[2] The issue is one of perspective: Given the present low level of knowledge about the culturally shared standards of choice in Communist China, the answers of a respondent who gives incomplete or distorted explanations of his behavior may be useful for such a study, provided only that he continues to think and talk within the Chinese frame of reference. Literal truthfulness may be less important in such a study under such conditions than in other cases.

Furthermore, the researchers believe that the complexity and form of the interviews afforded significant safeguards against gross fabrication of personal experiences and attitudes. Each interview focused attention on the concrete social context in which the respondent had lived. Against the background of detailed questions and answers on this topic, it was more difficult for him to attribute to himself invented motives, conversations, and actions than it would have been had the questions concerned only these latter.

[2] This consideration is also relevant to the possibility of gross falsification deliberately introduced by agents of the opposition camp. It is possible that one or two of the interviewees was a Communist agent, but there is no reason to suppose that there were more than one or two, if any, among the forty-three respondents. Also, even an agent would have had to think up a likely story—one that could have happened and seemed credible to the teller as a Chinese and therefore contained important elements of psychological truth.

Competence

The forty-three respondents included a disproportionate number of highly educated individuals; also, the authors believe that the PW experience in Korea provided the interviewees with a good occasion for reflection on the meaning of their experiences with the Communists. These considerations argue for the competence of the informants, and examination of the interview transcripts, especially the responses to probing questions, reinforces this judgment. Competence to describe personal experiences, and especially attitudes, differed among the respondents, however; the analysts therefore made every effort to interpret appropriately responses which differed in precision and completeness and to avoid overvaluing the responses of the more articulate and reflective while undervaluing those of the less.

Internal Consistency

No formal test was undertaken to discover the extent to which interviewees would give the same answers more than once for a given question. However, each of the interviews covered a great deal of ground and doubled back repeatedly to touch, in different contexts, matters discussed previously. Also, each dealt with many interrelated questions and was long and seemingly rambling enough to provide many opportunities for—even invitations to—inconsistency. In this sense, some parts of each interview constitute a partial check on the accuracy of other parts. Discrepancies within single interviews were few and were confined almost entirely to points of secondary importance.

Correspondence with Other Sources

The closest approximation to a formal test of reliability was the comparison, in the eleven cases where such comparison was possible, of the interview transcripts with other military reports on the same individuals. In almost all these cases, the military interviews date from a much earlier point in the subject's internment and were conducted in a different atmosphere and by different methods. Where information overlaps, correspondence is high. Discrepancies show no consistent direction or pattern; in a good many instances respondents made admissions to the research interviewers about their experiences and actions that would seem more damaging to their self-esteem and personal safety than those they had made to the military interrogators. Even closer correspondence appears in the three cases for which interviews and an autobiography acquired by personnel of the Civil Information and Education Program can be compared with ours. The analysts, of course, discounted discrepant responses.

While other studies of CCF soldier adaptation and attitudes are not directly relevant to the truthfulness of the respondents about themselves, it is reassuring to know that studies conducted by the RAND Corporation, the Operations Research Office, and others have produced findings consistent with the data of this study and in some areas closely similar. This is also true of the data and findings of studies of civilian brainwashing and other Communist practices in China.

Assessment by Competent Judges

All the interpreters who assisted in the interviews were of Chinese origin.

All were experienced in dealing with and judging the frankness of PW's. They often suggested probes, and occasionally expressed suspicion that a man was not being frank. Repeatedly consulted by interviewers about the probable truthfulness of responses, they expressed a belief that the respondents were telling, with few exceptions, the truth and were being open and frank.

It is the consensus not only of the interviewers and analysts but of recognized students of Chinese society who have studied the interview transcripts [3] that the interviews are not only usually "live," revealing documents but essentially accurate ones.

The Role of Current Organizational Pressures

The research staff expected that the respondents' membership at the time of the interviews in powerful, disciplined prisoner-of-war organizations, whether pro-Communist (repatriate) or anti-Communist (non-repatriate), would influence their responses in two ways.

First, descriptions of and opinions about Communist policies and methods might be stereotyped in accordance with the official lines of the organizations. Some common phrases possibly attributable to such pressures did appear, but the interviewers generally insisted that respondents talk from and about their own experiences, and in the resulting interchange this kind of uniformity of response was greatly reduced. In the case of the anti-Communist prisoners, moreover, the line itself was not a statement of a definite political position; instead, it consisted principally of rejection of Communism on whatever grounds. The terms of the official rejection seem to have been a distillation of the actual experiences and reactions of thousands of former Communist soldiers, not something imposed upon them by a few ideologists.

Second, respondents might tend to minimize, or even to deny, earlier attitudes which differed from their current position. There was, however, no evidence that having formerly been pro-Communist was considered anything to be ashamed of in the anti-Communist compounds. Nine of the thirty-four non-repatriates freely described their member-

[3] The research staff was assisted at numerous points in its work by the consultant services of two recognized experts on Chinese culture and political behavior: David N. Rowe of Yale University and Lucian W. Pye of the Massachusetts Institute of Technology.

ship in the Communist party, four others spoke of their once vigorously pro-Communist attitudes, and most of the group acknowledged having seen some good in the movement at one time. Repatriates appeared similarly frank about onerous aspects of Communist control. More generally, the study as a whole provided no evidence that Chinese soldiers as a group are much interested in or concerned about the intellectual or ideological consistency of their views, either at a particular moment or over time.

Ingratiation versus Frankness

Since the Chinese are traditionally oriented more toward establishing a pleasant negotiating relationship in all social situations than toward either getting at the truth or expressing themselves, it was supposed that the informants might tend to tell the interviewers what they thought the latter wanted to hear. However, the interviewer's self-introduction suggested explicitly that he would be satisfied and pleased if the respondent would simply tell his own story and report his own opinions—that frankness would best achieve the desired kind of relationship.

The relatively unstructured character of the interview itself, together with selective probing, provided an additional safeguard against mere ingratiation. Evasiveness was more than balanced by the frequently evident emotionality of respondents as they relived events that had been especially traumatic; also a respondent's occasional evasiveness sometimes revealed as much as a frank answer would have. Lastly, repatriate PW's did not hesitate to defend the Communists, and, as mentioned earlier, former pro-Communists among the non-repatriates by no means hid their former attitudes.

The environment of the interviews should be considered in evaluating these facts. As a group the PW's had long since concluded that their fate did not depend upon the good will of individual Americans. They had noted also that Americans rigorously limited their efforts to control the lives of the PW's and seemed often to value and respect the free speech they preached. Thus, while some individual interviews contain internal evidence of mere ingratiation at some points, the analysts do not believe that ingratiation was a source of serious distortion in the interviews as a whole.

Estimate of Effects of PW Experience on Content of Responses

It has been postulated above that the special organizational interests in which the respondents were caught up at the time of the interviews did not greatly affect the content of the interview responses. But the great majority of the respondents had been prisoners of war—and therefore free from Communist surveillance and controls on information—for well over a year. Most respondents had spent most of this period in groups led by anti-Communist fellow prisoners. The analysts

suspect that, while this experience did not in any apparent way stereo-
type the responses obtained, it probably had some effect upon their
content and particularly their articulateness, that it gave the respondents more insight into their experiences under Communist control and
enabled them to communicate more effectively with Americans than
they could have when they first came into U.N. custody.[4] Many offered
remarkably trenchant general characterizations and judgments of the
purposes and effects of Communist practices. That a group of Chinese
soldiers should be psychologically penetrating and socially perceptive is
not surprising; that they should offer numerous sweeping general statements is.

From one point of view, the effect hypothesized is distortion. Some
of the experiences and feelings respondents described to the interviewers happened in a more fragmentary and inchoate form than that in
which they were described. But the wholeness and clarity added during
the PW experience may have enhanced rather than reduced the practical utility of the responses. The selectivity of memory is not necessarily
a curse; human beings live on it, and even researchers may benefit from
it. The crucial question is: What is the principle of selection?

In the present case, this question means: What were the sources and
what was the character of the PW-camp culture which contributed to
the unity and clarity of the interviewees' thinking? The crucial fact is
that this culture was a creation of the PW's themselves. American
intervention within the compounds was minimal; even the education
program initiated by the U.N. Command seemed to the PW's largely
irrelevant to their concerns and needs. And further, as has already been
suggested, available evidence indicates that the non-Communist compounds did not have any single official interpretation of the Communist
experience and that such common interpretations as appeared were not
the inventions of a few ideologists. On the contrary, the extensive
interpretations to which a PW was eventually able to give voice seem to
have been products of: intercommunication with persons who had had
comparable experience, and reflection on his own experience.

Such an estimate implies that the responses were products of, among
other things, selective memory. So far as this was the case, not all the
interpretations and reactions to Communist control reported by the
respondents were fully present to them at the time they were reported as
having occurred, but all were present, so to speak, in embryo. The
estimate also implies that the process of selection was not arbitrary or
irrelevant but tended to emphasize that which was really important in
the process of adjusting to Communist control and forming one's judgment about it, not that which seemed important at some particular
moment during the process.

[4] Respondents captured later were not markedly less articulate, but the researchers suspect that this was partly due to these men's rapid assimilation into a PW
society and culture that was well established by the time they were captured.

Getting the Most out of the Data

This study aimed to identify in the responses of the interviewees those factors which are at once elements of contemporary Chinese culture and elements of the typical or basic personality of Chinese soldiers. This objective was to be achieved indirectly, by asking respondents to describe particular incidents and reactions and then identifying in these accounts the value standards employed.

The value factors in soldier reactions could be identified only if a considerable variety of information was gathered about the context of particular reactions. As has been pointed out, each of the interviews includes, not only information on the social origins and career of the respondent and the social structure—the system of roles, communication, and sanctions—within which given incidents took place, but data on each reported reaction—its specific stimulus, the evaluative reaction itself, the reasons for it, and the overt behavior which accompanied it. For readers familiar with Chinese life, each of the interviews provides a relatively full-bodied picture of a Chinese individual. And the interviews as a group provide a relatively clear picture of the operation of Chinese Communists military-political controls on the lower echelons of the CCF.

The Uses and Limits of Given Reasons

In their effort to identify common standards of valuation, the analysts could not assume that the reasons a respondent gave for his evaluative reactions to Communist authority—his answer to the question "Why did you feel that way?"—adequately described the standards of judgment that had actually been operative. (This caution is independent of any judgment about response distortion; it is based on two normal characteristics of internalized cultural values in all societies. In the psychology of the individual, such beliefs are seldom articulated because they are only partly conscious. In the life of the group, they are seldom articulated because they are held in common and are therefore taken for granted in communication.)

This caution turned out to be somewhat less necessary in studying this group of respondents than it would have been in, say, a study of a group of U.S. soldiers, because the respondents had been subjected to a series of cultural shocks. The experiences of culture conflict which they had undergone—their subjection to the new goals, rules, and forms of social relationship imposed by their Communist rulers, followed by experience as prisoners of war in the custody of Americans—had brought some of their deeply held and previously taken-for-granted values and beliefs to the surface of their consciousness and made these explicit. Thus, as the quotations in the text of the report suggest, sometimes the reasons given by a respondent for his reaction to Communist authority referred explicitly to a general standard of judgment and reflected accurately a culturally shared value.

Even when this seemed to be the case, however, it had to be demonstrated by further analysis of the response. And more often than not, the given reasons left the value criteria themselves largely implicit. The latter had to be dug out by inference—by additional interpretation of the incident in the light of reasons given and the rich contextual data of other kinds provided by the interview. We move on now to a general discussion of the premises on which these inferences were based.

Action Systems and the Uses of Contextual Data

The belief that data on individual character and on social structure are useful in interpreting data on personal feelings and identifications needs no defense. Where the research objective is to identify cultural values, these must be distinguished from purely individual values and styles of behavior, and information about individual character helps the analyst to make the distinction correctly. General value elements must be distinguished from expectations specific to the situation in which a reaction occurs, and data on social structure and specific circumstances help the analyst make this distinction correctly.

The contextual data contained in the interviews have, however, provided additional guides and checks for the analysis which are less commonly recognized. These additional uses depend on the characteristics of systems of human action.

The point must be introduced abstractly. Different social practices are interrelated and are probably best thought of as a system of social roles; values, beliefs, styles, and attitudes as individual phenomena are interrelated and together constitute a system called personality; and shared values and beliefs are interrelated and together constitute a system called culture. Furthermore, and equally important, all three of these systems—social, psychological, and cultural—are mutually dependent.

A change in any one element of one system requires and induces some change in each of the others, and these responsive changes do not occur at random. That is to say, social roles, individual perceptions and motives, and enduring group values and beliefs interlock. A competent social scientist who makes a statement about any one item or system recognizes that it has implications for the others. This is not merely an abstract recognition; the development of the behavioral sciences consists of growth in the number and certainty of propositions about specific interdependences. Consequently, in analyzing behavior in a particular group, the scientist finds as his study proceeds that he can often spot an error in his analysis by discovering that a particular finding does not fit in with information on closely related elements of the action system, and that he can often make a highly educated estimate of the character of an element on which he has little or no data by, so to speak, "triangulating" on it from the points with which it necessarily or most probably interlocks.

This interdependence of elements in social behavior is always taken account of, consciously or otherwise, in the initial formulation and design of social research problems, and usually in the interpretation of findings as well. Where rigorous experimental design and sampling are not possible, knowledge of this kind must enter also into both the selection of sources of data and the analysis of those data. The findings of this study were tested in this way at every stage in the analysis, and such testing often proved useful in pointing up errors and suggesting the character of specific elements of the action system.

In the analysis, the conception of the study as one in the interdisciplinary field of personality and culture [5] was kept constantly in mind. The analysts approached the identification of common value criteria through study of persons, of communication and other group processes, and of expressed ideas as such. They consistently sought out meaningful unities in the apparent variety of the data, avoiding preoccupation with "average" responses or with particular social conditions and personalities. Taking account in their interpretations of the different social-cultural backgrounds of the respondents and the different social positions from which the latter observed and participated in the Communist control system, the analysts attempted to use to the maximum the multiplicity of clues offered by the many kinds of information contained in the interview data. In this process, understandings about the interdependence of elements in action systems were constantly used.

Considerations of this kind largely account, I believe, for the great contribution made by the two area-expert consultants. Their ability to fill in information about traditional value orientations, traditional role expectations, and historically frequent patterns of personal motivation—information which was often only suggested by the interview

[5] The three subsystems of action mentioned are the objects of investigation of three generic behavioral sciences. Thus, sociology may be conceived as the study of social structure, which means the system of expectations people have about each other's behavior (including the mechanisms of social control which allocate reward and punishment)—the system of roles which makes up society. Anthropology consists in part of the study of the system of valuations and beliefs which are shared by the members of a society and which influence social action. Psychology is concerned in part with the study of personality as a system of action, and thus with the persistent mechanisms of adjustment and character trends which characterize individuals. When the practitioners of any one of these disciplines "explain" social behavior, they do so principally in the terms appropriate to their own discipline. The development of interdisciplinary fields like social psychology, the sociology of ideas, and personality and culture results in large part from awareness that findings arrived at by the methods and concepts of any one discipline have limited value in predicting behavior.

Methodologically, the present work, as a study in personality and culture, lies on the borderline of personality psychology and cultural anthropology. Such interdisciplinary researches, whether they deal with political (as this one does), economic, or other behavior, commonly mix the methodological weapons and languages of the three basic disciplines. Moreover, if they are appropriately staffed they can also take advantage of the substantive understandings previously achieved in the several social sciences—not in just one of them—to converge on a particular problem. This is the essence of the point I wish to make in this section.

data—and to relate this to the information on personal history, social situation, attitudinal response, and specific reasons which the interviews provided richly, contributed vitally to organization and interpretation of the data. As a consequence of these procedures, the authors believe that the findings deserve some additional confidence.

Determining the Generalizability of Findings

When a small group which is a genuine random sample of the larger population is studied, all applications of findings are of course direct; the characteristics of the small group are asserted to be those of the populations, and the degree of confidence each such generalization deserves can be stated mathematically. In principle, every departure from randomness renders these measures useless and requires that applications be indirect—they must result from inferences which are based in part on premises imported from outside the primary data of the research. In practice, the less plausible it is to assume that a non-random sample resembles a random one, the more the research analyst must use qualitative judgments in both deriving and applying his findings.

The first question that must be dealt with, however, is whether the objectives of this research required a representative sample of the military population with which it was concerned.

The Problem of Sampling in Research on Culture

In analyzing the experiences of the respondents, the researchers sought to penetrate below the level of manifest perceptions and attitudes and to identify the standards of valuation which, together with particular stimuli, had determined the content and intensity of those perceptions and attitudes. If this alone had been the objective, some kind of population sample would have been mandatory as a basis for generalization. The objective, however, went farther: It was to identify those elements which were common to the standards of judgment of almost all Chinese soldiers under Communist control or of almost all members of particular social-cultural groups among them. The objective was not to describe the curve of distribution of any attitude or other personal characteristic in the CCF but to identify cultural phenomena. As has been said, the analytic procedures used to identify them consisted, not of treating each respondent as an isolated unit of data, but rather of relating what could be learned about particular respondents as persons to what was known of the social structure in which the group members were enmeshed and the systems of values and beliefs to which they had been exposed. All findings which the analysts have sought to apply to larger Chinese soldier populations concern common value criteria, not the distribution of variable personal characteristics in a population.

While such value criteria are necessarily in individuals, I believe that the problem of sampling in a study of this kind differs from that in one where the reality of culture and social structure is not assumed or identified and used. In studies of individual traits, the respondents are treated only as subjects, and the population being studied should be sampled. In studies of social structure, respondents may be treated strictly as informants, and the problem of selecting informants is not one of sampling but of finding the most knowledgeable individuals. Studies of culture—studies of systems of shared values and beliefs— probably fall somewhere between these two extremes, although no definite set of principles for selecting sources in such studies has been formulated. The point can perhaps best be made through a hypothetical case.

A well-trained, perceptive anthropologist can usefully begin his study of a strange culture by watching and talking with almost any socially varied handful of members of the society in question. Why is it that he can at this stage dispense with representative sampling?

The answer to this question has two parts. In the first place, if the differences between his own culture and that which he is studying are great, he will be struck by manifestations of these differences very early in his inquiry, regardless of the identity of his informants—almost as he would be struck by a difference in skin color.

It is important, I believe, to recognize that the present study shares this characteristic. It is an early empirical study of a strange culture adapting to new circumstances, and it must seek, as the anthropologist must initially try, to identify the principles or premises in the thinking of Chinese soldiers which account for the most striking differences between their reactions and those of Westerners.

To use an analogy: At this stage in investigation, the present research staff and the anthropologist are in the position of the boy who wants to find out whether the white crystals in a bowl are sugar, salt, or something else—tasting a pinch or two of crystals from the top will tell him what he wants to know. Other questions could be raised—and would be raised in any extended study of the bowlful of crystals—which would require systematic sampling of them. For answering certain kinds of questions, however, it can be assumed that one crystal—or one member of a society—resembles the next one.

The second part of the answer to the question about the anthropologist's failure to insist upon representative sampling concerns the methods of analysis he uses. He can learn a great deal about the alien culture from contact with a non-representative sample of its participants, because he systematically takes account of the influence that each informant's special social position and immediate circumstances exert upon what that informant does and says. He learns about the social systems as he learns about persons, and he interprets each respondent's attitudes and beliefs in the light of his social environment and personal history. Furthermore, he makes communication contents themselves a part of his investigation. As has been pointed out, the present investigation shares these characteristics with studies in cultural anthropology.

Thus, for analysis which seeks to identify elements of culture and of typical or basic personality, the randomness with which subjects have been selected is less important than it is when the research concerns the distribution of variable personal attributes in a population; it is less useful to know whether the respondents have been randomly selected than it is to know the degree to which they are creatures of and immersed in one or more specifiable social-cultural systems; and the representativeness of the sample as a whole decreases in importance as the techniques of analysis in the social sciences—in particular, an ability to "triangulate" from sociological and psychological to cultural variables and back—become more varied and efficient.

All this by no means signifies that in the effort to identify cultural frames of reference the researcher can be indifferent to the social characteristics of his respondents. He can interpret their responses correctly only if he can identify the social positions which condition those responses. And in order to generalize the uniformities he finds in his subjects, he must be able to answer the question: Which culture or subculture are these patterns characteristic of? Thus, he must know, not only the social-cultural group affiliations of his subjects, but also which social-cultural groups are not represented.

I did not have all the data on prevalent patterns and discontinuities of communication and socialization in modern Chinese society which would be required to answer this question definitively. All generalization of findings has, however, been based on careful evaluation of the character of the respondent group and the degree to which it contains representatives of the principal social-cultural groups present in the CCF in Korea. The methods used to make this evaluation were referred to above; they are now described more fully.

Checks on the Sample of Types

As has been pointed out, the interviewers attempted to sample the range of backgrounds and personal orientations that existed in the PW population, or—putting the point differently—to sample the subcultures that existed in the CCF. But if the analysts were to be able to generalize about the degree to which the shared standards of value could be ascribed to larger populations, they had to have some guides external to the interview responses themselves—guides which would enable them to estimate: the degree to which the various types in the CCF were represented in the respondent group, and which respondents exemplified which types with what variations from the norm.

Sources of Guidance.—Since it was impossible to devise selection procedures which would guarantee the desired type of sample, the analysts had to apply such checks as they could intellectually, after the data had been collected, to provide the needed guidance. Such guidance was drawn from three sources:

Demographic studies of the Chinese prisoner-of-war population in Korea. These enabled the research staff to determine, with respect to each of a number of key personal-background characteristics, whether the full range of the characteristic in the prisoner population was represented among the respondents and which respondents represented various points on the continuum of that range.

A description, in each interview report, of the conditions and procedures which accounted for the respondent having been chosen. These indicated certain special influences that had operated differentially in the selection of various categories of respondents.

Consultant services of two recognized experts on Chinese political behavior and culture. These experts reviewed the interviews and pointed out ways in which the personal histories and orientations of individual respondents seemed to typify or vary from the norm of the informants' respective regional, economic, and social strata. One member of the analysis staff, an American-trained sociologist of Chinese origin, contributed a similar perspective on the data.

Inferences.—On the basis of these after-the-fact intellectual guides, certain preliminary judgments were made about the character of the respondent group.

It became clear that, as had been hoped, the forty-three respondents whose interviews constitute the principal data for this report included a very wide range of types of Chinese soldiers, both socially and psychologically. The reader is referred to the statistical appendix for partial documentation of this judgment. The researchers therefore believe that the interview responses contain an adequate sampling of the principal cultural value systems operative in the members of the CCF in Korea.

Not only were the analysts made aware at the start that the respondent group was not a representative sample of a military population, but they were able to determine that its characteristics differed from those of the relevant populations in definite ways as a result of the criteria and conditions that affected the selection of respondents.[6]

For example, knowing that the highly educated constituted a far larger proportion of the respondents than of any representative slice of the PW population or a Chinese Communist army of the near future (and that most of the highly educated were more articulate than others), the analysts were warned in advance that they might

[6] See "Coming in Contact with Communist Authority," below, and Appendix A —Tables, 1, 3, 6, 10, and 17.

tend to impute to the whole Chinese Communist soldiery modes of response to Communist control which characterize only highly educated soldiers.

It was concluded that, while any observed differences between values characteristic of certain social-cultural subgroups could not be generalized, the differences between other subgroups could be. This judgment was made on the basis of the number of respondents in the several social-cultural subgroups and the degree to which the criteria and conditions of respondent selection made comparison between one subgroup and another meaningless.

Thus, the responses of soldiers from poor-farmer backgrounds cannot be compared, on the basis of this study, with those of soldiers from middle-farmer backgrounds, because only five and nine respondents, respectively, fell into the two classes. However, the responses of soldiers with ten years or more of schooling (N-13) can be compared with those soldiers with three years or less of schooling (N-16). All findings with respect to subgroup differences deserve, of course, less confidence than do those that apply to the respondent group as a whole.

Each pair of subgroups which passed the test of numbers had also to pass that of similarity in criteria of selection. Suppose, for example, that the highly educated respondents had been selected in such a way that the average length of their exposure to Communist control was much greater than that of the poorly educated, or that most of them were men from coastal cities while most of the uneducated were former inhabitants of inland villages. Then the differences in the standards of judgment of the two groups would reflect, not only the difference in education, but these other differences as well. Considerations like these prevented the generalization of observed differences in values which paralleled certain other social-cultural background groupings. Similarly, in the making of projections into the future, a sustained effort was made to take account of differences between the patterns of valuation of men who had had pre-Communist military service and special reindoctrination and men without such experience, in order not to impute to future CCF soldiers orientations traceable to specific experiences which few of them will have had.

Derivation of the Findings

The China specialists commented at length on the substance of the interviews, relating the reactions and generalizations of individual respondents to major criteria of valuation in traditional and modern Chinese society. These commentaries supplemented the analysts' own reading and provided an important basis for interpretation of the data.

Identification of Reasons.—The next step was to identify those experiences and judgments which had influenced the respondents' attitudes toward the Communist system of military-political authority, and then to group these reasons on the basis of the underlying standards of judgment which the men seemed to be applying.

Two kinds of statements were abstracted from every interview: every explicit statement by the respondent that this or that fact influenced his attitude, and any description of an event or thought process which was so recounted as to strongly imply its influence. Each reason was treated as an item of data, regardless of the identity of the respondent (this did not preclude return to the transcripts for subsequent interpretation of a statement within the context of the individual interview).

The analysts now had a list of about a thousand reasons, of this order: "At first the Communist cadres treated us kindly, and I thought they were sincere"; "The first time they made me a target for criticism it was almost unbearable"; "Because of land reform everybody has enough to eat"; "I believed them when they said those who joined the party would be trusted and have good jobs."

Some reasons could be grouped together rather easily on the basis of similarity of external conditions and stimuli or of wording; others were not so easily classified. Study of the interview transcripts indicated that some of the latter did belong together but that others appeared to reflect reactions based on quite different standards of judgment.

Expert opinion and background reading on Chinese culture and social structure and on Chinese Communist ideology and methods of control provided numerous hypotheses which guided the efforts to group the reasons on the basis of underlying criteria. The comments by the consultants provided explanations for some of the groupings empirically identified and additional hypotheses about common standards of judgment which could be tested in the data. Both consultants had commented, for example, on the pragmatic and calculating character of the interviewees' reactions to Communist control, and had related this to traditional Chinese attitudes toward government and to the social upheaval that has characterized China in recent decades.

Hypotheses of another kind were derived deductively. After a group of reasons had been stabilized and a common criterion identified, the analyst asked, "If the respondents reacted on this basis, then what else should follow?" For example, it was found that agreement or disagreement with Communist ideology as such was not a major determinant of political loyalty; from this were derived a number of corollaries which could be tested on other parts of the data. Verification of these served in turn to reinforce confidence in the original finding.[7]

Identification of the Four Faces of Communism.—It became evident that the still numerous groups of reasons clustered into much larger, discrete groups. Four such classes of reasons made their appearances. What differentiated them from one another?

The four seemed to represent kinds of value criteria, different and

---

[7] See "Ideology and Programs of Reform," below.

discontinuous aspects of respondents' relations with Communist authority. Endeavoring to characterize in some way these four groups, the analysts concluded that these series represented four ways of looking at the Communist military-political system—four different faces or aspects.

The analysts gave names to these large groups: "sincerity," "controls," "ideology," and "personal career." From this point on, the data were classified in accordance with these distinct "faces."

Development of Findings

Development of more general findings led also to definition of those subgroups among the respondents—the highly educated men, the long-time professional soldiers, and the like—in which special standards of judgment appeared.

It became apparent also that the experiences and reactions of respondents which occurred before or just after their contact with Communist power differed significantly from those occurring after they had become enmeshed in the Communist-controlled social order. The staff decided to emphasize these differences by treating the first impressions separately in the background analysis preceding the more detailed sections on experience under Communist control.

A number of loose ends of course remain. In some cases, relatively important attitudinal reactions and choices have had to be reported much as they were described by the respondents, in their particular social setting, without identification of the standards of value which were central in these responses. In numerous other cases, the unifying interpretation is tentative. It is hoped, however, that the manner in which the findings and generalizations are stated will make clear the character of the tasks that will face follow-up research.

COMING INTO CONTACT WITH COMMUNIST AUTHORITY

What were the backgrounds of the forty-three soldiers on whose experiences and judgments this report is based? Under what circumstances did they first encounter Communist power? What did they expect, and what were their initial experiences and reactions? How successfully did they adjust to the new system of authority and standards of conduct?

The answers to these questions serve to introduce and provide necessary context for the subsequent analysis of experiences under the Communist regime. More detailed data are presented in Appendix A.[8]

Pre-Communist Backgrounds

Basic to the reactions of the Chinese people to present-day Communist control is the fact that most of them were born and grew up in a non-Communist and still largely tradition-bound society. All of the

[8] See Appendix A, Tables 1–7.

respondents lived their first, formative years in the older setting. The youngest of the respondents became a Communist subject at fourteen, the oldest at thirty-five; for the group as a whole, the median number of years lived in the old China was twenty-three. What kinds of material did these soldiers constitute for their new rulers?

The respondents were a highly diversified group. North China was the commonest region of origin, but one soldier came from far northern Manchuria near the Soviet border, another from Kwangtung on the south coast. One is the son of a Manchukuo magistrate, two the sons of Shensi landlords; five came from urban business families, a few from landless peasant stock, but most were from relatively well-to-do farm families. Very few mentioned religious aspects of their upbringing, but one belonged to a Christian family.

While two respondents had no formal schooling and one-third of the group had no more than three years, another third had been in school for ten years or longer. The average was five years of formal schooling. Eight were students at the time the Communists overran their areas, four were doing what could be called white-collar work, four were peddlers, and four more were farmers or fishermen.

Twenty-one men had had no military experience before they entered the Communist forces. Of the twenty-two who were soldiering, a few were in local or provincial forces, but the majority were in the Nationalist army; two had served for less than a year, one for seventeen years, with average service being four years. Most had been officers or non-commissioned officers.

The varied individual backgrounds represented in the group are not in the proportions in which they occur in China's young adult male population, but they do make possible some useful analyses of differential treatment by the Communists and differential responses to this treatment. For example, the highly educated have always occupied a key role in Chinese society; the Communists regard them as a special problem for control and reorientation. The fact that one-third of the respondents had ten or more years of schooling—making them, in Chinese eyes, members of the intelligentsia—permits us to examine the patterns of response to Communist persuasion and organization shown by well-educated Chinese and to compare their responses with those of men with little education.

Contact [9]

Pre-Communist background influenced adjustment to Communism in many and sometimes unexpected ways. It influenced the circumstances in which a man first encountered the Communists, and the knowledge, feelings, and expectations he brought to the meeting. Nationalist officers, students, and poor farmers, for example, drew from their environments different kinds and amounts of information—or misinforma-

[9] See Appendix A, Tables 7 and 9.

tion—about who the Communists were, what they were trying to do, and what could be expected of them. These early impressions in turn colored their subsequent adjustment to life under Communist control.

Throughout the twenty years of latent or active civil war, the Communists constituted an armed state within a state, insulated and almost self-contained. From their original bases, first in Kiangsi province, then in the northwest, they chewed and hacked away at the old social order through guerilla forays, land reform, disruption of transportation, looting, coordinated propaganda, and manpower levies.

Using its army as the primary instrument of expansion, political propaganda, recruitment, and social control, the party hierarchy gradually gained a stable source of supply and manpower. The Japanese war enabled the Communists to extend their sway within China; after receiving Manchuria from the Soviets in 1945–46, they were ready to meet Nationalist armies head on. Wherever they conquered they became *de facto* rulers, and by the time the Nationalist remnant fled the mainland, millions of Chinese had already lived for ten years or more under intermittent or continuous Communist control.

Pre-contact Perspectives

Sources of Information.—A young man's initial contact with organized Communism depended on when his area, his class, or his military unit became a Communist target. How he reacted depended in part on his pre-contact impressions and in part on what happened to him in the first days and weeks following capture.

The principal sources of information about the Communists available to the forty-three before they entered the orbit of Communist power were:

> Information disseminated by the Nationalist government, through classes for army officers and soldiers, through posters, and by provincial and local authorities.
>
> Direct or secondhand reports from refugees, soldiers, or others who had lived under Communist control, usually briefly.
>
> Word-of-mouth propaganda spread by agents of the Communist guerilla forces, primarily among civilians in areas of active operations and in normal schools and universities.
>
> Publications prepared by the Communists and circulated widely, particularly in university circles and generally among urban intellectuals.

The informants recall much more evidence of Communist than of government propaganda effort. Nowhere is the contrast sharper than among university students—a key group in modern Chinese society. Communist books and pamphlets were distributed in large quantities; crypto-Communists agitated among the students, organized discussion groups, and infiltrated student organizations.

The now widespread impression that the Communist line and program gained wide currency in university communities is confirmed by the informants. The relative silence of the Nationalists, together with existing dissatisfaction over their "failure to govern," left the Communists a wide-open field. A non-repatriate who became a Communist sympathizer at Nankai University sums up the situation suggested by others:

> The case for the Communists was made in great numbers of conferences and books which were widely circulated among the students. The Communists made students a major propaganda target. The textbooks used at the university tended to agree with the Communists, and by 1947 the Communists had gained control of more than 60 per cent of student organizations. Therefore, everything I learned in school and out of school was favorable to the Communists. The Nationalists, to the contrary, made no efforts to fight Communist propaganda either with propaganda of their own or by explaining to the students their view of the civil war and reasons for fighting the Communists. (F-4) [10]

The government devoted some time and effort to orienting troops on the Communist threat. Former Nationalist soldiers recall lectures on political subjects, including why the Communists were bad for China. These sporadic attempts at indoctrination seem, however, to have left only a vague impression. Several former Nationalist army men report that they had heard almost nothing about their military adversaries except that they were guerillas or bandits. Officers were somewhat better informed—some had had special political training which included systematic briefing on the character and development of the Communist movement—but most described their experiences and attitudes before capture in ways which suggest they had little awareness of the political significance in the struggle.

The fundamental difference between the Kuomintang and the Communists is strikingly illustrated by their respective emphases on political indoctrination of troops. The Nationalist attempt was spotty and casual; it suggests almost exclusive reliance on traditional ties and authority to achieve adequate combat morale. The Communists, on the other hand, gave troop indoctrination high priority. Impressive amounts of time and ingenuity were devoted to converting politically illiterate and apathetic farmers; even the most antipolitical respondents could recite agitational slogans about the people's revolution. The Communists were fighting an ideological war, and they carried its typical emphasis on

[10] The symbol (F-4) refers to the individual respondent quoted and to the transcript of the interview with him. Quotations and paraphrases throughout the report will be similarly documented. The identifying symbols N-1 through N-31 refer to non-repatriate PW respondents; the symbols R-1 through R-9 to repatriate PW respondents; and the symbols F-4 through F-6 to former non-repatriate PW's interviewed in the United States in 1954.

politics, values, and morale based in a historic mission straight to the consciousness of every soldier.

Interviewees who were neither students nor soldiers during the civil war learned whatever they knew about the Communists from soldiers who passed through their villages, refugees from areas where Communists had gained control, government posters, or the experience of a few months of guerilla rule.

Images of the Communists.—What kinds of information did the forty-three young men acquire from these varied sources? What were their conceptions of the identity and purposes of the Communists? And what was their idea of their own relations to nation, government, and politics generally?

By all odds the most striking aspect is ignorance about the nature of the struggle that was racking China. Only one of the interviewees, a former Nationalist officer assigned to counterintelligence and civilian organization in areas retaken from the guerillas, had developed an understanding of Communism and the civil war that was at once broad and detailed.[11]

A few other officers had a general picture of the issues and stakes. They saw the Communists as a highly organized group intent on capturing the government by force, and understood that Communist victory would mean drastic changes in Chinese society. But these officers were in general more aware of methods than of goals; they did not describe themselves as having held any strong attitudes, either positive or negative, toward Communist goals. Nevertheless, their conception of Communists as ruthless, divisive, and cruel, combined with their attachment to some aspects of the old order and concern about their personal fate, led them to fear and dislike the insurgents.

Several of the informants who were university students during the civil war similarly understood the struggle as one for control of the government, but their attention was focused on goals. They preferred the Communists because they promised reforms these students regarded as urgently needed. Efficiency would replace bungling, mass poverty would be eliminated through land reform, sound economic policy would halt inflation, resolution and unity would ensure international respect for China. With an image of the Communists derived from propaganda designed for their consumption, many of these young intellectuals hoped for Communist military victory and were ready, even eager, to cooperate.

However, intellectuals and Nationalist officers who saw the Communist drive as national and political in meaning constituted less than a fourth of the respondent group—and almost certainly a much smaller proportion of the Chinese population of military age. Most of the respondents, including several of the highly educated and a few Nationalist officers, either had no impression of the Communists or had a

[11] See chapter 3, below.

parochial image of them and the civil war. Ten indicated that they had almost no information about the Communists from any source until Red forces approached and seized power in their own localities.

The conception of the guerilla forces as bandits was probably most widespread. This label carried with it frightening traditional connotations of looting, kidnapping, extortion, and murder. For example, when the guerillas took over part of Kiangsu in 1940, the son of a public official "was very young and didn't know very much about Communism; but from the posters put on the walls by the government [he] knew the Communists were very cruel" (N-4). And a shrewd young Nationalist volunteer, later a principal anti-Communist leader in the U.N. prison camps, recalled that when he entered a Nationalist officers' school in 1946, "my understanding of the Communists was only that they were a bunch of bandits, robbers, murderers. . . . I had no political understanding or other feeling toward them. This idea remained with me until my capture by the Communists in 1950" (N-24).

The picture was often confused by contradictory rumors. Where Communist guerilla forces held sway even briefly, these rumors were sometimes reinforced by the propaganda of the deed. The son of a Kiangsu farmer said:

> During the Japanese occupation . . . as early as 1940, when the Communist guerilla activities were very strong in the area, they left a very good impression because of the good discipline of the soldiers. . . . When the Communist soldiers stayed in the homes of the peasants, they helped the farmer carry water; they helped the farmer light the fire. . . . [Later, after the Japanese were defeated and the Nationalist government returned,] the Nationalist soldiers' discipline was very bad, and the local officials were very corrupt. (N-2)

Also useful to the Communists were the reports of some People's Army veterans and covert agents in villages nominally under Nationalist control:

> They said it was a people's army and how well disciplined it was and friendly to the people. . . . A lot of people in the village had joined the [Eighth Route] Army. What they had seen, they thought was pretty good. In the army there were no beatings, and they were treated very nicely. (R-9)

Attitudes toward the Communists.—Of the informants who reported an impression definite enough to be called an attitude, the majority were clearly unfriendly to the Communists. The interviews as a whole, however, suggest that the impressions in different areas varied greatly, and indicate little feeling for the national and profoundly moral and political character of the civil conflict.

Nationalist soldiers were uniformly anxious about falling into the enemy's hands. A machine gunner said: "I figured they would make me do dangerous work, that I would be sent to the front to sacrifice my life in battle, or that they would kill me" (N-12). In some areas, this personal fear of the bandits was shared by civilians of all classes. The son of a rich farmer in Hopei first heard of the Communists when a relative returned from the Communist army:

> He was wounded and tired. He said the Communists always oppress and cheat the people; they compel workers to join the army; they take away all the food of families; and in the Communist army you must work or be considered an enemy. He was homesick constantly. He came back in tears saying that he didn't like the Communist army but was compelled to join. (N-6)

A man's social class did not determine how he felt about the Communists. Many civilians were indifferent to and even unaware of the civil war; few saw it as a definitely class-centered struggle. However, in some areas members of different classes tended to view the Communists differently. For example, "Before the Communist troops came to my area, I thought they would kill all the people. But the poor people thought that they would be less killed by the Communists. . . . In the beginning, the poor farmers welcomed the Communist troops." (N-4).

Entering the New China

The vast majority of the Chinese first knowingly came into contact with the Communist movement when its armies overran their home communities. They passively submitted as, at first gradually and then in a rush of conquest, it extended its sway over the mainland.

In this respect the respondents are fairly typical. Only four said they sought out the Communist forces and joined them voluntarily. Almost half came in as prisoners of war from anti-Communist armies, eighteen as residents of areas overrun by Communist forces, and two as travelers whom the guerillas impressed into service.

Two-thirds of the informants, like an even larger proportion of the Chinese population, were introduced into the Communist sphere between 1947 and 1949, when one province, city, and army after another was falling before the Red military advance. Most of the others were absorbed earlier, one as early as 1939.

First Impressions.—The Chinese Communist party generally imposed upon its armies a rigorous "love the people" policy, although in the guerilla period the necessity for haste and the policy of "disturbing the order of society" (N-4) had sometimes called for stern, swift measures and even for looting. But for the most part, and especially in the 1947–49 expansion, Communist soldiers in newly occupied areas treated civilians with impressive consideration. Purges were deferred while dossiers were collected; only a few top officials of the former local administration were likely to be placed in custody at the start.

In these circumstances, the most common single impression the respondents recall of their first weeks under Communist control is surprise and pleasure at the apparent kindness and warm, personal concern for the people shown by the new authorities. Anxieties were lulled; many who had feared the Communists as bandits felt they had been mistaken or misled; those who had expected good saw their expectations confirmed. Even those who experienced no special generosity were surprised by the discipline of the Communist soldiers. Furthermore, their behavior contrasted favorably with that of Nationalist armies during this crucial period.

Captured Nationalist soldiers were similarly well treated. For several weeks, while dossiers were being prepared and before reindoctrination got under way, the captives "were treated like brothers" (N-18) not prisoners. This welcome to those who had been most fearful made them more hopeful and more tractable than they would otherwise have been. An officer who had made repeated efforts to break out of the Communist encirclement and was shortly sent off to a "military-political university" described his initial impression as follows:

> My first reaction and that of [my fellow officers] was that it was not so bad. They treated us very well. . . . The environment was very good, and we had a lot of freedom. All of the students were greatly impressed . . . since we had anticipated no such freedom. Many had received little education. They thought that now they could get a college education. They were told that after they had finished their training they would be able to get home and if they were willing to work with the people this training would make them better qualified. . . . I was ready to give them [the Communists] the benefit of the doubt this time and make the best of it. (N-1)

Naturally, civilians and soldiers alike assessed this behavior in the context of their previous experiences with authority. Often the Communists compared most favorably. The unprecedented fact that troops did not beat civilians, nor officers common soldiers, and that Communist officials did not engage in the traditional squeeze, was widely noted and approved. The revolutionary notion that these traditional privileges of office were not natural laws but something to be prevented by human effort was first planted, in the minds of many Chinese of all ages, by Communist conduct and Communist-led discussion. The new rulers exploited every known abuse of the previous government through propaganda, through meetings for the airing of grievances, and through carefully planned contrasting behavior. A peddler from Shansi province, for example, said:

> Before the Communists came into the province, the Nationalist government deceived us. They said: "If the Communists come in, they will kill all the people in the province; and they will confiscate your property, your rent, your houses." At that time I trusted the propa-

ganda of the Nationalist government, but after the Communists came
in [I could see] that everything the Nationalists told us was wrong.
The Communists were very kind to us and helped us in every way. So
I thought the Nationalist government had deceived us, and I changed
by mind. (R-4)

In general, only informants from Manchuria reported use of coercive
measures to control the population immediately after the Communist
take-over; elsewhere such measures were initiated only after a period of
systematic wooing. But the period of wooing varied considerably for
individuals. Not all had time to lose their skepticism about the eventual
objectives of the conquerors.

Isolating the effects of the interaction of pre-contact images and first
impressions of the Communists is not only difficult but, at this distance,
risky. Nevertheless, the data seem to justify a few generalizations.

Most of the respondents had reason to be intensely anxious about
what was going to happen to their social positions, their property, or
their very lives. Nationalist military personnel at least half expected to
be treated as conquered enemies in the traditional Chinese fashion;
most local officials and the well-to-do had some reason to fear the new
rulers. Even the many who were apathetic about the struggle except
where it impinged directly upon their families were unsure of what
would happen to them, precisely because they knew so little about the
conquerors. To all those who were worried, the initial kind treatment by
the Communists was doubly impressive, and willingness to collaborate
as well as to conform increased.

The nature of the response depended to some degree upon whether
the pre-contact image was favorable or unfavorable to the Communists.
Of the respondents who had been unfavorable, a few regarded the
initial good treatment as a trick, but most were inclined to revise their
picture of Communist intentions and to drop their guard somewhat.
Where the pre-contact image had been favorable, the behavior of the
Communists strengthened it. The general tendency was to interpret
policies and events in a light favorable to the new rulers and to move
actively to cooperate with them.

Another factor was the extent to which a man had been influenced by
abstract and national as opposed to concrete and local considerations in
forming his first image of the Communists. For example, educated
informants who had based their opinions, positive or negative, on abstract ideas of national policy were greatly impressed by the "sincerity"
of the Communist soldiers and officers and their "desire to serve the
people." They quickly began to work out a *modus vivendi* or a career
within the new power system.

On the other hand, for many respondents the first concrete impressions counted most. Their life experiences had given them little or no
sense of personal relationship to nation, national policies, or the politi-

cal process; their perspectives were local and concrete, personal and familial. They became involved in the civil war only when it had a direct impact on their communities or military units. Subjected to Communist control, they reacted directly and simply to their personal experiences. And those initial experiences spoke a language they understood—the language of plain interpersonal morality. They were soon ready to go along, with a minimum of personal anxiety and a good deal of enthusiasm.

The importance of all these effects is pointed up in the relatively few cases where initial treatment was harsh or even merely impersonal. These men were as anxious and as ready to conform as were the others, but their initial experiences led them to retain a shell of reserve and predisposed them to notice distasteful aspects of Communist control. For them, the Communist myth of democratic reasonableness never took shape.

Careers in the Communist World [12]

This report is principally concerned with longer-term reactions to Communist control. Undoubtedly the Communist policies which most of the respondents encountered as new subjects created a climate favorable to the development of pro-Communist attitudes. At the same time, the evident military power of the new rulers created widespread anxiety to get along with them.

The Communists were not slow to exploit their gains. Gradually they tightened the screws, at once impressing people with the extent of their power, making clear the new rules of the game, and manipulating social pressures brilliantly to achieve a high level of conformity with a minimum of sheer coercion.

Nationalist captives were put into special reindoctrination programs. At the big military-political universities, created by the party to remold the minds of representatives of the old regime and train potential cadres, former Nationalist officers rubbed shoulders with pro-Communist university students. In the villages, agitation was begun which would lead quickly to public trials and executions and to redistribution of land. Young men from all classes were maneuvered into "volunteering" for the army.

Kinds of Experience

The respondents averaged a little more than four years under Communist control, most of this time as members of military units.

Former Nationalist enlisted men were given as much as three months of reindoctrination under military auspices. This included "airing grievances" and "speaking bitterness" against their former officers and the old regime, learning the "purposes of the revolution" and the character

[12] See Appendix A, Tables 8–11.

of the Communist army, and declaring their penitence for "crimes against the people" committed before their capture. It also included learning to criticize themselves and their fellows in strictly Communist terms; "volunteering" to "serve the people" as soldiers of the revolution; and being classified by their teachers as "reliable," "promising," "doubtful," or "reactionary" raw material.

Nationalist officers and students went through a longer and considerably more intensive program. They were subjected to more psychological strain, but they also had more opportunity to learn the intellectual and organizational ropes; some went on into their line units with junior officer ratings.

Only nine respondents spent as much as a year as civilians under Communist control. Most civilians of military age "volunteered" within a few months and, unless they were highly educated, were assigned to regular units. Here too, political training held precedence over military, so that these men had indoctrination experiences in many respects similar to the others'.

The informants had spent an average of three and a half years as regularly assigned members of Communist army units, with service ranging from seven months to twelve years. Regardless of length of service, not one respondent regarded his experience as a routine stint of military service. In the years after the conquest of the mainland, the army remained the regime's principal agency of political reeducation and social control. The Communist army was in fact a new kind of social order, and it employed a complete array of social controls to ensure uniformly high levels of conformity in speech as well as action. Soldiers had to learn a new way of life.

Success in the New Regime

Judged in terms of the ranks they achieved, our informants were unusually successful in the new society. Almost half became officers, of platoon leader or higher rank; [13] one was a general officer, the political commissar of a division, and five were regimental or battalion officers. Five were NCO's with duties ranging from assistant platoon leader to assistant squad leader, and sixteen were common "warriors." Moreover, thirteen of the respondents (30 per cent) became full members of the Communist party.[14] This percentage was probably somewhat above the average for the CCF in Korea.

[13] Roughly equivalent to U.S. commissioned ranks.
[14] This probably understates the number of party members in the group. In a few cases, the informant's background and reported attitudes were such that interviewers considered party affiliation so unlikely that they did not ask. Subsequent comparison of cases suggested that some of these individuals were party members, and the military reports confirm it in two such cases, N-31 and R-2. The latter was expelled for grafting, however, and only the former is counted among the thirteen party members.

FIVE INDIVIDUAL CAREERS

Just what elements determined the attitudes varied individuals developed toward their new rulers? Later, we shall try to isolate the value criteria that controlled the commitment or withholding of loyalty. Excerpts from case history as told by the subjects themselves are used to give reality to the more abstract statements.[15]

In reading these brief biographies, the reader should keep in mind the central issues explored in this report: What did the informants think about in deciding how to behave toward the Communists? What kinds of things determined how they felt about the Communists? What purposes did they intend to serve by allying themselves with the Communists? In choosing non-repatriation, what were they trying to escape? What actions persuade Chinese soldiers that a ruling elite is good or bad?

Kao, Hero of the Red Army

Kao (N-10) was interviewed in a Pusan restaurant. He had been taken prisoner by U.S. forces while wounded and then had refused repatriation. He had escaped internment in June, 1953, a few weeks before the interview, during the confusion created by the mass breakout of Korean PW's which the Republic of Korea government engineered. He was born in Manchuria in 1930. His father was a landlord and a magistrate in the Manchukuo government. The Communists occupied his area immediately after the Japanese surrender in 1945.

When the Communists came in, they moved right into our house and stayed there. They said I had to join the army—everybody had to join the army. My father said he didn't want me to be a soldier, that at most I could serve as an interpreter. I spoke Mongolian as well as Chinese. So when I was fifteen years old I joined the Communist army as an interpreter, with the rank of a platoon-level officer. In the beginning, it was through me that the Communists were able to talk to the Mongolian people. In the course of time, they organized a division of four thousand men, all Mongolian, and I took part in that.

The year after I joined the army, both of my parents were killed by the Communists. My father was killed at the time of the land reform because he belonged to the landlord class and was an official of the Manchukuo government. I was not at home at the time and didn't know about it. Ordinarily the Communists don't trust the sons of the

---

[15] These case histories have been constructed from transcripts of the interviews. Essentially, the accounts are presented in the subjects' own words as translated by the interpreter. Only statements most directly relevant to the processes by which the respondents form their attitudes toward the Communist authorities have been included here.

capitalist class, because their parents will be killed in the purges and the Communists are always afraid that they will avenge the death of their parents. They didn't trust me too much in the beginning, but I had joined them when I was very young, and I expressed no sorrow on the surface when I learned that my parents had been killed. There was no use—I couldn't do anything to avenge their death. I had already served in the army for a year, and even in those days I had to hide my emotions. The Communists thought I passed the test.

In 1947 I was sent to a military-political college for four months. I received purely political training: Mao Tse-tung's teachings and then the purpose of the revolution. One of the things I remember about Mao's teaching is that everybody must contribute to the cause of the nation and that in serving the cause of the revolution we must not be afraid of struggle and hardship. The purpose of the revolution is to benefit the proletarians. By proletarians they mean workers, poor peasants, and middle-class peasants. Anything above that are capitalists. The Nationalists protected the enemies of the proletariat. As the cause of the proletariat, the revolution is invincible and victory is inevitable.

The bulk of the Communist army was made up of people who were very poor originally. The Communists explained that in the beginning all the people of the world were equal and the reason there are poor people is that they are exploited by the rich. This is very effective with the majority of these poor people. They believe the Communists are fighting for the welfare of the poor and will give them a good deal.

I myself didn't believe their teaching. I don't consider myself a highly intelligent person, but people of a higher educational level have greater doubts. That is why the Communists won't trust them. In my own case, I was young and I saw there was no alternative. The only thing I could do was to join them so my position would be more secure.

Every day we had small group discussions. For instance, we would discuss the proletariat and the capitalist classes. The discussion might take the line that the proletariat always work hard and do an honest day's labor, whereas the capitalists eat the fruit of the laborer and take life easy. If this was the topic, nobody could talk outside the topic or defend capitalism. In the beginning I didn't know this, so I was locked up in isolation for five days. I argued that if the country was prosperous everybody would attain a high level of culture and comfort like the capitalist classes, but that the Communists wanted to make everybody equal at the level of the proletariat. I asked whether they wouldn't need the high level of the intellectual classes to uphold the culture and civilization of China. All this talk got me into serious trouble.

They don't say they are punishing you when they put you in

isolation. They say you have to think it out alone to cool off. When I was in isolation they still questioned me every day and tried to get me to confess my error. You can either write your own confession or wait until they come in to talk to you. I couldn't write very well, so I had to wait until they came. They came every day. Then they skipped a day, and the next day they asked me whether I had changed my mind. Finally I said yes—I decided it was better to say what they wanted me to say—and I was released. After that I recognized that to protect myself I must be the most progressive element. In time I built up their confidence.

In the discussions and criticism meetings everyone must talk. Whether the class has eight people or twenty, everyone just has to say something. If you don't talk, it is the same as opposing them. They encourage you to talk, but if you say something wrong you will be in serious trouble. Everybody had to go through being criticized; it makes no difference whether you feel shy or hurt. I didn't feel so good about being criticized in public. They told me that if I was afraid of being criticized I could talk properly from then on and I wouldn't be criticized. Later on, after I had learned, I was the first one to criticize others. I think I was more lenient than a lot of other guys, but I was very persistent. If a guy didn't say the right thing, I would keep going until I finally had him saying the right thing.

I graduated from the school in the middle of the class. I was already a full-fledged cadre, although I was still very young. In June, 1947, I was accepted for membership in the party. Then I was rewarded because of my leadership in fighting and promoted to a company-level officer. Then they trusted me.

The discipline is very strict. You just couldn't take anything from the people or harm them, and you couldn't have anything to do with women. The penalties for violation were very severe. You might get three or four or five years of severe reform by hard labor, or you might even be executed. Only regimental commanders who had five years of military service and three years of party service could get married, and men who resented the rule were told that if they worked hard enough they would be regimental commanders. There are always some cadres in any group. Each cadre watches the others, and jointly they watch the other men and immediately report any violation. Nobody can get away with it.

I was married in 1949. By that time I was a regimental commander. My wife was not a party member, but she had to be approved by the party. My situation was unusual because I had established a lot of merits. I don't think I was promoted exceptionally fast. As an interpreter, I had started with the rank of platoon leader. I was a little young for my rank, but all the men were about eighteen or nineteen. There were no older persons.

I was called a Hero of the Communist army in China. I had established merit in five campaigns, so I got great praise. Very few people get that many merits.

I went to Peking in March, 1951, when Mao Tse-tung invited all the heroes and gave them a big party. That included war heroes of the air force and navy and labor heroes. From there, a group of two hundred of us were selected to go to Moscow, Warsaw, Prague, Berlin, and other places. We attended a dinner in Moscow with Stalin.

At the banquet, only the Chinese and Russian representatives were served both white and black bread; the representatives of all the other satellite countries received only white bread. The Chinese delegates ate only the white bread. At the end of the banquet Stalin made a speech. He said: "You may have noticed that only the Russians and the Chinese are given both white and black bread, but you may not know why. The reason is that we Russians regard the Chinese as our closest allies in the Communist revolution, and black bread represents the food of the proletariat. It was not correct for you"—pointing to the Chinese representatives—"who have just won your revolution to forget so soon about your proletarian people."

Then Stalin went on to talk about the Korean war. Korea would be unified, he said, but the Korean war was complicated because it was only a part of a universal conflict, and, just as there could not be a divided Korea, there could not be a divided world. The struggle would be long, he said, but in time there must be a defeat of the capitalist society in America. After the speech I thought war was imminent, unavoidable.

I began to have doubts about the Communists as early as 1949. I had seen that people had no freedom, no movement, or anything like that. And I had heard that changes were taking place in Formosa. Then in 1950 I got in trouble because of a woman. I divorced my first wife. I wanted to marry another one, and there were complications. I had already had the woman and I asked permission to get married. They wouldn't give me permission, so I said, "Whether you give me permission or not, I want to get married." Then I was publicly criticized. They demoted me from regimental commander to platoon leader in October, 1950. I went to Peking as a hero, but the fact that I was a person in trouble and had already been demoted was an indication that my future would be limited.

From the time of my demotion I harbored thoughts of dissatisfaction. I volunteered to come to Korea, hoping I would have a chance to join the Nationalists. Before, I had to follow all the discipline because there was no alternative; the Nationalists were taking a licking and retreating. But now we heard, over the radio, rumors that there was an army corps of Nationalist soldiers in Korea, and I thought there would be a way out. I could go to Korea and have a chance to get out

of the whole setup. In the beginning the Communists wouldn't let me
go, but I petitioned again and again, so finally they let me go.

The Communists try to indoctrinate you, to remove all your personal feelings, but that doesn't mean personal feelings no longer
exist. They are still there, but they are covered up. When you see a
chance you will expose them. The Communists create people who
cheat the people, and the people in turn learn how to cheat them.

Hsu, Supply Officer

At the time of the interview, Hsu (R-9) was thirty-three years old. He
had been captured by U.N. forces in 1952. As a prisoner of war, he had
at first refused repatriation but then changed his mind. He had come
from the countryside in North China. He had a wife and two sons,
fourteen and fifteen years old.

My father was an herb doctor. He died when I was four years old,
so I didn't have a chance to learn his trade. My mother is still alive. I
had two years of schooling, and after that I became a worker in the
shoe factory. This was in 1939. The factory was a small cooperative.
In the beginning the products of the factory were used to supply the
Communist army. Later, under Japanese pressure, the Communist
army withdrew and I continued to work, but now the products were
supplying the Nationalist army.

While I worked at the factory we had meetings, but they were just
concerned with production and the workers' welfare. Privately, workers discussed Communism and other things. At that time the government authorities didn't bother with such conversations.

When the Japanese moved into the area in force, the factory was
closed and I returned home for over a year. Between 1944 and 1947 I
was a peddler and sometimes I worked on the farm. We had some
land, not very much [about half an acre], but I managed to work it.

Meanwhile, the Communist guerillas began to infiltrate the area.
They came first during the time of the Japanese occupation and
continued afterward. At first I had no contact with them. There were
no formally organized political activities, but there were a number of
Communist agents going around talking to people. Everybody knew
these people were Communists, but they didn't talk about land reform
or anything. They just talked about how good the Eighth Route Army
was. They said it was the people's army and very well disciplined and
friendly to the people.

In 1947 some of my old co-workers in the shoe factory who had
been in the Communist army came back and tried to persuade me to
join the army. A lot of people in the village had joined the Communist army too. They thought what they had seen was pretty good. In
the army there were no beatings, and everyone was treated very
nicely. They asked me if I would join the army—if my mother would

let me go. My mother thought it was all right because the Communist army gives an initial payment for the family; for each of the four seasons the village is supposed to contribute a share of food for the family. I thought my wife could look after my mother and the kids. I felt their living would be assured, so I joined. In the Nationalist army, they just drafted people into the army and didn't bother about the family left behind. But with the Communists, it was all voluntary.

In the Communist army, we had to attend literacy classes and educational classes. We were taught about land reform and how it was being justly carried out. I also received letters from home.

The whole picture at home is much better than before. As a result of the Communist land reform we got about 12 mow [about two acres], because the amount was based on the size of the family. The bulk of the land we received was from my first cousin. His family had held a much larger portion of land—about thirty-two to thirty-five mow. Now he had about fifteen. There were no real landlords in my village. The largest holders had no more than fifty mow, and there were no killings in the village. There were some disciplinary measures, but not many. Now all the people have some land. There was no sign of resentment from those who surrendered land to the others.

The main difference between local government under the Nationalists and now is that the heads of the province and the cities and villages are elected. In my village they have already gone through several elections. Each family has one vote. In the old days the Kuomintang officials "squeezed" the people. They took money and never told the people how they spent it, they beat the people, they forced the people to labor; they never served the people. This is undemocratic. All Kuomintang officials were corrupt—even the very young ones.

Now anyone can be elected, provided the people see that he is good, unselfish, and never commits crimes against others. Such a man will become known as a good man, and naturally the people will elect him. Then there will be records of what he has done for the people, and if he has done a bad job he won't be in office. Chairman Mao Tse-tung was the son of a middle-class farmer, but he had contributed all his money to the cause of the people and so he was elected. The Communists operate more on the basis of practical considerations than on the basis of personal relationships. If a man's work is considered unsatisfactory, that is what counts most. The people's will and feelings will be made known, because the officials send agents to ascertain the people's reactions to the official policies.

All the news from home I got through letters. From 1947 on I was fighting against the Nationalists. By the beginning of 1950 we had completely conquered China; formal resistance from the Nationalists ceased.

Every year the recruitment system was better, and more people wanted to join the army than could be accepted. This is because the Communist army is a good army. They treat you well. You eat better—very decent food. There is no class distinction. Soldiers and officers are alike—they eat the same thing, wear the same kind of suit, and in battle the officers are always ahead of the soldiers leading them.

I never got in any serious trouble. Other people knew exactly what you were doing, and if you did anything wrong somebody would tell you it was wrong right away. So you don't have very much chance to make mistakes. A group of three men made up a cell, with one of them elected as cell leader. So you were living with three guys all together and you were being closely observed. Suppose a man went down to buy some vegetables for the troops and the farmer refused, saying these vegetables were for his own use. If the man insisted and got mad and then came back to his unit and talked about this thing, the chief of the cell would criticize him.

If problems came up that the cell leader couldn't solve, he would report them to the squad leader, who was in charge of ten to twelve men. If they had discussions there and criticized the men and still couldn't solve the problems, they would go to a higher level. Each man can criticize the cell leader, class leader, or even the compound or battalion leader. You can always criticize if a man has done something wrong and you saw it.

Usually you report yourself if you have done wrong, because you realize you have done something wrong; you might as well tell it; if other people report it, you will be in more serious trouble. If you report it and confess it, you won't have any trouble. It's very difficult to hide anything, especially anything to do with money. After all, everybody knows how much you get. If you suddenly exposed yourself as having a little more money than other people, they would immediately ask you where the hell the money came from. With two other guys living so close in the cell, you just don't know where to put things privately. In the army we had to record every single item we got—down to a little fountain pen, a handkerchief, or pocket money.

If you try to hide anything, the longer you hold out the more serious the problem becomes. You might as well confess it earlier and get it over with. Naturally, there are people who will not report themselves, but eventually they will be found out and then the criticism will be really serious.

I had never experienced criticism and confession before. I was very embarrassed to think that after making a mistake I had to admit it before the public, but I found the ordeal wasn't too bad. I felt relieved to a certain extent. There was no penalty in my case. I found that this process of confession and self-criticism and mutual criticism did increase efficiency. I found it very good, not only in the military organization, but also in civilian life. If a particular criticism is not correct, you can point out that the facts are not right. You cannot argue about the morals of the case.

Naturally, I aspired to be a party member, but supply men are not very important in politics. To be a party member you have to be progressive and firm in your work; you have to act courageously in battle; you have to be obedient to superiors—to the organization; you cannot play around with women; you have to be honest; and all that sort of thing.

There are cases when you become a party member directly, and there are cases when you can just be a reserve. It depends on your background, personal history, personal contribution, and so on. At the time I was captured in Korea I was neither a party member nor a reserve, but I thought my chances were pretty good. For a supply man, it is not difficult if you are honest and never take a bribe, if you adhere to the discipline of the organization, and if you are courageous. A supply man can gain merit by taking the soldiers their food when they are in battle and seeing that the food is properly delivered.

In the winter of 1950–51 we started to move. We were not told we were going to Korea, but we started receiving education about the Korean war and how we should mobilize against the American imperialists. In Hopeh we got a month of intensive education and then moved to Manchuria. The reason we went to Korea was that the Americans had joined the South Koreans and were attempting to invade China. They had even fired across the Yalu. We were shown pictures in newspapers from the Manchurian border. So the people, who are now having a better life in China, asked the government to organize a resistance against the invasion. The government responded to the people's request and rallied the forces.

The cadres told us about how China had prospered under Communism, how even the poor people could go to school, how everyone had food to eat and work to do, how the country was becoming more and more beautiful, and how happy the people were living under the Communist leadership. Then they said: "Now the Americans are beginning to invade China again. Shall we defend China inside our boundaries, or shall we try to stop aggression beyond our boundaries?" Of course the men answered that all military men know it is better to defend yourself outside your boundaries. Then each regiment and each battalion volunteered to come over.

I was captured in June, 1952, after a year in Korea as a platoon-level officer. At first I was in a prison compound of non-repatriates, but I felt I was not accepted by the non-repatriates. I felt that my life was in danger, and I asked to be transferred to a repatriate group.

The Communist policy in dealing with us when we return will be generous. I think we will be sent to a rest camp and be fed well and then sent home. The main reason I want to go home is to see my mother. She has been very kind to me. My personal desire is to remain with my mother till the end of her life. I like my village. They are nice people, and they are very nice to my mother. If possible I would like to become a peddler again and remain there. Of course that is just my personal wish, and you have to abide by the Communists' decision.

The Communists realize the importance of the home, but the nation comes first. While you are in the service you have to think of your country first, and after that you can go home.

According to the new PW's, family life is much better now. They say the countryside is mechanized and that there are electric lights in all the main villages. Last year they began to have mechanized equipment for farming—tractors and so on—in my own village.

I myself saw Manchuria, where the Russians had technicians who helped the Chinese to rebuild the factories which made the tractors and equipment. I think China is very much indebted to Russian technical help. Only by Russia's help is China now capable of producing airplanes, motor cars, and locomotive engines. I myself have seen some of these Russian workers, and they are particularly courteous toward the Chinese people. They wear simple dress just like the Chinese, and they show the highest respect toward Chinese women. Russia helps China because just after the Communists established the People's Republic the treaty of mutual aid was signed. Then, with the establishment of Soviet-Chinese cultural relations and friendship organizations, Russia and China became one family. Russia is willing to help China because of this. There is no other motive.

Lee, Combat Officer

Lee (N-8) was thirty years old when he was interviewed in a U.N. prison camp. He defected in October, 1951, and subsequently refused repatriation to Communist China. He had grown up in North China in a medium-sized city and in the nearby countryside. His father had had eight years of schooling, some of which was in a mission school, and was a Christian. Lee's single year of schooling was acquired at a mission school when he was sixteen.

My father was a farmer, and the family made its living from the land. We had two hundred mow [over 30 acres]. Because the family was rich, I just played all day long with my younger brother. My brother actually went through eight years of school. He wanted to go to school, but I didn't so I had only one year of it.

Between 1937 and 1948 the Communists and the provincial warlord fought for control of the city. Seven times the Communists came to the town then left. They tried to enter ten times, but three times they were repulsed. Of the seven actual entries, only three were contested.

When I was sixteen, even though my father wanted me to stay in school, I joined the anti-Communist militia in the town. I wanted to be a soldier, but I entered the organization, not only for a military life, but also to fight the possibility of Communist control. The Communist party threatened the liquidation of my family. In the militia we were always on the move chasing the Communist guerillas. We had daily drills and classes, including some propaganda classes, mainly concerning the cruelty and banditry of the Communists. An educated middle-class farmer was the chief, but usually only the rich and educated upper classes were members. Some of the poor actually did join because they were afraid of a Communist attack on the city, but most of them didn't because they were opposed to the militia. The poor who favored the Communists believed the Communists would give them land. They favored the Communist party, so the militia also served to keep the poor under control—though we never fought with the poor.

Each time the Communists took a village or town in the region, they organized the poor and took all the land of the landlords and rich farmers and divided it among the poor. When the Communists were forced to withdraw again, the militia would return the land to the previous owners. The Communists always urged the poor to fight the rich. They stirred up controversy between the rich and poor to use for their own benefit.

Through this long seesaw struggle, the size of the Communist army based in the mountains nearby was increasing. Each time they captured and then left the city, some of the poor left with them voluntarily, and some personnel of the anti-Communist military organization, students, and merchants would be forcibly taken to carry the loot when they retreated.

After a year and a half the local militia was absorbed into the provincial army, but I kept my job as messenger in battalion headquarters. On the surface, the provincial army was a part of the Nationalist army; we fought with them against the Communists, but we were not really in the Nationalist army. In August, 1942, I was captured by the Communists. I was still only nineteen, but by now I had the rank of assistant platoon leader.

After my capture, the Communists said, "You were in the Nationalist army," and threatened me if I wanted to fight with the Nationalists again. They said that since a young man must join one army and the Communist army was the best because they were for the people, I should join them. The Communists didn't beat me. They told me the Nationalist army was no good and they listed their defects.[16] There was special training for former Nationalists. There were "liberation groups" assigned to work on the Nationalist units. Most of the cadres

[16] For the Communist version of the defects of the Nationalist army, see the cases of Fu, Kao, and Hsu.

were Communist party members, but if there were only a few former Nationalists then perhaps civilians would instruct them.

I don't remember much about the actual classes; I only remember that we were told to change our thinking and be gallant, stand hardship, obey orders, and say nothing against the Communist party.

There was a public class to change thinking. You had to speak frankly about mistakes you had committed in the Nationalist army, such as robbing people. Class members would then argue these matters. Sometimes the classmates would criticize and embarrass me. That night the instructor would come and console me in my sadness. He would tell me to change my thinking so that I would not be criticized any more. I wasn't criticized very seriously, because I had been in the Nationalist army only a short time, but I was also criticized because my family were landlords and Christians. I was asked if I was a Kuomintang member and what I thought of the Kuomintang.

I was also asked why I had killed Communist party members. I had killed two party members in my native city. When I was captured by the Communists I was with others who knew about it, and they told the Communists. I had admitted only one, so I was accused of not being frank in the class. I didn't confess the other because the instructor told the rest of the class that it was enough to know I had killed one Communist party member and that I should not be further embarrassed. I didn't think it was kindness in the instructor but a trick to make me more favorable to the Communist party. I was very scared and promised to kill more Nationalists to make up.

My chief critic was a poor man who had been forced into the militia. The Communists always used the trick of contradiction between two people. After the discussion of the killing, all the others criticized me at the urging of the leader. If anyone hadn't criticized me, he would have been regarded as a sympathizer of mine. There were some sympathizers, but they spoke only in private. They joined in the criticism but explained later that they had had to criticize me. If anyone was identified as a friend of mine or of anyone else being criticized, the Communists said that there were no personal friends in the Communist party and that the man should not be afraid to criticize. The instructor took notes and later stated some conclusions—usually that the crime was only that of the Nationalist officers, because they compelled the common soldiers.

The Communists instructed us on working hard and on their efforts to serve the people, and promised us a comfortable life when the Nationalists were defeated. All were to have the rights of free speech, equal living, freedom to join the party, and—at first—freedom of religion. At that time I believed their teaching, but also I had no choice about joining the army. So after a few months in the "liberation group," I was assigned as a common soldier. Over the next few years I had six promotions, up through all the unit commands, and was made assistant battalion commander in 1948. My duties were purely soldierly. It was my bravery that won these promotions; I was a good marksman, strong in command, and I won battles.

After three years in the army I became a candidate for the party, and in 1948 a party member. I would have wanted to enter the party sooner—as soon as possible—but they required a three-year investigation period because I came from a rich family and had been a Nationalist soldier. Poor men who had not been in the Nationalists could become members in only two months. Only superior people could join the party. You had to be very honest, work hard, be eager to learn, and not talk much. You must want to join; that was evidence of your trustworthiness. Your knowledge of Communism and of Russia—especially Russia—was very important. There were classes to teach Communist party history and theory and many textbooks to read. I was much interested in these things at the time, but later my interest was reduced when I came to understand all their tricks and cruelty, which were worse than those of the Kuomintang.

You had to be eager to serve the party and obey party orders. Even if your family asked you to return home, you must disobey or the Communists' work would be handicapped. The idea is to eliminate family ties. You are not supposed to be concerned over a death in the family. Another thing you had to promise was that when you were fighting you would not surrender until death. This was an oath only party members took.

When I was a platoon leader I was publicly criticized once. Some of the enlisted men said I was not concerned about my men. I felt that the Communist army was democratic and criticism like that was in order. The criticism did me no good; I felt very sad because somebody might doubt my thinking. The political officer told me that this meeting was to make the Communist army different from the Nationalist.

Anyone from a squad leader up can call meetings to discuss the mistakes of subordinates: bothering civilians, fighting with other soldiers, or even disobeying garrison orders. The meetings for self-criticism and mutual criticism are planned by the directing committee of the company. They are party members. Each meeting is planned for a particular person; no one else can be criticized. The witnesses are arranged and well prepared. The purpose of the meeting is to instruct people how not to make mistakes like those being criticized. They were very effective. There were many young soldiers who understood little and thought the meetings were not so bad. But they are no good, because they are controlled by the party and there is no freedom of speaking.

I had no real political interest; my good fighting was my sole recommendation for promotion. In peacetime I could not have been a regimental commander, but in war I could be because I could show my ability to fight. That is my personal opinion. To rise in peacetime, you must have a good mind, be a Communist party member, believe strongly, and obey the party orders; I couldn't be a regimental commander because of my small education and because I didn't like political meetings.

Sometimes I argued with party members because I held different opinions. My superior officer asked, "With your different opinions, how can you direct men to fight?" He meant that since I cared little for politics I couldn't lead my men well. The Communist party believes politics are more important than fighting, and I was only interested in fighting. Therefore, my promotions were slower than others.

The great strength of the Communist army lies in its use of political tricks to control the army. The tricks changed from year to year; there were too many to tell about. After the Japanese surrender they had a "morale-correcting campaign" to purge the Japanese and Kuomintang spies. Many were killed. Another trick was the "anti-pride and hatred campaign." The political officer made contradictions between the officers and enlisted men; the men had to make complaints against the officers to political agents who went around for the purpose. Another was the "three-check meetings" to check officers on their concern for the enlisted men.[17]

I came to understand all their tricks and their cruelty, for example, the brutal liquidation—the expropriation or killing—of the rich and former officials. They were killed by brutal means, such as being tied with rope and pulled by a bull along the street or being placed on a red-hot iron plate until dead.

I remember being impressed by the public trial meetings. The sentence was decided upon in advance by the Communist party committee at the division level; the trial was for the purpose of making an example for the people. The chairman asked everyone to express an opinion; but because of the very large numbers present, only representatives of the people could actually speak. The killing is what impressed me. If the man was to be executed, the killing was done right on the spot. The prisoner was taken under the platform and shot, and then a representative of each unit would come and take a look.

Finally, I received letters announcing the deaths of my mother and father. I learned that the Communists had captured my native city in 1948. When they were coming in, an American missionary, who was a good friend of my father's and whose church my father had joined,

---

[17] When an individual committed an error, a "three-check meeting" was held in which three aspects of his life were investigated—his family status, his occupation, and his thinking.

fled by air and left my father in charge. After the Communists captured the city my father was accused of being a U.S. spy. My mother was killed too, because she was of landlord status and was charged with spying for the missionary. She was tortured. Finally, she admitted the charge, but neither of them had any spy materials. I learned of their execution through three letters received on the same day. The mail room had changed the words about the deaths to say they were both well, but a friend of mine in the mail room gave me the straight information.

Because of this, I began to hate the Communists and, when I was sent to Korea, I decided to surrender. In October, 1951, a U.S. plane was shot down while I was on patrol. With the three members of my patrol I brought the one survivor back to the U.N. lines. They broadcast my story across the lines to the Communist army, and it was written up in *Stars and Stripes*.

Fu, Old Noncom

Fu (N-22) is a large man with a forceful personality. At the time he was interviewed he was thirty-five years old and a major leader among the anti-Communist PW's interned on Cheju Island. He came from a family of poor farmers in North China and had three years of education. He had spent ten years in the Nationalist army, fighting first the Japanese and then the Communists, and had achieved the rank of master sergeant. As a Communist soldier, Fu tried three times to desert before he succeeded in crossing the U.N. lines in Korea in November, 1950. He was one of the first hundred Chinese PW's taken in Korea.

I first heard about the Communists in 1939. The Nationalist army was fighting the Japanese, and I heard there was a Red army assisting us. But then in 1945, the year the Japanese surrendered, my unit was dispatched to take over Paotow in Inner Mongolia. The Communists began to attack the city. They used loudspeakers to make propaganda; they claimed that the city should be taken over by them, not by the Nationalists. At this time I thought that the Communist troops were a great threat to the Nationalist army.

I was captured by the Communists in December, 1948, when our unit was encircled near Peking. Before I was captured I saw a lot of the intrigue and the despotic nature of the Communist army; so I hated them very much. When I was captured I was disappointed, but the only thing I could do was join the army. After my unit was captured, all the officers above platoon leader were transferred to one place, all the noncommissioned officers were gathered in another place, and all the soldiers put in a third place. We were trained by the Communists in a "liberation group" for about three months.

The longer I lived there, the more I understood the real menace of Communism. The first step of this training was for the Communists to tell us that we had belonged to reactionary troops and that now we were lucky to have a chance to join the People's Liberation Troops so we should serve the people. Second, the Communists wanted all of us to admit our guilt in persecuting the people before we were captured.

If anyone told the Communist leaders he didn't do anything wrong in the Nationalist army—never hurt any people—the Communist leaders would ask him, "Did your regiment fight with the Communist army?" If the answer was yes, the Communist leader would then ask him if he had damaged any people's houses. The answer would be, "I damaged a house, because you can't prevent damaging a house during fighting." Then the Communist leader would accuse him, "You damaged the people's houses, and so you are guilty; so be criticized." The Communist leader then would ask, "Did you kill any people during battle?" If the man answered, "I never killed any people during the battle," the Communist leader would ask him if he had killed any poultry. Maybe the man answered, "Yes, I killed some poultry." Then the Communist leader would accuse him, "You damaged some property of the people, and so you are guilty."

If someone admitted his guilt in the Nationalist army—if he even admitted that his unit killed poultry or damaged houses—the Communists would tell him that since he had done some wrong to the people he must do some good in the People's Army so that the people would forgive him. The only thing you can do is promise them what they ask, and so we promised the Communist leaders we would do what they wanted us to do.

In fact, all the promises that we made to the Communist leaders were only superficial. In our hearts we disagreed with them but we were afraid that if we didn't promise, maybe they would accuse us of other guilts. If someone swore he didn't do anything wrong to the people and never admitted his guilt, the Communist leaders would send him to division headquarters and court-martial him. If his sentence was light he might be put in jail for one or two months, but if it was very serious he was transferred to another place. None of us knew what happened to such a man; the Communists never killed any of our liberation group in the presence of a group of people.

Or maybe if a man didn't promise, the Communist leaders would say that before he was captured he belonged to the reactionary troops and now he still didn't want to obey the orders of the People's Army. They would say he was a reactionary agent and he would be killed right away. I didn't see anyone who was killed by the Communists right away during the criticizing meetings. But there was a man in my company who, because he didn't admit his guilt, was sentenced to be court-martialed; because life in jail was very hard, he died in twenty days.

There was also another step. The Communist leaders held complaining meetings and let all of us complain about our superiors in the Nationalist army. They encouraged us to blow off steam. If one man complained about how a superior officer oppressed him or beat him, and another said he was never persecuted by his superiors in the Nationalist army, then the Communist leaders wanted the second man to sympathize with the first. In this step they didn't force everyone to complain about their superiors.

Once a political instructor told us that the Eighth Route Army deserved all the credit for the eight-year anti-Japanese war and that the Nationalists did not do a single thing against the Japanese. Hearing this, I was indignant, and so I jumped up and said: "Ever since Generalissimo Chiang declared war against Japan, China has been divided into eight war districts. These were divided later into twelve, and I can even tell you the names of several district commanders. They were Han Fu-chiu, Yen Shih-shan, Hsiu Yueh, and Chen Cheng. Were they Nationalist or Communist leaders?"

When the Communists heard that, they were all startled. Then I continued: "Do the Communists have any conscience?" Everybody was dumbfounded. At last one Communist cadre stood up and pointed at me, saying, "You are a reactionary!" I was taken away by the police. What I told them was true, but they jailed me for a week, giving me two bowls of rice daily; I didn't even get any salted vegetables with my meals or any blanket or comforter. From that time I began to understand the Communists. I learned that they called black white and white black. The thought of trying to make my escape first occurred to me then.

In the liberation group I didn't admit any personal guilt, but I did admit that my unit had hurt some poultry and damaged some people's houses. So the leaders said that if I did something for the good of the army they would excuse me. I was assigned to a squad where I was the only one who had been in the Nationalist army. My rating was private. I was ordered to do all the hard work. I had to sweep the ground and cook the meals. When we marched from one place to another, after we reached our destination all my comrades could lie down and rest, but I had to cook, sweep, boil the water, and so on. And if we carried shells, the rest of the men only carried three shells, but I had to carry five. If I complained about the hard work, the Communist leaders would accuse me again. They would say, "He doesn't want to do hard labor, and he doesn't want to do anything for the good of the army, and so he is a reactionary agent." When I saw they were going to make some accusation against me, I would work hard. Sometimes I saw they weren't worried about me, and then I could slack off.

In the squad the first meeting after breakfast was the political class, usually for an hour. After the class they held discussion meetings, usually another hour, and then a twenty- or thirty-minute meeting for criticism. There was another mutual criticism meeting for about thirty minutes in the afternoon. Actually there were three criticism meetings every day. The rest of the time we worked.

In the political classes the first thing they wanted to teach us was the theory of Marx and Lenin, and how under the leadership of the Communists the whole law could be reformed and improved. The second thing was about the U.S. as an imperialist country and how the U.S. wanted to invade other countries. In the discussion and criticism meetings the Communists only obtained verbal agreement, never agreement from the heart. No one dared to say anything. If anyone disagreed with the Communist party he would be criticized.

I was never promoted, because I was put in jail three times in the space of a year. Twice it was for trying to desert, once for speaking my mind. I had no opportunity to talk to other people in the squad during this period. Only occasionally the party members wanted to talk to me.

I was always dreaming about this very painful situation. Often I dreamed I saw a Nationalist unit with some of my friends and wanted to desert to them, but upon my desertion I was discovered by the Communist army. I always woke up at that point. Once I shouted in the dream so that I was heard by other people in my hut. And these people asked me, "Why do you shout so loudly?" I said, "Nothing, nothing, I only dreamed." When I was in the Nationalist army I dreamed different dreams. It was always about fighting with another man whom I couldn't stand, and I always escaped from the fighting because I could run very fast.

Sometimes people were criticized for talking in their sleep. There were two cases in my platoon. One had been in the Nationalist army and was very dissatisfied with the Communists. One night he shouted, "I want to fight with you!" The squad leader woke him up and asked, "Why do you shout, 'I want to fight with you'?" The man said, "I just dreamed I was fighting with you in the battlefront, and because I dreamed it I shouted it." The squad leader told him: "You haven't forgotten your reactionary thinking. If you don't remove your reactionary thinking from your mind, you will not be excused by the party or the army."

There was another case—one of my comrades. His father was a landlord whose property had been confiscated. He was very unhappy in the army, and one night he shouted that the Communist government would fail and that if he had a machine gun he would kill the squad leader, the platoon leader, and the political instructor. He could not tell them the reason he shouted, and so they put him in jail.

All of us in the Communist army were just like puppets. Although you have eyes, you cannot see; although you have ears, you cannot hear anything; although you have a mouth, you cannot say anything.

Two times during the first year I tried to desert. Once the district government discovered me, and I was sent back and confined in the regimental jail. After my release I went back to the battalion, where I faced a "struggle meeting" [18] attended by the entire battalion.

In February, 1950, we moved to Manchuria. My work was to load and unload freight. I saw daily with my own eyes the trains carrying great quantities of soybeans and bean cake. One day a deputy commissioner came to our place just as I was carrying a bag of soybeans over my shoulder. I asked him where all the soybeans were going. He said: "Don't you know, those are for our Russian brothers. This is only a token of friendship we have been showing to the Russians since the signing of the Sino-Russian agreement." I asked him why I didn't see things coming back to us from the Russian side. He told me that the time had not come yet. This conversation gave me a further understanding of Communism. I realized that the Communist government was like Wang Ching-wei's government [the Japanese puppet regime in Manchuria], that they were not for the people and that the signing of the Russian agreement was a deed of high treason.

In July, 1950, the bandits—the Communist officers—called for study of the aggression of the American imperialists in Korea. They taught us to give aid to our Korean brothers and root out American imperialists. I was very glad to hear all this, because I knew I was going to get a chance to escape pretty soon. But many of the soldiers, because they had suffered very much under the control of the Japanese, were afraid of being controlled by the U.S.

They told us lots of lies in the classroom. Once the platoon leader said, "American imperialist airplanes are no good, and Americans are only paper tigers." I asked: "Are the American planes really bad? Look at all the destruction they caused in Anshan. Also, even the authorities once told us that the reason we couldn't liberate Taiwan is because the American Imperialist Seventh Fleet is there." The platoon leader was very angry and said I was pro-American. He sent me to the security section at regimental headquarters. My name was listed for spying, but they couldn't find anything to prove it. I was held for twenty-seven days. I got only two meals a day. For each meal I got only a very small bowl of rice, and in the morning I had to get up when the bugle blew, and so I couldn't get enough food to eat or enough time to sleep. They wanted me to confess I was a spy. Finally, I was released from jail because the unit was about to enter Korea. This was in October, 1950.

When we entered Korea the Communist leaders told us that U.S. troops had just invaded Korea, and the Nationalist government had dispatched thirty-three thousand men to assist U.N. troops in attacking

[18] A quasi–trial, quasi–camp-meeting at which the culprit is publicly charged with wrongdoing by the chairman, the wrongness of his behavior is elaborated and emphasized by fellow soldiers in the audience, and a full confession and promise to improve are exacted from the culprit or he is sentenced. See Lee's references to "public trial meetings."

Korea, so that we must defend our nation and enter Korea to fight with them. I was forced to enter Korea, but I thought this was a chance for me—maybe I could meet the Nationalist soldiers.

Chien, Medical Aid Man

Chien (F-5) was interviewed in the United States in 1954. He had deserted from the CCF and had been picked up by advancing U.N. forces in June, 1951. As one of the fourteen thousand PW's who refused repatriation, he had finally been sent to Formosa. There the Nationalist government had selected him as a member of a delegation to "tell the story of the PW's" to the United States. Chien was born in 1928. His father, a well-to-do businessman, operated a construction company and an ice factory. Later, the family moved to Kweichow province, in southwest China. Chien was in his second year of college when the Communist forces occupied his home town in December, 1949.

I first came into contact with Communists some time before they took over. I was studying history. After the end of World War II the Communists in the university student body agitated constantly to arouse dissatisfaction with the Nationalist government.

One of the things they stressed that was important to me was the uncertainty of our professional future under the Nationalist government. They pointed out that highly trained students had great difficulty getting jobs when they left the university and often ended by doing menial chores. They described this as just one example of the uneconomical use of Chinese resources by the Nationalists. They said that under the Communists students would get good jobs and have a secure and happy future, and that China would grow powerful because her resources would be fully used. This was a very effective line. The Communists also stressed the inefficiency and corruption of the Nationalist government, and insisted the Communists would build a strong China, free from Western exploitation.

When the Communists infiltrated the city they did two things. They spread Communist propaganda generally, and told everyone there was nothing to fear and so they should not resist or flee. They said the Communists were concerned with the welfare of the people and would treat them well. And, in fact, when the Communists first took over the city they behaved extraordinarily well toward civilians; everyone was very favorably impressed. All my previous judgments were reinforced.

It took me a year to alter my favorable impression. The only doubt I had in the beginning was because almost immediately all the students who had been giving me Communist propaganda were appointed officers in the army or officials in the government. I realized suddenly that they had been covert party members, whereas I had thought that they were only convinced students without any definite political ties. Soon I began also to notice that the Communists took food from the peasants, and I was disturbed by the cruelty of the struggle meetings and purges.

My family's assets were confiscated, and my father was arrested and sent away—I do not know where he is or what happened to him. At the time I felt this was all right. I felt that in order to build a new social structure it was necessary to destroy the old, and I did not feel bitter about the personal deprivation involved.

Naturally, I had no more income and could not continue my studies at the university. The Communists said that I should not feel badly, that I had always received the benefits of the rich and that I must learn to share the hardships of the people. I agreed with them. They told me I could continue my education at a military-political college, at which I would be charged nothing. They said that afterward I could go to work for the party in any job I chose.

At the military-political university I was completely cut off from the outside world. All of the students were assigned to hard manual labor in order to gain a proletarian point of view. Each evening we participated in meetings for self-investigation, to reform our thoughts and purge us of our bourgeois class consciousness. Each student was made responsible for reporting, not only on his own thoughts, feelings, doubts, and failings as a worker, but also on those of the others. In this way the Communists created an atmosphere of constant mutual watchfulness and suspicion. While all this was unpleasant, I felt it was necessary if I was to learn to serve the people, and generally I tried very, very hard to fulfill my work quota so that I would not be criticized and because I wanted to make a good record.

When we finished at the college, we were told that we must join the army. This was in direct contradiction to what had been promised, and one man questioned the Communist political officer about it. The Communists were very angry and called the student a counter-revolutionary. He disappeared, and everyone thought he had been given a different kind of job. Later we learned he had been arrested. At the time of this episode the Communists repeated that the party did not trust intellectuals, because they tended to waver in their loyalty. In order to be trusted, intellectuals must try very hard to remake themselves and must report on themselves, their friends, and their families. I was disappointed, but I thought that a particular Communist, rather than the party or government, was responsible for the unkept promise.

We were told that now, with the civil war over, the task of the army was to defend China's borders. I thought I was going to Manchuria to defend the Manchurian border. Only when we crossed the Yalu did I realize we were going to Korea; there had been no mention of this possibility. It was at this time that I began to hate the Communists for their deceitfulness.

Although I was nominally a cultural officer [an educational function without political or administrative responsibility], in Korea my duty was to take care of the wounded. I was very disturbed by the way the Communists decided who should be saved. Communist party members and cadremen have special insignia inside their jackets. We were told to look first inside the jacket of a wounded man and see if he had such insignia. If he did, he was to be saved if at all possible; as far as the others were concerned, it didn't matter. If non-party soldiers were wounded and could not walk, they were either left or shot. I realized at this time that I would not be among those saved if I were wounded.

I not only had to pick up the wounded on the battlefield but I had to accompany them a hundred miles to safety. This meant walking there and back. My physical condition was very bad at this time—I had tuberculosis—and often I could not walk the distance. My political officer told me I must do better, that I was not progressive. I then started leaving two days in advance of the other people in order to get a head start, so that I wouldn't have to walk so far each day. This worked for a time, but I became weaker. Finally, in a big retreat in June, 1951, I fell behind and hid for a while, then found the U.N. lines and surrendered.

I also hated the Communists because of their "human-sea" methods. In the pre-battle meetings the Communists said there were only two enemies left—the three divisions on Taiwan, and the Americans. They said the Americans were afraid of close fighting and were soft and would run from hand-to-hand combat, so that even though American weapons were good they would be useless. The political officer asked for volunteers to make pledges. One man would volunteer to kill fifteen Americans, and another would volunteer to destroy two tanks. The political officer then made the volunteers write out these pledges and sign them. At the time of the battle he would call these men out and say: "You have volunteered to fight especially bravely today and to kill fifteen Americans or destroy two tanks. You must lead the charge." They would run forward because there were guns behind them and they were afraid of the Communists as well as because they wanted to fight the Americans. I was much disturbed because the Communists valued their equipment much more than they did human lives. They were much too cruel to their own soldiers.

These five men thus include three from relatively well-to-do families, two from poor families. Two are highly educated, three have had little formal schooling. Two entered the Communist world as prisoners of war; one was drafted for his special skills; one was a rare genuine volunteer; and one was a university student, idealistic and strongly pro-Communist. Their experience under the Communists ranges from eighteen months to ten years. Two had attended intensive indoctrination centers; none had spent much time as a civilian under Communist control. Two became party members. Two were what we would call field-grade officers, two were low-echelon staff officers, one was a private. The most successful of the lot, a regimental commander and Hero of the Red Army, was on the skids as a Communist at the time of his capture by the U.N.

The experiences of these five exemplify also the wide variety of techniques and sanctions the Communists employ to persuade and to exact conformity. In adjustment to the new regime, the men represent a gallery of extremes. Hsu volunteered, and the longer he stayed in the CCF the more pro-Communist he seems to have become. Fu disliked the Communists before he met them, and grew to hate them more with every passing month. Kao was a highly effective opportunist, but eventually got in trouble through outright defiance of party authority. Chien wanted deeply to identify with the proletariat, but eventually became disaffected because of the discomforts and risks to which he himself was subjected.

As a gallery of variant combinations of motive and circumstance, these five may be said to represent the forty-three. They illustrate the wide variety of factors that entered into the behavior and attitudes of Chinese soldiers under Communist control. These case histories should serve to:

> Convey an idea of the kinds of human beings we are here concerned with.
> Illustrate the basic social organization of the Chinese Communist Forces, and thus the kinds of demands and opportunities which the respondents met as they tried to adjust to this new social order.
> Suggest many of the factors that entered into the process of political judgment and some of the ways in which these factors interacted to produce pro- or anti-Communist attitudes.

LEARNING TO LIVE WITH COMMUNIST AUTHORITY

Arthur Koestler once remarked that "statistics don't bleed." Neither do analytical descriptions by social scientists. Accounts of the experiences of Kao, Hsu, Chien, Lee, and Fu should help to bridge the gap between the analysis presented in this report and the human experience of living through a totalitarian revolution.[19] Their stories can serve to clarify and illustrate general elements explored in this chapter to provide background for the more detailed analysis that follows.

Characteristics of the Regime

Out of the experiences of these five men and the thirty-eight others interviewed in such detail emerge the outlines of social organization and control in the Chinese Communist armed forces.

[19] See also Chapter 3, below.

In large part the new system is a repetition of structure and techniques already familiar in other totalitarian movements: the politicalization of every phase of living; the destruction of existing social groups and the attempt to construct a political community in which all relations among men are a function of their relation to the state; the insistent emphasis on official ideology, the demands for positive loyalty, and the centrality of the "thought crime"; the systematic surveillance and reporting to enforce conformity and isolate the individual; the hierarchical classification and differential treatment of subjects according to a group identification derived from the ideology. All these have been present to a greater or lesser degree in the Soviet Union, Nazi Germany, and the "people's democracies" of Eastern Europe. The details of totalitarianism vary, however, with doctrine, national traditions, and experience, and Communist China differs from other totalitarian states in a number of significant ways.

Class Structure and Differential Opportunity

In the usual Communist attempt to invert the social order, a landlord or rich farmer or other capitalist and feudal background does constitute an obstacle to the achievement of rank or power in the new Chinese society. However, such a background by no means precludes acceptance or advancement, as the experience of Lee, the combat officer, and Kao, the regimental commander, indicates. Much the same thing can be said of previous service in the Nationalist army, advanced education, and religion.

Mass Thought Reform as a Serious Objective

Evidence from the case histories serves to emphasize that the Chinese Communist leaders have as an operational goal the restructuring of individual consciousness to conform to new ways of thinking, feeling, and acting. They are not willing to accept the passive conformity to the demands of national authority which seems to have been traditional in China.

While some kind of thought reform is a characteristic aim of all totalitarian regimes, the Chinese have set about its accomplishment on a mass basis more purposefully and more effectively than have others. In their reeducation processes they have utilized techniques never before applied on a mass basis.[20]

New Techniques of Social Control

It is clear that the Chinese have developed new techniques for social control or, at a minimum, have applied known techniques in new ways. Self-criticism and mutual criticism, for example, are utilized, not only in special indoctrination camps, but throughout the army, to expose

[20] See, for example, Chapter 3, below.

error and to probe the minds and emotions of soldiers. Such criticism becomes the point at which surveillance, overt sanctions, and education intersect to expose, censure, and correct shortcomings of attitude and conduct. Kao, Lee, and Fu, the old Nationalist noncom, see criticism as a part of the system of coercive controls. To Hsu, an avowed Communist, it is a technique for educating people and enabling them to stay out of trouble. In the light of their personal experiences, this difference in viewpoint is understandable.

Although four of these five informants were disaffected and had gotten into trouble with authority, it is noteworthy that neither they nor any of the other thirty-eight referred to a special secret police apparatus—a distinct group, apart from the regular party organization, with special responsibility for surveillance and the enforcement of conformity.[21] The role of a secret police—in fact, the existence of such a force—is vitally important in an inquiry such as ours because its presence in any given group is a symptom of the regime's inability to achieve its objectives without coercion.

Instead, the informants picture a system of detailed surveillance and reporting carried on by each against all—a system in which even the opponents of the regime participate in forcing conformity on themselves and others. Party members and cadres are described as important in the system of social control, but only in the sense that they have more responsibility for organizing and are more vigilant in performing functions expected of all.

The absence of references to a secret police in these interviews is especially striking by contrast with reports of Soviet and East European defectors, who almost invariably identify the secret police as a major focus of anxiety. Possibly the respondents had failed to recognize a covert informer system and independent counterintelligence operation like that of the MGB in the Soviet Army. What is important for the purposes of this report is that the respondents did not think and react on the assumption that the Communists had a secret police apparatus.

The data suggest a hypothesis that the Chinese Communist army does not have, because it does not need, a distinct body of informers tied to an independent chain of command for counterintelligence collection and police intervention. Apparently the Chinese Communist leaders have devised effective techniques for ensuring universal surveillance. In the presence of high levels of fear, ambition, and anxiety to conform, these techniques perform for the lower echelons of the army many of the functions of a secret police system, and perform them with greater efficiency and economy.

It is entirely conceivable that the Chinese Communists, unlike their Soviet counterparts, will also succeed in achieving effective totalitarian

---

[21] They spoke of both security forces and local police. The existence and character of these forces have long been recognized in Communist China, and neither is properly referred to as a national secret police.

control of behavior in civil life without the need for a secret police of the Soviet type and size. Traditional Chinese society lacks any conception of individual privacy; the general assumption that the business of each family ought to be known to the others has been a vital stabilizing element in village life and in commerce. If the Communists are able to exploit these attitudes and habits as successfully in the villages as they have in the army, they have cracked a fundamental factor in the local community's historic ability to prevent governmental control of the pattern of Chinese life.

Furthermore, in doing so they will have avoided the disadvantages of using a secret police system, which would be a major source of population alienation and capable of becoming an important power center in its own right. Such an outcome would be even more dangerous to the future of freedom in China than would a repetition of the Soviet development.[22]

Conformity versus Identification

Traditionally in China the ordinary individual accepts political authority but identifies with it only slightly. He regards some rulers as better than others, but in general he does what he must and tries to protect his own interests, which are closely related to those of his family. This acceptance of situations beyond one's control involves an effort to come to terms with the holders of power while keeping them psychologically at arm's length.

The Communists, however, are not content with this relationship. They demand that their subjects actively identify with them and give them allegiance along with obedience. At the same time, they are trying to transform the social order and overhaul the lives of their subjects. This effort creates innumerable points of potential conflict. New demands conflict with old customs and expectations; the new morality offends and denies the old.

The case histories suggest both the wide range of matters on which the Communists require their soldiers to reverse habitual patterns of conduct and speech and the intensity of the Communist demand for loyalty. The interviews show overwhelmingly that the respondents tried very hard to conform to the demands of the new rulers, and succeeded very well. Kao's defiance of authority when he wanted to remarry and Fu's insistence, long after he had presumably learned the dangers of reactionary speech, that American weapons are potent—both find few

[22] The role that a secret police may or may not play in Chinese civil life badly needs clarification (see W. W. Rostow *et al.*, *The Prospects for Chinese Communist Society*, 1, 165). Most recent sources assert that secret police organizations exist, but acknowledge that precise information is difficult to obtain; a CENIS unpublished paper, "Chinese Communist Police System"; Richard L. Walker, *China under Communism*. None of these sources shows that a secret police organization penetrates down to the rank-and-file level either in the cities and villages or in functional organizations.

parallels in the other forty-one interviews. On the whole, the picture is one of great zeal to conform and considerable skill in learning how.

Conformity does not necessarily indicate sympathy for the regime. Indeed, even positive and active conformity, fluent verbal conformity, and leadership in conformity do not, as shown in the case histories, signify that the conformer identifies, in any sense familiar to us, with the Communist movement and power hierarchy.

The continuous pressure for high conformity and the strenuous efforts to conform do, however, affect the formation of attitudes. Consequently, a man's attitudes toward the Communists may depend to a considerable extent upon how easy or how difficult it is for him to conform to the new rules, whether he is able to feel at ease in the face of the day-to-day controls imposed by the Communists.

Hsu, the supply officer, and Chien, the medical aid man, illustrate this relationship clearly. Hsu described his adaptation as relatively painless, and his attitudes are positive. He has experienced no acute conflicts between the new and the old ways; small discomforts— criticism, self- and mutual, once unpleasant—seem to have been resolved with little difficulty. The process of adjustment to a Communist society which began when he joined the Eighth Route Army in 1947 has proceeded without encountering serious obstacles. A poor farmer and trader without previous military service and a rare genuine volunteer for the Communist army, he faced none of the problems arising from class origin or education which made adjustment difficult for Chien and others.

He remains strongly attached to his family, but he has not had to face a basic conflict between loyalty to family and loyalty to government; on the contrary, his family has profited from land reform and, as far as he knows, is better off than before. Knowing little of present-day civil life, he seems to accept at face value the Communist claims to democratic government.

Hsu's total acceptance of the Communist position is unusual even among the repatriate interviewees. His story to date, however, resembles those of others in suggesting that adjustment to the Communists' demands is not always painful and that attitudes toward the system of authority may be influenced by this fact.

Chien's story, on the other hand, like those of some other upper-class informants, leaves one with a feeling that the difficulty of learning to be a proletarian and the hardships of being one were a considerable factor in the eroding of his initial faith. Chien never managed to feel at home in the CCF.

On a somewhat different level, the initial hostility to the Communists felt by Fu, the old Nationalist noncom, was deepened by his sense of being continuously coerced, while Kao's lack of agreement seems to have become academic as soon as he learned enough about Communist ways to deal with them opportunistically.

Of the respondents who at one time or another felt at ease in the Communist control system, some (like Hsu) reached this point quickly and easily, others (like Lee, the combat officer) only after prolonged readjustment. Either way, the feeling appears to have affected their political attitudes. It was not, however, a guarantee against subsequent disaffection, as the experiences of both Lee and Kao vividly show.

Success versus Identification

Closely related to ease of adaptation to the Communist control system is a man's ability to achieve personal safety and career advancement. The case histories suggest that these factors were important determinants of political attitudes. Chien's disaffection, for example, was largely a product of frustrated ambition and of Communist indifference to his illness, while Kao seems to have been won over by success and alienated principally by demotion. Fu's hostility was fed by his knowledge that the authorities distrusted him as a former Nationalist NCO, while Hsu's knowledge that they regarded and treated him as a natural ally and friend must have promoted his identification.

Correlates of Success

What kinds of men got ahead in the CCF? How far does the hypothesized relation between success and identification with the authority system hold up in the group of interviewees? If a man's success in the Communist system is measured by the highest rank he achieved in the CCF and by whether he became a member of the Communist party, some simple tabulations on the respondents can shed light on these questions.

In the first place, high rank and party membership are not confined to the proletarians in the group. It is true that men from upper-class origins, the highly educated, and former members of the Nationalist forces (especially officers) were repeatedly told by the Communists that they were unreliable elements and must make ever more active efforts to turn over and become useful agents of the revolution. In actuality, however, a man's eventual rank and the likelihood of his joining the party were closely related to the sheer length of his service in the CCF—more closely than to any other objective factor.[23] This relationship holds up even when education, class origin, or pre-Communist military service is held constant.

Furthermore, among respondents with similar terms of service, the most highly educated and those from feudal or bourgeois class origins were more likely than the others to become CCF officers and at least as likely to become party members. The only factor somewhat unfavorable

[23] See Tables 12–15, Appendix A. The relationship between length of service and rank, familiar in all armies, is enhanced in the CCF by the absence of a distinction between enlisted and commissioned ranks; the ladder of promotion is continuous.

to both promotion and party membership was previous service in the Nationalist army, especially for a long time or as an officer.[24]

In this group of respondents, there is no unequivocal relationship between either CCF rank or party membership and the ways respondents said they felt about the Communists at the time they became PW's.[25] Disaffection could begin or become serious at any stage of a man's career in the Communist world. Several who moved up the ladder felt less at home when they reached high levels than they had initially.

Career Lines and Sources of Disaffection

Here it will be useful to suggest some sources of alienation which were independent of the individual's own rank and relation to the party.

One common source was a sense of being persistently discriminated against, a feeling that one would never be fully accepted. Some men who felt this seem to have been decisively alienated at an early stage; others, only after prolonged effort and perhaps considerable advancement. One interviewee, for example, served five years in the CCF and became a divisional staff officer and party member before he deserted to the United Nations. His story throws light on the feelings of a good many people with similar backgrounds:

> [At the time my CNA unit was captured] the educational level of the Communist army was very, very low. When they found that I had been a student, they made use of me. They thought I was a college student; they didn't even know the difference between high school and college. I was the only one around who could read and write. But I realized from the start that my background would not fit the Communists. I was a student and my family capitalist. . . . I realized they would never let me break away and go back to school, so I just did everything . . . they wanted and played along with them. I went through the whole process of self-criticism and exposing my past and remaking myself. But I found out that . . . they still maintained doubts, because I had better education than the rest. . . . Even their own books I could read and could explain certain things, whereas they could not, and I would always be distrusted because of that. . . . They always charge that the educated people are wavering elements, not firm in

[24] Tables 13, 14, Appendix A, show, in somewhat distorted form, the relationships between success in the CCF and education, class origin, or previous military service. As Table 15 suggests, when length of service in the CCF is held constant, these relationships change their form somewhat and only what is said in the text above appears clearly.

[25] This lack of relationship may be a function of the conditions that controlled selection of repatriate respondents in the PW camps. A survey of most of the Chinese PW population, conducted in 1952 by CIE, AFFE, indicates that PW's with longer terms of service in the CCF were more likely to choose repatriation than those who had served briefly. If we assume that length of service was closely correlated with rank, as seems likely, then it follows that higher-ranking PW's were probably somewhat more likely than those of low rank to choose repatriation, and in this sense to have been pro-Communist while in the PW camps.

their convictions. The most important [real] reason is that they [the highly educated] are the kind of people who will reason about things. In the first few weeks after our capture by the Communists, they put two men on me to keep their eyes on me all the time. . . . [Subsequently, I was even a political officer for a while. But more than four years later, just before I deserted to the U.N.] I was working in the headquarters, and they had been watching me all along. (N-31)

A second source of disaffection in the face of personal success was personal injury—or serious injury to loved ones—at the hands of the Communists. The moment when Lee learned of the liquidation of his parents was clearly crucial in the development of his hatred for the system (his reaction was far more typical of the respondents than were those of Kao and Chien). Chien's awareness that the Communists were indifferent to his illness helped him to perceive that indifference to human feeling was a general characteristic of their way of ruling. Such experiences might occur at any stage in a man's career but, provided he kept his thoughts to himself, might not affect its outward course.

Third, many of the respondents were alienated by experiences which led them to perceive the Communists as deceitful. Chien finally realized when he found himself in Korea that the series of broken promises by which he had been victimized was not just the work of a few insincere individuals. Similarly, Lee began to perceive the continual movements in the army, not as high-minded efforts to eliminate corruption and injustice, but as tricks designed to tighten party control. A man could stumble upon such insights at any point in his experience with the Communists. Indeed, a man was more likely to be forced to face the fact of Communist trickery as he moved toward the inner circle and had to participate in cynical manipulation of the masses. More than one Communist officer became progressively more disillusioned as he climbed higher in the ranks and the party. Correspondingly, he might redouble his efforts to prove himself reliable because he was more aware of the penalties for failure to conform.

Agreement versus Identification

Political principles and views on national policies played a small and ambiguous role in the judgments formed by Kao, Lee, and the others. Programmatic propaganda did contribute importantly to Chien's initial sympathy for the Communists. But Hsu, the only other man among the five who approached them voluntarily, did so for elementary reasons of moral and personal interest, and Chien's eventual anti-Communism was based on similar considerations. While it can hardly be said that Kao ever identified fully with his masters, he was an effective and apparently content arm of the authority system despite his unbelief. Lee more nearly identified for a considerable period, although he said he only believed about the land reform.

This generally secondary role of political ideas characterizes the interviews as a whole. It is important to remember that most of the informants, like the vast majority of Chinese, did not have highly developed political ideas at the time they became subject to Communist power, under conditions which took no account of their preferences. The problem they faced was that of working out a concrete *modus vivendi* under conditions of continuous pressure. Among the things to which they had to adjust was a new body of Western-type ideas about politics.

In working at this problem, many learned a great deal about the operational meaning of Communism—its practical consequences for human personality, social organization, and social values. The eloquence and penetration of their final judgments on the regime reflect this political education. But the much-talked-of war for men's minds fought on the level of explicit propaganda seems to have had much less impact upon their attitudes than we are wont to suppose.

Who Are the Communists?

Upon reading the case histories, the reader may find himself asking: "If Kao and Lee felt the way they said they did even while they were commanding battalions of soldiers in battle for the Communists, then where is the real hard core of the Chinese Communist movement?"

American experience in a relatively free society leads us to think that much human action is voluntary in the true sense of the word. If we see people taking serious risks in the service of a cause, we tend to assume that they believe in that cause. Communist soldiers do take such risks; the "human-sea" attacks and the prisoner-of-war demonstrations in Korea are only striking examples of what occurs repeatedly. Still, we have ample evidence—for example, in the action of the fourteen thousand Chinese PW's who refused repatriation—that the experience of living under Communist control creates widespread dissatisfaction, disillusionment, fear, even repugnance. How are we to reconcile these viewpoints?

The most common way is to assume we are dealing with two quite different groups: the masses of ordinary folk, who are victimized—manipulated or coerced—and the hard core, a relatively small group of fanatically dedicated Communists who have managed to gain control of the levers of social power. This hypothesis makes a good deal of sense when applied to the data. The highest-ranking respondent, the divisional political commissar (R-1), is indeed a convinced and dedicated Leninist. He identifies almost unequivocally with the whole system of controls and with the principle of absolute party discipline; his thinking is a closed system which permits no real communication with non-Communists, and adversity only strengthens his faith. At the other extreme, many respondents make it clear that they felt coerced, and some give evidence of having been manipulated without understanding what was being done to them.

This hypothesis, however, is oversimple. People like Kao and Lee moved up to positions only a little below that of the general but never approached his fanatical dedication. And the reasons for conformity on the part of people at all levels appear too complex to be summed up as coercion and deception.

Subjectively, few of the informants, even the party members and high-ranking officers, committed their loyalties to the Communist movement for any considerable time and identified unequivocally with their roles. Objectively—that is, judged on their actions and how they would have appeared to us and did appear to their fellows—many were members of the hard core. It seems reasonable to hypothesize that this distinction is widely applicable in Communist China.

For example, when he sat at the banquet table with Stalin as a Red Army Hero, even after his demotion, Kao must have appeared the epitome of identification with the regime. Up to the moment of his desertion, Lee would have appeared to be a hard-core officer strongly identified with Communist goals. Even Chien, who had accepted without complaint his father's arrest, the impoverishment of his wealthy family, and the grueling labor associated with learning a proletarian point of view—would we not have described him as an example of dedicated youth?

In the absence of Korea and the line it enabled them to walk across, these three would probably have gone on acting out the roles of dedicated men. Many of the informants had become habituated to their roles in the CCF. But, with the single exception of the general, those men never lost sight of the party hierarchy as a "they" capable of imposing unforeseen demands or penalties upon them. They learned the concept, unfamiliar in Chinese thought, of the organization. Kao is not unique in his perception that a mode of social organization can create people who cheat the people and can indeed traduce a whole population into adopting deceit as a way of life. For each man, there was always a "they," distinct from himself and his values, which could make him do things he would not choose to do. From his point of view, the real Communists—what we would call the hard core—were those a step or two above him and on up to Mao himself.

This distinction between self and party, sensed even while one participates in party councils, appears repeatedly in the interviews. It may be that men need the distinction desperately. Indeed, one of the most remarkable—and, to Americans, morally horrifying—aspects of fully developed Bolshevik social control is that it makes conscience almost irrelevant to conduct, except where a man, like the general, genuinely internalizes the whole system of Leninist theory and morality, or where there is a line a man can step across, as so many did in Korea. Perhaps the most striking aspect of Chinese Communism is that, with respect to its soldiers, it has achieved this level of human control so speedily.

The Faces of Chinese Communism

The over-all attitudes of the respondents toward Communist control were not determined by any single, simple, consistent standard of judgment. The varied circumstances in which these attitudes developed indicate that the new system of military-political authority presented four general aspects to the respondents—the major points of view from which they regarded and reacted to Communism. At one time or another every interviewee had perceived each of these faces of Communism:

Ideas.—It propagated an extensive ideology and a set of national social policies of programs of reform. One might agree or disagree.

Conditions of personal status and security.—The new social order, military and civilian, appeared as a set of rules that the individual had to learn to come to terms with. It stratified men in new ways and offered them new conditions for achieving personal safety, respectability, and power. One might feel secure, accepted, and successful, or "live in a fearful state."

Controls.—It appeared as a system of controls that continually impinged on the individual—demanding, exposing, teaching, warning, rewarding, punishing, and defining in great detail what he could or must do and say. A man might regard the controls as reasonable, or as inhuman and unnatural.

Morality.—The movement as a whole and many of its particular aspects were not merely conditions which a man had to accept but human creations which he must judge as good or bad. One might conclude that the Communists were sincere or deceitful rulers.

Almost any element of the system—indoctrination, "human sea" attacks, self-criticism and mutual criticism, land reform, the new social stratification, surveillance—may be looked at from any one or all of the four points of view. Correspondingly, the individual might react in terms of one or more of four kinds of interests: as a rational citizen, as a status seeker, as a man trying to be at ease in his environment, as a moral agent and judge.

This classification does more than serve as a tool for the research analyst; it represents one of the findings from the study. The distinctions it implies between kinds of interests—and, in part, between kinds of persons—are seldom made explicit by the interviewees, but we believe the distinctions are implicit in the interview content.

Some of the most complex questions about how the interviewees' attitudes toward the Communists developed and changed can be explained in terms of shifts in the relative importance of these four aspects. The university student Chien began by responding principally to ideological and programmatic appeals, and was decisively alienated only by the Communists' persistent indifference to his personal welfare. Fu, the old soldier, reacted ethically from the first, but his hatred was greatly reinforced by the coercive impact of the control system upon himself. Kao, who became a Hero, appears to have been primarily career-oriented throughout. Hsu, a less ambitious man, seems to have been oriented toward adapting to the controls and, less strongly, toward programmatic (though not ideological) considerations.

The sections that follow deal with this fourfold classification of interests in or aspects of Communism. Each was studied in turn as a source of identification with and disaffection from the Communist authority system. The authors asked such questions as:

How important was this aspect to the informants? Was it more important to some groups than to others?

What attracted them about this aspect? What repelled them? Which attractions and repulsions were most intense?

Above all, in terms of what criteria did the men organize their experiences and form their attitudes toward each aspect?

IDEOLOGY AND PROGRAMS OF REFORM

One important question about the political orientation of a man (or group) concerns the level of abstractness on which he perceives politics. Does he feel himself to be a member of a nation? Does he identify with national goals? Do his political attitudes and behavior result in part from convictions or feelings about how men should be governed, or solely from the course of his own or his group's fortunes?

In the modern West, wars and elections alike are fought in the name of abstract principles: liberty, democracy, justice, and others which command widespread moral approval. Among the widely accepted generalizations about the Chinese, on the other hand, is the idea that they are opportunistic—most heavily influenced by considerations of personal interest.

The political abstractions put out in large doses by the ideologically oriented Communist rulers of China fall into three major categories:

Pure Communist ideology found in the writings of party leaders and theoreticians from Marx to Liu Shao-chi. Knowledge of it is considered essential for party leaders.

The sloganized version of this ideology designed for mass consumption. The Communists seek everywhere to communicate Communist truth in a form palatable to all, regardless of education, sophistication, or interest. Such mottoes as "Expel the imperialist exploiters!" and "Death to the landlord!" communicate the notion that society is divided into hostile economic groups.

The broad policies of social reform publicly advocated by the Communists. These refer not to the basic world view or ethical-historical position of the Communists but to temporary, instrumental goals such as land reform, collectivization, the development of heavy industry, and equality for women.

What these three categories have in common is the generality of their reference. Their subject matter is history, the nation, the economic system, and other impersonal, invisible phenomena. The implementation of a general principle or policy may take on specific and personal meaning when it impinges on an individual with practical consequences which he likes or dislikes. In this section, however, we are concerned with the informants' responses to Communist ideas, slogans, and reforms as generalizations. To what extent and why did the men agree or disagree with the ideas? How important were these agreements and disagreements in their judgments of the Communists?

All the respondents had been exposed to sloganized versions of Marxist ideology in political classes and knew something about the salient reforms advertised by the Communists. But both ideological and social policy propaganda were less important than several other factors in determining loyalty or disaffection. The respondents' final attitudes toward the regime were influenced more heavily by the system of detailed human control and their estimates of their chances of personal security and advancement. These personal matters were judged with little reference to the general programs and the political principles in terms of which the Communists explained and justified them.

Pure Ideology

Communist ideology proper appears to have played an insignificant role in attracting support. Some highly educated informants had been exposed to the basic texts in military-political academies, and some of them had gladly supported the Communists. In general, however, they showed little knowledge of or interest in these basic ideas.

Among the other respondents who had supported the Communists, several mentioned studying and believing Marxism-Leninism; probing, however, revealed that they referred, not to a doctrine about history, politics, and society, but to agitational slogans often related to particular social programs. Some of the less literate seem to have liked the idea of a movement which had answers to all conceivable questions. "The lectures sound so logical that, no matter how highly educated you are or how much worldly experience you have, you can't hold out against their reasoning. I never saw anybody who could not be converted" (R-3). The attraction of being associated with a comprehensive, persuasive doctrine did not, however, lead these people to develop any great interest in the content of the doctrine, much less an understanding of it.

Similarly, Marxist-Leninist ideology as such was not an important factor in alienation from the regime. Few informants appeared concerned about the Communists' attack on the old moral code or the institutions which embodied it, except when the attack had touched some personal interest. Those who disliked the Communists tended to see ideology as a part of the attempt to control the thinking of everyone, and resented it as such.

This relative indifference to ideology has important implications. It suggests that most Chinese party members and sympathizers in the lower and middle echelons did not believe in Communism in the religious sense so often ascribed to Communists in the West. It suggests that their commitment to the party was relatively superficial and limited, and that alienation from the party is not for Chinese the soul-shaking experience it often is for highly indoctrinated Western Communists.[26]

Rich versus Poor

One tenet of Communist doctrine, a sloganized version of the concept of class conflict, was widely known and approved. The interviews reveal that the Communists gained widespread acceptance for the view that the civil war was a struggle of the poor against the rich. As defenders of the poor, the Communists gained approval, not only from poor farmers, but from the sons of rich manufacturers and landlords as well. Describing their reasons for joining or supporting the party, informants referred repeatedly to a belief that "the poor people would be richer" (N-14, a village mayor later publicly tried for squeezing the poor) or "there would be no more poor people if the Communists controlled the country" (N-2, the son of a middle-class farmer).

After the Communist triumph this crude notion of class struggle lost its appeal for many, when violence cast the struggle in a new light. The nature of the conflict had been ambiguous; for many it had been equated simply with land reform, and involved no notion that the capitalists and feudal elements would be physically destroyed. The identity of poor and rich had also been ambiguous; several informants had been stunned when their own families, whom they had not expected to be classed as enemies of the people, were purged. The struggle began to appear to many not as a humanitarian effort to benefit the poor but as an attempt to "turn society upside down in order to establish and tighten up the control of the Communist organization" (N-26).

Nonetheless, the respondents appeared not only to notice class differences but to regard class origins as important differentiators of men's interests and sense of community. Whether this represents real acceptance of a specifically Marxist idea, or merely a reappearance of popular

[26] See Gabriel A. Almond *et al., The Appeals of Communism,* Chaps. 11 and 12, pp. 297–370.

attitudes that have characterized previous periods of social upheaval in China, is not clear.

Land Reform

In China the only specific program widely linked with the Communists even before their victory was land reform. For domestic as well as foreign consumption, the Communists placed land reform at the heart of their program; it was the principal means by which rich and poor were to be made equal. They relied heavily on the promise of land reform—or, in areas even temporarily under Communist control, the actual redistribution of holdings—to undermine existing authority, to gain support from the poor farmers and landless tenants, university students, and professional people, and at least to neutralize all other groups except the landlords themselves.

The promise of land reform appears to have been a widely effective propaganda appeal. Almost all the respondents who were party members and sympathizers mentioned it as a reason for having supported or approved of the Communists, although only the divisional political commissar, son of a landlord, appears to have joined the movement largely for this reason. Some approved primarily because they saw land reform as evidence of Communist concern for the poor and of Communist purposefulness. Only a few of the informants were members of the class which stood to gain materially from redistribution; the attitudes of these few, where apparent, seem to reflect gratitude for concrete, personal (or family) gains rather than agreement with a policy.

Among the informants (a relatively young but disproportionately propertied group) the promise of redistribution—or the general proposition that land holdings ought to be equalized—initially provoked either favorable reactions or no reaction at all. In no case did general disagreement with the concept appear to have contributed importantly to disaffection. As implemented, however, the program became a major source of dissatisfaction and alienation.

To finance industrialization and the military machine, the Chinese Communists have followed up their land reform with substantial taxation of agricultural output, forced sale of grain at prices fixed to favor the government, and the promotion of producers' cooperatives. The farmer is working, in effect, for a new landlord who is at least as demanding as the old one. Even without full collectivization, with which the regime is proceeding cautiously, these policies constitute partial socialization of the land.

Consequently, the most important current question about the impact of Communist agrarian policies upon soldiers' loyalties is: How do they react to this quasi-socialization of the newly redistributed land? Of the informants, only a handful had lived close enough to civilians after the land reform to see any clear effects of the new policies. It is important that these few who did have firsthand knowledge reacted in terms of uncertainty as to whether the poor really had gained anything. They are actively interested in the level of taxation,[27] although a few simply regard taxes as inescapable, like death. Most of the respondents, who had been in military life throughout land reform, had little or nothing to say about its aftermath.

Nationalism

The growth of nationalistic aspirations among the Chinese masses has been the subject of a good deal of discussion by Western scholars. In the respondent group, however, only those with university education expressed keen interest in China's position among the nations and based their judgment of the Communists to a significant extent on nationalistic considerations. During the civil war at least, most of these men had felt that the Kuomintang was unable or unwilling to defend the nation from economic and territorial encroachments. Because these men "Witnessed the humiliating picture of the country's degradation" (N-13), their sympathy went to the Communists, who promised a future of national independence.

Among the less educated, even the staunchest supporters of Communism did not spontaneously refer to nationalist aspirations as a reason for their approval of Communist goals and behavior. While they showed some interest in China's international position, patriotism as such seemed to play only a small part in their thinking. Furthermore, the readiness with which the highly educated ignored nationalism when other values were at stake argues that it is a relatively weak factor even in their political calculations and loyalties.

Some of the reactions to the new government's relations with the U.S.S.R. indicate that nationalist feelings sometimes may motivate opposition to the Communists. A number of informants said they resented the privileged status of Russians in China, and the shipments of foodstuffs to the Soviet Union while the Chinese did not have enough to eat; and they expressed suspicion of Russian intentions toward China. However, these factors were not a major source of disaffection.

None of the respondents spoke of Chinese participation in the Korean conflict as a great national crusade, although the data suggest that the Communists have tried to instill nationalistic motives for purposes of military morale, linking patriotism with defense of one's own home and family. While some accepted the official Communist definition of the Korean conflict as a "defense of the nation from imperialism," there was

[27] See also Allen S. Whiting, "The New Chinese Communist," pp. 600 and 605. Whiting interviewed a random sample of the former cadres among the fourteen thousand non-repatriate PW's who returned to Formosa in 1954. They unanimously favored the principle of land reform and were much interested in the peaceful land reform in Formosa. They criticized implementation of land reform on the mainland on two grounds: first and most serious, because of the executions that accompanied it; second, because of the heavy taxes that followed and their belief that the poor had gained nothing.

little indication that this belief had drawn them toward identification with the Communists. In no case was it a major source of loyalty. On the other hand, the trickery by which the Communists manipulated whole units into volunteering for Korea, or sent them across the border before they knew where they were going, was a significant source of disaffection.

Though inconclusive, the data suggest that much recent Western writing on China exaggerates the extent and intensity of nationalist feelings among Chinese soldiers, and especially the importance of such feelings as a source of either loyalty to or disaffection from the Communists.

Purposefulness

Besides responding to the appeal of specific social reforms, the highly educated were attracted by the fact that the Communists had a body of planned reforms. Seeing the nation rent by civil war and weakened by scarcity and spiraling inflation, these respondents believed the Nationalist government was incapable of the planning and resolution necessary to solve these problems, as it had been unable to eject the Japanese from China. The fact that the Communists seemed to have a "definite aim and definite policies" (N-13) and "knew where they were going" (N-27) impressed ambitious or idealistic members of the intelligentsia.

This element lost much of its appeal when respondents found concrete aspects of Communist control oppressive. What many had once seen as a source of unity they now might see as a chain enslaving them and their fellows.

SAFETY AND STATUS

It has been suggested that the first question a present-day Chinese is likely to raise when contending forces struggle for power is: "Who is the likely victor and what must I do to get on with him?" [28] While the political attitudes of the interviewees do not appear to have been determined wholly on this expediential basis, a man's estimates of whether he had or could achieve personal security and professional advancement in the Communist system were often crucial in determining the willingness with which he worked for the Communists or the intensity of his interest in escape.

While such considerations enter into political choices everywhere, the Chinese orientation appears to have special characteristics. First, among the respondents, estimates seem to have been based on individual rather than on class or group interest. Second, the informants seem to have made compromises to protect their interests without the sense

[28] Lucian W. Pye, *Some Observations on the Political Behavior of Overseas Chinese*, p. 14.

of guilt that a Westerner might feel over similarly opportunistic behavior.

This relatively guilt-free adaptation probably results from the traditional Chinese view of life. Living is seen as a process, not of struggle, much less of progress, but of adaptation to given reality. No system or creed is absolutely good or true, and anything which succeeds probably embodies some good. The man who can accurately appraise the forces outside him and negotiate a compromise with them which preserves his interests is a wise man; such an action is not betrayal but common sense.

Most relationships in traditional Chinese society were personal rather than bureaucratically impersonal; the Chinese has typically depended upon his social relationships for his personal security and respectability. Consequently, one should not be surprised to find that Chinese soldiers seldom distinguish clearly three elements which Westerners regard somewhat differently: being physically safe; belonging, being trusted and protected by one's friends, or being honored by one's fellows as a superior person; and having authority and power in a formal hierarchy.

Promises and Prospects

Almost all the informants say or imply that at some stage in their relations with the Communists they were willing to make the best of their situation and cooperate with the new rulers. Once the Communists gained control of an area or an army unit, they controlled the life and future of every person in the group; the individual felt isolated from, and unsure of, protection in conventional social alliances. Furthermore, these people had none of the Westerner's sense of duty to resist evil even unto death. They did not perceive their former commitments as absolute, and those who were offered an opportunity to be accepted generally took it, even when the price was intensive reindoctrination.

Promises of acceptance and professional advancement were commonly made to university students and were very effective in securing their cooperation. Despite party distrust of these carriers of bourgeois culture, their education is a vitally important resource which the Communists need until the distant day when proletarians can be trained to man the vast bureaucracies of army, party, and government. For this group, appeals of ideology and social reform were skillfully coupled to the desire for good careers and membership in the elite. The Communists usually promised free choice of jobs or assignments to desirable party jobs.

The inducement held out to captured Nationalist enlisted men was that they need not fear for their lives or even remain under suspicion—in fact they could begin a new life—if only they would renounce their former loyalties and vow sincerely to serve the people in the Communist way. In general this tactic paid great dividends in overt behavior and substantial ones in the attitudes of the captives.

The prospect of personal gain was an important—sometimes the only—motive for seeking party membership. Particularly before the final victory on the mainland, promising young men were told they could gain "special privileges and special promotions" (N-7) and "a bright future" (N-14) if they would join.

The appeal of party membership was not always so gross, however. Cadres stressed that only superior people were taken into the party. Several felt the appeal of being a leader and of "being trusted and allowed to know confidential things" (N-7). Less material considerations seem to be reflected along with the more evident ones in such statements as, for example, that party membership meant "getting a job . . . and being personally taken care of by the party" (N-30).

Achievement and Identification

Most of the respondents worked hard and long in the service of the Communist system, not only because they were prodded constantly, but because they badly wanted the security and position that they were told hard work would bring. Most of those who worked hard and "spoke properly" earned promotions largely in proportion to the length of their service. Party membership was another prized achievement which some won quickly, others only after a long interval of proving themselves by their actions. How did the experience of advancement affect attitudes toward the regime?

On the whole, advancement seems to have shored up pro-Communist feelings. Not only did it bring concrete good to the individual; he felt that promises were being kept and effort rewarded, and that his original bargain had been a good one. He was less likely to think about alternatives to Communist control.

The effect was not always so clear-cut, however. Promotion and party membership did not necessarily bring a sense of personal safety or put the individual at ease. He might, for example, awaken to the fact that nobody is ever really trusted and that Communist comradeship is a myth. Promotion exposed him more directly to the persistent trickery of the party. Some found that being promoted still did not free them from criticism of their unreliable backgrounds. If advancement had any of these effects, it backfired on the individual's identification with the system.

Promotion and party membership also exposed the individual to additional sanctions for deviation. A battalion political officer, speaking at this point principally about ideological conformity, says:

> I had some opposing opinions about the lectures, but none of us dared to raise such a question. The instructor would tell a questioner that he did not have confidence in the Communist system. Then maybe he would be punished, or warned, or perhaps they would take away his party membership. . . . We were all afraid of losing it; we were all

afraid of making mistakes. . . . It's not only a feeling of being afraid, it's an actual fact. . . . If the leaders want to confiscate the membership of a party man, they hold a purging assembly. They let all the people of the assembly curse that member and criticize his shortcomings. That man will be shamed; he will have to stand it. . . . Even as a party member he has no friends. And after he is thrown out of the party no one will talk to him. So we were afraid of forfeiting our membership. (N-4)

Demotion

The importance of career prospects to some who had attained party membership and rapid military advancement is further suggested by the speed with which disaffection followed demotion. A successful man did not have to feel that his physical security was threatened; if he felt only that he "would have no future" (N-10), he was likely to begin looking for a way out of the system. The frankness with which these informants related their disaffection to considerations of personal gain suggests not only the habit but the moral acceptability of making choices on the basis of "what's in it for me."

The Unreliables

The importance a man attached to a negative opinion of his chances for acceptance and advancement is demonstrated by the reaction of the "unreliables." Each man under Communist control was investigated as to family (class) background, education, occupation, and attitudes, and classified as "reliable" or as "unreliable" and "suspect."

The groupings shifted with circumstances, but in general unskilled workers, poor farmers, tenant farmers, and those without any regular source of livelihood were considered reliable. Middle- and upper-class origins, personal or family ties with the previous government or the Kuomintang, service as an officer or NCO in the Nationalist army, membership in religious organizations, and high education were considered adverse factors.

Some distinctions were made on the basis of the individual's apparent degree of personal commitment to the old society. The young were presumed to be less contaminated than the old, the Nationalist soldier less guilty and incorrigible than the officer, the middle-class farmer less doubtful than the rich farmer. Some form of cleansing, however, was required of all.

Some, trying to get along with the new regime, were alienated by the initial experience of being regarded as unreliable; the strenuous process of reeducation alienated others. Still others were alienated by the discovery that, even after they had been reformed and achieved some status in Communist society, their backgrounds followed them like a prison record, affecting the degree of surveillance to which they were subject, their promotions, assignments, and punishments.

Intellectuals

According to the respondents, the Communists regard intellectuals as unreliable because the latter, coming from upper- and middle-class backgrounds, do not "understand the aspirations of the proletariat" (N-26), and have "a tendency to think" (N-23) and not to "follow blindly" (N-13). Party officials described them as "the first to doubt" and to "realize they have been fooled and used" (N-2), as "changing and wavering" (N-13), therefore "less easy to control" (N-2).

Since the intellectuals' education makes them necessary to the Communists at the same time that it renders them suspect, the Communists attempt to resolve this problem by promising intellectuals career and status rewards to secure their cooperation, by subjecting them to intensive thought reform designed to "remake them into a type of worker and peasant" (N-26), and by awarding them some prestige symbols (for example, the title "cultural instructor" with platoon-officer rank) while withholding power and authority.

During the process of thought reform, which typically lasted about six months, the promises seem to have won the desired cooperation. The process itself had either a neutral or an adverse effect in motivating intellectuals to serve the regime. The data indicate that the Communists take quite seriously the objective of "making intellectuals live and think like the proletariat," [29] but that they do not succeed in transforming the subjects in the way they intend—or in the way the subjects learn to tell them they have done.

Thought reform did not alter the value the informants placed on achieving prestige and power through their job careers, nor did it eradicate their traditional assumption that they had a right to positions of respect and authority. Young intellectuals were rudely shocked, therefore, to discover that even after intensive reindoctrination and assignment as officers they were "more closely observed" than others (N-26), and that "although we had the same pay and clothing [as other cadres], we had no power or command function whatsoever" (N-23). This led them to feel that "intellectuals will never be trusted" (N-26). Disappointment and discriminatory treatment tended to alienate them, and this effect was multiplied, as will be seen, by their belief that the Communist leaders had deceived and used them.

Nationalist Officers

The "remaking" of former Nationalist officers was considerably more harsh; their treatment was more severe and their chances of gaining

[29] W. W. Rostow, director of the CENIS China Project, concludes from his study of these thought-reform techniques: "One senses that the purpose of all this is to produce not Marxists but men who, having cut themselves off from their past, will serve the state efficiently" (*A Comparison of Russian and Chinese Societies Under Communism*, p. 13). The interviews, which came from both victims of intense thought reform and men who have administered parts of it, argue strongly that the Communists took their announced purposes quite seriously. See also, Walter Gourlay, *The Chinese Communist Cadres: Key to Political Control*.

acceptance smaller than was true for the intellectuals. Many officers attended military-political universities along with intellectuals and junior cadres, but were subject to more open threats and coercion both during and after formal reindoctrination. Occasional executions—"I would say that every month some one of us was sentenced to death" (N-6)—were used to warn the rest. Minor breaches of conformity (even talking in one's sleep, which the Communists considered a form of rebellion) were penalized.

The techniques by which the Communists induce men "voluntarily" to destroy their old social ties and to "volunteer to serve the people" were used with great overt effect. The supposed freedom from compulsion, however, neither fooled these men nor won their loyalties. Regardless of their subsequent treatment, this initiation seems to have prevented many captured officers from identifying with or even truly accepting the new regime.

Even those who had been prepared to make the best of the situation were likely to be embittered by feeling themselves a special target for criticism. The painful experiences of confession, self-criticism, and public renunciation of old ties bred hostility; Communist harping on their backwardness and unreliability bred the conviction that access to authority, respect, and even physical safety was closed to them.

Resentment and anxiety led to redoubled efforts to conform and demonstrate loyalty.

I became more obedient to the biddings of the Communists. I followed orders and criticized myself for whatever errors I committed—real or fancied. Each criticism, each confession intensified my resentment until I often cried in my dreams. I controlled myself, but I lost weight. (N-21)

I became very keen and alert to the danger I was in; I was always alert to what was going on around me. I felt a great bitterness growing in me toward the whole system. My desire for revenge and my desire to preserve my life so that I could have this revenge were strengthened. [At a later stage,] it was necessary always to explain to oneself that it is necessary to submit in order to reduce tension. The only way anyone could get control of himself was to see it as an absolute necessity to submit to what the Communists were saying. (N-1)

The smallness of the rewards these efforts earned, as well as the humiliation they entailed and the fatigue they induced, tended further to intensify resentment.

Nationalist Enlisted Men

Most enlisted men captured by Communist forces during the civil war were also subjected to a program designed to induce them to "turn over" and serve the new organization willingly. They were required to participate in "airing of grievances" and "speak bitterness" meetings oriented to their "crimes" as Nationalist soldiers, to "confess" and publicly disavow their former ties, and—in effect—to "volunteer" for service in the People's Liberation Army. The program lasted from two weeks to three months.

The facade of reasonableness and genuine interest in them as individuals often convinced these soldiers that the Communists were really what they depicted themselves to be. More important, Communist cadres made it clear to these soldiers: that they need not continue to be regarded as suspect or reactionary, particularly if they came from poor families; but because of their previous actions they owed a special debt to the people, which could be repaid only by extraordinary devotion and service; and their future performance would be judged in the light of their past errors. These were the terms on which they were to enter the new society.

Their accounts suggest that on the whole they considered this set of terms reasonable and acceptable. Only a few felt from the start that they were in a bad position and could not get into the good graces of their superiors; most were prepared to accept the terms and buckle down to work. Subsequent experience with having their past thrown up to them, however, contributed to the alienation of several.

Uneducated Volunteers: A Contrast Group

The significance of knowing that one was considered unreliable is vividly illustrated by comparing the ways in which the uneducated "volunteers" (from poor farmer families) and the intellectuals and former Nationalist personnel reacted to Communist domination.

Most of the uneducated had much less skill and vigor to offer than did the three groups of unreliables; their military usefulness was undoubtedly smaller. Nevertheless, the few such men in the interviewee group showed none of the corroding anxiety experienced by these others. Generally, of course, they were not ambitious and did not have the intellectuals' conception of a right to preferment, and they were accustomed to being ordered about. It is clear, however, that they were treated in a friendly way; they were assumed to be acceptable until proved otherwise. They had none of the sense of physical or social insecurity that dogged the unreliables, and they expressed none of the corresponding reasons for disaffection.

For many such men the fact that the CCF fed its soldiers well was itself a factor in their sense of security. A young farmer from Honan, whose family holdings were unchanged by land reform, explains that he volunteered for the army in 1952 because "life is better in the army. They eat much better. [Question: Isn't it true that you might get killed?] Well, not everybody gets killed, and mostly you don't get killed. . . . You will die anyway—everybody does. The main thing is that I would eat better, have a better life, in the army" (R-8). On the other

side, the occasional withholding of food as a sanction against noncon-
formists [30] enhanced their sense of insecurity.

Family Safety and Status

For most of the respondents, willingness to support Communist authority seems to have been affected almost as strongly by the fate of
their families—especially their parents—as by their personal experiences and prospects. The few who came from families which profited
from the land reform clearly regarded this as a significant reason for
supporting the new rulers. The Communists exploited this gratitude in
their recruiting campaigns, calling on the sons of former poor farmers
to volunteer for the army in order to protect their new holdings. Communist promises to take care of their families made such men more
willing to join, and those respondents who believe, like Hsu, that this
promise is being kept are clearly comforted by it.

Although the respondents generally approved the policy of land reform, its implementation was strikingly important in antagonizing a
number of them. The reasons provide insight into the values that
control the political choices of present-day Chinese soldiers.

Under the banner of land reform the Communists carried through
four distinct kinds of actions:

> Equalization of agricultural land holdings among village families.
> Total impoverishment of rich farmer and landlord families in
> many villages through confiscation of all their holdings.
> Confiscation of all land and personal property belonging to families
> which, regardless of their wealth, had been associated with the for-
> mer village or provincial administration or militia.
> The execution, deportation, imprisonment, or beating of rich farm-
> ers, landlords, and former civil servants, and members of their fami-
> lies.

Only the first and, to a much lesser extent, the second of these
practices attracted support. As for the third and fourth, there is no
evidence whatever in the data that they created support and much
evidence that they created serious disaffection. Although respondents
whose parents suffered special punishment were by no means the only
ones who reacted negatively, the effects on their attitudes were most
striking.

At the time of the interviews nearly half of the respondents either
knew or assumed that the Communists had deprived their families of at
least some of their property. Of these, fewer than half described the loss
as one of their reasons for dissatisfaction, and most of those who did so
ascribed less importance to it than to other reasons. In only one case, in
which the respondent himself was the head of the family, does the loss
of property seem to have been a major reason for disaffection.

[30] See, for example, the case history of Fu, above.

On the other hand, of the thirteen respondents who knew or believed that their parents had been killed, exiled, or impoverished by the new regime, most expressed strong resentment.[31] For several, including some Communist party members of long standing, the purging of their parents was a crucial factor in their alienation. Resentment was even greater where the parents were known to have been humiliated in public trials.

In short, the informants placed a much higher value on the physical safety and social respectability of their families than on their family property holdings. These respondents identified to a high degree with their parental families. That this should be true in a group disproportionately highly educated and urbanized may argue that, despite the changes of recent decades, the Chinese family remains a powerful focus of personal loyalty.

COMMUNIST CONTROLS

Even if no other evidence were available, it could be inferred from the interviews alone that the Chinese Communist leaders aim at destroying the warp and woof of the previous society and weaving a new institutional and value fabric. Such an effort necessarily brings the regime into conflict with its subjects at innumerable points where their values, habits, relationships, and self-images reflect the old society.

The Communists recognize that the characters and interests of their subjects cannot be reshaped overnight. They are, however, determined to build the new social order, and they apparently believe that forcing people to act and talk as if they were dedicated to the new system of values will contribute to their conversion. Consequently, the regime needs a comprehensive system of controls which at once ensures near-universal conformity and provides favorable conditions for internalizing these controls in the subjects.

With respect to persons who are already adult this is a larger order, but the Chinese Communists have been extraordinarily inventive in attempting to fill it. In large part they employ the same techniques to produce conformed behavior and conformed thinking. Indeed, the development of an interlocking network of controls which at once persuades and coerces almost every facet of behavior may be their supreme contribution to the arsenal of modern totalitarianism.

The success of this apparatus in achieving overt conformity cannot be doubted, but its effectiveness in securing subjective consent from adult Chinese is another matter. The data clearly indicate that in

---

[31] Two young intellectuals learned of the confiscation of family property some time before they learned of their fathers' executions. Knowing the former, one (F-4) continued to sympathize with the Communists, while the other (N-26) remained ambivalent in his feeling toward them. Both said they began to hate the party when they learned of the executions.

Communist China, as in other totalitarian states, the amount of manipulation and coercion utilized to silence opposition and secure protestations of loyalty is an important cause of permanent alienation from the authority system.

All social orders include procedures for the control of unapproved behavior; all employ some manipulation and some coercion. But while no one who feels coerced likes it, not all coercion breeds significant alienation from the social order itself. Since the Chinese in general lack absolute standards of personal conduct, they might be expected to be somewhat more malleable than others to the demands imposed upon them. The crucial question, therefore, is not simply: "Did the respondents feel coerced, pushed around by the new social order?" Rather, we must ask whether they perceived the techniques of control as unreasonably, unnaturally coercive and confining.

The fact that this system for controlling individual behavior at once teaches and coerces permits those subject to it to see it in either light. To some respondents, like Hsu, the demands seemed on the whole reasonable, although exacting; to others, the system of controls seemed inhuman, wholly manipulative and coercive. The apparatus itself was not a major source of loyalty; it was, however, a vitally important source of disaffection for those who regarded it as unnatural.

The impact of selected elements of the control apparatus is examined in the following sections: surveillance and self- and mutual criticism, which occupy a central place in the system of control, and which many of the respondents came to regard as symbolizing the nature of the regime; two specific sanctions—hard labor and public execution; the ways in which the regime intervenes to control the soldier's relations with the civilian world, especially with his family. In all these cases, some soldiers regarded the controls as reasonable while others resented them acutely. In each case, we must ask what accounts for the difference and whether any common criteria underlie the diversity of apparent attitudes.

Surveillance and Criticism: A Major
Focus of Sentiment

To provide systematically for detailed surveillance of each soldier in the CCF, the Communists rely on several interlocking practices which check and reinforce each other. The smallest organizational unit in the CCF is the three-man cell; these men live so closely and constantly together that the actions of one are known to all. Not only within the cell, but in the squad and platoon, each soldier has the duty of observing and reporting on the behavior—including even the moods and silences—of the others. The individual who does not report any transgression, however small, of any other squad or platoon member is treated as an accessory. Each squad includes members of the Communist party or Youth Corps, who have a special obligation to watch and report on all other squad members and on each other. Frequently they are assigned to observe with special care the behavior of particular suspect members. Unit censorship of a soldier's mail provides additional information about him.

Surveillance in itself is not foreign to Chinese tradition, since within the village community or other close-knit group the concept of individual privacy, as we know it, is absent. Tactful, confidential correction of a man's errors by his friends and superiors is part of this picture but criticism in public is traditionally shocking and disruptive.[32] Yet the Communists have made such criticism a major instrument of social control—an instrument which realizes maximum social effect from the information that surveillance provides.

Although self-criticism has long been employed within the U.S.S.R. and other Communist nations and parties, the Chinese adaptation is sufficiently distinctive that it should probably rank as social invention. Elsewhere, self-criticism has been confined to limited goals among limited party or occupational groups. In Communist China, the process has been applied so widely and so intensely that it ranks as one of the basic institutions of social control. As utilized there, criticism, self- and mutual, constitutes a new method for gaining and exercising total control over the individual and therefore an advance in the techniques of totalitarianism. It is at the same time a mode of instruction in revolutionary standards and a mode of punishment for their infraction.

Fundamentally, criticism is a group process in which each group member is required to examine orally in the presence of his fellows his own and their behavior and to criticize these in the light of Communist standards of virtue. Thoughts and feelings are to be dredged up and fully discussed; in principle, privacy has no place whatever.

Criticism meetings may be used to call attention to meritorious behavior, but more commonly they serve to identify and correct mistakes. Not every infraction of discipline or deviation from the spirit of the proletariat is brought up for group criticism; most minor matters are handled in essentially traditional ways. Still, the Communists want to teach through the example of a man's behavior, to mobilize group opinion with respect to him and conduct like his, and to enhance his anxiety about his acceptability. Consequently, group criticism is a regular, daily part of the routine of every group sponsored by Chinese Communists, occurring as often as four times a day in reindoctrination schools. Being public and being focused on an individual, criticism exploits the extreme need of Chinese individuals for group acceptance and approval.

Criticism sessions are a part of the routine to which the soldier is required to conform; not even respondents who accept the utility of

[32] Public denunciation is not unknown in village society, but occurs only when the denouncer wishes to cut off all relations with the other person.

criticism described participation as voluntary. In regular military units, such meetings were held at the end of each day's activities, "even if we marched 120 [Chinese] miles or were in a short break from combat" (N-9). Second, if a man fails to criticize himself, "other people will criticize him. It is much worse than if he did it himself" (N-23). Soldiers quickly learn that a man who criticizes himself before others do can even win praise, and spontaneous self-criticism becomes the rule rather than the exception. Third, if a man does not participate in criticizing another, "he will be asked about his connection with the person being criticized" (N-8) and will find himself a target. Consistent failure to participate in either aspect of the process means that a man "will be under closer surveillance, even when he goes to the toilet" (N-25). For all these reasons, the informants uniformly concluded that "you were forced to talk. You had no freedom to be silent. You were not only forced to talk, you were forced to talk according to the Communist rules" (N-13).

In these circumstances, criticism tends strongly to become self-operating and self-enforcing. Nevertheless, unit cadres prearrange the meetings and are constantly on hand to prevent men from slipping back into traditional forms of judgment. Not only the offenses and offenders to be exposed, but even the witnesses who are to talk and the line they are to take, are often selected in advance. In the criticism meeting itself, cadres may lead off and set the tone, but rank-and-filers carry the burden of accusation and questioning against an offender.

The cadres take special care to see that Communist standards of virtue are adhered to. If a wrongdoer confesses his errors and promises to do better but states his self-criticism in bourgeois terms, the questioning and probing will continue until he acknowledges his reactionary mentality and learns to "talk correctly." If he refuses to admit the errors his fellow squad members charged him with or they are not satisfied with his explanations, he is criticized in a platoon meeting. If the matter is not resolved there, he must face a meeting of the whole company, then of the battalion. The seriousness of the original offense is compounded by refusal to confess and repent in the appropriate terms.

Some of the respondents recall the typical criticism meeting as one devoted to exposing a wide range of shortcomings in the thought and action of some individual. All those who had undergone such an experience, even if only once, had experienced something akin to shock. The repetition of such experiences is a principal means by which unreliables become aware that they are not and will not be trusted.

Eventually, a stubborn reactionary is removed to regimental head-quarters for more conventional disciplinary action; a persistent one may simply disappear. No such heavy-handed hints are required, however, for the great majority; the data indicate that most of those who are subjected to the many-sided pressures of criticism learn their lesson at the squad level and quickly become active contributors to the process of mutual and self-correction.

By these techniques the Communists have created a remarkably effective and largely self-operating system of human control. Supporters and silent opponents of the regime alike cooperate in securing the conformity of themselves and others, by giving each man the impression that the others are solid "progressives," and by creating a pervasive "atmosphere of mutual suspicion and watchfulness" (N-13) which tends more than any other single condition to isolate the individual.

Viewed as a Reasonable Demand

Only one respondent, the divisional political commissar, identifies unequivocally with this system and defends it on principle.

[We determine a man's reliability] through the observation of his activity. A man's behavior is always guided by his thinking. Therefore . . . when a man is discovered to be deviating in his actions, we try to reason with him through a very slow process until he begins to understand. . . . Admittedly, there are groups of people who, because of their backgrounds and so forth cannot be convinced of the ideology of Communism. . . . And there are people who "lean east and eat pork, lean west and eat mutton." There are a lot of these people on the mainland, and they are not only in the rank and file. But we Communists are very realistic people. We observe them and make use of them. If they are doing the right thing now . . . we tolerate them and they have a place. But . . . the best test of a party member is a time of change, a time of attrition. Then you really test these people and only use the most reliable elements. . . .

Although the political workers have the complete trust of the soldiers, when they make mistakes the soldiers can report them. . . . In the case of the common masses, it is the same thing. They put each other under surveillance. . . . [Chairman Mao Tse-tung once said that] the only difference between the Communist and other political parties lies in the Communists' use of criticism and self-criticism. You see, criticism and self-criticism are the weapons used to solve the conflicts between one's personal interest and the public interest. The old Chinese saying "A gentleman examines himself three times a day" amounts to the same thing. However, the Communists believe that self-criticism is not always adequate because one may not be able to examine and criticize himself thoroughly all the time. Therefore, mutual criticism is also necessary. . . . Through criticism and self-criticism one can develop a kind of faith, a faith of serving others with complete disregard of one's own personal interest. And here lies the power of criticism and self-criticism. (R-1)

Some of the other respondents thought of criticism as cathartic and as beneficial to *esprit de corps* or efficiency; even some non-repatriates once regarded the system as reasonable. Those who do not object to it did describe participation as uncomfortable, but they felt that criticism is on the whole helpful or harmless, or it is a necessary or appropriate means to acceptable ends. For example,

> I felt very embarrassed at first, but I got used to it over time. I have never been through a session in which I was the big target—only on small stuff. These sessions were good for the work because they helped to avoid repetition of the errors. There were no false tales involved. (R-2, a squad leader and party member)

> Why would a man criticize himself in the presence of other people? Well, in the first place we all know the things we have violated, and we know they are wrong. Sometimes it makes you feel better to confess, sometimes not. If you are criticized and you don't admit it, you just have to go through it again, and every time they get harder on you. But if nobody knows what you did, then you don't tell it. As far as having to criticize your friends is concerned, that is beyond control. (R-3, a regimental staff officer and party member)

Viewed as a Source of Disaffection

That continuous surveillance and daily criticism may have negative effects even on soldiers who approve the system is suggested by the quotations just given. Because of the importance to Chinese of face and social approval, the respondents in general found the experience almost intolerable when they first faced criticism, whether they were targets or merely sensed that they must attack an associate. One of them described it as "worse than being killed in battle" (N-15).

Even after men began to learn how to take criticism, most of them felt under pressure. The sense of personal isolation and the need to be constantly wary grew with time. Some described the surveillance-criticism system as "just a way of cutting you off from all association with your fellow men" (N-31) and as "creating universal distrust" (N-25).

Those who disliked the Communists for other reasons, or who continued to be watched and criticized closely, reported a sense of extreme tension. This was especially true in the centers for intensive reindoctrination. A Nationalist major assigned to a Communist unit after a three-month reindoctrination speaks of criticism as

> the most powerful weapon the Communists have. First, it forces a man to control what he says, etc., then he becomes afraid that even if he harbors thoughts, these thoughts might expose him and get him

into serious trouble. By this time you have no more individuality. Then it is natural for them to lead and control you. (N-25)

For a number of respondents, surveillance and criticism became the symbol of the most objectionable features of the Communist regime. These informants perceive criticism in particular as the principal arm of a systematic effort to "control everyone through deep fear and terror" (N-27), and to dehumanize everyone and destroy all nonpolitical human relations.

Although it is difficult to disentangle the effects of the several elements of the control system upon the individual's attitudes, the surveillance-criticism system clearly had a strong influence. A Nationalist officer whose reindoctrination was unusually lengthy described the reactions of several:

> [In a political-military university, where we found ourselves confessing to and criticizing one another for all manner of crimes,] most of us became dumb and without feelings, as if we were stunned by this assault on our emotions and our forced participation in these kinds of actions. After all these things . . . I never really lost the view of myself as being against Communism. . . . [Later, in a "reform through labor" camp] we were reduced to animal existence. Our senses were practically destroyed. . . . We became like tools. . . . We were mostly exhausted all the time, but we kept a tight rein on our thinking. . . . To preserve oneself, one had to be extraordinarily careful not to betray oneself at any time. A lot of the men just go crazy. It's like two people inside themselves, they are always fighting. . . . I don't know of anyone who completely gave up or surrendered to this Communist thought control. It is impossible to surrender completely to it. (N-1)

A university-educated man, who worked in an uncle's factory in Peking and was initially very pro-Communist, told why he volunteered for the army:

> The Communists were deliberately trying to humiliate people with a good background to go through certain manual labor which was considered very dirty in order to test you out. . . . If they see that you are not taking it all in, the atmosphere can be quite unpleasant. . . . Politically, I couldn't stand the blind obedience. But the second thing is personal. The intensity of the living environment was almost unbearable. You were supposed to work eight hours—that is what they said—but actually it is eleven hours [because of the political class early in the morning and the criticism meeting in the evening]. There is nothing but tension. . . .
> I was never blamed, because I was not in a responsible position. But I have had to criticize other people. . . . The impression I got is that they build up habits of telling falsehoods. . . . You feel you are

being humiliated, but you can only swallow your pride. There is no alternative. . . . This . . . criticism is so directly opposed to my conceptions of a human being that I resented it extremely. . . .[33]

In spare time, the only thing I wanted was to sleep. . . . Before, I had lots of friends, but gradually I had no more friends. I was afraid and they were afraid, so I had nobody to talk to. In those days you could still talk freely with your family [but I had to live in the factory most of the time]. . . . Formerly I was very lively, but under these circumstances I became very despondent. . . . I joined the army because that environment was becoming impossible. (N-13)

Determinants of Responses

Why do some regard Communist surveillance and criticism as reasonable while others regard them as unnatural and destructive? Are there in the responses of the interviewees any common elements which can be expected to persist into the future?

Differential Responses.—In part, of course, a man's attitudes toward surveillance and criticism reflect his attitudes toward the whole Communist authority system which evolve from other things: the fate of his family, his own career success and sense of safety, his judgment of the morality of the rulers, and to some extent even his agreement with their ideas. It should be remembered, however, that criticism itself greatly influenced a man's sense of security or insecurity. Also, to most of the respondents, the standards enforced through criticism and implied by the institution of criticism itself were Communist ideas, more genuinely representative of the system than the abstractions the Communists tried to inculcate as basic principles.

Differences in attitudes also reflect different personal backgrounds. Some respondents, especially the poor and ill-educated, were accustomed to accepting their situation passively. A young middle-class farmer from Shensi with three scattered years of schooling said:

[At first I was in a unit with a lot of others from my village, and] we talked about all sorts of things, but when we saw the party cadres, then we had to be careful. [In 1952 I was transferred to another unit, and from that time on] I had no friends. I just had to be more careful. I didn't know these men. . . . [As for criticism,] in the beginning it was very uncomfortable, but in time you get used to it. They are not scolding you, just criticizing you. . . . Maybe sometimes your friends will expose you. But it is not deliberate, it is just mutual criticism. We are the same group and we know more or less that everybody is under

[33] In a statement written for a staff interviewer after the interview itself, this respondent adds: "Of all the evils of Communist techniques, none is worse than mutual criticism and self-criticism, their most important method for the control of the people. Through this means of exploiting human conflict and contradiction, the Communists destroy a person's character, deaden his senses, and wipe out his natural human instincts."

the same conditions. You have just got to go along. There is no other way. There were times when, after I was talked to individually, I had to say things in criticism meetings that I knew were not true. I just had to say them. . . .

[When I am repatriated] I want to go back to my farm. I want to see my parents. For one thing, you are more free as a civilian. You don't have to be fearful. You don't have to be ruled by others. (R-7)

Clearly this man and others like him are conscious of the same kind of confinement and pressure that anti-Communists bitterly resent. They will be glad to escape from it, but they do not perceive surveillance and criticism as reasons for especially disliking Communists. Such men have always lived under conditions beyond their control. They would not be so shocked by surveillance and criticism, would not find them so unnatural as do men accustomed to being on the other end of the pole of power and initiative.

The difference is not merely a matter of social class. Former Nationalist enlisted men were commonly alienated by Communist surveillance and criticism; experience with a different kind of military system presumably predisposed them to resist. And in comparison with little-educated respondents from the landlord or official classes, the highly educated place more stress on the assault that criticism makes upon personality; they appear to have acquired a quasi-Western conception of individuality which they value.

Finally, the Communist hierarchy, distrusting soldiers from certain backgrounds, presumably feels an especial need to "impress them that the organization is all-powerful" (N-13). Such men would more often be targets of public criticism, and would feel more coerced and resentful.

Generic Elements.—Despite variations in individual responses, surveillance and criticism can still be properly described as an important and potentially general source of soldier dissatisfaction with Chinese Communist authority.

Regardless of class, Chinese seem to need, almost as they need air, some sense of freedom in their relations with others. The traditional social order was not feudal; status was not fixed; the small farmer as well as the city dweller was used to a good deal of independent negotiation and compromise; the standards that governed his relations with others were personal and aesthetic, not impersonal and logical. Communist surveillance and criticism not only confine him directly but circumscribe all his relations with his fellows.

Several respondents who had served three years or more in the Nationalist forces gave evidence of having made close friends and of having identified to some extent with their military units. There is no comparable evidence of friendships, except on a covert basis, among the respondents who had served three or more years in the Communist forces. On the contrary, many reported that their sense of isolation and their watchfulness grew as the months went by. All were acutely aware of Communist opposition to personal ties. The interviews suggest that this basis for unit identification has been largely suppressed on the lower army echelons [34] without development of the new kind of comradeship and small-group morale based on common political convictions which the Communists persistently preach.

So far as the Communists have succeeded in suppressing traditional bargaining and friendship without creating a substitute cement for personal relationships in the army, they have created, not loyalty, but an important source of disaffection. This loss of mobility in personal relations seems to sum up a good deal of what the anti-Communist respondents meant when they said that the Communists are trying to destroy them as persons. The feeling that they have been trapped into participating in their own dehumanization only made it more painful.

Unreasonable Sanctions

Finally, insofar as soldiers began to perceive that the Communists were using surveillance and criticism, not merely as practical operating techniques, but for the sake of control—"by weakening each individual, they exercise control" (N-26)—these institutions tended to become central symbols of the real nature of the Communist authority system.

Public Executions and Beatings

The Communists' systematic exploitation of the traditional Chinese dread of public humiliation and the fear of death in their efforts to secure conformity, and the public killings that contributed importantly to the fearful state in which many soldiers lived, convinced a number of respondents that their masters were cruel and inhuman. Nor was revulsion at such brutality limited to those who had had personal experience or been closely related to victims.

For example, a respondent from a middle-class farmer family in Kiangsu reported no suffering on their part. However, after a period as a party member in which he had "acted from the bottom of his heart," he

> began to doubt the ideas of Communism because I began to learn more about the results of the land reform in Manchuria and . . . to realize the cruelty of the land reform and the number of people who were being liquidated. That is when I began to doubt the system. I began to learn the terror, the system of terror, that the Communists used in the land reform. It impressed me so much because I myself came up from the farmer class. I began to find some of these things [that I had been doing in good conscience] distasteful. (N-2)

[34] The data are by no means complete on these important points.

Pro- and anti-Communist respondents differ markedly on the amount of bloodshed they reported having seen in the course of the revolution. This discrepancy occurs, not between those who once voluntarily supported the Communists and those who never did, but between almost all who are now disaffected (non-repatriates) and almost all who are not disaffected (repatriates). The different experiences of the two groups may partly explain their different attutides toward the Communists. Among the nine repatriates there were no unreliables who had undergone intensive reindoctrination in which terror was systematically employed; some of the repatriates came from areas where redistribution of land was accomplished with almost no violence. To the extent that their experience has not included exposure to blood purges and mass trials, one can only estimate their probable future reaction to these practices, in the light of the reactions of former supporters who are now non-repatriates.

Reform through Labor

Most of the respondents subjected to forced labor clearly resented as inhuman the extreme pressure that was placed upon them to work harder and still harder, and the extreme exhaustion they experienced. The anti-Communists among them felt that the Communists were trying to humiliate them by making them undertake such labor. The interviews do not, however, show unequivocally that the subjects felt insulted or humiliated, or regarded manual labor as unnatural. A normal-school student who attended a political-military university explained his reaction to it:

> The purpose of the indoctrination of this student group is—the Communists coin this phrase—to remake the intellectuals into the type of the worker and peasant. During this process, they have to learn to live just like workers and peasants. They deliberately make those who like to keep themselves clean, dirty. . . . Naturally, we didn't like it. It's against all our habits and our knowledge, but in the conditions we didn't dare say anything. . . . After you go through six months of this indoctrination and they reduce you to . . . this way of living, it makes it easier to work in the army. The trouble is that part of the indoctrination is based on your guilt complex. Because you are of the bourgeois classes, you have been living on the exploitation of peasants and workers. . . . I myself refused to believe this was true, because I knew that my father never made any money exploiting other people. As far as that part is concerned, the students still harbor a lot of resentment. . . . But this six months did make it easier to adjust to living in the army. (N-26)

This equivocal response to a traditionally repugnant demand may reflect, not only flexibility, but also the character of the judgments that

Chinese make of others: While manual labor would have been unthinkable in the context of the old society, it does not seem so unnatural or unreasonable as part of the system developed by the Communists, who have consistently linked themselves with the workers and peasants.

Control over Contact with the Civilian World

In its effort to harness individual loyalties to the state, the Communist party is a major long-term enemy of the Chinese family. Consequently, among the devices employed to control the behavior and thinking of CCF personnel is the detailed regulation of their contact with the civilian world. In the experience of the respondents, such regulation included promulgating and enforcing detailed rules of conduct *vis-à-vis* civilians,[35] censoring and altering mail sent and received by CCF personnel, attempting to weaken ties to the parental family, determining whether soldiers might marry and whom the eligibles might marry, and prohibiting relations with women other than wives.

Censorship of Mail

CCF cadres not only read the mail a soldier received but altered it when it seemed likely to damage his morale. This practice was known to many of the informants and actively resented.[36] Attitudes toward mail censorship seem closely related to feelings about Communist interference with family relations.

Family Loyalties

The prescribed position with respect to family loyalties varied from one category of military personnel to another. Junior party members were told "to give up the idea of family," that it was "a personal privilege which must be sacrificed for the revolution" (N-7). Sons of landlords were "encouraged to kill or report their fathers and mothers if they were not loyal to the regime" (N-23). Ordinary soldiers not of doubtful social origin were asked only to let their duty to the revolution take precedence over their family obligations for a time; they were assured that their families would be provided for during their absence. A few respondents disapproved of the general Communist position, subordinating filial to political duties, but most did not react strongly to it. However, as has been pointed out, serious maltreatment of an individual's own family was an extremely important source of disaffection among all classes of informants, including party members of long standing.

[35] See "Coming into Contact with Communist Authority," above.
[36] That this attitude is widespread is further suggested by the number of respondents who were told by mail clerks about the alteration of their letters. Willingness to violate discipline to give such information suggests a feeling that a man has a right to news from his family.

Control of Marriage and Sex Relations

Before and during the Korean conflict, only regimental and higher officers were ordinarily permitted to marry.[37] For those who were eligible to marry, the party asserted a veto power over their choice of partners. Sexual relations between soldiers and women to whom they were not married were rigidly prohibited.

Probing revealed that these policies created far less dissatisfaction with authority than they would among soldiers in Western armies.[38] Most violators of the rule on illicit sex relations seem to feel that the rule itself was legitimate. Although informants mention thoughts about women as a frequent subject of self-criticism and mutual criticism, in no instance does this prohibition appear to have been a major factor in disaffection. Only the prohibition on marriage seemed to induce serious disaffection, and then only when it frustrated a specific desire to marry.

As regards the party's veto power over a man's choice of a wife, again there was little reaction to the policy as such, although a few single men expressed resentment. The case of Kao is one illustration of this conflict. Neither the execution of his parents nor his own landlord origin interfered seriously with his adaptation to and success under the new regime, but the denial of his request to remarry set in motion a cycle of insubordination, demotion, and disaffection. In other instances, resentment resulted when soldiers had to break engagements of long standing because of the doubtful social origin of the girl.

Several who expressed resentment about regulations governing marriage and sexual relations linked the complaint about their own deprivation with resentment against the high party members or government officials, who were not so deprived. This is only one of several kinds of statements which suggest awareness that a new privileged class is growing up in China and suggest that tensions of many kinds may develop between that class and the masses. One informant, for example, related that his wife was forced to divorce him and marry a Communist civilian official. Such officials, he further charged, "always have more than one wife. To get a divorce, a Communist party member need only accuse his wife's family of something" (N-6). Another stated that Communist officials "can have any woman they choose" (N-1). And still another complained that, while he was not permitted even to think about women, higher-level party members "get wives and also, if they like, another girl, and if there is mutual consent and if they can get approval of a higher authority, they can go to bed any time" (R-3).

Only the divisional political commissar identifies with and defends

---

[37] According to the divisional political commissar, the only dedicated Communist in the respondent group, the prohibition of marriage is an economic measure—the party cannot assume responsibility for supporting men's families and lower-echelon soldiers are unable to do so without help.

[38] Resentment appears to be considerably more intense among Soviet defectors subjected to the non-fraternization regulations in Germany and Austria.

the policy governing marriage by low-echelon military personnel; his defense, while it makes sense if the regime's goals are assumed to be urgent, is as likely as not to infuriate the personally oriented soldiers and junior officers who have to live with the policy.

MORALITY

Traditionally, interpersonal relations have had a peculiar importance and role in Chinese culture. In China, unlike the West, politics and business alike have proceeded on the basis of negotiation between individuals, each of whom is acting according to rules appropriate to particular situations and kinds of relationships.

One consequence is that, in any given situation, in comparison with a Westerner a Chinese is more sensitized to personalities, motives, and character and less sensitized to logical consistency, abstract argument, and general principles. The first concern of the Chinese is to determine whether the other is a sincere man, whose interests are compatible with his own. The factor of personal interest, itself vitally important in the political choices of Chinese, is here woven into his moral judgments.

When the other man is indifferent to one's well-being, this readily becomes a basis for judging him to be insincere. When he combines such indifference with protestations of deep interest, or when he is positively antagonistic to one's interests while protesting friendship, he is likely to be regarded as worse than insincere—namely, deceitful. No man, or group, with whom mutually considerate relations are impossible will be judged moral.

The data make clear this connection between morality and self-interest, and demonstrate the importance of moral judgments of this kind as an influence upon the political loyalties and identifications of Chinese soldiers.

Sincerity as an Appeal

One of the most important reasons given by informants for initially supporting the Communists was the belief that Communists were reliable and trustworthy men who had a warm, personal concern for the people. The consideration, unprecedented in China's military history, with which the Communist armies treated both civilians and prisoners of war during the period of expansion was impressive. Among the respondents, even those who were most apprehensive, and were to suffer most as unreliable, felt during these first weeks that "it was not so bad" and that "maybe the Communists would treat us well after all" (N-1).

These policies bore important fruits for the Communists. The reader will recall that, except for university students and some Nationalist officers, few informants had had any but the vaguest notions about the Communists before falling under their control. Many thought of them as bandits and feared them not as a rival political organization but as robbers, kidnappers, and murderers. The initial good treatment was the more impressive for being unexpected. It suggested the possibility of establishing friendly relations with the new rulers on an individual basis. At the same time it established the Communists as sincere men ("They did what they said they would."—F-4), and cast an aura of moral respectability about the movement which led people to feel that by allying themselves with it they were serving a good cause as well as protecting their interests.

Similarly, these policies were explained to Communist soldiers as a simple set of principles. As such they contributed markedly to the loyalty these men accorded their leaders and the degree to which they identified with their jobs.

Communist Deceit

No complaint is so often repeated by the non-repatriates as the charge that the Communists are deceitful. Here the former party member, the professional soldier, the intellectual, the successful and the unsuccessful adapter alike find common ground. The repetition of this charge by men who had observed the regime from a wide range of vantage points implies the existence of a widespread criterion for political judgments—and a criterion which the Communists were repeatedly failing to measure up to.

The same criteria which led informants to support the Communists as sincere led many of them later to conclude that the movement deserved no support because it was based on deception. The instances in which such a judgment was made show that "deceitful," like "sincere," is a broad term, used to characterize the morality of a wide range of actions. The charge that a man or group is deceitful is a serious and final condemnation.

The respondents were speaking not so much about lies, tricks, half-truths, and manipulation in general as about their own personal experiences. The subtle relation between personal interest and general moral judgment was the same whether the judgment was one of deceit or one of sincerity. The judgment was not merely a rationalization of personal interest but the consequence of a moral standard according to which a man or movement is bad if he or it behaves so as to make friendly mutual trust impossible. In making these charges the informants were explaining simultaneously why the Communists were evil and why it was impossible to find personal security in the new regime.

Despite the absence of a concept of absolute truth and the expectation that authority operates deviously, the informants did not show unlimited tolerance of lies, distortions, and manipulation. On the contrary, the interviews suggest that some Western observers may have exaggerated Chinese admiration for the shrewd manipulator. It is clear that some informants were impressed much more by the dishonesty than by the effectiveness of tactical promises that the Communists made and broke.

Nor was personal involvement necessarily a prerequisite of disapproval. Watching the Communists manipulate another by playing on his anxieties or making promises "opened one's eyes" (N-5); it "made one not trust the Communist party" and "revolted the sense of justice" (N-7). Awareness of lies and tricks was not enough by itself to initiate alienation in many respondents, but the Communists' consistent use of such tactics was an important factor in total disaffection, total refusal of loyalty. Seeing the Communists betray others who had made a bargain with them seems to have suggested to some and confirmed for others that the Communists as persons were tricky and exploitative, deceitful men who "talk sweetly though their mind is malicious" (N-5). Personal experience was readily generalized when similar deceits were perpetrated on others.

"They Deceived Me"

A number of informants related their initial perception of Communist deceit to some matter directly involving their personal or family interests.

For several, the feeling that Communists do not keep their promises and "do not follow their own programs" (N-5) grew out of the purges accompanying redistribution of property. The discrepancy between what the informants understood to be the stated policy and what the regime actually did was an important proof and example of Communist unreliability.

Other respondents—primarily intellectuals—related Communist deceit to unfulfilled promises of good jobs. These men had submitted voluntarily to unpleasant thought-reform courses in the belief that their futures would be assured after graduation. When the expected rewards were not forthcoming, they felt exploited. Communist cheating had prevented their attempt at negotiation from working out in a mutually profitable way, and they therefore judged the Communists to be deceivers.

"They Do Not Tell the Truth"

Many respondents reported resenting the Communists' lies about facts which did not suit their arguments. The most impressive of these, perhaps because its falsity was most widely recognized, was the Communists' claim that they had won the war against Japan in China and that Russia had won the general war against Japan. To former Nationalists who fought against the Japanese for years the former claim was absurd. Furthermore, their own face was involved. The fact that they had not only to accept but to repeat such distortions increased their personal bitterness at the same time that it alerted them to the Communist use of falsehood.

"The Form of the Public Will"

Widely condemned as deceitful were Communist efforts to make prearranged meetings appear spontaneous, coerced action appear voluntary, and deliberate policies appear accidental. Several informants described the careful staging of public trials so that they would seem like spontaneous outbursts of popular resentment. A member of the Youth League, for example, recalled:

> One day a man violated a regulation. The party decided that the penalty would be death. My political boss called a meeting of all party cadres, and [since I was working directly under the political commissar] the instructions were given to me from that meeting. They said: "Well, we've been talking about democracy and all that. It was decided at the meeting that the man shall be executed, but we don't want to just hand out execution orders. They have to have the form of the public will." So a meeting was ordered at which all the public— that is, all the soldiers—were to be present.
>
> In the meantime all the party cadres were prepared, and they were planted and spread out in the crowd. The guilty man was on the platform. [After the crime had been described and condemned,] the company political commissar asked the public what the penalty should be. One of the party cadres called for the execution of the man. Immediately he was joined and echoed by all the others. In time, the whole group was saying the same thing. . . . Because I understood how this worked, I realized how undemocratic they are in reality. The so-called will of the people was a form of deception. (N-26)

Criticism meetings, the recruitment of "volunteers," lectures, the "mass demands" of soldiers to go into Korea—all were similarly prearranged. So far as interviewees were aware of the advance arrangements, they interpreted them as attempts to deceive, confuse, and coerce. Party members and officers were, of course, much more likely to know of this stage management and to participate in it. No less than others, they interpreted it as evidence of Communist untrustworthiness; more than one first began the toboggan slide of disaffection when he realized that he had been maneuvered into deceiving his subordinates and gradually began to recognize that he too was being utilized.

A System Based on Deceit

Seeing Communist efforts to trick and manipulate themselves and others, and knowing of their own attempts to deceive the Communists—"the Communists create people who cheat the people and are in turn cheated by them" (N-10)—many informants came to see the entire system as one operating through deception and coercion.

Many finally believed that Communist power itself is a myth sustained only by the mutual supervision and distrust of men who hate the system. "The strength of the Communist organization is not really a strength. It's a temporary strength because they adopt measures of deceit which will only fool the people for a time" (N-31). Whether they expected the regime to collapse or not, men who perceived that their masters regarded them as mere tools to be used at will were infuriated by the discovery.

SUMMARY AND CONCLUSIONS

This research deals with the questions: How far have Marxist-Leninist standards replaced or blended with traditional Chinese standards in the soldiers' judgments of their Communist superiors and the Communist system of military-political authority as a whole? By what criteria do these men give or refuse loyalty to the Communist leadership?

Answers to these questions are based principally on long, intensive life-history interviews with soldiers of the Chinese Communist Forces who became prisoners of war in Korea. The interviews were analyzed by qualitative methods to identify the standards of judgment which underlay particular reactions to Communist authority, and to discover which of these standards were common to all or to definite groups among the respondents.

Interviews with forty-three Chinese PW's comprise the primary data for the study. The interviews ranged from two to twenty hours in length, the average being nine hours. Interview conditions were permissive, but the principal topics covered were uniform. Each interview dealt with specific events in the man's life and his reactions to Communist goals, demands, and control techniques; full information was sought on the social conditions and cultural context of such incidents and responses.

Characteristics of Respondents

In the selection of prisoners to be interviewed, the objective was to obtain men of widely varied background and experience who could be expected to be competent and articulate reporters on Chinese Communism and its impact on the people under very different circumstances. Although their number is not large, with respect to certain basic background and personal characteristics the respondents exemplify the range of variation that existed among Chinese Communist soldiers in Korea. They appear to embody the principal social-cultural subgroups represented in the CCF.

All the regions and almost all the provinces of China were represented, as were all social classes. The fathers of some were farmers, rich to marginal; others were landlords, urban capitalists, officials, peddlers, or artisans. The educational levels of the respondents ranged from no schooling to university graduation, and their occupations before their contact with Communist power were similarly varied. Half had served in the Nationalist army.

All but four had come under Communist control involuntarily—as prisoners of war or when their home areas were occupied—and initial contact with the new rulers ranged from 1939 to 1950. Some respondents were as young as fourteen at the time, others as old as thirty-five. Length of time under Chinese Communist control ranged from seven months to twelve years, the average being slightly over four years. For almost all of this time the men were in the Communist army or in special political indoctrination programs under army control.

As Communist soldiers, their ranks ranged from general to private. Half were privates ("warriors") or NCO's, and most of the rest were platoon and company officers. Thirteen were full members of the Communist party, and five had been political officers for considerable periods. Some of the men were captured by U.N. forces in Korea as early as November, 1950, others as late as July, 1953. Nine wanted to be repatriated to Communist China, thirty-four had refused. Four had changed their allegiance while interned; seven others had been segregated by the U.N. Command because of uncertainty about where their loyalties lay.

In view of this wide range of backgrounds, careers, and attitudes toward Communist control, the standards of judgment found to characterize the entire range of respondents can plausibly be supposed to have characterized CCF soldiers generally. Also, since nearly one-third have at least ten years of education—and by Chinese standards are members of the intelligentsia—the special value criteria of this criticially important group could be studied.

Identification of Common Values

In analyzing the interview data, the research staff identified every attitudinal response to any aspect of the Communist system, favorable or unfavorable. The approximately one thousand specific indications of loyalty or disloyalty were then studied to identify the underlying standards of judgment which were common to all or particular categories of respondents. Hypotheses about common standards were derived from explanations provided by individual respondents and from interpretive comments by consultant experts.

Findings

Adjustment to Authority

Initial Reactions to Communism.—Until the time they became subject to Communist power, most of the respondents knew little about the Communists or the civil war in China; the most common impression was that the Communists were bandits. Some university students and Nationalist officers were more aware of the issues involved; some of the former, feeling the country's need for reform and a sense of national purpose, were strongly pro-Communist.

In dealing with newly captured Nationalist units and newly occupied communities, the Communist forces showed unprecedented kindness. Even respondents who experienced no special generosity were pleasantly surprised by the self-restraint and discipline of the new rulers. The Communists exploited every known abuse of the Kuomintang and Nationalist army through carefully planned contrasting behavior as well as through propaganda and meetings for the airing of grievances. This approach led people of almost all classes to feel that the Communists were serving the people and deserved support. Young men tended to believe that they could come to terms with the new rulers and work out a satisfactory life in the still unknown new order. Outward conformity to Communist orders and standards of conduct was high from the start.

Communist Mobilization of Minds.—While some kind of thought reform is a characteristic aim of all totalitarian regimes, the Chinese Communists have set about it more purposefully, more massively, and more intensively than have other ruling groups. At a minimum, they have applied known techniques in new ways. In daily meetings for self- and mutual criticism, for example, surveillance and overt sanctions are united with education to expose, censure, and correct shortcomings of attitude and conduct. Simultaneously, the Communist leaders attack all personal attachments between soldiers which are not based on common political convictions. By these and other techniques they exploit social pressures and personal anxieties brilliantly to ensure conformity.

In sharp contrast to former soldiers of the U.S.S.R. and its satellites, none of the respondents referred to a special secret police apparatus. Instead, the interviews depict a system of detailed surveillance and reporting carried on by each against all—a system in which even opponents of the regime force conformity on themselves and others, and the apparent consensus of one's peers is used continuously as a pressure for conformity. Party members and cadres were described as important elements of the control system, but only in the sense that they have more responsibility for organizing and are more vigilant in performing the functions expected of all.

Conformity and Advancement.—The respondents conformed zealously to Communist demands; many of them held responsible posts and were promoted repeatedly. High rank and party membership were by no means confined to the proletarian respondents, even though men of upper-class origin, the highly educated, and former members of the Nationalist forces were harassed by the Communists as unreliable elements. A man's eventual rank and the likelihood of his being allowed to join the party were closely related to the sheer length of his service in the CCF—more closely than to any other objective factor. Of the respondents with similar terms of service, the most highly educated and those from feudal or bourgeois origins were more likely than the others to become officers and at least as likely to become party members. The only factor somewhat unfavorable to both promotion and party membership was previous service in the Nationalist army, especially for a long time or as an officer.

Conformity and Loyalty.—Judged objectively, on the basis of their overt actions, many of the respondents were members of the hard core of the Communist movement. Subjectively, however, few even among the party members and high-ranking officers had committed their loyalties to the movement and identified with their roles in it for any considerable length of time. Out of their experience they had learned the concept, unfamiliar in Chinese thought, of the organization. With the single exception of a general officer, a divisional political commissar, the respondents never lost sight of the party hierarchy as a "they" capable of imposing urgent demands or penalties upon them without advance notice. As each of them saw it, the real Communists—what we would call the hard core—were those a step or two above him and on up to Mao himself.

This distinction between the self and the party appeared repeatedly in the interviews. It applies equally to men with long and short service in the Communist army, to intellectuals who went through intensive reindoctrination, to youngsters drafted off the farms, to men who held responsible party posts, and to men who were always suspect. We hypothesize that this distinction between overt conformity and private allegiance is widespread in Communist China.

The respondents did not feel guilty when they acted contrary to their own preferences and ideas of propriety. Those who were under suspicion felt anxious, but their problems were not complicated by moral conflict. Even the concept of the Mandate of Heaven, which implies that any effective government must have some good in it and so would justify loyalty to Communist authority, seemed to be understood merely as a practical warning against trying to fight the inevitable.

Determinants of Soldier Loyalty

The respondents expressed attitudes ranging from absolute, unqualified support to absolute, unqualified condemnation of the Communists. Only one exhibited the ideologically based identification of self with the Communist party which the party itself preaches and tries to foster; others differed markedly in the firmness with which they approved or rejected various aspects of the system.

About one-third of the group described themselves as having been at some time genuinely pro-Communist—in their own terms, willing supporters of the new rulers. Many of the others had at one time or another passively accepted Communist authority without any wish to escape or change it. Although nearly all saw some qualities in the new rulers that deserved praise and support, some had always resented and hoped to escape from Communist control.

What, then, were the standards of judgment that formed the basis of their allegiance or disaffection? Let us consider first the groups with which soldiers identified—the groups whose fate they considered to be tied to their own—and then the principal criteria they used in deciding whether political authority was being exercised in a way that deserved their support.

Identification with Groups. Family.—The treatment of their parents influenced the attitudes of the respondents almost as deeply as did their personal experiences. In the abstract, they did not react strongly against the Communist contention, so contrary to Chinese tradition, that family ties should be subordinate to political ones, although most of them disagreed with it. They did, however, react strongly when implementation of this policy affected their own families. Those whose families profited from land reform regarded this as a reason for supporting the new rulers. Pauperization, public humiliation, or execution of a man's parents, on the other hand, was likely to have a violent and immediate effect upon his loyalties; even some party members of long standing were decisively alienated by it.

The men also resented censorship of news from home. Party control over the marriage of soldiers created a strong adverse reaction when it blocked a man's own engagement or broke up his home, though as a policy it provoked only mild resentment. Men recently taken from civilian life identified to some degree with their local communities; long-time soldiers did not.

Military unit.—Respondents with service in the Nationalist army reported close personal friendships and some bonds of personal loyalty between officers and men; they did not report such ties in the Communist forces. All respondents agreed that it was dangerous to have a close personal friend. The Communist leadership persistently tried to build morale on the basis of common political convictions and persistently attacked: "individual unit-ism," such as, for example, failure to turn over booty to higher headquarters, and all personal bargains or friendships which might threaten the primacy of the party's claims. The techniques of surveillance and public criticism employed to enforce these and other objectives bred an atmosphere of mutual distrust which tended to suppress close ties to fellow soldiers and to the unit.

Nation.—During the civil war, Communist propaganda to university students emphasized the government's weakness in domestic affairs and its inability to defend China from economic and territorial encroachments. Several respondents were drawn to the Communists by their desire for a united, respected nation.

Otherwise, however, the data suggest that nationalism is not a major determinant of loyalty to Communist authority. The less educated respondents did not appear to have any particular interest in the subject; they did not spontaneously refer to nationalist aspirations, and even their dislike of the Japanese seemed much more closely related to personal experiences with oppression than to any general patriotism. Even the intellectuals, once they became subject to Communist control, reacted primarily to personal aspects of their experience rather than to anti-imperialist slogans or to the fact that the Communists were making China a power to be reckoned with. Distrust of Russian intentions toward China, for example, was stated more as an expression of the traditional Chinese suspicion of foreigners than as an expression of modern political nationalism.

The Faces of Chinese Communism.—The four aspects of Communism, which we outlined earlier, correspond on the whole to the major points of view from which the respondents regarded and reacted to Chinese Communism. The relative importance of the four as influences upon soldiers' attitudes toward Communist authority differed from one respondent to another, and from one time to another for single respondents. All, however, reacted in some degree to all four. This classification of interests represents one of the major findings from the study, and the research staff hypothesizes that most Chinese soldiers formulate their judgments of Communist authority on the basis of these four aspects.

Communist ideas.—Agreement or disagreement with Communist political principles and national policy proposals was not a major focus of either loyalty or disaffection among the respondents. At the time they became subject to Communist power most of them, like the majority of Chinese, did not have any general ideas of the kind that characterize Western political debates. Some of the better educated, however, judged the Communists initially on the basis of their land reform and nationalistic propaganda.

Regardless of class origins, the respondents favored the idea of land reform and the objective of improving the lot of the poor; many accepted the Communist view that this entailed a struggle against the power of the rich.

Some of the poorly educated respondents liked the idea of being connected with a movement that had answers to apparently important questions. The better educated were likely to be impressed by the sloganized version of Marxism which they were taught. Neither group, however, had a sustained interest in political principles as such. Since almost all the respondents became subject to Communist power involuntarily, their crucial problem was that of working out a *modus vivendi,* under conditions of continuous pressure. Among the things to which they had to adjust was a new body of Western-type ideas about politics.

Many of them learned a great deal about the operational meaning of Communism—its practical consequences for human personality, social organization, and social values; the eloquence and penetration of their final judgments reflect this political education. But the "war for men's minds" that is fought on the level of explicit propaganda about programs and principles seems to have influenced their attitudes much less than we are wont to suppose.

Everyone learned Marxist slogans in order to get along in the new order, but the longer they lived with the Communist movement the more their interest shifted to the non-ideological faces. In shaping the mature loyalties of the respondents, the practical impact of Communist principles and policies upon their own specific interests played a much greater role than the policies and principles as ideas.

Status and security.—The desire for safety and status in the new order was extremely strong and a most important influence on the men's loyalty. They were, by Western standards, remarkably frank in relating their feelings about the Communists to considerations of personal welfare.

Intellectuals were promised good jobs if they would undergo intensive thought reform, and Nationalist soldiers were promised forgiveness if they would work hard in the service of the people. Both groups considered these terms reasonable and tended to conform willingly. The prospect of additional status and security was also a major reason for wanting to join the Communist party.

On the whole, advancement strengthened pro-Communist feelings. It suggested to the individual that promises were being kept and effort rewarded, and that his bargain had been a good one. Some men discovered, however, that even after they had been promoted or admitted to the party their bourgeois or landlord backgrounds were cited, like a prison record, to compound the seriousness of their mistakes. Intellectuals were commonly assigned as cultural instructors with junior officer rank but without real respect or authority. Such men were likely to conclude that they would never be trusted and to become disaffected.

Promotion with apparent full acceptance was not a guarantee against defection; the execution or humiliation of a man's parents might outweigh, in his thinking, even rapid personal advancement. Furthermore, promotion and admission to the party exposed men more directly to the trickery and deceit of the Communist organization. As they moved up in the ranks they were watched as carefully as ever and, knowing this, concluded that Communist comradeship was a myth.

Methods of control.—In their effort to revolutionize Chinese society the Communists must fight all the traditional patterns which have characterized the people's relations with one another and with the government. In the army they seek to impose an impersonal, bureaucratic organization and a morale based on universal political principles. However, their techniques for controlling the behavior and thinking of individuals, though remarkably ingenious, are only partly effective.

Many of the respondents developed strong feelings about the control techniques themselves; these attitudes became important determinants of attitudes toward Communist authority. Most of the men were impressed at first by the Communists' reasonableness and use of open discussion. At the same time, however, they were shocked and embarrassed by having to participate in public criticism of themselves and others—a practice far removed from traditional Chinese interpersonal relationships with their extreme consideration for the face of all parties. In time they got over the shock, but universal surveillance and daily criticism meetings tended to create an atmosphere of mutual suspicion and a sense of undue coercion. The respondents' reactions were even stronger when they recognized that the Communists were using these techniques for the sake of total control and not merely to achieve particular objectives.

The traditional freedom of individuals to negotiate personal relationships was severely curtailed; the sense of personal isolation and helplessness bred anxiety in many. According to Chinese Communist policy, public criticism is the principal weapon for reconciling individual and group interests; for many disaffected respondents, however, it became the principal symbol of the Communist effort to dehumanize them and reduce them to the status of mere tools.

Similarly, Communist public trials and executions, designed to whip up mass enthusiasm and mass participation, created fear and resentment. Although they heartily approved of land reform, respondents of all classes, including party members, were seriously alienated by the cruel public humiliation and execution of landlords and former officials. Respondents whose parents suffered in the land reform resented their loss of face more than they resented the loss of property. Intellectuals required to engage in manual labor interpreted this demand as a deliberate effort to humiliate them, but they were alienated more by exhaustion and continuous exhortation than by the degrading work itself.

Communist regulation of the relations between soldiers and civilians was often considered legitimate, but censorship of letters from home and party interference with the marriage plans of individuals aroused serious resentment while increasing men's loneliness.

Morality.—The morality of Communist behavior was a major influence on loyalty among the respondents. While Chinese soldiers appear to many Westerners to be relatively lacking in a concept of absolute truth or propriety, and while they do assume that authority operates deviously, an unlimited tolerance of distortion and manipulation should not be inferred.

No characteristic of the new rulers won so much praise and stimulated so much loyalty as the sincerity with which they treated common people and soldiers who had just come under their control—their seeming willingness to negotiate in good faith. And no long-term characteristic of Communist rule won so much hatred as the deceitfulness with which cadres broke the promises made to individuals, lied about facts that did not suit their purposes but were important to individual respondents, and put a false front of spontaneity and democratic decision on actions that had been carefully rigged by the party organization. The most disaffected respondents felt that they had definitely characterized the Communist order when they spoke of it as a regime based on deceit.

PART II

Chinese Responses to Communist Military-Political Control

THE ROLE OF TRADITIONAL ORIENTATIONS TOWARD SOCIAL RELATIONS IN CHINESE RESPONSES TO COMMUNIST MILITARY-POLITICAL CONTROL

Samuel M. Meyers

The success of the Chinese Communists in manipulating lower-echelon officers and soldiers has been shown by Bradbury and Kirkpatrick in Chapter I. This led research personnel to give a great deal of consideration to the techniques of manipulation and control employed by the Chinese Communist regime.

The information elicited from soldiers of the Chinese Communist armies—except those who remain firmly pro-Communist—tended to give a picture of persons forced to comply with the demands of the regime by heavy physical and mental pressures. Interviews with Chinese PW's conducted for this research project do not provide any reasons for believing that these informants were in truth convinced pro-Communists but were trying to create the opposite impression by stating they had been forced to comply. Nonetheless, their descriptions of their experience hint that something more is involved. They describe force as being in the background though seldom used, but their descriptions of particular situations in which they had no choice but to conform have not always convinced their interrogators.

Furthermore, human beings do not merely react to external forces mechanically, but respond according to how they perceive or define the situation. Consequently, some knowledge of how the Chinese tend to define social situations, and in particular of the meaning they ascribe to the control measures employed by the Communists, is needed in order to guard against a distorted view of such control. The question is: What combination of objective circumstances and subjective orientation results in a Chinese soldier's perception that he must conform to the demands of his superiors even when the substance of those demands is radically opposed to his previous loyalties and habits?

In attempting to answer this question, this chapter will:

> Set up certain assumptions about the orientation of typical, traditionally reared Chinese toward social relations and authority.
>
> Reconstruct imaginatively, on the basis of the assumptions, their definition of certain common situations presented by Communist efforts to control their behavior.
>
> On this basis, predict how they would respond to these situations.
>
> Examine, in general terms, how these predictions conform to the actual responses that have been reported.

Methodologically, the predicted patterns of behavior are hypotheses to be tested by comparison both with data available at present and with data that may become available in the future.

This analysis is not concerned principally with long-time Communist cadres who, because of their intensive indoctrination and their immersion in the peculiar, highly disciplined, social structure of the party, are less likely than others to manifest traditional Chinese characteristics directly. It is assumed that, although these men cannot completely escape their cultural background, their perception and motivation have been remolded to a considerable extent. Rather, the analysis will deal principally with non-Communist Chinese under Communist control.

The general system of controls employed by the Chinese Communists need not be described; this system is now widely known. Particular elements will, however, be described and discussed as the analysis requires.

ASSUMPTIONS REGARDING ORIENTATION OF CHINESE TOWARD SOCIAL RELATIONS AND AUTHORITY

The assumptions about Chinese orientations are based on study of certain Chinese classics and the observations of contemporary students of Chinese culture.[1] Although generalizations about a vast, highly differentiated culture like that of China are very likely to prove oversimple, the premises selected for this analysis are salient among the generalizations frequently stated to apply to Chinese social behavior. They are:

---

[1] See, for example: Unpublished Army China Area Manual; Bradbury and Kirkpatrick, Chapter 1, above. Lucian W. Pye, *Some Observations on the Political Behavior of Overseas Chinese;* Ruth Bunzel and John H. Weakland, *An Anthropological Approach to Chinese Communism;* Francis L. K. Hsu, *Under the Ancestors' Shadow;* Francis L. K. Hsu, *Americans and Chinese: Two Ways of Life;* H. C. Hu, "The Chinese Concepts of 'Face' "; James Legge (ed. and transl.), *The Four Books: Confucian Analects, The Great Learning, The Doctrine of the Mean, Works of Mencius;* H. H. Dubbs, *Hsuntze Works;* Max Weber, *The Religion of China;* Herrlee G. Creel, *Chinese Thought From Confucius to Mao Tse-tung.*

Chinese typically seek to establish harmonious social relations.

Harmony, according to the Chinese view, will be established and maintained if each person carefully observes rules of behavior prescribed for particular situations and for specific roles. Acting properly, according to the rules, is an important moral injunction.

Shaming, or loss of face through public disapproval, is a potent sanction for enforcing group rules of conduct.

Desire for social recognition or gaining face is a strong motivating principle.

Fate, the Chinese believe, is an important consideration in success. One cannot fight against the environment, nor can one manipulate external factors and relationships; one must accept them even though they may seem capricious. Only by adjusting to this pattern of relations can one hope to influence events. Thus, one cannot plan too far ahead. One should wait and act correctly in the situation, hoping that by so doing one will be favored.

It is not asserted or assumed here that the foregoing are the only important traditional factors in Chinese social behavior, or even the most important. Rather, the analysis to follow is intended to assist in answering the question: To what extent can the observed patterns of responses to Communist control be accounted for in terms of the assumptions selected here, and in what respects are these assumptions inadequate? Additional premises will be suggested at points where the data seem to require them.

COMMUNIST CONTROL TECHNIQUES

Manipulating Captured Nationalist Soldiers into Volunteering for the CCF

Many Chinese soldiers first experienced Communist control as prisoners of war when Nationalist army units were captured by or surrendered to the Communists during the civil war. In their treatment of captured soldiers, the Communist leaders followed a unique policy,[2] the principal features of which were substantially as follows.

All captured soldiers and officers were welcomed and entertained. In return, the prisoners of war were encouraged to make speeches expressing their gratitude. Officers and enlisted men were segregated, investigated, and classified. Then, the men were given an intensive political orientation in which the two regimes were compared, the Chinese Communist Forces praised and the Chinese Nationalist army con-

[2] This policy has been in process of development since 1928. At the 1928 Futien Conference of the Central Committee of the Chinese Communist Party, Mao Tse-tung presented a basic document on personnel policy in the Red army, and directed particular attention to the treatment and disposition of captured soldiers. The principles laid down at that conference set policy which with minor exceptions continued through the Korean conflict.

demned. The "speak bitterness" meetings were held. Here stooges expressed grievances against the old regime, and compared the considerate treatment accorded them by the Chinese Communist Forces with their former life in the Chinese Nationalist army. Occasionally, a unit's former officers would encourage their men to join the Communist forces. All were urged to express their grievances; some meetings became so emotionally charged that many men sobbed. At the conclusion of these meetings, which lasted up to eight hours, the soldiers were given an opportunity to volunteer for the CCF. Those who wished to be released were given funds to return home, but were generally given more political indoctrination before their actual release. Those who elected to join were dispatched to units in the Communist army. The scattered evidence now available (largely from military sources) indicates that when additional manpower was needed by the CCF an overwhelming majority of the men in a captured unit volunteered to join.

That such a large percentage of the prisoners volunteered to join the CCF, especially since they were allegedly given a choice, raises some doubt about the voluntary nature of the decision. However, on the premises adopted for this analysis, one would not expect many Chinese to buck the tide of a well-organized movement, since they habitually seek the praise and esteem of others. The "speak bitterness" meetings were planned to produce some action, and when a soldier saw others volunteering he would usually conform to the will of the group, regardless of his personal inclinations. Since these meetings were attended by complete captured units of the Nationalist army, where presumably everyone was acquainted and some measure of cohesion existed, violation of what appeared to be a group norm was unthinkable. In other words, the situation was manipulated by the Communists so that the prisoner felt he had only one choice—to volunteer.

It is also possible that in their orientation sessions the Communists succeeded in convincing many individual soldiers of the merits of their case, and that such soldiers chose to join the CCF on a basis of at least subjective rationality.

Another factor whose role in this behavior needs further investigation is this: In some cases the voluntary choice was made under the extreme tension and emotion characteristic of certain types of crowds. Descriptions of "speak bitterness" meetings show that the tension and excitement which developed were sometimes sufficiently intense to permit easy manipulation of the crowd by an agitator. In civilian "speak bitterness" meetings concerning landlords, it is said that the excitement sometimes became so intense that only an act of violence against the landlord would satisfy the crowd. At the soldiers' meetings, however, no concrete figure was available upon whom the group could vent its anger. Instead, an image of the Kuomintang regime was held before the soldiers, and a promise to fight was extracted.

Any one of these three possible reasons, by itself or in combination with the others, might constitute sufficient impetus to volunteering, but I believe that the first reason bears the most weight.

Captured Nationalist officers and certain classes of non-commissioned officers (NCO's) underwent a more intensive period of orientation, lasting up to three months. One new element was added to this orientation. Whereas the rank-and-file soldier merely expressed his grievances against the former Kuomintang regime, officers and NCO's had to identify themselves with the old regime by confessing wrongs they had committed against the people. This admission of wrongdoing was manipulated in such a way that the confessors experienced great shame and humiliation and asked for a chance to expiate their past by working for the Communists. From such evidence as was available to the research staff, it appears that groups were formed and a standard of behavior was established by the Communists, and that under the circumstances the officers and NCO's, having no alternative, conformed to the standard, even going so far as to fabricate confessions to show the proper attitude.

While in general the NCO's and officers volunteered for reasons essentially similar to those of the enlisted men, fear of violent action taken against them by the Communist regime must be considered an additional factor in their decision to join the Communist forces. As responsible members of the Nationalist army they were, by definition, enemies of the people. Failure to associate themselves with the Communists would have signified clearly their continuing loyalty to the Nationalists and would have left them open to the clear and present threat of purging, the terrible consequences of which were well known to them.

Just what proportion of former Nationalist soldiers were accepted as volunteers for the Chinese Communist Forces is unknown. Enlisted men were sent into line outfits immediately after their decision to volunteer. The officers and NCO's who were accepted were generally required to undergo more intensive indoctrination, lasting up to nine months in exceptional cases, before they were considered safe enough for assignment to duty.

Chinese persons also came in contact with the Communist regime during recruiting drives carried on by Communist cadres in the cities and villages. Here again, an act of volunteering was involved. Typically, the recruitment drive took place in a well-organized group. The more extremist or "progressive" elements began the movement to volunteer, and others followed suit, apparently regardless of their private inclinations. Again, as with captured Nationalist soldiers, a well-organized group has set a standard and the individual member of the group cannot refuse to volunteer, for that implies unwillingness to abide by group norms, which is contrary to Chinese cultural standards. At the same time, the individual may well recognize that he is confronted by a powerful organization with which he cannot cope, and feel that in these conditions he can only accept his fate and go along, hoping that fortune will favor him.

That the Chinese Communists take such pains to require voluntary action seems strange to Westerners. Time and time again their writings have emphasized its importance.[3] The Communists apparently believe that if Chinese are forced against their will to engage in some activity, dangerous problems of morale and discipline will beset the organization. Certainly this is a reasonable assumption and one which is also applicable in the West, but Westerners do not ordinarily take such pains to manipulate a situation so that a voluntary act is the only course of action left open. It may very well be, however, that in Chinese society a voluntary act has wider implications, in the sense that if a person volunteers for anything a chain of mutual obligations is set up which is binding upon both parties. If this is true, then the Communists have a club to use over the individual who, having volunteered, begins to backslide. They can then easily accuse such a person of not living up to the obligations he has undertaken. Failure to live up to one's obligations in Chinese society engenders loss of face, the threat of which is generally sufficient to keep a person in line. By the same token, however, disaffection may set in when individual volunteers recognize that the Communist leadership is not fulfilling the obligations it has implicitly assumed toward them in accepting their service.[4]

Inducing Conformity in the CCF

Guidance Structure

In the CCF, former Nationalist soldiers and new recruits are confronted by a new situation. New rules and regulations must be obeyed, and a different type of conduct is required in relations with civilians. The units are well organized, with strategic positions held by Communist cadres, who set the standards and goals of the group.

What can be expected of these soldiers? Chinese tradition creates a strong preference for living in well-defined situations and acting in well-defined reciprocal roles. It could be expected that, if such persons were placed in an unstructured situation, they would be uneasy and would search for clues leading to the correct behavior. Since the Communist leadership actively provides guidance—and further, since there is no clearly patterned alternative—it would be expected that the rank and file would realistically adjust to the situation and quickly bring their conduct into conformity with the prescribed standards. They would do this not because they are forced, in the literal sense—for most,

---

[3] See Mao Tse-tung, *Selected Works;* Boyd Compton (transl. and ed.), *Mao's China: Party Reform Documents, 1942–44;* Liu Shao-chi, *How to Be a Good Communist* (Peking: Foreign Language Publishing House, 1951).

[4] See Chapter 1, above.

the threat of force remains far in the background, is not a clear and present danger—but rather because it is the correct and reasonable thing to do.

To help the new soldiers learn new ways of thinking and acting, various educational techniques are employed by the Communists. Personal interviews, lectures, discussions, dramas, and other standard pedagogical tools are all used to redirect the thinking and consequently the conduct of the new soldiers. But the most potent educational tool—one that, if not invented by the Chinese Communists, is applied uniquely by them—is self- and mutual criticism.

Criticism

Criticism has its immediate roots in early Bolshevik doctrine: Lenin pointed out that what distinguished the Communist party from other political parties was its willingness to examine its past conduct in the light of party principles and to redirect its efforts on the basis of such criticism. Not only have the Chinese Communists extended this party concept to include the entire citizenry, but they have made it a weapon of extraordinary effectiveness in promoting mass conformity. This may be because criticism, particularly self-criticism, also has roots in ancient Chinese philosophy. A high-ranking Chinese Communist held as a prisoner of war in Korea and interviewed by the research team has suggested that Mao Tse-tung took a famous Confucian saying, "A gentleman examines himself three times a day," and extended it to the masses. At any rate, criticism is a most important tool in the Communist scheme for correcting thinking and behavior. Effective utilization of this technique requires cadres who have the correct ideological viewpoint and who know the rules that have been devised. One major rule states that criticism should be employed only when a principle is involved; thus criticism must be constructive. Through criticism the thought and conduct of the individual are brought into harmony with party principles.

While constructive criticism is an effective teaching technique, it can be predicted to promote internalization of the desired conduct only if the individual identifies strongly with the group and/or its purposes to begin with. Therefore, a good Communist (or a man who has decided to conform maximally in order to get ahead) would welcome criticism, for it would enable him to correct shortcomings that prevent him from working effectively. For most persons, however, criticism is unpleasant; it may merely lead a soldier to suppress acts and words for which he might be criticized. Thus, depending on the degree of group identification, criticism may be principally a technique for obtaining maximum conformity rather than a way of achieving genuine learning, understanding, and internalization of party goals and ideas. The extent to which genuine commitment is achieved, as opposed to mere conformity, cannot be determined. Under normal circumstances the difference may not be significant so long as behavior follows the required pattern. But in critical situations the difference may be all important if one wishes to exploit and activate passive disaffection.

Either way, all observers agree that criticism is an effective technique for inducing correct conduct. This is not unexpected if the phenomenon is viewed against a background of Chinese cultural traits. Traditionally, the Chinese seek to establish and maintain harmony; to do this, they must act properly according to the rules. Consequently, one seeks to conform to the situational demands, in this instance, Chinese Communist army standards. If one is then criticized publicly for a violation of army standards, it is a shameful and humiliating experience. One has lost face since one has violated behavior patterns deemed to be correct by the group.

Westerners find it difficult to comprehend the anguish which Chinese suffer when publicly criticized. Such criticism induces them to take steps to ensure that the experience will not be repeated. They will make determined efforts to reestablish a position in the group by acting correctly in the future. Even though the criticism is leveled at a man by the leader and is given constructively, this will not detract from the man's feeling that he has met with group disapproval. And as stated earlier, group disapproval is a dreaded punishment, for it means that the individual can no longer depend upon the group for support.

However, disapproval is not expressed only by the leader. It is a cardinal principle among the Chinese Communists that everyone in the group should criticize the culprit. Criticism of one's fellows is contrary to traditional Chinese conduct norms; public criticism causes the person criticized to lose face, and it is a principle of traditional Chinese behavior that one never makes another feel insignificant publicly. Nevertheless, since criticism of one's fellows is a clearly prescribed norm of conduct in the CCF, and since the man who does not engage in such criticism is himself likely to be criticized by the group, he resolves the conflict in his own favor and criticizes others. From the offender's point of view, the full weight of group disapproval is brought to bear upon him; this is a tremendous burden for a Chinese to carry without bowing to the will of a group. The only way one can avoid this humiliating experience is to act correctly. Our premises would lead us to expect that, subjected to this continual, serious pressure, the Chinese Communist troops would be well disciplined and orderly.

Nevertheless, individuals are bound to make mistakes or yield to contrary private impulses. Then, rather than face the group criticism which is sure to come, particularly if the mistake was committed in the sight of others, it is the lesser of two evils to criticize oneself. From the point of view of the actor, self-criticism serves two functions, provided it is made in terms of the appropriate criteria. First, it effectively undercuts criticism from others and enables one to control the situation. If a man allows himself to be criticized by others, he cannot know just what they will say; he has lost his defenses against what may prove a jarring and bitter experience. Second, self-criticism provides a positive sign that the actor recognizes its importance in correcting mistakes; it is evidence to the Communist leadership that he sincerely wishes to change himself. If the self-criticism is to be performed properly, the individual must provide a correct political analysis of his conduct, further supplying proof of his good intent. Such behavior will evoke praise, signifying that his position in the group is secure. It will also add to his prestige, since criticism typically occurs in public and since, among the Chinese probably even more than among persons from other societies, A's acceptance of and respect for B is a function of the reaction to B exhibited by other members of the group to which both A and B belong. Such approbation will constitute an encouragement to work harder, and thus the individual is drawn closer to the organization and perhaps to more genuine identification with it.

One would expect, then, that soldiers would choose to engage in self-criticism rather than to subject themselves to the risks of mutual criticism. At the same time, they will actively avoid serious violations of prescribed conduct, since, even though they resort to self-criticism, Communist cadres and "progressive" elements in the unit may subject the individual who has criticized himself to severe additional criticism before the group if the violation is serious. On the other hand, in order to show the proper attitude, minor violations will be criticized by the perpetrator whenever committed, or even invented and criticized.

Over time, criticism becomes more tolerable, not merely because persons become used to it, but because gross violations have been brought under control, either through commitment to the regime, with the obligations such commitment imposes, or in response to severe group disapproval or additional sanctions. In these conditions criticism, both self- and mutual, continues, but deals almost solely with minor incidents where group disapproval is minimal and/or for effect. Thus criticism tends to become ritualized.

Pressure for Increased Work Output

Besides playing on the orientation of new CCF soldiers in such a way as to train them effectively, the system of control is useful in other situations. As an illustration, I suggest that the system has a significant role in increasing the work output of former Nationalist officers and NCO's now in the Chinese Communist forces; the basic operation will be somewhat the same for other men as well.

Formerly, the policy of the CCF required that all recruitment and enlistment be voluntary. As has been pointed out, before being accepted for service in the CCF some volunteers were required to admit their personal guilt for crimes against the people, and others had to admit guilt by association because the Nationalist units to which they belonged had committed such criminal acts. Whether their guilt was personal or by association, this admission would be expected, on the basis of the assumptions made for this analysis, to cause them to feel intense shame and anguish, which they would desire to expiate by working for the new regime. But they were required to do more than ordinary work, since only through extra labor could they make restitution and regain status. Consequently, they were expected to do much of the heavy and menial labor. Some of these men had formerly held command positions exempted from physical labor, and for others any work beyond the quota of hard labor in which Chinese traditionally engage must have been especially onerous. It is therefore likely that some of them complained about the work they were doing and/or did a minimum. Such a reformee would immediately be criticized for not showing the true spirit of the proletariat and "blowing hot and cold," or he might be called a "lagging particle" or a "backward element."

Criticism of this nature would strike a vital spot in Chinese character, since it implies that the offender lacks sincerity, that he joined the CCF under false pretenses, that he did not mean what he said when he promised to erase his former crimes, that he was not living up to his obligations. In the face of such criticism, supreme efforts would normally be made to erase that judgment by performing in the manner required. Thus, it appears that any level of performance up to the limits of physical endurance can be set and achieved through the use of group control and criticism.[5]

SOLDIER RESPONSES TO DISAFFECTION IMPULSES AND COMMUNIST COUNTERMEASURES AGAINST DISAFFECTION

Individual Management

Might not the policies referred to, together with other policies of the regime both within the army and outside, create disaffection on the part of various elements in the military forces? Interviews with Chinese prisoners of war in Korea indicate clearly that such disaffection existed, but they also show that this disaffection did not lead to expressions of mass dissatisfaction or to nonconformity. This lack of relation between disaffection and overt conduct suggests that a man who is disaffected must determine whether the situation is such that he can act on his disaffection without threat to his values. If we assume that he perceives the situation as prohibiting overt acts of hostility or escape, there remain several ways in which such a man might deal with his dissatisfactions.

The disaffected soldier knows that if he allows his overt conduct to reflect his disaffection, he will be criticized immediately by cadres and "progressive" elements. Since criticism is humiliating and embarrassing, and since in addition he may be severely punished, he cannot afford to risk deviation. However, he knows that he is judged by the

[5] See Chapter 3, below.

Communists according to the consequences of his conduct. In other words, if his conduct has good consequences for the regime, his political thoughts will be assumed to be correct; if the consequences of his act are detrimental to the cause of the regime, then his thoughts will be politically suspect. Thus, he is likely to conclude that the safest and most reasonable course of conduct is to adjust in the traditional manner—namely, to act according to the rules and bide his time. If his disaffection becomes stronger, he may correspondingly increase his efforts to conform. This may lead not only to praise but to promotion, and such a man may find himself in a paradoxical situation in which he is at once increasingly disaffected, maximally aiding the Communist regime, increasingly accepted as reliable, and more and more enmeshed in its machinery.

Alternatively, disaffection may be changed to acceptance through continuous social interaction with the members of his unit. The disaffected individual can perceive only that he is disaffected, since others in his unit are acting and speaking correctly. He would therefore tend to feel socially isolated—an unpleasant position for anyone, but especially for a Chinese person. This fact, together with the constant pressure for genuine commitment, the necessity for acting and speaking correctly, and the discomfort of nurturing feelings which cannot be acted upon or expressed, may lead to a change in attitude from disaffection to acceptance and even to recognition of positive reasons for supporting the regime.[6]

Disaffection may be managed in a third way. The disaffected man can rationally conclude that the objective situation denies him any alternative course of action and that it is reasonable and sensible to conform outwardly, but through private, symbolic acts—for example, the use of irony, mockery, Ketman,[7] fantasy—he may carry on a symbolic fight with the regime and maintain a private dignity.

Group Formation

The management of disaffection discussed in the preceding paragraphs involves only the responses of isolated individuals. It may be, however, that the disaffection is so intense and overwhelming and the individual feels so urgent a need to share his feelings that, despite the risks, he will seek to communicate with others. Because of the highly effective surveillance system, such communication requires that special channels and forms of communication, as well as a specialized language, be developed. Embryonic and amorphous groups, whose members are bound together by common states of disaffection, may then evolve.

In normal circumstances such groups can create only limited diffi-

[6] A. Doak Barnett, *Hsueh Hsi: Weapon of Ideological Revolution in China.* See also Chapter 3, below.

[7] Czeslaw Milosz, *The Captive Mind.*

culty for the regime, but the regime cannot allow them to grow because, in a crisis situation, they would act as magnets, attracting other dissident elements toward them to form resistance groups. Therefore, the regime must constantly seek to undermine the development of any group whose tendency is counter-revolutionary or conspiratorial. It does so primarily through preventing all clearly disaffected communication, restricting the formation of groups which do not directly serve official purposes, and thus depriving disaffection impulses of linkage to objects.

This constant war of attrition against disaffection must eventually convince the disaffected of the futility of continued resistance, particularly since it is so difficult to gain any measure of support for one's views. Aside from the special dependence on group opinion exhibited by Chinese, it has long been held in the West that in the absence of support from others a nonconforming position can be maintained only with extreme difficulty by anybody. At the same time, positive rewards for acceptance are constantly held out before the disaffected Chinese soldiers by the Communists. It follows that, unless the disaffected elements in the CCF receive additional assurance that continued resistance will pay off, and can be persuaded that a more desirable alternative will be presented to them within a reasonable time, such elements will make their peace, however reluctantly, with the regime.

CONCLUSION

This chapter has sought to account for the observed conformity of Chinese to Communist military and political control in terms of traditional orientations toward social relations. While it has not been proved that such orientations were major factors in conformity, this chapter has nevertheless shown that the observed behavior of Chinese soldiers which surprised American investigators can be understood in terms of assumptions about these orientations. However, additional investigation would be needed to clarify the role of these orientations in Chinese conformity to Communist control.

: III :

WANG TSUN-MING, ANTI-COMMUNIST: AN AUTOBIOGRAPHICAL ACCOUNT OF CHINESE COMMUNIST THOUGHT REFORM

Wang Tsun-ming, the subject of the following autobiographical account, has been labeled by Radio Peking "a reactionary agent of Chiang Kai-shek." As a Chinese Nationalist officer, Wang fought the Communists in various roles for three years but was finally captured in 1949. After an unusually long, intense reindoctrination he was put into the Communist army and then sent to Korea, where he deserted to the United Nations. He subsequently became a major leader among anti-Communist Chinese prisoners-of-war, and has now been repatriated to Formosa, where he has resumed his career in the Nationalist army. The present report is based upon interviews conducted while he was a PW.

The bulk of Wang's story concerns his reindoctrination by the Communists. It reveals with exceptional clarity the emotional and intellectual elements of brainwashing and its effects upon a dynamic, natural leader of men. Especially noteworthy in Wang's detailed account of his thought reform are the progressive narrowing of the choices open to him, the devices by which the Communists wrecked his traditional and Nationalist social ties, and the way in which he simultaneously served the purposes of the Communists and developed a bitter-end will for revenge. The story makes it crystal clear that the effectiveness of Communist brainwashing with Chinese subjects is not traceable to the inherent moral and intellectual power of Marxist-Leninist views, or to their special affinity to Chinese culture. The ingenious use of teaching procedures, especially the close interweaving of formal instruction, group discussion, confession, and self- and mutual criticism, has a great deal to do with Communist success, but the preparation of detailed dossiers on the pupils, intimate surveillance of their actions, physical

Two long interviews, conducted by Lloyd E. Ohlin and Richard P. Harris, form the principal basis of the case history. Major contributions in the editing of these materials were made by Richard P. Harris, Helen Piazza, and the late William C. Bradbury.

exhaustion, and threats of severe penalties are indispensable—indeed crucial—parts of the process. Wang seems to have been an unusually difficult pupil, and was subjected to formal remolding for a period three times as long as that prescribed for captured Nationalist officers. That his brain was not "washed clean" should warn us against exaggerating the potency of Communist techniques in reshaping Chinese values and personality patterns.

At the same time, the reader should recognize that Wang's personal response to these controls is unique in some respects: he had unusually strong reasons to distrust and dislike the Communists, and their consequent effort to remold and control him reinforced this hatred even as it taught him to conform. Yet he is aware that his conformity was not a mere surface yielding.

Wang Tsun-ming is clearly a vigorous man of action; he is also unusually lucid and articulate. He is tall, with an impressive military bearing, and speaks with an air of authority and conviction. He was selected for interview because of his breadth of experience in the Nationalist Army during the civil-war period, Communist indoctrination schools, the Chinese Communist Forces, and the U.N. PW camps, and because of his understanding of, and persistence in resisting, Communist control. Because of his position of leadership in the PW compounds, the interviews upon which this report is based were interrupted repeatedly by other prisoners demanding Wang's advice and decision on internal administrative problems. But he is evidently proud of his record as an anti-Communist fighter; he tells the story freely and expresses willingness to have it widely known. In telling the story of his life, he grows most intense when he describes his reeducation and "reform through labor" at the hands of the Communists. Indeed, he regarded the lessons of his experience under the Communists as so important that he made great efforts, unusual for him, to delegate his responsibilities as a PW leader in order to keep the long interview periods free of distraction.

The bulk of the following narrative is presented in the first person; it represents a nearly verbatim record of Wang's replies as translated by a highly qualified interpreter in the course of a three-day series of interviews conducted at Mosulp'o on Cheju-do in August, 1953. Parts of the story are, however, summarized in the third person. These represent additional information acquired several weeks later through another series of interviews. A few highly specific items of information are from a routine interrogation of Wang which was conducted shortly after he became a prisoner of war.

With one significant exception (which is noted in the text), these three sources of data on Wang Tsun-ming are mutually consistent at the many points of overlap; each of the three provides some information omitted by the others. The objective aspects of Wang's account of Communist techniques for consolidating power in the villages and of brainwashing are, of course, corroborated by many existing reports.

FAMILY AND SCHOOLING

Wang Tsun-ming was born in Shenmu-hsien, about 160 miles north of Yenan in Shensi province, northwest China, in September, 1926. He was the second of three sons in a family of five children. His father was a minor Nationalist government official, and the major source of the family's income was his position as personnel chief of the county government. But the family also owned a small clothes shop and one hundred mow of land (about sixteen acres). By Chinese standards, therefore, Wang came from wealthy, landowning origins. While Wang and his younger brother were still students, the oldest brother became a chief of police.

At home with Wang's parents lived the two daughters, the three sons, the oldest brother's wife and eventually their three children. Wang's father's brothers and their families, similar in size and composition, also lived in the immediate family circle. This was, Wang tells us, "an old-fashioned Chinese family. The discipline was very strict, because I came from a rural family. When I did something wrong I used to be punished by being made to kneel in the corner or at the place of ancestor worship. I was instructed at great length in the moral code of China, and great stress was laid on filial piety."

As Wang approached his tenth birthday (1936), the Communist Eighth Route Army, having completed the now famous long march from the south of China, installed itself in northern Shensi. The southern part of the province was still controlled by the Nationalists, and even in the north the lines of Communist control were constantly shifting. Wang did not know what the word "Communist" meant; he recalls that the Communist forces were always referred to as bandits and described as cruel by his relatives and friends. Until he was eleven and left Shensi, Wang was not allowed to go out on the streets alone, since the Communist guerillas often kidnapped boys in the outskirts of the cities and in the rural areas.

The Communists were not the only source of disorder and violence. A Manchurian army under General Chang Hsueh-liang, driven out of its home area by the Japanese, was in southern Shensi, ostensibly under Kuomintang orders to attack the Communists. But when Generalissimo Chiang Kai-shek visited the area late in 1936, Chang kidnapped him and attempted to force the Generalissimo to agree to a united front of Communist and Kuomintang forces against the Japanese. This policy was confirmed when the Japanese forces moved south from Manchuria into China proper in 1937. But the Communists used this period of domestic cooperation primarily to expand their own power.

Thus, during 1938 the Communist armies became a close threat to the Shenmu-hsien area, and many boys were sent off to the Nationalist army schools. Wang says: "The local government had been ousted, and my parents were very much afraid. They obtained a promise from a friend, an officer in the Nationalist army, to take me with him and go away from the area. I stayed with him for a number of years and went to school wherever he was stationed." In the next few years Wang traveled over much of North China; at first the pair was in Anwhei, then in Honan until 1945. Here Wang completed two years of a senior middle school (high school) run by the Nationalist army. In addition to his regular classes, he received one hour of political study and two of military drill each week. The political course was principally anti-Japanese and had no anti-Communist content.

As he was finishing his second year, the Japanese surrendered and the school moved from Honan to Suchow in coastal Kiangsu province. The government then withdrew its support, and Wang was forced to leave for lack of funds. He entered government service and never saw his family again.

As for the family, Wang says: "I got one letter from home in 1940, and had no further word until 1951. My family had stayed in Shenmu until the Communists came in 1940 to take over on a fairly permanent basis. At that time the whole family moved to the country where we own land—all the uncles as well. Eventually, I heard through friends in 1951, the family lost even their farmlands and had to escape to save their lives. They moved to the city of Sian [in central Shensi]. My older brother was dead." Then they were sent by the Communists to Suiyuan province beyond the Great Wall, northwest of Shensi, "to open up the country. I do not know if they are still alive, since I have heard nothing more about them." Wang has no idea where his parents may be, and thinks they are probably dead. He speaks of his family with little emotion and in the past tense, as if resigned to the fact of their death or disappearance.

OBSERVATIONS ON COMMUNIST PROCEDURES
FOR TAKING AND CONSOLIDATING POWER

After the Japanese surrender, a race developed between the Nationalists and Communists to secure the weapons, territory, and productive capacity that had been under Japanese control. With Russian help, the Communists won easily in Manchuria. By the end of 1946 they had captured Japanese arms deposits, isolated the province, and secured key locations throughout North China. Elsewhere, during 1946 and 1947, they employed their now famous hit-and-run guerilla tactics to destroy Kuomintang armies piecemeal and to gain a stranglehold on communication centers in central China. At the same time they built up strength and reorganized their forces for the final campaigns of conventional positional warfare.

In this situation, according to Wang, the Political Department of the Ministry of National Defense issued a secret appeal to numerous young people to serve in the anti-Communist cause. Because "I always wanted to join the army, to revenge myself for what the Communists had done to me and my family," Wang joined a People's Service Team in March, 1946 at the age of nineteen. He became a warrant officer in Suchow and received four months of political training, including for the first time some formal briefing on the Communist threat. For a while he served as a liaison officer with the civilian population, arranging billets and supplies for the militia. Later, he was given the job of organizing an anti-Communist intelligence network among the civilians, first in a part of Kiangsu province and the next year in neighboring southern Shantung.

Organizing Newly Captured Areas

In this job Wang became intimately familiar with Communist techniques for organizing newly captured territories.[1]

In general it was a situation of vacillating conflict where control of an area passed from the Nationalists to the Communists and back again repeatedly. I did not see much evidence of indoctrination of the peasants by the Communists at that time. The Communist activity was guerilla activity. They were interested in fighting and concentrated on that, moving in and then pulling back again. Under these conditions the Communist policy when they took over a village was one of mutual purging of people. This policy was pursued as follows: The first step would be to mobilize the riffraff[2] in the area. The Communists told the riffraff that now the tables had been turned and it was they who would purge the capitalist class. The second step was to make use of the poor farmers to purge the well-to-do farmers. After each struggle for control of an area a number of rich farmers and capitalists were killed. Thus the vacillating conflict gradually led to the killing of rich merchants and those in the landowning class. The third step was then to mobilize the middle-class farmers to purge the riffraff, because they had committed robbery, theft, and other crimes which were essentially crimes against the people. By that time large groups of recruits were ready to move with the Communists when they pulled out of the village, because they feared the revenge of their victims.

The first job the Communists had, of course, was to organize the government. They pulled together party workers, "progressive" elements, and people like that. The gangsters, riffraff, and thieves were used as goon squads and progressive elements at first. The first job was to mobilize these men. Then the Communists issued directives to the "progressives." Then they would have the first public meeting, a people's assembly of the village. This is the beginning of the second

[1] Wang's description of these procedures is confirmed by the personal experiences of other informants as well as by several published accounts.

[2] Asked what he meant by riffraff, Wang made it clear that in his vocabulary the term covered petty thieves and people who were poor or destitute or down-and-out.

step. During the assembly the progressives would be planted as stool
pigeons in the audience, and they would air grievances against well-
to-do people. In this way victims are identified and charged. The
victims are then told to confess their exploitation of the people. Of
course their confessions can never be satisfactory. The goon squads
would then kick and beat the victims and continue to air grievances
against them and other people. I remember one village where a
farmer was accused by a fellow of taking an egg. It was not the
farmer who took it but his great-grandfather. The fellow charged that
this egg became a chicken and this chicken made many eggs and so
later there were many eggs and many chickens. Thus, this farmer
would have to pay a huge fine on his exploitation of the original
stolen egg. In this way and by such devices, it would eventually be
possible to confiscate all his property to pay for his—or his ancestors'—exploitations of other people in the area. The next step would
be for the poor people—the agitators—to move into the rich farmer's
house, claiming he had exploited them. The farmer would be told to
borrow from friends and relatives to pay the fines which were assessed against him. The fines were usually levied by a vote of the poor
classes in the public assembly. The final stage, after the man had
been stripped of all his property, was to force a confession from him.
This confession would be rejected on the grounds that the man was a
perpetual liar, that his guilt had been established, and that he had
reactionary elements in his makeup which could not be changed. An
agitator would cry out that the man should be beaten to death.
Planted progressives in the assembly would respond and agree. Sometimes all the members of the assembly would be forced to participate
in the execution. Each person would be given a bamboo stick. They
would parade by in single file and whip the victim. Thus the blood of
the victim and his final death would be on each man's hands. Sometimes even women and children would have to participate. All families in the area were made to participate in such executions in public,
and thus they all in some measure shared the guilt of them.

The Communists took money and food themselves. They distributed the land and the property to those who claimed the most exploitation. In this way people were encouraged to air grievances, since by
airing grievances they could lay a claim to land and property.

The third stage is when the purging gets turned around. The
middle-class farmers in China are those who just manage to plant
their land and get along. The Communists talk to them. They point
out the criminal threat, the thefts, and the unworthiness of the
riffraff. Thus, they even use the middle class to fight the tenant
farmers who are too obedient to the landlords, insisting that the
middle-class farmers suffered from subservience of the tenant farmers to the landlords. Now another public meeting is held. The riffraff
are charged and also the very poor tenant farmers because they were
too obedient to the landlords. Members of the middle-class farmers

are planted in the assembly. These party members or progressive middle-class farmers then say: "Let's give these people another chance, since they are part of the proletariat. Henceforth, if they serve the people they will redeem themselves." Then the Communist party members call for the poor peasants, the tenant farmers, and the riffraff to join the army. These people knew that it was either a case of joining the army or being purged by the assembly, so they usually joined the army. The poor peasants did not have to be accused of bad action as much as the riffraff group did. The poor peasants had received land in the purging of the upper-class wealthy farmers and so they were told: "Now that you have benefited from the people, you must serve the interest of the people." They were also advised that by joining the army they would serve to protect their new holdings. Thus the poor peasants were appealed to less for redeeming their former crimes than for protecting the new benefits they had won.

The Communists operated on a very different time schedule when they had firm control of an area than they did when they were moving in and out in the guerilla days. When they were operating as guerillas they had to speed the process up, and it was not so thorough as later on. After firm control is established in an area the process may last as long as eight months. In the first stage, three months are spent in which no apparent action is taken. Everything is calm on the surface. This time is spent in research and investigation by the Communists. The Communists appeared to do things openly and aboveboard. They had simple slogans which were easily understood, and there was a great deal of easy explanation for everything that was wrong. The soldiers treat the people well and even help with the farm work. At this time many people become converts to the Communist cause, but in reality the Communists are finding out all about everyone in the village and their relations with each other. In the second stage, a village committee is organized consisting of the poor farmers. The third stage consists of the purging of landlords and rich farmers; and the fourth stage, of land redistribution. Thereafter, purging is continuous as the need arises. With the guerillas this whole process was speeded up and might take place within a month. Under these conditions many landlords escaped. Where the control was firm in the later days, the Communists were able to make their restrictions on the movement of people stick and no one escaped. During the period of land reform no one is allowed to leave the village without a permit. In this way everyone is kept under control. After the land reform is completed, restrictions are relaxed and people can move about more freely.

Resistance, Submission, and Commitment

I do not think any effective resistance against this process is possible. I found that rich people preferred to commit suicide rather than to fight. They tried to keep everything, to hold on to it to the last minute. When the Communists take away their farm, they try to save their house. When they lose their house, they try to save their clothes. When they lose their clothes, they try to save their lives. Finally there is nothing left, and they commit suicide. These people will not resist. They are poor fighters. They always try to compromise with the Communists. Furthermore, there is close surveillance of rich people. They are usually imprisoned after they are charged at the very beginning. Under these conditions the man tries to protect his family after he has lost everything else. Then he tries to kill himself rather than fight, hoping that this will protect his family and they will leave the family alone. These people are not used to fighting. They hope that at some point they will be let alone. Frequently old men and women also kill themselves rather than fight. The able-bodied men who could resist the Communists and might be inclined to are rounded up and imprisoned. This leaves only the older people and the very young left at home, and they are unable to fight. Of course the Communists do not call it imprisonment; they call it protective custody.[3]

Under these conditions there is no real physical resistance. Most of the resistance seems to come from people who have tended to collaborate with the Communists before. They may even have sons in the Communist army, but during the period of land reform perhaps their landholdings are reduced. They protest verbally. They argue that they have supported the Communists and should not lose the land. Penalties are levied on them for making this protest. They are charged by the Communists with not being honest; usually they are middle-class peasants who hold up to maybe twenty mow of land [about three acres]. Each member of the family is entitled to three mow of land. If there are four members, then the family is entitled to twelve; if they hold twenty now, they must lose eight. If they protest, they are penalized for the protest. Instead of losing eight they may lose ten or twelve now, so no one protests. The system varies from one locality to another, but the amount of land depends on how many people there are in the area and what the local conditions are as regards their being able to farm the land.

Some resistance comes from the poor tenant farmers who refuse to accuse certain landowning "capitalists." Some of the landowners were very benevolent and very friendly to the tenant farmers. These farmers were loyal to their friends and to the proprietors. Some tenants therefore refused to be used by the Communists and refused to denounce the landlord during the purgings. Failure to cooperate in

---

[3] Here Wang adds: "The Communists are always turning words upside down. When they say 'protective custody,' they try to make you believe that they are protecting the man from the mob or from the public assembly and from purging. In the same way they refer to the places where they reform men and brainwash them as 'military colleges.'"

this way meant they either had to run away, or some might join the Communist army to escape, or some were charged as running dogs of the landlords and penalized accordingly. The way these people acted shows that the Chinese have a strong moral code. The real problem with our people is their general ignorance. That is why the Communists are so successful.

In my job I found the peasants very cooperative. In general the local people seemed to think that the Communists were oppressive in recruiting for guerilla activity and for labor and in their methods of collecting food. The first thing we did when we came back into a village that had been occupied by the Communists was to call a meeting of the whole people. We told them we were aware that the Communists forced everyone to participate, and we assured them that only under the Communists do they have to do things like this. The worst elements had usually departed with the Communists. We got some complaints by relatives of people who had been the victims, but these complaints were reconciled for the purpose of restoring order and for the purpose of conserving the popular support for the Nationalist cause in the area. We tried to help the victims of the Communist terror and to reorganize the countryside for the Nationalist cause. We recruited peasants and other people in the area to serve as informants for such a time as Communists might again move into the area. People who had served as purgers for the Communists were given a chance to repent and again serve as Nationalist supporters. Nonetheless, in this process the Communists always gained strength, since they had involved people in actions for which these people feared to be called to account by the Nationalists when the Nationalists returned. [Such people became tied to the Communist wagon.] Under these conditions the Nationalists were continually losing strength.

I recall one case in Lini, in Shantung province. It happened in 1947. The Communists occupied this area, and then it was recovered by our side. I had to help organize the people. When we got there we found a tremendous welcome. The people killed chickens and everything to welcome us. This included all classes except those who left with the Communists. I found that many poor people still believed strongly in the old moral code of the Chinese. The Communists violated this code. We rounded up the old village heads who had fled from the Communists. There were Nationalist Youth members who had become Nationalist guerillas when the Communists came in, and they returned too. We also used the poor peasants who were willing to cooperate with us. The government was reinstated with little change. The poor tenant farmers returned to the government the land they had received from the landlords—that is, the land taken from those people whom the Communists had killed.

In the beginning, as I said, the Communists got many converts and got a great deal of active support. But gradually the people find out that Communism has a way of increasing its demands after the organization is firmly established. The freedom of movement of the people is restricted; the taxes become even greater than those levied by the former landlords; the people have to make continuous contributions to the government; they must give manpower to the army. They begin to feel trapped and to see no escape. I will tell you how the Communists operated. They had what they called a "Three Step" campaign in the early days—and in the later days too—of their conquests. The first step was the strict discipline of the army—strong disciplinary measures for all the troops. The second step they called a "love people" campaign, and the third step was to instill terror and fear psychologically. I found—and people told me too—that the Communist army was far more disciplined than the Nationalist army. The soldiers were taught that they had a mission to serve Communism and that they could perform this mission by treating the people well. They were forbidden to steal or commit any act of disregard for the rights of civilians. They were urged to help the people in many ways. They helped with farm work, carried water, and did other things. In this way they won friends. This was part of their discipline and their "love people" campaign in the early stages. Later, they began the purgings by exploiting the resentments of the peasants against the rich landlords. These purgings instilled fear and terror. Then later, the people are told by the Communists to build a militia to protect the Communist organization against raids by the Nationalists or against sabotage. They are told they will get better food in the militia and they will be treated well. But after they join up they are moved to another place to get training. Then suddenly they find themselves very far away from home, out of touch with everybody, and incorporated into the Communist army. These people then become very resentful because they feel they have been tricked into it.

Destruction of Traditional Loyalties and Moral Code

Repeatedly in his interviews with U.S. personnel, Wang reverted to the theme of the destructive impact of Communism upon old loyalties and moral precepts, which is so well illustrated in his own experience.

It must be clear that the Communists are a revolutionary party. Their only chance to gain power is through chaos. It is also clear that in China the teachings of Confucius are the backbone of the Chinese people and help to maintain the social order of China. Some of the details of these teachings are obsolete, but the principles still stand and serve to govern effectively all relations between family members, friends, and strangers in China. The Communists blame the poverty and weakness of China in the past on her moral heritage. They charge that the restrictions of the moral code kept China backward and kept her from moving ahead in the world.

They would usually start with the family. Filial piety is one of the highest virtues, according to the old code of Confucius. The Communists tried to promote dissension between family members. They persuaded sons to denounce their parents as reactionaries. They tried to break up husband-and-wife relationships by giving the wife greater emancipation and by organizing women generally into various women's groups. They also created dissension among brothers, trying to get one brother to report on another. They tried to exploit the feelings of rivalry between brothers which have always existed. They tried to exploit conflict between different age groups, the old and the young. They tried to split all these groups up. The slogan that they used was, "Everything for the younger generation."

I have seen them try to break up the family system very early, especially in the early school years. They taught the children that parents brought you to this world by accident, but Mao Tse-tung will educate and care for you; you needn't depend on your parents any longer but depend on Mao Tse-tung. Another thing they did was publicly to praise the children as being intelligent and patriotic. They would urge them to report on their home life. They would pick out a child as a shining example if that child reported on his parents as reactionary. They would say to the child and the other children, "By getting his parent arrested, this child has served hundreds of people." Another thing they would do is to plant questions for the child to ask his parents and then he would report back to the school. They would make use of the children's reports about their parents to build up a case against the parents. They usually use such techniques on specially identified targets that they want to purge or eliminate.

In the old Chinese family, dissension among the members or splitting up of the family property was regarded by everyone as reflecting on the honor of the family. There was very little quarreling between family members, because this too was regarded as reflecting on the family honor. I believe it is easier to break up the families in the cities. In the rural areas they are more conservative and the children adhere much closer to the old moral code, but in the city there are more influences outside the family which affect their behavior. When I was at home, discipline was very strict, because I came from a rural family. . . .

I will tell you an example of what I saw, showing how the Communists try to break up the family. During the indoctrination program which I went through after I was captured, we were told by the Communist authorities at the military college that we were going to visit a ten-day Youth League meeting. This meeting of boys that we watched concerned the case of a father who had beaten his son. The son reported the beating at the meeting, and the father was called up to be questioned and lectured by the authorities and then questioned by other children in the group through prepared questions. They asked: "Do you not know it is a feudalistic practice to beat one's son? Do you not know children have liberty and self-respect? Children are the masters of tomorrow. Do you not know they are treasures of the country?" Finally the son was told to hit his father back before the group. After the meeting the Communists lectured our [former Nationalist] officers from the military college, and told us: "We took your group to see this because you all have old feudalistic ideas. Henceforth you must realize that the feudalistic practice is to be wiped out." After this we all had to discuss the case and justify this interpretation, though we were all sick at heart at what we had seen.

Another way they tried to do it was to break up relationships between friends. Friends have always been sacred, and the bonds of friendship have been honored. An example of this is what they did between me and my troops. They forced us to denounce each other and become suspicious of each other. They also tried to work on the attitude toward the nation. They tried to replace the loyalty to the family and the country with loyalties to the leaders of the Communist party. They also systematically went about burning the old books and rewrote history in an effort to blank out the teachings which lay in the historical writings of the Chinese people.

Do you know that the Communists taught that no sentiments are to be allowed between people? The only sentiment allowed is stated by the Communists as follows: "There is no sentiment between individuals. Emotion is only to be built on the revolutionary basis. Revolution purges all decadent thoughts. Everyone should worship Mao Tsetung." [4] The Communists do not like wise people. One is not supposed to use his brain to think but to learn the true—that is, the Communist—precepts. Letting your brain become too well developed, the Communists say, is dangerous.

Communist Substitutes for Traditional Sentiments

Of all the emotions the Communists taught, the most important is revolutionary emotion. This means obedience to Mao Tse-tung and his party. One becomes a comrade by virtue of this emotion. Only this emotion is permitted. Let me give you an example. They teach us about revolutionary love. This is one of the accepted emotions of love. When an old party member has sought the favor of a young woman of the party, it is necessary to get her to submit willingly. Other women party members will persuade her. They will say to her: "We know that this man is ugly and old, but he has contributed greatly to the revolution. You are not going to bed with this man but with what

[4] The quotation is a literal translation from Chinese characters which Wang wrote down from memory.

he represents. You will be serving the party and be duly rewarded for your action. Your refusal will be a refusal of the cause and not the man." [5] Thus you can see that everything between persons—all kinds of sentimental relationships—must always have some kind of revolutionary reason.

Among the parents, mostly there was just a kind of passive depression, despondency, fear, and anxiety in response to these Communist tactics. They did not know how to resist or to fight. It was mostly passive resistance. Sometimes they refused to support the son at school. But there were too many outside influences at work dividing and splitting the family members from each other. All the members belonged to different organizations. They became members of units outside the home, which separated them. They found gradually they had more in common with these outside organizations than they did with the family or other members of the family. These outside units always kept trying to promote trouble in the home. The family members could no longer share their thoughts and experiences because of fear of betrayal by the others in the family at their organization meetings. The family members were warned by the Communists not to discuss outside the organization what went on in the meetings, so they could not talk at home about what happened outside the home. The most important teaching that was always drummed into them in these organizations was that they must always follow Mao Tse-tung and his leadership of the party and the demands of the Communist organization. This takes precedence over all other loyalties including those to family members.

COMBAT AND CAPTURE BY THE COMMUNISTS

In 1947 Wang joined the Kuomintang youth affiliate, and late that year volunteered for service in the regular Nationalist army. Early in 1948 he was transferred to a select central cadre in Nanking for training as a political officer. Here he had three months of anti-Communist training, including courses in the three principles of Sun Yat-sen and the Four-Open Movement, an anti-graft campaign. He then asked for assignment in his home province of Shensi, served briefly as a political instructor in a school for military police officers in Sian, and was again transferred at his own request to a regular military unit, the 181st Regiment, 61st Division, 90th Army, at Pucheng, Shensi. Here as a second lieutenant he gave political instruction at the company level. A few months later he was promoted to first lieutenant. In 1949 he became a regular member of the Kuomintang.

Morale was high in the 61st Division, according to Wang; the division was noted for its bravery and fighting spirit. Wang states that at one

---

[5] Wang laughed repeatedly as he gave this illustration, as if at the transparency of this disguise for a seduction.

time the Communists were ready to sacrifice three armies in order to crush this division. The Communists were particularly afraid to fight the 61st since this division was the top of the cream. The 90th Army was the best of the three Northwest armies which were Chiang's most loyal troops (under General Hu Chun-nam) and had been sent to prevent a Russian move to the south. They were armed with American weapons. Wang says he thoroughly enjoyed fighting the Communists. His division, he recalls, always tried to take Communist prisoners alive since prizes were offered for captives.

One of the most courageous and well-known fights of this division, according to Wang, occurred when it was surrounded by four Communist armies in October, 1948. Almost the entire 181st Regiment was wiped out in six months of fighting. Forty men, including Wang, attempted to fight out of the encirclement in two hours, but only twenty-one men lived to tell the story. For this daring escape Wang was given a decoration certificate, thirty silver dollars, and a captaincy.

The 181st was reorganized, and the army retreated westward to Kansu province. There in 1949 Wang received another month of officer training and then was reassigned to his regiment as an infantry company commander. His job was to guide troops across the mountains in the battle zone. But after fighting only a month, the troops were transferred.

> The Nationalist troops were ordered to fight as guerillas in the rear of the Communists, and we were among them. But very shortly we were ordered to Szechwan province, where a huge showdown battle was scheduled to take place. There were many conflicting orders at this time, and everybody was very confused. The Communists were already in possession of the territory to which we were finally ordered, and the local Szechwan forces had rebelled and were fighting our troops. These rebel troops were under Generals Liu Wen-whei, Ten Hsi-ho, and Pan Chun-san, who sold out to the Communists before the Nationalist army could effect plans to retreat to Tibet. The armies of these warlords surrounded our units. They ordered us to disarm, but as a company commander I refused. I organized two platoons to serve as guerillas, and we tried to break out of the encirclement. The Communists captured the generals of our division and corps. These senior officers advised us to surrender, but we broke out with one battalion. We were surrounded again by the Szechwan Army. Again I was returned to my unit, and I tried to negotiate and build up more resistance against the Communists.

At this point, Wang launched into a long, impassioned description of his attempts to break out of the encirclement. He seemed to place a great deal of stress on his own participation in organizing these breakouts, particularly as evidence of his resistance to Communism. There follows a brief outline of his several escape attempts.

> I organized three escape attempts in an effort to return to a guerilla status and break out of the encirclement. The first time it was successful—one platoon got away. But before I could get the rest of the platoons out, the plot was discovered. We were then moved to another place, and for a second time I mobilized my company and other companies as well. But this was discovered before we had a chance to make the break. A few of the officers had gone over to the Communist side, and we didn't know it. They had become progressives. The Communists reorganized the battalion command. I then made a third attempt. I organized two companies. The company from the other battalion was discovered, and we had no chance to break out. The Communists seized me and talked to me for two hours. They did not dare discipline me too much, because they knew I was not only an officer but a leader; they were afraid I would fight, and they were trying to win the confidence of the men. The regimental commanders, who were siding with the Communists at that point, asked the Communists to remove me away from the men. That's when they took me out as a disturbing element. After they first arrested me they kept me seven days and nights in a dark room.

REFORM AT THE HANDS OF THE COMMUNISTS

The 181st Regiment was interned at Liangshan, Szechwan, late in December, 1949. Wang and forty of his fellow officers were segregated, and in March, 1950 were moved to a large nearby installation. Here he began his political reeducation. That his troops were subjected to a similar though less intense indoctrination is indicated in the following.

> I was no longer with my troops, but later in Korea I met some of the men and they told me what had happened. At first there was no change. The Nationalist army was not disbanded; they were only lectured by the Communists. They were told that those with no guilt would be forgiven and that others could redeem themselves. Only a few cadre of persons from the Communist side stayed to promote better relations among the Nationalist troops. The Communists more or less stayed under cover, but they conducted individual interviews. After two months the Communists fully understood all the individual backgrounds of the men and the organization of the Nationalist troops. The food was excellent. The troops had meat every day— better even than the Communist army.
> Then general discussion meetings were held, organized by units. They started the airing of grievances and then the liquidation of a

few targets. After that there was a systematic elimination and weeding out of reactionary and unreliable elements.

First Indoctrination Period: Military Political Academy

Wang and other captured officers became students at the Political Military Academy near Liangshan. The period of indoctrination here was three and a half months. There were over one thousand students, some of them men who had been selected for training as party members, but most of them officers captured from the Nationalist forces. Wang recognized many of the students as former officers of the 1st, 3rd, and 90th Nationalist Armies. During the first three weeks they were permitted contact with one another, but after that all contact was suspect since cells of opposition might develop. The class was broken up into groups of forty persons, the members of each group living together with assigned leaders.

The Winning-Over Period

The impression I got was that of a military and political college, because that was just the way it looked. My first reaction and that of the other men was that it was not so bad. They treated us very well, and we thought that maybe the Communists would treat us well after all. The environment was very good, and we had a lot of freedom at first. All of the students were greatly impressed by this two-week period, since we had anticipated no such freedom. Many had received little education, and they thought that now they would get a college education. They were told that after they had finished their training they would be able to get home and, if they were willing to work with the people, this training would make them better qualified. I felt frustrated by the failure of the guerilla movement and the failure to break out of the encirclement. I was ready to give them the benefit of the doubt and make the best of it.

There were three main steps in the training program. The first step was one of management, which was placed in the hands of the students. We conducted our own elections and we disciplined ourselves, and the Communists did not interfere with our activities at all.

The second step was one in which the Communists began to promote activities designed for our spiritual and physical well-being. There was still no coercion and no indoctrination. We had sports and games and dancing—just plain recreation, and no coercion at all. For the first two weeks we had been given complete freedom by the Communists.

Indoctrination, Confession, Criticism: The Screws Tighten

After these first two weeks, the groups of forty were divided up into separate classes and the real indoctrination stage began. This lasted the rest of the time we were at Liangshan. The main themes of the classes were that the old way was false while the new way brings theory and practice together; that action always follows discussion; and that labor is the foundation of the world. Heavy work always went along with the instruction in theory, even when the work was not closely related to the subject we were studying.

They started off first with lectures which explained the wrongdoing of the Nationalist regime and attributed many evil schemes to General Chiang Kai-shek. After the lectures we had discussions in the evenings. Now we had to do more and more what the Communists wanted us to do, such as dancing and singing and holding discussion meetings, and the schedule became very heavy. We had less and less time to ourselves. Subsequent lessons were on the purpose of society and the history of social evolution.

After the first few weeks of theory and discussion, the airing of grievances began. Each of us had to accuse the others in group meetings for their past or present failings; we all had to criticize ourselves and each other. Soon began the period when we had to write our personal histories. These autobiographies went into the files and were used to check our activities in the past. Then came the period of greater understanding of each individual, the purpose of which was to probe into our backgrounds and build up the file. All our own confessions in response to accusations by others were included. The next step was the lectures on the history of social evolution— many lectures and much discussion. And finally, there was the period of coordination of mind and action. The purpose of this was to firmly establish recognition of the proletarian class and to identify ourselves with it in mind and action. After the first two weeks of gentle introduction to life in the college, all these stages took the remaining three months.

I do not remember too much about [the economic theories taught at Liangshan]. But one point impressed me. They said there was no such thing as basic economic laws, but if one set goals according to Marxism it was possible to control the course of economic development. If certain things are regarded as favorable to Communism, it is possible to adapt the theory of Marxism to rationalize them. It was most important above all to understand the rise of the proletariat.

In this school, after the first few weeks, there were generally six class days and one free day. But on the free day the students were never allowed to rest, since almost every minute had some planned activity, usually heavy labor. Everyone volunteered to occupy himself usefully on these days. The other days were divided into class days, when the majority of time was spent in lecture and discussion, and occasional work days, when the students volunteered to do heavy work such as carrying sacks of rice. Work was always emphasized and held in high esteem, because here theory is put into practice.

On class days much of the time was spent in planning or discussion before work and in criticism and resolutions for improvement afterward. There were times when we worked only half a day and spent the rest of the day in discussion. But we were always kept busy, and everyone was under great pressure to participate actively.

Wang describes a typical class day as follows.

5:00 A.M.	Get out of bed, and immediately divide into small groups of four or five persons to resolve good behavior for the day—for example, "We must work hard and study hard. We must not let our heads nod in class."
5:20	Twenty-minute rest period
5:40	Breakfast
6:00	Big Class. A two-hour lecture on the current subject matter. Students must take voluminous notes.
8:00	Twenty-minute rest period
8:20	Small Class. Students in small groups read their notes from the Big Class and discuss the topic for three and a half hours. Everyone participates actively.
12:00	Lunch
12:15 P.M.	Fifteen-minute rest period
12:30	Small group discussion. Questions asked about aspects of the current topic that are still not understood.
1:00	Big Class
3:00	Small Class
5:00	Supper
5:15	Folk dance. Everyone participates.
5:45	Thirty-minute rest period
6:15	Small Cell discussion. Four or five students report to each instructor. Personal criticism and the leader indicates where improvement can be or has been made. Sample topic: how to become eligible for the Communist Party.
6:45	Ten-minute rest period
7:00	Small Class. Three cells with a total of twelve persons. Criticism of daily behavior—for example, "You carried only forty sacks of rice."
7:30	Singing session. All songs have an ideological content
8:30	Roll call. As names are called, the leader gives praise or blame to the student for his behavior during the day.

[Here is the way the accusation system worked.] Not far away my enlisted men were also being given special training. Among other activities, they accused their former platoon leaders and officers. I was accused of three errors: squeeze [graft], slapping enlisted men, and having a big-shot complex. I was taken back to the compound where I had lived before being removed from the unit, and I faced four enlisted men who were my accusers. I confessed to my errors and said that now my mind had been reconstructed. It was fortunate for me that I was a good athlete and was respected by my men; they could have made things much worse for me.

The Price of Self-Preservation

I will tell you everything that happened and just how my first impression changed. I had been there a little over a month and had been writing all these personal histories and everything, and the Communists knew about my past and knew that my father had been a landowner. It was in April, 1950, and they were beginning to conduct land reforms in my home town in Shensi. Four soldiers from Shensi addressed a letter to me. They told me to return and face land-reform procedures at home. I knew this meant I would be liquidated if I went back, and I tried to find ways so that I wouldn't have to go back and face the purgings in the village. I went and spoke to the authorities of the school. I said, "I wish to learn to be a new man here." The military authorities at the school said that I had to talk to the four soldiers. I talked to them very courteously. I explained to the leader that I had never indulged in corruption. I admitted I had beaten one man in my command. I agreed to apologize before the people.

The four soldiers said they had no authority not to take me back to the province with them, unless it was approved by the school authorities. Now I was a good basketball player at the school, and the school authorities knew me well. Also, many teammates spoke in my behalf. I wrote a seven-page letter to give to the soldiers to take back to the province with them. In the letter I gave a thorough confession of everything. I confessed that I was from the landlord class, that I had accepted their practices, that I knew this was wrong, and that I wished wholeheartedly to be a member of the proletarian class. I would even be willing to confess irregularities before the people to show my humility to them. I had one fountain pen as my only possession, and I would surrender it for proper use by the people. I begged them for another chance, so that men like me could become useful to the new China. I also wrote a second letter to the squad leaders in my old unit. This letter was sent back to the unit. I urged these men to accept the Communist program, so that they might benefit and work for the people. I told them I had given up everything to work and to learn under the new Communist system.

Under these conditions some of the students were taken back to face charges at home, and some were permitted to stay. It all depended where the authorities thought the men could be put to the best use to further the Communist cause, either at home or at the school. I believe that the school authorities engineered this whole thing. They had my record, and they knew where I came from, so they notified the home authorities. This was not used on all men, but it was used mostly on those in a position of leadership, like commanding officers. In this way the resistance of the commanding officers is broken down, and their willingness to cooperate is then used to educate others in the school and among the troops back in their old units.

It all depended on the individual case. Those who were best supported by the men at the school were allowed to remain as an example that could be used with their troops. Those who were very corrupt would be used for a better purpose back home.

I think that this trick they played on me occurred about one and a half months after I arrived. All this time the educational process or indoctrination was going on among my old troops too, so these old troops were more receptive to this. The Communists thoroughly planned everything, and they ensured the success of techniques like this. They used them to convince my former soldiers to follow their bidding. They are diabolically clever. They destroy all personal relationships and feelings. After such an action, I could no longer reorganize my men to resist, even if I tried. I am convinced the men would not respond after the letter I wrote. The loyalty that used to be between us was destroyed. [I am sure that this was the result because, I was able to learn what was going on among the enlisted men.] There was a lieutenant colonel from the same Nationalist unit there at the school going through the training. He had an aide who was able to bring messages from the outside, so we knew about activities back in our old company. We knew the Communists had mobilized the men to use him as a target. They had mobilized the men against me as a target too. They had mobilized those whom I had beaten, and the beaten ones helped to mobilize the rest against me. The entire company was forced unanimously to condemn me as a person. They worked individually on those who would not do this; they intimidated and forced them to agree to criticize me.

I knew that all the men felt guilty in violating the old moral code between officers and men, and I knew that they would not hold me strictly responsible for the letter I had written, because they too had realized that I had been forced to do what I did. Nevertheless, it broke up something between us.[6]

Furthermore, I felt badly hurt in my feelings because of the unfair charges they had directed against me. I knew that the confession that I had to make was not true. I knew that I was not corrupt, but I also

[6] As he told this story, Wang gave evidence of being highly emotional and upset. This seems to have been an extremely distressing experience, and it was surely a distressing confession to make to strangers. Moreover, he manifested great bitterness toward the Communist pressure and trickery which had forced this kind of behavior.

knew that the Communists wanted to kill without having victim's blood on one's hands. This meant that they wanted physical and mental liquidation of oneself by oneself, so that no one could say they had done it, but rather the person had brought it upon himself by the nature of his previous actions. In this way they could kill without having the victim's blood on their hands.

I was struck with a great fear. This was the first time I really realized the danger I was in. I became very keen and alert to the danger, and I was always alert to what was going on around me. I felt a great bitterness growing in me toward the whole system, and my desire for revenge was strengthened, though it also strengthened my precaution to preserve myself alive so that I could have this revenge. At the time of writing the letter, I knew there was no alternative. I must write it or perish. I became aware then of the great deception by the Communists. From that time on, the frequent review of my case and my confessions insulted and hurt me further, and my resolve was strengthened to fight the Communists with everything I had. At the time I acted out of fear of being returned home. I desperately looked around and sought an alternative; this was the only way out.

The only consolation I had was that it was customary for people to have to do this sort of thing. I knew that it was serving the Communist purpose, but I could not help myself. I felt that my troops would not believe it at heart, though they had to appear to believe it.

The Communists also forced Wang to confess his past errors through writing and rewriting his personal history. Hours were spent dredging up all past events. This personal history became a part of his file.

False Confessions and Their Uses

The diaries and autobiographies the men wrote were rarely acceptable upon first writing, but were written over and over until all sins were discussed and rejected with sufficient fervor.

After all the autobiographies were handed in, the leaders gave talks to the group, stating in very polite language that "some of us are still not honest." No one was specifically pointed out, but everyone was afraid that he was the one being censured. Some students were pointed out as models. The leader would say, "This man has been most honest, but others of us have not done so well." Wang felt guilty because he had not been so honest a man as these, but his fear kept him from telling the whole story.[7]

The group was also given blanks to fill in. Such questions were asked

[7] Wang's sense of guilt about his dishonesty indicates that, despite his hatred of the Communists, he had already partly internalized—that is, had partly accepted and was partly acting on—the Communist standards of conduct. Evidently membership in a group which is undergoing thought reform and a sense of obligation to measure up to the group standards, even though these standards have been foisted on the group, comprise one of the strongest weapons the Communists possess.

as: "How many Communists have you killed?" "How many women have you raped?" At first Wang refused to fill in these blanks, and the Communist leader asked him to come to the office. There the leader continually asked questions, keeping Wang in the same seat for hours. This process continued for three or four days, the strain becoming greater and greater. Wang says he became confused because there was no time for rest or thought and finally capitulated. Never did the Communist leader use open threats. Rather, the leader would continually ask questions, keeping Wang constantly defending himself, and would use such veiled threats as: "You know the people have treated you very well in spite of all your past errors. Now you, in turn, must tell the whole story and hold nothing back." Everyone knew that even more severe reeducation awaited those who did not measure up to the people's generosity.

All former Nationalists, Wang believes, were afraid of revealing the wrong things. For example, confession that one had killed any Communists, he believed, might result in public trial and death. He knew that one of his former enlisted men was killed after admitting killing Communists. Wang remembered bayoneting several Communists in battle, but he never mentioned these in his diary. To be safe, he wrote that he did not know whether or not he killed any Communist soldiers, since all fighting had been at long range. However, to compensate for his assertions of innocence in this dangerous area, he wildly exaggerated the number of prostitutes he had visited and invented stories of rape. These sexual errors were particularly necessary since "the Communists believed that all Nationalists had committed rape." If no such incidents were confessed, the individual was put under heavy social pressure, until he was finally forced to admit such crimes, whether he had committed them or not. Other members of the group also read and helped one to write one's diary, particularly where one failed to mention certain errors in one's past.

> Inside, one felt ashamed for confessing anything at all, but outwardly one must appear to have strong feelings of guilt for these past acts. One always had to rationalize this guilt by blaming it on the old society. One showed progress by saying that one was making this confession for the new society.
>
> I felt great shame in confessing homosexual acts, even though I didn't do them, since homosexuality is highly condemned in the old moral code.
>
> After each lecture it was necessary to have an airing of grievances or confession meeting, and in this meeting we might say how we were inspired by a lecture, phrase, or by the action of a comrade. We must cite the turning point at each stage of our learning of Communism. Each new insight that we got had to be aired and our former erroneous thinking condemned. Thus, each time I confessed my past

errors I dealt with a different area, because I was always learning new insights and therefore had to condemn new past errors. At the end of the three-month indoctrination period, I had to make a list of all previous wrongs that I had discovered I had committed. I had to list how many chickens I killed, how many beatings I gave, how many women I raped or seduced, and how many homosexual acts I committed. I had to tell this whether I had done it or not. I used to invent these things. Everybody did.

When asked by the interviewer whether the great amount of time allotted for discussion did not make the discussion drag and become stilted, Wang replied that the contrary was true. There was never enough time to criticize all the bad things. For example, on the topic of criticism of Chiang Kai-shek, everyone was competing to speak. "The environment forced everyone to participate. 'No one can throw away his reactionary burden,' the Communists said, 'unless he speaks in a progressive way.'" Wang emphasized that he had to talk—to confess, to resolve to do better, to analyze the past and present errors of others—in order to save his life, and added that his conscience hurt him for talking so much.

During these discussion periods we also had mutual criticism. Each man pointed to another man and accused him. We all accused each other of killing a chicken on such and such a day. We were always killing animals. When we accused another man of killing a chicken, he would accept the criticism and apologize; so both of us got merit: one for criticizing, the other for accepting the criticism.[8] We thanked the person for the criticism, but both of us knew it was not true. Every day the Communists thus promoted the public acceptance of these falsehoods and lies. The Communists knew it was false, but they didn't mind because it went on the record and it could be used against a man in the future.

The New Chinese Man

In writing my personal history I would say: "I had bourgeois habits, I felt shy about criticism, but now I will reveal my whole life because I realize there is no need for shame. I have no such thing as personal friendships any more. That is bourgeois. Now all are working for the same cause. I have enlarged my friendship to all and to Mao Tse-tung." I denounced the old idea I had of personal liberty. "I confess now that I must realize I must always identify myself with the group. I have begun to appreciate the new society, so now I have the spirit of learning." Sometimes I would confess I saw a woman on the street. I would confess unholy bourgeois thoughts I had about her.

[8] Wang described this tactic with considerable humor and laughter, as if he and his fellows felt they had outwitted and deceived the Communists.

"But now I realize she is my sister, and such a thought is incestuous. All women are sisters, all men are brothers. All the nation is a family, and Mao Tse-tung is the father. The only sex relations are the ones approved by the party." I could use the word "family" only in connection with Mao Tse-tung and the people as his children.

I think the Communists were trying to get us used to accepting all the lies in their doctrine. They tried to break down our respect for truth. For example, one would learn to say, "I could not understand how the proletariat could lead the revolution, but I see the good work of Mr. X and now I understand." Mr. X was usually a person of very low mentality—some ignorant peasant. This falsehood would be stated with a great conviction of truth.

The Communists were always telling us to cut off the burden of our family. We had to write how corrupt and feudalistic the old family was, and say that we would follow the leadership of Mao Tse-tung. We had always to denounce our past life as corrupt and admit that everything there was wrong. I remember a fellow once said that in the old days his father was a landlord, and that during a bad year his father opened the granary to the people, and that later the people killed the father. This was a very serious error, and the Communists turned on this man and he became a target for serious criticism.

The Communists have no truth. It is hard to say what is truth for them. If a Communist asks you to kill a man, and you kill him, that is the concept of truth at that moment. Later it may be defined as an error. Only that which serves the current party line is really the truth.

A man is always made to be wrong, never the party. So the man must confess his guilt. Then he is taken elsewhere and promoted for his party loyalty. The local situation is satisfied, and the face of the party is saved. This happened in the selling of victory bonds. They sold all the government bonds they were supposed to and more, but too much force was used, which resulted in much local dissatisfaction. So then the Communist party condemned the use of force, and the men who used force were moved away elsewhere to repeat the same tactics again.

A man's personal intentions mean nothing. Everything has to be done for the organization. It is the objectives of the party, and not the personal intentions of the men, that matter.

One time while we were at the military college, I had to witness the execution of two friends of mine. They were the regiment and battalion leaders of the unit in which I used to serve. When they were tried, I and the other men had to acknowledge the correctness of the charges. We had to hold back the tears and to smile during the execution. I knew then that my men, my troops, would feel the same at heart about the letter that I wrote. The trial of these two leaders was called without the knowledge of anyone. These men were identified as targets. They were given a chance to prove themselves. Outside persons were brought in to make the charges. Everyone was called to the meeting and the trial. The senior party members of the school were on the platform. The outsiders that were brought in charged these two men for several days with all kinds of crimes. Two intimate friends of these men were taken out from their quarters at night and disappeared. The fact that these two close friends of the victims were spirited away at night impressed on the rest of us the need to cooperate or face "unknown fate and terror by night." After three days of such charges, all the men were called upon to vote for the execution. The men, the party members on the platform asked for objections. They asked all who voted yes to raise their hands. Gradually the hands were raised higher and higher as the leaders on the platform closely watched the actions of everybody. Everyone knew they were condemning their friends to death, but they had no alternative. When they all voted, they were praised by the Communists: "At last you understand and accept Communist indoctrination. These people are enemies of Communism and you voted their execution." Then they shot the men down right in front of everybody, and then every party member and any of the cadre workers there had to walk by and shoot the men too. They mutilated the dead bodies with all of us looking on. Later they were buried next to our quarters under only six inches of earth. That night it rained. One of the men tried to clear the water from the grave with a cup. I will never forget this picture.[9]

I think the Communists intended to numb one's senses and one's feelings through such experiences. There were many cases of men who have gone through this experience who have committed suicide. Most of us became dumb and feelingless, as if we were stunned by this assault on our emotions and our forced participation in these kinds of actions. After all these things I felt that my men, my troops, could understand about my letter, and I never really lost the view of myself as being against Communism.

I fortified myself repeatedly with an old historical story that gave me faith in the future, that made me believe that I could preserve myself, escape Communism, and eventually get revenge. I had this faith in the future, and that was all I had to live by. I will tell you the story. There was a captive prince who had to eat the feces of the conquering prince for ten years. Eventually he was returned by the victorious prince as supposedly a defeated and completely degraded man. But ten years later the former captive prince came back with an army and defeated the former conquering prince. I had to keep telling myself this story repeatedly, and it helped to keep my faith alive and my will to resist. There were really two things that helped me to resist. One is this faith in the future, and the other is the feeling that

[9] Again, in telling this story, Wang gave evidence of being under severe emotional stress. Apparently these were memories which he seldom permitted himself to dwell upon.

the Communists by deception of this kind could not control the country in the long run. Through these lies they could not control the people. The outbreak of the Korean War helped to keep this hope alive.

None of the three schools Wang attended was walled or fenced in, but guards were posted at the four corners of the building and the students were not allowed to leave a designated area. During the period at Liangshan, three students escaped and were never found. Wang believes they would have been killed if they had been caught. Even if the students had obtained permission—as they could not—they could not have gone shopping since they had so little money. They were paid seven thousand yuan in People's Currency per month—enough to buy about half a pound of native tobacco. From time to time they were allowed to go to public meetings of the people for self-criticism, accusations, and public trial of class enemies.

> During the rest periods between classes we were able to smoke. All we had was tobacco on a stick. We sang between classes too. We were always watched. There was no chance to talk to anyone except about approved things. One greeting that the men used to use between each other was "meeting of the dumb" [literally: "Greeting from one dumb fellow to another"]—but we only exchanged this greeting at the latrine.

Second Indoctrination Period: Reform by Work

> The first school lasted until June, 1950 at Liangshan. Then I was moved to another place, Wan-hsien [also in Szechwan], for further indoctrination of the same kind. The Communists were not satisfied with the performance of the whole group at Liangshan, and felt that further indoctrination was needed. This indoctrination took place much further removed from our old military units. They decided that more manual labor was needed, and we had that at Wan-hsien. They called it "reform by work" or "productive education."

At Liangshan all the officers were mixed together. At the new school the senior officers, majors and higher, were kept separate.

At Wan-hsien the students lived in the mountains with much poorer living conditions than in Liangshan. They grew vegetables and built houses. Whereas in the first school the men were able to see their families once a week, now they could see their families only once a month, although all the wives and children of the men had been moved to Wan-hsien. The wives and the children lived in a compound far away from the officer group, and they also were indoctrinated. The families totaled about three hundred persons. Children's groups were organized; only infants stayed with the mothers. Occasionally, they would have very big classes, where all the family members would get together.

The wife and the husband got together only when a mass assembly was held, and even then they must stay in their own groups far apart. This was conducted only every three weeks. It was very painful to see them simply look and wave at each other. The Communists started to indoctrinate the wives and children because they found when the husbands went home for visits the indoctrination would not stand up under the critical talk of the wives and children at home. Thus now, in the new place, all the men were told that their families had been organized into groups and were being indoctrinated for the good of the men. The Communists pointed out that it was an economic necessity to do this. The state had to support their families, since the men were supported by the state; then too, the families would become more useful through indoctrination. They would think in revolutionary terms, and thus the men would be better off.

Emphasis in the second indoctrination period was on understanding the spirit of the proletariat through action.

The main texts were Marx's *Das Kapital* and Mao-Tse-tung's *Modern History of China*. They lectured and covered many topics. We learned and studied about the proletariat. We learned about the modern history of China for the past hundred years. We received lectures on basic economic theory. They also held airing-of-grievances meetings, and meetings for the reexamination of individual personal histories. During these meetings we practiced mutual criticism and self-criticism.

When we were lectured on the proletariat, we were told we must learn by practice. We must labor, carry coal and honey buckets [10] and water, and help the peasants. In this way we would better understand the philosophy of the proletariat through action. The Communists had a saying: "Theory must coincide with practice." They taught that we must bring thinking and behavior together by doing. This proletarian work was carried on in July. The Communists started a campaign which they called "Challenge to Other Units." Everyone was very hot. They knew they had to work hard. Each unit had to challenge other units. They couldn't resist. The Communists had teaching units who spent day and night persuading you if you were tempted to resist these work efforts.

Everybody felt they were being exploited by the Communists, and their labor was being used. We were urged to do our utmost to live in other people's praise and esteem.

The Need for Praise

I will tell you about something that happened to me. Every member in the camp where we were had been praised at one time or another

[10] Buckets of human excreta to be used as fertilizer.

for his manual effort at labor. No matter how hard I worked, they did not praise me. I was the last one and still not praised. I became very worried and fearful because I knew that this was bad not to be praised. A man who is praised is then sure that he is in good standing. I was not used to carrying heavy loads like the other men. I could carry only fifty-pound loads instead of one hundred pounds. The praise that they give you is an insurance that you are secure. So one day we were going out to move rice bags to the quarters. I was determined this day to do my utmost—to kill myself if necessary to win praise—because I knew if I did not I would be lost. I picked the biggest load I could find, over one hundred and fifty pounds, and I carried it up the slope. I had to rest. The instructor was watching. He said, "Today you expressed the true spirit of the proletariat." I fell under the heavy load, but I asked no assistance. I spit blood, but I won evidence of security through the praise of the instructor. This is what they mean by the spirit of the proletariat. It means to run off and do the impossible with great faith and willingness.

The purpose [of the Communist efforts to inculcate this spirit of the proletariat] was threefold, I think. First, they wanted to create a situation of utter mental and physical exhaustion. We were reduced to animal existence. Our senses were practically destroyed. We could think of nothing else. We could think of nothing. Our movements were mechanical. We became like tools. [Second,] the Communists made use of my group for educational purposes. Occasionally we would receive outside Communist newspapers. In that paper would be the story of our group, our work, our progressiveness, and so on. We were exalted and praised. I think this was intended to impress the civilians that these former Nationalist officers had accepted the doctrine completely. I think also it was designed to impress the Communist soldiers that former Nationalist officers were converts to true proletarianism, and that this then was a real challenge to all Communist soldiers to follow their example. All Communist soldiers must take up the challenge and be urged on by this great example. And the third reason, I think, is that this group was never thoroughly trusted. It was intended that we were to be liquidated in this process—that we were to die of exhaustion, commit suicide, or violate the code of the Communists and be punished accordingly. This to me is proof of the Communist deception: that while we were being praised in the Communist newspapers and cited as an example, we were privately being called parasites of society by the instructors. They would say: "You do not understand the spirit of the proletariat. You committed crimes as Nationalist soldiers. You are still nothing but parasites." All the men knew they were being deceived, but when they would mouth the progressive slogans of the Communists they felt that they in turn were in some measure deceiving the Communists.

Wang was asked how he could know what the secret feelings of the other men were if he could not communicate with them.

There were some chances to communicate, though one had to be very careful. The only chance for an exchange of words was in the latrine. Sometimes one could say half a sentence or show by an expression or blink of the eye what one was feeling. One had to be very careful whom he spoke to, but it was possible to feel the sympathy and the mutual feelings of understanding of others. The latrine was the only chance to casually pass half a remark to a friend.

Wang describes the different types of organization meetings held at this second military college.

I think there were about five different types or maybe even more. The first could be called the smallest. It was a cell meeting of three men. We met after work each night. We made a summary of the work of the day and we criticized how the work was done. The idea was to develop a spirit of improvement. We discussed all the events of the day, everything that happened: the food, the meetings, the conversations; and we shared all individual experiences that we had. We made suggestions to the others. This was called the "nightly review of the day's events." The second type was a squad-size meeting of twelve men. It was conducted early in the morning. The platoon leader would outline the working schedule for the day. He would comment on the previous day's events. He would criticize those who had been non-progressive, and he would urge the men to improve. The third type was a platoon-size meeting, of three or four squads. This was usually a weekly meeting. It handled mostly administrative and organization problems. The squad leaders would report daily to the platoon leaders, and the platoon leaders would review the obstinate cases reported by the squad leaders at the weekly meetings. The fourth type was a company-size meeting, which was held weekly or biweekly. A political commissar would initiate the meeting by a lecture. This would be followed by extensive discussion lasting a day or even three days. The leader of the meeting would also cite those to be praised for their work or criticize those who had been backward. Some were very severely criticized; this was very bad—they knew that this was dangerous. The fifth type was a secret meeting, and this was reserved for cadre or party members. They met every night. They were concerned with the thinking of the people—the way we thought and the way we acted. They would submit reports on those they thought were unreliable elements among the men. They would work out programs of handling or dealing with these men and of trying to get them to reform.

You know, it is not hard to be a Communist man in a cadre. All his work is done according to stereotyped patterns of praise, criticism, reporting, and so forth. They do not show originality. They just do the same thing over and over and over again. The only time they develop new ways of doing things is in the secret meetings where they discuss ways of handling people who resist. When we were at these military colleges, these cadremen took all our possessions from us by claiming that we gained them by exploitation.

Well, one of the ways the Communists attempted to root out our deep feelings was through the newspaper. We used to publish a newspaper in the camp. The squad published one once a week, and the company would publish one every month. Those men who could write were supposed to write and prepare articles in their spare time for the newspaper. In writing for the newspaper it was important that you express your thoughts. This was the most important thing to do. One had to criticize deviation in thought or practice on the part of others and to praise correct thinking. He must also do this for himself. We would frequently have to quote Mao Tse-tung and the impressions we had received from his writings. We were supposed to indicate where we got our inspiration and what had changed our thinking. In lectures, if we were inspired by certain phrases in the talk, we had to use those phrases to reexamine our past and to criticize it. For example, a man would write, "I have been depressed, but because of one incident I have seen the light and step by step am becoming a new man." It was very important to analyze the turning point in your thinking; the Communists placed a great deal of stress on this. We had to analyze the turning points in our thinking about Communism and the subsequent stages of our education. All writings had to be censored. The Communists were continually trying to force men to describe in complete detail the steps leading up to each change in thinking and to reveal all the incidents and thoughts which made them see the light and the truth of Communism.

I also had to tell how many Communist soldiers I had killed. I was forced to admit them though they were not true. The first time I wrote a summation, at the end of my first indoctrination course, I admitted everything, but I did not admit killing Communist soldiers. In writing my summation after the second indoctrination, I increased the number of times I had done all the other things, and I also told of killing one Communist soldier. I said that I had now learned that I had nothing to fear, and so I could admit everything, even those things I had formerly hid way down deep in myself. This was accepted by the Communists as showing improvement and progressiveness.

Conditions of constant surveillance and examination of one's thoughts and actions created unbearable tensions for some of the men.

Self-Control, Exhaustion, Breaking Points

We were exhausted most of the time, but we kept a tight rein on our thinking. There was a case of a man who spoke at night in his sleep. He was overheard by the cadre of the Communist instructors, and the next day he was severely criticized in the meeting. Usually when one is criticized before the group, one lowers one's head. This man was ordered not to lower his head, and they put a chopstick between his chest and his head to force his head to be held up, so that he would have to look at the group. For self-preservation, one had to be extraordinarily careful not to betray oneself at any time.

A lot of the men just go crazy. Like two people inside themselves, they are always fighting. It was a common sight at night to see men yell and jump in their sleep. But most of the time they wouldn't say anything. They were so alert and so defensive against betraying themselves, they would even protect themselves in sleep. One time I dreamed that I was running. It was a sort of nightmare. I was running and couldn't run, and I dreamed that I wanted to say something and couldn't say it. I used to have this nightmare frequently. But even this shows the control people kept over themselves. These things would happen most frequently during the period of airing of grievances. The Communists knew that this kind of conflict was going on inside all of the men, and they would try to scare it out of them or repress it. Occasionally in class the Communist cadre would say: "On a certain night someone said that the Communist army was bad. We must find out who said this." Usually a man who was accused of talking in his sleep would maintain that he did not know anything about it and frequently he was not penalized, but thereafter they would keep a very close surveillance on him.

Random accusations of deviation during sleep were frequently made by the Communists.

This used to happen frequently, but everybody knew that they didn't have anyone in mind, so there was no result. But it did have the effect of impressing on everybody that such thoughts were forbidden, consciously or unconsciously.

The conflict between what a man was told and what he really believed was resolved in varying degree.

It was necessary always to explain to oneself that it is necessary to submit in order to reduce tension. The only way anyone could get control of himself was to see it as an absolute necessity to submit to what the Communists were saying. What I used to do was always to look at nature. I'd admire the tree or the moon and do anything to distract my thoughts from all this trouble. It seemed to me that almost all the men at the camp were neurotic. It was just a matter of degree. The extreme cases were just sent away. The less serious cases were interviewed by party members. It was explained by the party members in class that reactionary ideas poisoned these men's minds and that everyone had to get rid of these reactionary ideas. I don't know of anyone who completely gave up or surrendered to this Communist thought control. It is impossible to surrender completely to it. On the surface it is necessary to appear to be calm and confident. In the beginning everyone appears to submit to the Communist doctrine, but as time goes on it is possible for anyone to escape the deception that the Communists are practicing.

Third Indoctrination Period: Near Chungking

In October, 1950, I was moved to another military college near Chungking for three more months. The Communists didn't tell us why they were moving us. I had been three and a half months at the military college at Liangshan and an equal amount of time at Wan-hsien. The men believed that the Communists felt we needed more indoctrination.

In this third school, current news commentary was used, with stress upon American imperialism and the capitalist menace. There were four different periods of teaching. The first was a period for teaching of current affairs. This consisted of three phases. The first was a lecture phase on historical and current affairs; the second was a case history phase; and the third was the airing of grievances. In the lectures we were taught the history of American imperialism in China. After the initial lectures there was a period in which we gave case histories. The purpose was the mobilization of thinking about American atrocities. We had to cite case histories of American atrocities. Each member had to contribute from his own knowledge to such stories. We were taught about the Korean War and the American imperialism, and we were asked to air grievances against American imperialism. The second period of the indoctrination was called "digging the root." This involved another attempt by the Communists to develop a penetrating understanding of each individual. It involved dipping into his personal background and exploiting the confessions that he would write. The third period was known as "tail cutting." This period was devoted to getting rid of bourgeois thoughts and habits, particularly those related to family loyalties and all other reactionary thoughts. The fourth period was devoted to obedience to organization. We must all listen to the people and to the organization. There must be unquestioned obedience by all to the Communist party.

The uneducated and laborers were described again as having the highest status. The instructor said that the world was under the control of the laborer and the peasant and that everyone must follow these two classes.

Throughout this training, as in the second school, Wang describes his feeling as one of constant physical and mental exhaustion. There was never time for relaxed conversation. Joking was unknown, and a sense of constant threat was felt. One of the men in an adjoining class lost his sanity under the strain, and the instructor explained that it was because he did not reveal everything in his reactionary past. Most students seemed to become mechanical robots who responded when the right button was pressed.

In this third school, children under seven accompanied their mothers, those from seven to fifteen went into a special class, and children above fifteen were considered adult.

WITH THE CHINESE COMMUNIST FORCES

Wang's group was indoctrinated until January, 1951. At this time many of the group joined a Communist army unit near Chungking for three weeks, and then many were sent to Korea. Others were sent to Sinkiang province to open up the country. This is the Chinese equivalent of Siberia in Russia—it represents forced labor from which there is little or no escape. Wang himself was assigned as a "warrior" (private) [11] to a mortar company in the 91st Regiment, 31st Division, 12th Army.

This unit had just returned from Kweichow province in South China. They had been issued new clothes, rested, and were obtaining replacements. We were immediately placed under very close surveillance in this army unit. Our records from all of our indoctrination training were turned over to the unit. At this time we were told that the place where the unit was located was unsettled. It was better to move to older, liberated territory.

Ten days later the division was moved from Yutong in Szechwan to Hankow. When asked by the interviewer if he volunteered for the CCF, Wang replied that during all the time he was being reeducated he was still considered to be a soldier, and it was as a soldier that he was assigned to the 12th Army. Almost all students in his last school were assigned to different units.

After three days in Hankow, the army moved to the Ching district of Hopeh, which is known to the Communists as Old Liberation Home. A week after arrival their American and Chinese weapons were exchanged for Russian types. Here Wang recalled with a grin, "We always called the Russians 'Elder Brother.'"

We stayed in Hankow two days. After we got there, we were told that there were too many troops near Hankow; there was a problem

[11] In a military report Wang is reported as saying that in the CCF he became a platoon level officer with the duty of drill instructor. The discrepancy between this and his interview statements is unexplained.

of supply; we must go to Hopeh province near Tientsin. We were then told by the Communists that the United States had invaded North Korea and that we must volunteer to give assistance to our brother country. We were told, "We are going to the border, and by our very presence at the border we boost the morale of our brothers in North Korea." We were told that we would receive three months of political and military training, but actually we got much less. They changed all our weapons. We had American weapons, but these were discarded and we got Russian weapons. When we got the Russian guns in exchange for the American ones, we didn't like them. They were not as good as the American ones. They were old-style rifles. Many men asked, "Why do we change?" The instructors charged them with "unfirm" thoughts, and with having pro-American sentiments despite the fact that America was now our enemy. No one dared protest about the rifles any more. We practiced with this new equipment and got political education concerning American atrocities and plans.

After the new weapons were distributed, a scheduled three-month training course began. However, within two months the army moved north "to defend the border." During the entire period of training, the troops were always kept busy. If they were not exercising, they were conducting political discussions. The officers never struck their men. Such tactics were unnecessary since all discipline was taken care of through mutual criticism.

Among the Communist rank-and-file members, particularly the soldiers, the resentment was very great over sexual restrictions. The Communists tried to destroy the sense of sex among the soldiers. They were very strict. They tried to benumb the sexual instinct, because soldiers could not afford families or sexual ties.

One could not get married unless one was a colonel or higher or a major who had participated in the Sino-Japanese War. Those who had families could visit them once a week. The Communists explained that they could not marry because of the war situation, but the men knew that the top Communists were very corrupt sexually. This promoted and excused secret affairs on the part of the men. They realized that this struggle—the world struggle—would never end, that they must fight America and England. This was one of the greatest problems the Communists had to deal with, for the men felt there would never be a time when the party would allow them to have adequate sexual relations. Only party members were very careful not to run against this restriction, if they were not officially allowed, since the greatest fear of the party member is that he would not know what to do if he were kicked out of the party—he would be lost.

The higher one goes in the party, the greater one's fear is of being caught off base. Every sentence uttered must be carefully considered. Once a member of the party, a man has no choice but to devote his whole life to it. For those above the rank of colonel in the army, the discipline was not so strict. They had special mess, transportation, living quarters, and each was allowed to have a wife. The Communists explained this on the basis of the work they had to do: they needed these extra requirements to carry out their jobs. Others who complained were told that when they reached this level they would get these things too, since the higher functions require them, and these are awarded by the party.

Guarding the Border: Inside Korea

After the period of learning had been terminated, we were sent to Antung, a city on the border of North Korea, the object being border defense. Before the meetings in the indoctrination in South China, the Communists used to call out the northerners and instruct them to watch the southerners. They reversed this procedure in the north, talking to the southerners before each meeting and telling them to watch the northerners.

We had been at Antung only a week when the Communists explained to us: "We are here at border defense. North Koreans are deep in South Korean territory. They need manpower to guard the rear zone. You are to go as security forces to guard PW's." Before we left Antung we were given instructions. We were made to practice air raid protection. We were told not to talk and smoke in our travels "so as not to disturb the people." We were told that Americans have airplanes for bombing civilians, while all our planes are out fighting on the front lines. We were also told to unload ourselves of all excess equipment—that is, to travel light. I knew immediately that this meant we were going to the front, but the instructors said: "There are many supplies in the new areas where we are going. We may lose all our old things; so leave them behind till you come back."

Wang's unit learned to fire Russian anti-aircraft guns. They were told that they were preparing to shoot down American imperialist planes. The American planes, the instructors said, were inferior to the Communist models. They also were instructed how to build improved trenches.

The Communists, Wang recalled, entered the war at the end of 1950, and the 12th Army crossed the Yalu at midnight March 25, 1951.

After I crossed the Yalu with my company, it was still dark. At daybreak we stopped at a farmer's house. The party commissar talked to us. He said: "There are a lot of South Korean bandits around this area, who are robbing people. That is why the North Korean peasants are so poor. Everyone must stay with the unit, or he is liable to get killed by these robbers." I think this was supposed to prevent people from deserting. The second night we ran into an air raid. Bombs and flares were dropped. We walked until an hour before daybreak. Then we dug holes against the air raid. We did the same thing for five nights.

Many Americans were captured and used as guides. Shortly after crossing the Yalu, every man was ordered to clean out all needless materials from his pack, and the march to the south began. All marching was at night. The troops were instructed to look out for aircraft. They were constantly ordered to march faster and not to drop back. The greater part of their food was fried noodles. It was difficult to obtain hot water to drink.

After seven days of marching, two of the enlisted men of the unit were shot by their leader because they were too weak and could not keep up with the rest of their unit. There were many men lagging behind, so the leader shot these two as an object lesson. He then put a lamp beside the bodies and a note which read, "This is what happens to soldiers who drop back."

Each night the lecturer told us about bandits. We came across two policemen, and everybody saw them. They were dead. The lecturer told us "Some bandits have killed these two cops." I felt, and so did a number of other people, that the Communists might have killed these cops deliberately to impress the men that they should not desert. After arriving at Kasan, the regiment camped in the area a week to ten days to rest and receive training. During this period there were three projects: to reduce our pack and unnecessary equipment a second time and to increase the bullets and weapons carried; to recognize who had good discipline in marching—these were given a certificate; and to learn how to dig trenches. We were told to dig trenches. We were told to dig more holes for air raid protection. . . . This job had to be done very thoroughly wherever we stopped. We were also told that we were not going to fight . . . but that while advancing we might run into some remnants of the U.N. forces.

They made an effort to mobilize hatred against Americans. We were instructed that the Americans use napalm bombs to burn homes of peasants. We were told to assess our merit. "Those who march well show their progressiveness. . . . This is a chance to redeem ourselves"—especially those of us who had committed crimes against the people.

We were instructed in military discipline and notified that the penalty for disobedience was death. We were told that the Communists were increasing our munitions supply in case of trouble. At the end of ten days, the regiment started out again with much encouragement to march quickly to the second front line. There was no more talking about no fighting. We were now told that the Communist troops are all victorious.

However, again the marching became too slow. The original assignment of our unit was to take care of the Allied PW's, but because the unit was so slow the assignment was given to another unit. Therefore our regiment—the 91st—was then marched to the front.

During this march, I caught diarrhea and was forced to fall out. I was kept behind with other sick troops until May 20. In the meantime, the 91st fought in two large battles. I heard from fellow soldiers that the Allied fire was very heavy.

The Communists instilled a fighting spirit in the men at the front through the promotion of subordinates.

The Communists instilled a patriotic fighting spirit in the leadership of the troops by pulling out highly indoctrinated men at all levels of command and then promoting subordinates, who were then inspired to prove themselves. The ones who were pulled out—the highly indoctrinated ones—were saved for further indoctrination of other men.

New Evidence of Unreliability

When asked to explain why the Communists in the army did not trust him, Wang described two incidents.

Well, two incidents happened. I will tell you about them. The first incident happened while I was in Hopeh province. I received a letter from a friend in Nanking. The letter informed me that my parents had been ejected from the land where they had their home and were sent to Suiyuan province in order to open up the country there. The letter told me they were in very poor circumstances. I could understand this since my father was very old. I asked permission from the authorities to sell all my personal belongings and asked the Communist organization to give the money to my parents. I received immediate criticism. They said I still had money and I was harboring reactionary thoughts and had not confessed my background thoroughly. They gave me a receipt but did not remit the money to my parents. I had a gold bracelet purchased in 1942. As a result, I was most agitated and I planned to escape. I took up the problem with a friend by the name of Liu of similar background. Liu, also a member of the army, of middle-class background, lived nearby. I gave him the money and asked him to purchase civilian clothes. I planned to go to Nanking. I did not know that Liu was a member of the Youth group, and he betrayed me. They gave me the works. I really became a target. The only way I got out of it was by means of the following explanation: "It was not I who lacked confidence in the organization, but the organization who lacked confidence in me. I had revealed everything that I had done in the past, but the organization doesn't trust me. It didn't remit the money, and I still have the receipt. If the organization would trust me, I would do as well as I could because I would believe in it." This got me out of that particular trouble, but they still didn't remit the money to my parents. Instead, they kept me under very close surveillance, and I was never allowed to carry a gun. I just carried two hand grenades and two mortar shells.

The next incident happened in Kasan in Korea. We had to dig air raid holes. I was very tired, my hands were blistered, and I was in a bad mood. By careful observation the Communists noted this, and they criticized me again. They called me backward. I said, "The organization doesn't trust me, and the money has not been remitted." The indoctrinator assured me that the money would be remitted and that the organization trusted me. I felt maybe I made a mistake when I said, "You wait and see when the time comes." I meant by this that I would prove my worth to the organization, but it could be interpreted that I would prove myself troublesome. They questioned me further. They took away the two hand grenades that I was carrying and gave me two more mortar shells to carry.

Wang recalled only one friendship during the time he was under Communist control. This friend was a blacksmith whose job was to shoe the CCF horses and who was given the nickname Horseshoe—Wang did not know the real name of the soldier. Wang had known this man in the Nationalist army, and each knew that the other hated Communism, but neither ever spoke of this even when the two of them were alone. Once they slept together in a cave and talked late into the night about their personal backgrounds. This friend said, "Life in the CCF is very cruel." Neither discussed escape, but it was understood that both would attempt it if the opportunity presented itself. Each pledged that he would take care of the other in case of difficulty. Horseshoe was very kind to Wang during his illness, bringing him hot water and finding him a walking stick.

SURRENDER AND REPATRIATION

While his unit was on the front lines, Wang had an opportunity to read a U.N. pamphlet signed by General Ridgway and other leaflets dropped from U.N. planes. (He recalls that the Communists were making much propaganda at this time over the dismissal of General MacArthur.) After reading the pamphlets, Wang decided to surrender at the first opportunity.

On the night of May 20, 1951, Wang was working on his usual labor detail carrying shells and fried noodles up the mountains to the troops at the front. He knew the Americans were nearby beacuse he could see their searchlights. Wang was in charge of a labor detail of three men. He told them that he was going to the latrine, and instructed them to carefully guard the noodles and shells while he was away. Then he took off in the darkness and climbed two mountains, guided by the U.N. spotlight. Nobody followed him, but he heard them calling his name. He spent the night in the mountains and surrendered the following morning. Wang said that in surrendering, his main worries were that wolves would find him in the mountains or that he would not be able to find the Allied lines.

On the morning of May 21, Wang saw Allied troops; raising his hands, he walked toward them. One of the GIs suddenly raised his gun and shot Wang in the leg. The GIs were evidently taken by surprise since there were no other Chinese in that area. Four or five of the soldiers searched him. When they found nothing but the Ridgway pass, they apologized for shooting him and treated him well, giving him candy and cigarettes.

Wang was first placed in the hospital, Camp 2, Pusan area. He was subsequently transferred to Camp 3, and then, for his own protection after a dispute with the Communists in the camp, to Camp 10, and still later to Compound 86, Koje-do. In April, 1952, Wang signified his desire not to repatriate and was moved to Camp 3, Cheju-do, with fifteen thousand other non-repatriate Chinese, where he became chief of Enclosure 2, containing five thousand PW's. In January, 1954, he was repatriated to Formosa and, following a three-month rehabilitation program, recommissioned a lieutenant colonel in the Nationalist army.

ADJUSTMENT OF CHINESE SOLDIERS TO THE COMMUNIST DEMAND FOR IDEOLOGICAL PARTICIPATION

Jeane J. Kirkpatrick & Pio D. Uliassi

FOCUS OF THE RESEARCH

A distinctive feature of modern totalitarian regimes is their emphasis on remaking the whole of the society over which they rule. The victory of the Communists in China marked the beginning of such an effort. In their few years of rule, the Chinese Reds have shown a vigorous determination to replace traditional Chinese values with new values ostensibly derived from the basic ideological postulates of Communism. The ability of the most determined and ruthless rulers to remake society is, of course, not unlimited. The long-range program of molding men in accordance with the Communist model is tied to the growth of a new and malleable generation. Even in current Chinese society, however, some groups—with the armed forces as a notable example—are subjected to controls that are impressively intense and coordinated, and the political rulers' effort to remake men in the Communist image appears likely to have effects which are both quick and deep.

This chapter concerns one part of this effort—what the authors call the demand for ideological participation. Like the other parts of this volume, the present chapter is based on analyses of forty-three interviews conducted with Chinese prisoners of war in Korea by a research team.

All totalitarian regimes proclaim ideologies, and all require at least some lip service to them; all exercise, or try to exercise, rigid control over many areas of private life. The distinguishing feature of political training in the Chinese Communist Forces is the persistent linkage of these two demands. Not only are soldiers required to know and approve the ideology of the Communist revolution, and not only must they obey every demand of their rulers; they must also be able to explain, justify, or condemn the smallest detail of their daily behavior on the basis of criteria derived from the official party line. This leads, of course, to an extreme emphasis on political indoctrination in the ordinary sense of the term. But it also leads to an almost continuous process of self-analysis in which the individual must openly examine every act, thought, and wish and interpret it in approved ideological terms.

The pressure for ideological participation may be defined, then, as the demand that the totality of an individual's verbal and non-verbal communications conform to a system of social norms derived from official Communist ideology. In other words, all the writing, speech, gestures, acts—even moods—that have meaning for others are required to be consistent with the Communist way of life. To the extent that this demand is fulfilled, the individual becomes a carrier and exemplar of the new Communist culture, although at the same time he may remain internally a product and reflection of the traditional society.

The nature of ideological participation is of particular interest in the case of soldiers, since it involves factors that are important in determining whether soldiers identify with their roles. Bradbury and Kirkpatrick, above, suggested that with soldiers from the CCF such identification was determined by two general kinds of factors:

> Those bearing primarily on soldiers' loyalty to their leaders and to the symbols of authority in general.
> Those bearing on soldiers' psychological comfort in the performance of their everyday tasks.

In accordance with the objectives of the study, earlier chapters have dealt with the specifically Communist features of life in the CCF before and during the Korean war, and not with attitudes toward or adjustment to inherent features of military life. These chapters have dealt mainly with factors determining loyalty—that is, determining whether soldiers shared or rejected the values of their military and political authorities. This chapter is limited to one group of factors that bear more closely on how comfortable these soldiers were in this relationship; more specifically, it is restricted to the problem of adjustment or adaptation to the demand for ideological participation. Before we proceed, however, we must clarify some of the assumptions and considerations that underlie the description and analysis.

Ideological Participation as a Technique for Resocialization

The particular importance of ideological participation to soldiers in the CCF is suggested by two distinct but related functions which it performs or is meant to perform. It is, first of all, a major technique of social control intended to ensure complete conformity. But it is a control technique with a fundamentally pedagogical purpose, in the sense that its ultimate aim is to bring about the internalization of Communist values in the pupil or "patient." This aim is perhaps a natural development of the Communist view of ideology.

The Communist View of Ideology

In Communist literature, ideology as a concept resembles in some respects the concept of culture as used in American social science. Perhaps the best-known statement of this view is one by Marx himself:

> Upon the different forms of property, upon the social conditions of existence rises an entire superstructure of distinct and characteristically formed sentiments, illusions, modes of thought and views of life. The entire class creates and forms them out of its material foundations and out of the corresponding social relations. The single individual who derives them through tradition and education may imagine that they form the real motives and the starting point of his activity.[1]

In Marxist terms, then, ideology is a subculture, an aspect of the natural, inevitable outgrowth and rationalization of the interests of a particular economic class.

A significant modification of this theory—and one that is suggestive for our problem—was basic to Lenin's interpretation of Marxism. In Leninist theory, the working classes themselves tended toward trade unionism and could never develop a truly political proletarian outlook. The ideology for the inevitable revolution must therefore be developed by an intellectual and political elite which, organized as the vanguard of the proletariat, would transmit it to or impose it on the masses, to bring about revolution and a new world.

In theory, the success of a Communist revolution means the victory of the working classes—represented by the party. And the victory of the working classes means the supremacy of their ideology. This last point, however, must be qualified, for Communist ideology is victorious only in the sense that it is the ideology of what has become the ruling class. This does not mean that a new Communist culture suddenly and completely replaces older cultures or ideologies. Two reasons for this complex situation may be found in Communist literature.

First, the Communist seizure of power cannot immediately and completely alter or lead to the replacement of all old forms of production. Residues of older economic institutions continue to exist side by side with the new economy which is gradually created by the Communist state. These older forms of economic relations are accompanied by their own characteristic ideologies.

Second, even where older economic and social forms have been

[1] Karl Marx, *The Eighteenth Brumaire of Louis Bonaparte,* English translation edited by C. P. Dutt, p. 40.

replaced by new institutions, many individuals remain whose ideological formation took place under the old regime. These individuals then perpetuate the ideology of the former exploiting classes and may even contaminate others with their obsolete cultural heritage.

In such conditions, the Communist rulers aim to complete the revolution by gradually eradicating all remnants of the old culture that are not in harmony with Communist ideology. This means, in practice, a totalitarian revolution, in the sense that the shift in political power is followed by radical changes in the social system and eventually by fundamental changes in the whole system of values.

It is possible to see in Communist theory and policy two basic processes for advancing the desired cultural revolution. First, as the economic relations of society approach the Communist ideal, the rising generations of men presumably will gradually acquire the ideological (cultural) superstructure which reflects these new relations. This, however, is a long-term process. In the meantime, something must be done about those individuals or groups who live and function in the new society but who are in fact bearers of the old and condemned ideology and, as such, dangerous to the new order. The solution adopted by the Chinese Communists is intensive political indoctrination. In essence, this means that adult human beings must be stripped of old habits, values, and world views, and remade in the image of Communist man. This involves, as the material illustrates, a process of intense resocialization.[2]

Resocialization

The effort to transmit a new culture by means of intense indoctrination involves the Chinese soldier, who is subjected to it, in a learning process in which he must acquire new values, new goals, new concepts about himself and others. The amount and kind of learning required for such a transformation are comparable to those of the initial socialization period, which takes place in infancy and childhood. In other words, the Communists attempt what may properly be called the resocialization of the individual.

But the CCF soldiers involved in this learning process are adults or near adults; they have already been socialized through the acquisition of a traditional, pre-Communist Chinese culture. Instead of the *tabula rasa* of the infant, who learns from parents, siblings, and nurses what he must do to get along in his social group, they already had a fully developed frame of reference at the time they came under Communist control. They had a picture of themselves and their world. They had values, habits, and attachments to persons and objects; they had a fully developed set of expectations about the behavior and responses of

[2] For an elaboration of the Chinese Communist view on the relationship between economic class and ideology, see Chapter IV of Walter E. Gourlay, *The Chinese Communist Cadre: Key to Political Control.*

others. Because they lacked the plasticity of the infant, it must be assumed that some formidable obstacles to resocialization are inherent in the process itself.

Additional obstacles are created by the nature of the relationship between soldiers and their political mentors. First, of course, is the absence of the affective relationship that exists between infant and parents. Perhaps equally important, the very persons responsible for transmitting the orientations, values, and goals of the new culture are themselves products of a previous culture; remnants of the former culture live inside the men charged with eradicating it. This may have important consequences. The agents of resocialization may themselves commit errors or fail to perceive the errors of their charges. Furthermore, the soldier who is being indoctrinated may sometimes doubt that the indoctrinator himself believes in the ideology he is trying to transmit.[3]

Ideological Participation as a Technique

We have indicated that in one sense "ideology," when used by the Communists, really means "culture." Therefore, in a situation where the ruling power has a fully developed ideology and the means to create a totalitarian social order, what is involved is an attempt to replace an entire culture in a relatively brief passage of time. Since the cultural revolution cannot wait on the slow growth of new generations, the Chinese Communists are engaged in a dramatic effort to resocialize those who have fallen under their rule.

In the CCF at the time of the Korean war, this effort took the form of a persistent demand for ideological participation. As will be shown, this went far beyond casual attempts at political indoctrination as this process is sometimes understood in the West. In time alone, political training in the CCF formed a major part of the soldier's total training. But what was distinctive about this indoctrination was its thoroughness and intensity. The CCF soldier had to know the ideology of his rulers and indicate agreement with it; more than that, he had to apply it constantly and explicitly to judge his own behavior and that of his fellows. The pressures for participation were such that all soldiers in the CCF not only had to constantly verbalize the principles of Communism but also had to constantly act as if they believed in them.

The degree of control required for such ideological participation can be attained only in thoroughly disciplined groups. The demand for ideological participation in the CCF was applied in an ideal situation, and the effectiveness these techniques may have in bringing about conformity or resocialization could only be approximated in non-military situations.

[3] Some of these observations may also apply to the relationship between child and parents, of course, but differences of degree give them relevance at this point.

The Nature of Adaptation

Adaptation as Learning

The degree and kinds of adaptation to the demand for ideological participation will suggest the relative success or failure of the attempted resocialization. As used in this study, adaptation implies learning the forms and content of ideological participation and the consequences of conformity and nonconformity. The first of these categories must be examined more closely, for it raises problems of definition.

In a study such as this, it is important not to identify learning with any one kind of acquired behavior. In approaching the problems posed by the Communist efforts to resocialize adults or near adults, it is convenient to distinguish among three kinds of things that are learned in the process of socialization:

> Attachments to specific persons and basic values.
>
> Culturally acceptable ways of expressing these values or attachments.
>
> Culturally acceptable ways of behaving toward objects that are defined as value objects by those with the power to enforce social norms but are not accepted as such by the individual.

The ways of expressing values and attachments tend themselves to acquire intrinsic value status. Such ways of behaving tend to be unreflective and habitual, and gradually take on the qualities of permanence and desirability. Furthermore, in a given culture, a value and the approved way of expressing that value are normally not easily distinguished; for example, in Oriental societies respect for parents and the specific ways of expressing such respect tend to become indistinguishable.

In relation to the third category of things learned, it must be emphasized that "correct" behavior toward non-value objects is usually instrumental to the achievement of some value held by the individual. For example, the child entering school may conform to rules, not because he believes in the value of classroom discipline, but because he does not wish to displease his mother. Similarly, a Chinese soldier may engage in self-criticism, not because he believes in the value of public exposure, but because in doing so he protects himself from punishment.

The distinctions among the three categories are important as a means of emphasizing the varient relationship between values and ways of behaving. Human behavior is purposive; men calculate ways of achieving or protecting values. They are capable of ingratiation, of acting as though they valued a particular person or thing when in reality they have some other value which ingratiation will serve. The existence of words like "sly," "deceitful," "tricky," and "insincere" reflects the capacity of people to behave in ways that do not indicate their true feelings.

The confidence man, found in every complex society, is a living reminder of human ability successfully to play roles and manipulate
values that one has not internalized. In thinking about the assimilation
of Communist roles and values, the reader will do well to keep in mind
the capacity of people to learn without internalizing, to speak without
believing.

Three Aspects of the Respondents' Adaptation

The preceding observations suggest some of the main problems
treated in later sections. Bradbury and Kirkpatrick, who were concerned primarily with a description of the values or motives revealed by
the respondents, established that the degree of successful adaptation to
the Communist system by individual respondents had no relation to the
degree of loyalty. Nevertheless, it may reasonably be assumed that
Chinese Communists aim, not only at overt conformity, but at the
internalization of their new system of values. Consequently, the discussion which follows is centered on three main topics relating to soldiers'
adaptation to the Communist demands for ideological participation:

> The degree and kinds of overt conformity and non-conformity
> exhibited by the respondents.
> The major areas of conflict between the old values and attitudes
> and the behavior required by the Communists.
> The possible long-range effects of the demand and all its ramifica-
> tions on both the individual "pupil" and the operation of the Commu-
> nist-controlled social system.

BASIC REQUIREMENTS FOR IDEOLOGICAL PARTICIPATION

On coming under Communist control, the respondents were confronted
with a situation which required the development of entirely new conceptions of politics. The Communist insistence on continuous and explicit
understanding and application of political ideology in day-to-day activities was a completely novel demand in Chinese society. Initially, in
expounding the rudiments of Marxist ideology or stating even the simplest propositions about individual welfare and government policy or
reform, the Communists were usually dealing with questions which had
never before been raised in China. We will sketch the pre-Communist
political experience of the respondents and discuss the meaning of
ideological participation.

All the men interviewed in this study had lived a large part of their
lives in a pre-Communist environment, most of them in circumstances
that encouraged a parochial, non-political view of their world. Despite
the conventional picture of Asiatic masses being moved by a virulent
nationalism, the notion of membership in a nation seems to have been
nearly meaningless for many of the interviewees. It is true that most of

the intellectuals (men with more than ten years of education) did exhibit a fairly developed feeling of concern for the nation, and informants with previous Nationalist army service fighting against the Japanese had acquired some feeling for the nature of a foreign enemy. Nevertheless, it can be said that among the respondents nationalism as a concept and as a feeling was limited both in extent and in intensity.

Knowledge about political issues was similarly limited among the men interviewed. For more than a decade China had been rent by a civil war which had affected many parts of the country and the lives of millions of people, yet few among the informants had a clear conception of the issues. Some of the intellectuals were well aware that the civil war had been fought for control of the government and therefore the power to make policy for China; they had been familiar with salient slogans embodying proposed reforms. Apart from this group, however, there was little understanding of the relationship between the civil war and the government.

Even among former Nationalist officers there were individuals who said that before coming under Communist power they knew nothing about the Communists, and thought of them only as bandits and cruel lawbreakers. They had not pictured the Kuomintang—for which they fought—as standing for one kind of government and one kind of social organization, and the Communists as standing for an alternative. They therefore had no particular feelings of loyalty to the ideology or programmatic aspects of the Nationalist cause, though they were, in varying degrees, loyal as fighting men in the Nationalist army.

Such political ignorance and indifference cannot be attributed entirely to the undemocratic character of pre-Communist Chinese political life. Even in non-democratic societies, it is possible to acquire experience in thinking about and influencing politics. In Bismarckian Germany, for example, the trade unions provided a kind of training ground for political consciousness at a stage where members of the working class had no direct means for participating in national government. However, very few of our informants had had a comparable kind of membership which could have sensitized them to large political issues and to the stakes of political power. A small number had belonged to student political organizations. As for the rest, their affiliations had been restricted to the family, the army, and, in a few cases, secret societies. The secret societies were concerned with securing privileges for individuals as individuals, not with influencing general policy; army commanders did constitute a political elite, but the officers and men of the Nationalist army seem to have been un-self-conscious representatives of a political position. In short, although familiar with local, manipulative politics, the Chinese masses had little or no experience with politics of a national, programmatic type.

A cause as well as a consequence of this inexperience was that, in pre-Communist days, few of the interviewees had either seen or felt any relation between national public policy and their personal fates. They had not perceived their disappointments and problems as having political or social causes which might be alleviated by the government. The Communists were the first to make wide and effective efforts to instill such consciousness in the masses. In the words of one respondent,

> The Communists are very successful in giving them reasons why. In the beginning, not all the people understood; some said that they are being oppressed and that they are poor because it is their fate. But it was through the Communists that they saw that that was not the case; they saw that they were being exploited. They saw that their sufferings and their hardships and poverty were due to these different classes existing and that the Nationalist soldiers represented the force which defended those particular classes. (R-3)

It is against this background of ignorance and inexperience that the Communist demands for positive loyalty and ideological conformity must be examined. Membership in traditional Chinese society implied, not national political participation, but habitation of an area that fell within the territorial boundaries of China. Large-scale government impinged on the average citizen's life only when he was drafted into the army, when tax collectors descended on the village, or when the entrance of warring troops turned his village into a battleground. In these contacts, obedience rather than loyalty (i.e., internalized emotional or intellectual commitment) was the issue. The Chinese in pre-Communist society does not seem to have been required to agree with the actions of his rulers. No pretense was made that in obeying the ruler he was following his own will. Such demands for symbolic or actual participation—through consent—in government occur only in political societies where democratic doctrines and/or forces have demanded the reality, or the façade, of government by the people.

Communism is a pre-eminent example of such a body of doctrine. Its ideological basis rests partly on the historical prediction that the masses will rule themselves in the political, economic, and social realms, and partly on the ethical imperative that the masses should rule themselves. The development of a political structure in which the people are represented only through an assumed identity of rulers and ruled has not lessened, in the Communist view, the importance of popular support. However, this view of the central importance of the people's will is manifested, not by an effort to form policy to correspond to the public will, but by an attempt to re-form the public will to correspond to policy.

Consequently, a Chinese coming under Communist rule was confronted with the demand for continous positive support of the social revolution engineered by Communist leaders. He was required to know—with varying degrees of completeness and sophistication—the intellectual basis, the value hierarchy, the friends and enemies of these leaders; to agree with their evaluations; and to conform his whole behavior to these considerations. Although the demand that he obey was not new, the demand that he know, agree, and self-consciously conform his every act to the standards provided by a novel political ideology was new indeed.

The Meaning of Ideological Participation

What Participation Involves

As a process, ideological participation contains three important elements which may, for analytic purposes, be distinguished: knowledge, expression of agreement, and repeated justification or rationalization of all behavior in appropriate ideological terms.

Knowledge.—The first requirement in ideological participation was, of course, knowledge of Communist ideology. As has been noted, the very effort to transmit knowledge of political principles and ideals to the soldier was in itself a break with Chinese tradition. Nevertheless, not only was the CCF soldier expected to know the social and political aims of the revolution of which the Communist party and the People's Army were instruments, but the everyday details of his military tasks and discipline were related to these broad goals. Ideological knowledge, in other words, involved both a knowledge of the revolutionary ideals of Communism and an understanding of the relationship of these ideals to the soldier's daily behavior.

The average person was, however, seldom exposed to ideology in its pure form. Knowledge of ideology was in most cases limited to knowledge of Communist slogans and programmatic goals. This knowledge normally included three elements: a general picture of the revolutionary struggle, presented largely in terms of opposed forces of good and evil; a justification of particular Communist policies such as land reform and the Korean War; rationalizations, in terms of these broader considerations, of the particular demands placed on soldiers. The range in ideological sophistication was, of course, considerable.

Agreement.—Ideological participation involved not only knowledge but full agreement. The Communists would prefer to create real conviction, and their first step in this direction was always extensive reasoned argument. Nevertheless, whether or not there was such conviction, the whole process of ideological participation aimed to ensure that all overt expression conformed to Communist norms.

Agreement, first of all, must be verbal agreement. As one respondent put it, "If the Communists say something is good, you say it is good" (N-19). Those who attempted to argue soon learned that "You can never win by showing hostility to them. We tried our best to do whatever we were ordered to do—to say the things we were ordered to say" (F-6).

The Communists were also sensitive to non-verbal evidence of agreement or disagreement. "They not only observe your actions, your behavior, but they also observe your attitude, your mood" (N-13). The reasons for this were expressed as follows by one repatriate, a general and political commissar: "A man's behavior is always guided by his thinking. Therefore, when his actions exhibit deviation, his thinking must be deviating in the same manner" (R-1).

Communication in formal situations was, however, only one of several areas where control was exercised. Even his dreams could subject a soldier to criticism or more severe punishment. Discouragement of private friendships largely eliminated opportunities for expressing deviant opinion in informal situations. Interpersonal relationships outside official political or unit ties were discouraged, and men found to be forming such relationships were punished. Criticism and mutual surveillance were designed to prevent the formation of interpersonal ties, and generally were effective in so doing. Undoubtedly one of the reasons that personal relationships were discouraged was the desire to prevent the expression of dissident sentiments among the individuals; it is probably for this reason that, while non-work-connected talking among individuals was discouraged in all cases, it was considered especially dangerous in the case of men of doubtful social origin.

> There are two categories the Communists observe the closest. One [is] the more educated, intellectual classes. The other is the so-called upper bourgeois class or landlord class. For instance, if two college students are caught talking together, they will be in serious trouble; or if two people both from the same kind of [upper-class] background were caught talking, they would be in serious trouble. (N-25)

Continuous Application of Ideological Principles.—The third requirement of ideological participation meant that a soldier's whole range of behavior was constantly and openly interpreted in ideological terms, both by others and by himself. At discussions and criticism meetings, everyone was expected to take an active part.

> Everyone is forced to express his opinion about the discussion topic. If two or three men in the assembly don't express their opinions about the topic, the Communist instructors will claim that they are reactionary agents and will punish them. (N-23)

> The discussion seems to be very active. Even if one didn't want to discuss, one had to pretend to be interested and to speak. (N-5)

Reasons for Communist Emphasis

Although there can be no doubt about the intensity and persistence of the demand for ideological participation, the Communists' motives or aims must be largely inferred. An important reason for this demand is surely the desire to use military service as a school for training individuals to live in a Communist society. The CCF served as a major training ground for Communist citizenship as well as for service in battle.[4] Chinese Communist leaders appear to take very seriously the Leninist precept relating performance to ideological orthodoxy. The belief that how a man does his job will be determined by his total ideological development leads to a heavy emphasis on political morale—that is, on indoctrination and general ideological training. According to this view, the requirements for the good citizen and the good soldier are in large measure identical—as are those for the good citizen and the good peasant, industrial worker, or university student. Conversely, failure or bad performance even in technical tasks is often interpreted politically—that is, as resulting from ideological inadequacies.

The conflict of roles between Communist and pre-Communist society suggests another reason for the emphasis on ideological training in the CCF. Almost all social roles have been changed by the Communists in their unprecedented experiment in social engineering. Therefore, the fulfillment of any single new role (that of soldier, for example) often precludes the fulfillment of other, traditional roles. For the man entering the CCF, becoming a good Communist soldier necessitates becoming a new kind of citizen, son, husband, and so forth. Because he is expected to adopt roles that have not been acquired and internalized in the normal process of socialization, he has to be taught the principles that are to replace habit and spontaneous feeling as a guide to conduct.

The informants had been exposed to differing amounts of ideological training. Several of the highly educated—chiefly a few former Nationalist officers and those who were university students at the time their city or province fell under Communist control—were subjected to intensive indoctrination in military-political universities, special centers set up for the purpose of reforming selected representatives of the old order. These informants had been exposed to ideology in a more elaborate, sophisticated, and complete form than were those trained in regular army units. However, the basic propositions and emphases on ideological training were identical.

What, then, were these propositions, and what, precisely, did ideological participation involve for the CCF soldier? How did the Communists attempt to communicate the new value system, the policies, and the criteria by which men were henceforth to be judged? How did they seek to persuade their subjects of the moral and intellectual superiority and the tactical astuteness of Communist valuations and policy? In short, what was it that the interviewees had been required to learn?

The Content of Indoctrination

For the purposes of this study, the content of the indoctrination to which all new members of the Communist forces were exposed may be viewed under two major categories. First, the Communists explained to

---

[4] Until 1948–49, of course, the CCF was largely the Communist society.

them what Communism was, and then what it stood for in the domestic and international struggles. From such propositions about the nature of their mission, the Communists derived the duties and obligations of individual soldiers.

The Meaning of the Communist Struggle

Slogans, particular proposals for social reform, and simple ideological tenets were all combined to create a picture of the Communists and their struggles. The idea of struggle appears in all parts of the Communist effort to inculcate the minimal ideological consciousness in their soldiers. For as good Marxists, who see history in terms of dialectical oppositions, the Communists defined their mission as much in terms of whom or what they were against as in terms of whom or what they were for.

Thus, while the civil war was still being fought, in explaining the character of the group in which the new CCF member was expected to fight, and to which he was expected to grant total obedience, the Communists stressed their opposition to the existing society and the Nationalist government. Since in most cases the soldiers were unaware of a struggle between opposing social conceptions, the Communists had first to explain that such a struggle existed. This they did by positing the existence of two classes: proletariat and capitalist. They then explained that members of "the proletariat always work hard and do an honest day's labor, whereas the capitalists are eating the fruit of the laborer and taking life easy" (N-10). The capitalists were variously defined as the landlords, the rich, the exploiters, the Kuomintang reactionaries.

The Chinese Communist mission was, of course, to defeat these enemies of the people. Land reform—a central programmatic slogan of the Communist in the years preceding their triumph—was to bring about a state in which "the rich and the poor would be the same— everyone would be comfortable" (N-12). As summarized by one respondent, the basic items in the pre-Korea catechism for CCF soldiers were as follows.

> The purpose of the revolution is to help the proletarians. The Nationalists or the Kuomintang protect the enemies of the proletariat. As the cause of the proletariat, revolution is invincible and victory is inevitable. (N-10)

After the outbreak of the Korean hostilities new propositions were added, to explain to each soldier why he must fight in Korea.

> They told how . . . the reason we [China] were poor and the United States was rich was that we were being exploited, just as they had told poor farmers that their suffering was the responsibility of rich landlords. (N-26)

> They told us how in the whole world the strongest nations invade the weak nations. That, for instance, in the First World War the Germans

attacked Soviet Russia and in the Second Japan invaded China. And in this war American imperialists invade Korea. Maybe after they occupy all of Korea they may enter Manchuria and occupy all of China, so all Chinese people will be under the cruel control of the American people. So we must assist the Koreans to defend our nation. (N-19)

The Communists passed out books . . . saying that Americans wanted to conquer the world, and their first step was to invade China and then the Soviet Union. (N-11)

As these quotations show, in their treatment of both the domestic and the international scene, the Communists sought to present themselves simultaneously as representatives of the downtrodden and helpless and as the preordained victors in the struggles against oppression. This point is made specifically by another respondent.

In teaching what the Communist army was, emphasis was also laid on its invincibility. They told a story of how a band of a few tens of thousands of men eventually conquered the whole country and became an army of five million. They stressed the inevitability of the success of Communism, not only in China, but in the whole world. (N-26)

It is interesting to note here how readily the concept of dialectical opposition is converted into a devil theory of politics when popularized for mass consumption. Whatever qualifications appear in the writings of Marx and Lenin on the moral qualities of the proletariat and the capitalists were discarded in the formulation of a view which divided the world into forces of good and forces of evil. The fundamental premise to be inculcated in all new subjects was the identification of the Communists and their allies with good and the identification of their enemies with evil. It is, then, in the name of this good which the party represents that sacrifices are demanded from the individual.

The Role of the Individual in the Chinese Communist Struggle

The insistence on the application of ideology to everyday behavior—a significant characteristic of Chinese Communist political indoctrination—means that the individual is constantly aware both of his expectations under the new order and of his precise duties and obligations.

Expectations.—In the Communists' cosmic struggle, some of those who fell under their control inevitably belonged to the condemned classes. Some—for example, older landlords, high Nationalist officials—who were too deeply compromised by their past were, of course, to be liquidated, often executed. Others were unmistakably proletarian and had reason to expect favored treatment. But for a large number of persons the consequences of the Communist victory remained for some time ambiguous: first, because the line between the good proletarians and the evil capitalists was flexible; and second, because the treatment to be accorded members of the former exploiting classes was not immediately clear.

Because of such ambiguities in propaganda many respondents first encountered the Communists with a certain amount of anxiety. They soon discovered, however, that not all the exploiters were equally condemned. For the most part, regardless of background, they had been given the opportunity to ally themselves with the forces of good. As one—the general and political commissar previously quoted—put it,

> When the Communists took over Chinese society, it was made up of divergent peoples; these people had different background; it will take time for the non-proletarians to be converted to the Communist ideology. The Communists recognize this, and they are not forcing them—they know it will take time—but they believe that by actions, by effect, and by time they will be won over. (R-1)

Class background did not necessarily preclude acceptance or even advancement in the Communist army. Individuals were evaluated in multifarious ways, not least among which was a willingness or apparent willingness to conform.

> It's hard to say which classes are reliable to the party. As long as a man agrees with the Communists, he is reliable. If he disagrees with the Communists, he is unreliable. (N-4)

> The Communists considered me reliable, not because my family were farmers, but because I could fight better at the battle front. (N-19)

Nevertheless, class background and previous political activity did influence an individual's place in the new order, for the Communist revolution meant somewhat different things to the exploited and to the exploiters. Furthermore, these differences were not simply inferred from the treatment experienced by individuals representative of the old classes; they were explicitly spelled out in all indoctrination programs.

The exploited.—Two groups of respondents—volunteers from poor farmer backgrounds, and former Nationalist enlisted men—may be listed as members of the exploited classes to whom the Communist revolution was represented as meaning liberation and new opportunities. To the first group, the Communists presented the simple appeal of working for the people who worked for them. In addition to the chance to ally themselves with the proletarian revolution, these persons were offered new physical comforts, more food, and greater respect. It is this group among respondents which showed least anxiety about its fate under the new regime.

The former Nationalist enlisted men, on the other hand, did experience considerable anxiety. They too, like the poorest farmers, were described as victims of the old ruling class. But they had been compromised by their alliance with this ruling class in much the same way that Lenin described the workers of imperialist countries as compromised by their benefits from colonial territories. Consequently, before they could be fully accepted by the new order, they must air their grievances against former rulers, confess their own parts in crimes against the people, and devote themselves wholeheartedly to the new order. For members of this group, the successful revolution meant both the release from exploitation and the necessity for an expiation of their own past crimes.

The exploiters.—To members of the old exploiting classes—intellectuals, sons of wealthy families, and former Nationalist officers—the Communists could not immediately offer new material benefits or higher status. Instead, to these groups they stressed the necessity of seeking redemption by sharing the hardships of the classes from whose labor they had formerly lived.

It is true that considerable effort was devoted to winning students over to the revolution by promises of rewarding careers in the new society.

> One of the things [the Communists] stressed . . . was the uncertainty of the professional futures of the students under the Nationalist government. They pointed to the fact that highly trained students had great difficulty getting jobs when they left the university, and often ended by doing menial chores. They said that this was simply an example of the uneconomical use of China's resources by the Nationalists. They said that under the Communists, students would get good jobs, would have a secure and happy future under the new government, and that China would grow powerful because her resources would be fully used. (F-5)

Nevertheless, even to those intellectuals who collaborated willingly, the revolution meant an abolition of former privileges and a reduction in status in an effort to "make them live and think like the proletariat" (N-26). One former student described his own experience as follows.

> Naturally when the family assets were confiscated I had no more source of income and could not continue my studies at the university. The Communists in the university talked to me and said that I should not feel badly—that I had always received the benefits of the rich and that I must learn under the new regime to share the hardships of the people. . . . I was assigned to hard labor in order to gain a proletarian point of view and to help purge me of class consciousness. (F-5)

The treatment of former Nationalist officers was even more severe. They were expected to confess their crimes and errors, to criticize themselves and their fellow officers intensively, and repeatedly to renounce their old ties. Their eventual acceptance depended on the degree of their personal commitment to the old society and on the strength of their real or apparent commitment to the new.

It is important to point out, however, that none of these groups ever really succeeded in dispelling the suspicion that surrounded it. A student soon learned that "the Communists stressed the fact that intellectuals were not trustworthy, that the party did not trust intellectuals" (F-5). And a repatriate found that his mistakes were easily attributed to his tainted background. "They criticized me because I came from a background which is nonproletarian, so they told me that I had to be more careful" (R-7).

Duties and Obligations.—From this struggle between the old order and the revolution both within China and on the battlefields of Korea, and from the fact that every individual was involved—consciously or not—in the struggle and represented and aided either one side or the other, the Communists deduced the obligations of CCF soldiers. In the army, and in the military-political universities where some of the men in this study had been introduced to military service, political instructors placed particular emphasis on the implications of the ideological postulates for the life of each individual Chinese. From ideology was derived, in addition to a political rationale for military discipline, certain general moral qualities and many specific role demands. In fact, as the following few pages will illustrate, these ideological implications were largely identical with the requirements of the jobs that the respondents were expected to fill.

The soldier had to learn concern for the general welfare—"To serve the people and the country, even to die, is good." The nation, the people, and the revolution must be given priority over personal interest and all other obligations. "The nation comes first" (R-9). "One must work very hard for the people" (R-4). Even family life was "a personal privilege and must be sacrificed for the revolution" (N-7). "In a socialist society, personal problems should never block one from his endeavor for the party or public interest" (R-1).

Since the particular ways of serving the people were of course defined by the Communist leadership, the first requirement of such service was unquestioning obedience to the Communist party. The very definition of the counter-revolutionary is "anyone who does not agree with the Communists" (N-18). The authority of the party spread to the military hierarchy, and the importance of discipline as a political duty of the CCF soldier seems to have been emphasized.

The respondents, both repatriates and non-repatriates, also revealed the stress placed on the propagation of certain general moral qualities. Individuals were expected to be courageous, unselfish, honest, just, democratic, and fair to the people, and the specifics of these qualities were constantly spelled out in detail. In answer to a question as to how officials are known to be undemocratic, a respondent supplied the criteria. "They take money and they never tell the people how they spend it.

They beat the people. They force the people to labor. They never serve the people. This is undemocratic" (R-9). The qualities of good Communist leaders and soldiers were summarized as follows. "[They are] not corrupt . . . can stand a hard life . . . will take care of the lives of soldiers, and are willing to fight to their death" (N-19).

The pains taken to relate specific aspects of the role of soldier to general ideological principles are illustrated by the following quotation.

Mostly [in my unit] we violated these things: (1) wanting to go home; (2) wanting women; (3) quarreling among selves; (4) insubordination; (5) corruption; (6) not progressive enough; (7) fear when fighting. . . . When we were homesick, they [the Communists] said: "Well the revolution is not over. There is no time to be concerned with homesickness." Second, with women. They explained it like this: "You have your own sisters and wives, and you are taking advantage of somebody else's sister or wife." About personal quarrels they said, "These are your comrades; you are fighting against a common enemy; conserve your strength." Thus all men must adhere to the regulations, must obey the organization. Discipline is most important. When you come to corruption they said: "You are harboring thoughts which lead to exploiting other people. Being proletarians, you cannot exploit." If you were not progressive, they said: "Your stand is not firm. You do not understand the principles of revolutionary forces." As far as fear is concerned, they said that you place self-interest higher than the common welfare. (R-3)

This indicates the basic requirements for all soldiers. Some, because of social background, previous experience, or current position, had special obligations, also deduced from the basic ideological tenets. Intellectuals were expected to "remake themselves into a type of worker [in order to] understand the principles and aspirations of the proletariat" (N-26); and the obligation of the Nationalist officer was similiar. The party member, on the other hand, acquired special duties because of his superior status. In return for the privileges of party membership, greater self-lessness, zeal, and efficiency were required.

Everybody who joins the Communist party must give up his own rights and all relationships with his parents and brothers and sisters and friends, and all your thoughts must be for the nation and for the people. There is no personal feeling—you should have feeling only for the whole nation and for the people. (N-14)

The material in this section indicates the way in which ideological generalizations were applied to specific aspects of the soldier role. Tying the general principle to concrete rules of conduct provides an operational definition of the general principle. For example, putting the nation first or serving the revolution, means that the soldier will not be homesick, will avoid women, will not quarrel with his fellows, and will respect superiors. Conversely, tying the specific rule of conduct to a general principle or goal provides a rationale for the specific rule of conduct.

Here, then, are the political axioms and their corollaries. The basic principles, unadorned, might be nothing more than the Communist version of what every soldier hears in orientation lectures. It is their use, rather than their content, which is crucial, for it is this which gives operational importance to the principles themselves and which ensures their impact on the lives of Chinese soldiers. Simply as ideas or exhortations, they might or might not affect the lives of those who came into contact with them. But as axioms whose corollaries are enforced rules of conduct, their influence is as wide as the arc of power which enforces them. In the CCF the soldier or officer is forced, by a series of devices which reinforce each other, to keep the Communist frame of reference and orienting principles in the forefront of his attention. It is required that he learn these principles; that he be able to articulate them; that he relate his activities and thoughts to them; that he judge his behavior and that of his fellows in these terms; that he continuously reaffirm his loyalty to Communist goals, rules, and values.

The organizational techniques and the incentives that are manipulated to ensure such intensive participation are described in the following section.

THE ENFORCEMENT OF PARTICIPATION

For most of the informants, entrance into a Communist army marked their entrance into the Communist world. Indoctrination in Communist values and goals was woven into the lives of CCF personnel to such an extent that a period of army service might be described as a preparation for life in a Communist society. The program for restructuring the ideology of the individual began almost immediately after his entry into the army. In describing the ways in which the respondents learned their rulers' expectations and techniques for enforcing compliance, we will focus on several situations in which the learning process is most central, and therefore most clear. The airing-of-grievances sessions organized for captured Nationalist soldiers, the criticism meetings which were a regular part of a soldier's life, the lectures and discussion groups whose purpose was more nearly indoctrination as that term is commonly understood—all were directed at communication of the new culture and role requirements. These situations are therefore ideal for revealing the crucial elements in the process of learning and adapting to the new ideological demands. But it should be remembered that such learning experiences did not take place in isolation. The soldier's whole life was organized to reinforce the expectations and responses learned in these formal situations.

Three Learning Situations

Airing of Grievances

The interviews indicate that airing-of-grievances or "speak bitterness" meetings, organized to hear individuals' complaints against the Nationalist army, were a regular, institutionalized part of the process for inducting captured Nationalist troops into the Communist army. Generally enlisted men and noncommissioned officers were separated from their officers before this process began. The purpose of the meetings is explained by their name. They were held to hear the Nationalist soldier recite his sufferings at the hands of the organization and leaders from whom he had been "liberated." The crimes of the officers against their men were to be fully exposed; the evils of the landlord clique which governed the army were to be explicated. Soldiers were encouraged to articulate every resentment, and every injustice and hardship they had experienced in the Nationalist army. Former officers were forced to admit their own crimes, real or imagined, under the old regime.

According to one informant, the meetings sometimes became emotional as soldiers indicted their former leaders. Others said that they recognized the justice of some of the charges against the Nationalist army. Still others stated that "nobody believed the charges," that "they felt badly to say such things" but that they "had to do it."

This last type of response brings us to the function of the "speak bitterness" meetings in acquainting men, newly under Communist control, with the twofold concept of correct thinking and correct speaking. Every individual was quickly given to understand that he was supposed to condemn the army of which he had been a part. Failure to do this, or refusal to agree with another's condemnation, was evidence of incorrect thinking, and incorrect thinking was an offense of major proportions against the new rulers.

Nor did passivity—that is, acceptance without participation—escape censure. The requirement for positive loyalty meant that the individual had to do something—namely, to describe his own sufferings or sympathize with those who had suffered.

> In the complaining meetings, if one of them complained about how his superior officer in the Nationalist army oppressed him or persecuted him or beat him and another man said he was never persecuted or beaten by his superiors in the Nationalist army, then the Communist leaders wanted the man who had never been persecuted and had never been beaten by his superior officers to sympathize with the man who was persecuted or beaten in the Nationalist army. (N-22)

Doing either of these things implied already cutting ties with previous loyalties in the name of principles of conduct expounded by the new rulers.

In the respondents' reactions to these meetings can be seen the genesis of different modes of adaptation to the demand for verbal agreement and participation, and some of the reasons for these differences. In general the demand that former Nationalist soldiers articulately sever ties with that army produced three types of reactions: agreement, disagreement, indifference.

Although there were some who believed the complaints, and whose participation was characterized by agreement with the procedure, more reacted negatively and resented being forced to participate. One basis for the negative response of some Nationalist men was their knowledge that certain statements condemning the Nationalist army were untrue. Since the meetings were in part staged affairs, in which CCF cadres and political officers also participated, by no means all the charges made grew out of the experience of the new captives. For example, the charge that the Nationalist army never fought the Japanese was sometimes made in a group composed largely of men who had participated in campaigns against the Japanese.

Finally, some seem to have reacted out of neither agreement nor disagreement; they simply did what they felt was required of them without any significant feelings about the truth or falsity of the charges. This purely passive conformity was relatively rare (as compared, for example, to the passive compliance of peasant soldiers who had not taken an active part in the Japanese war).

It is significant that all three groups conformed verbally. Even charges that the respondents knew to be false were rarely contradicted, either by them or by their fellows. This suggests that verbal conformity was already the dominant pattern of behaving. In the rare cases when an individual expressed disagreement with prescribed views in these meetings, he brought strong censure on himself—and generally became convinced that non-conforming speech was unwise. The data strongly suggest, however, that for most captives direct punishment was not required in order to induce them not to disagree.

Another striking aspect of the response of captured Nationalists to the "speak bitterness" meetings is the apparently guilt-free nature of their conformity. Verbal denunciation of the organization and leaders they had formerly served appears to have caused almost no anguish of the kind associated in the West with betraying loyalty. We would not, of course, expect to find a sense of guilt in men who agreed with the condemnation; however, with two possible exceptions, there is no indication that the fairly large number of respondents who disagreed with what they considered false statements felt any guilt or shame about affirming them. The feeling that they were forced to do it was regarded as adequate justification for their behavior; the idea that their action might require any further justification seems not to have occurred to them.

Despite their overt conformity, however, some who felt they had been coerced into agreement were strongly resentful. This resentment was, naturally, most pronounced in those who had disagreed with the complaints against the Nationalists and had been punished before they capitulated. Those who reacted in this fashion began early to feel that the Communist system was coercive and that its representatives were all deceivers.

These two charges—deceit and coercion—were important factors in final disaffection from the regime.[5]

Lectures and Discussion Groups

A schedule for the period of basic training, supplied by one of the informants, reveals the heavy emphasis placed on political indoctrination in the CCF.

0530–0550	Reveille
0550–0750	Physical training
0820–0850	Breakfast
0850–1050	*Political training* [6]
1100–1200	*Political examination*
1200–1400	*Discussion of political training and critique of examination*
1400–1530	Rest period
1530–1600	Supper
1600–1830	Physical training
1830–1900	Roll call and report
1930–2030	*Analysis of day's work*
2100	Bed check

Considerable time was allotted to orientation lectures on Communism and its goals, and to group discussions whose purpose was to test the agreement and understanding of the listeners. The lectures treated such broad topics as "Why We Must Annihilate the American Imperialists," "On the Principles of Revolution," and "The Superiority of the Proletarian Class." They were an important means of communicating basic Communist orientations to those new to Communism, and of communicating additional new aims as they arose. Lectures were generally followed by discussion periods, for which the listeners were organized into small groups. In the discussions, the new CCF soldier once again met the demand for participation and active agreement. Again, he learned that "you had to speak," "you could not be silent," and again he learned that agreement was the only course open to him if he wanted to stay out of trouble.

The techniques used to induce agreement were sometimes imaginative and always persistent. Great pains were taken to convince the soldiers through rational persuasion, as the following quotation illustrates.

[5] Bradbury and Kirkpatrick, Chapter 1, above.
[6] Emphasis supplied.

This is the process of education which is applied to all cases. First, they explain to a man why he must not serve the cause of the capitalist and why he should serve the cause of the proletariat. That is fundamental. They will assign men with a greater knowledge than yourself to talk to you, to explain the things individually. After going through this process and talking and reasoning and explaining, then you go into group discussion to discuss the whole problem. First, his explanation why, the reason why; then if it still doesn't penetrate in the group discussion, we have individual interviews. In the beginning you are assigned to somebody who is more or less equal in intelligence to explain things to you. Then if he still can't win you over, you are assigned somebody with a superior intelligence than you. Well, in the long run they have so many that he will work on you and you are bound to see the light. (R-3)

Again the responses of informants fell into three major groups. Some agreed, and "believed it all very much." A larger group disagreed strongly. Finally, a few neither agreed nor disagreed strongly; they received the lectures simply as cues to what they were now expected to say, without much reaction one way or the other to the truth content of the lectures.

In fact, of course, the disbelievers as well as the passive conformers responded to the lectures as cues. For the disbelievers the lectures provided a means of learning what they were expected to say, and once this group had become convinced of the futility of disagreement most of them assiduously cultivated "correct speaking." Informants reported carefully "memorizing the slogans," "learning the slogans so I could say what they wanted me to say," and similar efforts toward conformity. However, those who disagreed resented the programs as one more means of arbitrarily controlling thinking.

As in the case of captured Nationalists in grievance sessions, those who believed what they were told escaped the pressures of feeling personally coerced. These soldiers approved the programs of lectures and discussions, and saw them as evidence that the Communists cared what they thought and were reasonable men.

When the Communists came, we noticed one thing—the Communists would permit the people to talk. They gave the people a chance to reason, and they wouldn't penalize the people without a cause. (R-5)

Nevertheless, even they were aware that agreement with the "lessons" was required.

In lectures and discussions, as in airing-of-grievances meetings, all informants adapted quickly to the demand for active agreement. And again, conformity did not create significant conflict, even for those who disagreed with the content of the propositions to which they gave assent. Their non-belief, by making them more alert to determine the requirements and more assiduous in their detailed fulfillment, may even have served a positive function in their advancement. Several informants who report "never having believed it at all" made successful careers in the CCF.

Criticism

A third situation in which the recruit learned the meaning and application of ideological participation was the self- and mutual criticism meeting, which in most cases was held daily.[7] The criticism meeting is perhaps the most striking example of a Communist institution serving the dual goals of control and reeducation. Fundamentally, criticism, self and mutual, is a group process in which each individual is expected to examine orally the thoughts, feelings, and behavior of himself and other members of the group and to criticize these in the light of Communist social norms.

Criticism meetings are perhaps the crucial institution in the enforcement of conformed speech. Every individual in the Communist army is a member of a criticism group. Since such a group is composed of men who live together continuously, it is the level at which an individual's total life becomes subject to state power. Anything a man says is likely to become the subject of discussion at a criticism meeting. His moods, his dreams, his remarks about his work, and his conversations with others are all subject to exposure.

Criticism is a multi-function institution, the point at which instruction, surveillance, and punitive sanctions intersect. From one perspective, the criticism meeting is an important part of the system for instructing persons in correct thinking and correct speaking. From another, it is an important component of the security system, the institutional guarantor of the system of mutual surveillance. From still another perspective, it is the lowest court of the Chinese Communist judicial system. Although its function in all these areas would have to be considered in any comprehensive study of the Chinese Communist Control system, here we will limit our attention to the ways in which the criticism meeting instructed recruits in the meaning of the demand for ideological participation and to the way it encouraged conformity to this demand.

The first contact with criticism meetings was, for all informants, a shocking experience.

> The first time I was criticized I could not stand it. I felt it was better to be killed in battle than to be criticized by other persons in the meetings. (N-15)

> I felt very miserable before this group. (N-19)

[7] See next to last item on training schedule, above.

At the mutual criticism session I felt very embarrassed at first. . . .
(R-2)

The first time you criticize yourself you feel you have lost face.
(N-23)

The pain of the experience naturally generated attempts to understand
the kinds of behavior which called forth punishment and the ways of
avoiding or mitigating it.

One of the chief errors for which men were criticized was failure to
speak correctly. Incorrect speaking opened the way to a range of errors
included in the general charge of improper understanding. It might
mean that a man had complained about hard work, or had failed to
participate in discussion groups or criticism meetings themselves; it
might mean he had disparaged a party or army policy when speaking to
an associate, or had failed to accept criticism in a progressive spirit. It
might even mean he had revealed an apathetic mood or talked in his
sleep. All these crimes and misdemeanors resulted from incorrect speaking in the sense that they resulted either from saying something that
should not have been said or from failing to say something that should
have been said. They could therefore be avoided by changing speaking.[8]

The interviewees quickly learned the price of nonparticipation.

You have to listen carefully and point out the mistakes of another. If
you do not do so, you will be criticized yourself, so you have to
criticize others. (N-26)

In case you lag behind in criticizing a man—in case you don't ask
questions and don't participate in the criticism—you will be observed
and criticized yourself. (N-25)

If you don't criticize another man, you will be asked about your
connection with him. (N-8)

They also learned the price of failure to criticize themselves.

It is better to criticize yourself in spite of losing face, because if you
don't criticize yourself the other people will criticize you. It is much
worse than if you criticize yourself. (N-23)

The most severe thing is when everybody jumps on you. That has to
be prevented. (R-3)

[8] The Communists classified these as errors of thinking. We have categorized
them as crimes of speaking rather than of thinking, because they became crimes,
operationally, when the thought or attitude was communicated, verbally or non-
verbally, and because this is the level at which most of the respondents received
them. Furthermore, it was possible, at least in the short run, to fulfill the
requirement by changing only the overt expression of the thought or feeling, not the
thought or feeling itself.

Such considerations as these led them to decide it was better to conform their speech to Communist demands.

At first the Communists criticized me for lack of understanding proletarian principles and for not having a firm stand. I had to follow along with this, and I memorized all the terms and the processes very well. (N-26)

During the criticism meetings there is only one way: the only thing you can do is promise them you would do what they wanted you to do. (N-22)

After a while you develop certain protective instincts. . . . In the first place, in actual work you will be the most aggressive worker. In case there are meetings, you will be the first to voice all the slogans. You become a master in deception, and even then you might make mistakes at times. Then, the moment you discover you made a mistake, you are the first one to admit that you made a mistake. (N-2)

They learned quickly that talking must be controlled all the time, that careless speech to anyone anywhere might make one a target of a criticism meeting.

When we [fellow villagers in the same army unit] talked to each other freely, somebody was bound to expose something once in a while; then we would all get criticized. (R-7)

There is no chance to talk with friends. Everybody is afraid of talking with other people. You trust no one. (N-23)

Thus, the pattern of anxiety, error, punishment, and conformity was similar to that in "speak bitterness" meetings and discussions. Again, conformity came quickly on the heels of learning the rules; again, the reasons for conformity varied. Some who agreed with Communist goals and values saw criticism as "good for work because it helped avoid future errors" (R-2), as a way of "increasing the efficiency of the people, the group organization, and the group movement" (R-9). Those who disagreed conformed from reasons of fear or expediency. In criticism meetings as elsewhere the fear of punishment was crucial to learning the demands and conforming to them. However, it should be remembered that, despite their prominence, punitive sanctions were combined at every stage with a range of other inducements to learning and conformity. The man guilty of wrong thinking or speaking was censured; simultaneously, the man who spoke correctly was praised as progressive, and might eventually be rewarded with promotion or a chance to join the party.

Most informants were more sensitive to the punishments than to the rewards associated with criticism meetings; conformity to the demand for correct speaking was motivated more purely and directly by fear than was conformity to other aspects of the demand for ideological participation. The explanation for this is found in the extreme dislike of being criticized felt by almost all informants.[9] Self- and mutual criticism, consequently, played an exceedingly important part in convincing the recruit that "you must say what they want you to say," both in the criticism meeting itself and outside it. Painful experience in a criticism meeting was a crucial factor in leading an individual to new efforts to conform his speaking to the Communist demands. To understand the crucial role of criticism in the adaptation process we should bear in mind these facts:

> Within the criticism sessions themselves, correct speaking is correct behavior.
> Criticism sessions were the chief arena in which all errors in speaking and acting were exposed and discussed.
> Correct speaking in criticism sessions depended on appropriate application of Communist ideological tenets.

The criticism meeting, therefore, constituted a kind of continuous examination of the participant's learning. In the meetings he had to prove his ability to identify reactionary thinking or behavior in himself and others and to explain its causes and consequences in acceptable Marxist terms.

Communist Manipulation of Incentives

General Pressures

As the preceding material has shown, the Communists do not limit the process of indoctrination to the repetition of goals or values by cadres and political officers alone. On the contrary, they create situations in which the individual is continuously forced to participate in discussion groups where ideological tenets are explored on both the abstract level and in their concrete implications.

One of the most important factors in the CCF indoctrination was its context. The soldiers learned as a group, and the group was manipulated to reflect consensus on Communist goals and values. The controls over everyone's speech had the effect of rigorously censoring the communications the individual received from his group. All these communications were supposed to reflect enthusiastic acceptance of the Communist roles and norms (and, as we have seen, most did). From the time a man entered the army there was little possibility of his being exposed to contrary views. By isolating individuals, mutual surveillance and criticism effectively inhibited the formation of friendship groups where

[9] For most, "gradually the pain lessened" (N-15), but this lessening was probably as much a consequence of increasingly effective conformity to the expected behavior as of habituation.

dissident views might be expressed. Censorship of mail was intended to ensure that the individual would receive no communications from outside which would contradict the indoctrination he received in the army. Severely restricted communication with the civilian world further reduced the possibility of contamination from that source.

Supplementing the pressures which an individual felt directed at himself was the pressure resulting from living in an environment where examples of the consequences of conformity and nonconformity were constantly before him. In punishing individuals, the Communists appear to have devoted the greatest possible effort to exploiting the pedagogic possibilities of each individual's errors. Trials were often public. Criticism meetings involved public criticism. Expulsion from the party climaxed group investigation of the errors of the expelled member. Executions also were often public. More than one informant described his personal terror at witnessing the trial and execution of a condemned man. Each man's punishment instilled fear in others, and each man's success carried its own explicit explanation.

These facts have one important consequence: the manipulation of group consensus is such that heterodoxy is punished and inhibited by the apparent disapproval of the whole group. Whereas an individual member who disagrees or doubts may suspect that the expression of group disapproval is only a response to the same pressures which he himself feels, he can never really know whether it is coerced or spontaneous; he cannot confirm his doubts or opposition through conversation with others. Therefore, he must live with the assumption, not only that all his actions, from dreams to casual conversation, are known, but that any heterodoxy will bring upon him the disapproval of his peers and superiors.

Let us now examine the major factors that operated to create conformity—the control techniques utilized by the Communists and found in all the learning situations described earlier.[10]

Control Techniques

Rationalization.—As was indicated in the section on lectures and discussions, the demand for affirmation of and conformity to the goals and values of the new China included a systematic effort to explain and justify this new ideology. The painstaking efforts to convince men of the rational and moral superiority of Communism attest to both the intensity of the new leaders' desire to induce consent (internalized belief) and their seriousness of purpose in engineering a cultural revolution.

To believe that the revolution proceeds simply by giving people orders

[10] Conformity was also induced by certain character traits which appear to be rather persistent and common in men who reached maturity in traditional Chinese society. For a detailed description of these and an analysis of their role in molding the behavior of Chinese soldiers, see Bradbury and Kirkpatrick, Chapter 1, above, and Meyers, Chapter 2, above.

would be to underestimate the ambition of the revolutionary aims. The informants were agreed that a chief characteristic of Communist leadership is that it gives reasons for everything. The request for volunteers, for example, followed on the heels of elaborate explanations of the nature of the enemy, the stakes of the war, the war aims of the Communists, and the meaning of the war to the individual. Likewise, the demand that men criticize themselves and others was founded on repeated explicit explanation of the functional purpose of criticism in a Communist society. The smallest policy or event was explicitly related to fundamental premises of the new society. The operational aim was achievement of perfect understanding and acceptance of the goals and policies, general and particular, and their relations to the individual.

When a man gave evidence, through passivity or disagreement, of misunderstanding any aspect of the role requirements or values, various techniques were utilized to correct his mistake. The political officer might talk to him individually and attempt to explain the basis of his error. All the members of a discussion group or a criticism group examined possible explanations of his misunderstanding and were overtly united in the desire to persuade him of his error. These efforts continued until the individual either was convinced or decided to appear to be convinced in order to escape the pressure of the teaching. Where normal efforts at explanation failed, political officers at higher levels were called in to speak to the heretic. Criticism meetings composed of higher-level officials or party members might be called for the same purpose. According to one informant quoted earlier, men of progressively greater intelligence attempted to satisfy an individual's doubts until he was finally convinced.

Approval and Disapproval.—Other positive techniques were utilized to motivate consent and voluntary support. Interviewees mentioned several rewards available to those who showed an interest in and knowledge of ideology and who demonstrated zeal in cultivating progressive thinking in themselves and in propagating it in others. One of these was simply praise by authorities. Informants told anecdotes which described their own and others' sensitivity to praise. The susceptibility of the masses to manipulation through their eagerness for praise was described as follows.

> Most of the Chinese people are ignorant, and with a little pat on the back they will do anything. All you have to do is pat them sometimes, they really give their lives to you; and the Communists know just how to do it. (N-25)

Informants who had at one time supported the Communists, as well as those who still supported them at the time of the interview, revealed their pleasure at receiving praise in such a way that it is clear that praise compensated them importantly for their painful experiences in self-criticism meetings and motivated them to try hard to fulfill Communist ideals. The informants who had never supported the Communists revealed a similar sensitivity to praise, but they appeared to value not so much the good opinion of the authorities as the feeling of security associated with being approved by authorities whom they fear.

> Every member in the camp where we were had been praised at one time or another for his manual effort at labor. No matter how hard I worked, they did not praise me. I was the last one and still not praised. I became very worried and fearful because I knew that this was bad not to be praised. To be praised, one is then sure that one is in good standing. (N-1)

In evaluating their responses, however, it will be well to keep in mind that in their completely controlled environment the only possibility of finding approval, from either authority figures or peers, was by behavior which reflected and confirmed Communist norms. The series of social control mechanisms devised to manipulate group opinion ensured that failure to learn and adequately apply ideology met with the apparent disapproval of the entire group. The individual who failed to participate adequately in group discussions or criticism meetings, or who in his work failed to express proper understanding of its relation to general goals, was met by disapproval from authorities (political and military officers, party members, and cadres) and by expressions of disapproval from his peers. The Chinese sensitivity to disapproval made the simple expression of approval and disapproval a more effective spur to conformity than might be the case in other cultures.

Status and Power.—In addition, all the means of acquiring status, security, power, and prestige were controlled by the Communists. Like the carrot on the proverbial stick, these universal social goods were held out as rewards—in this case for ideological zeal combined with hard work. The man who demonstrated progressive thinking and actions could be expected to have his efforts crowned by promotion or an invitation to party membership. These rewards in turn made available to him various goods associated with higher status in the new society. For example, during the Korean conflict soldiers below the rank of regimental commander were not permitted to marry. Men were told repeatedly that if they wanted to marry they must work hard and serve the revolution in order to rise to the required rank. Better living conditions were likewise a prerogative of rank. And perhaps most important of all, superior rank was felt to increase personal security.

Punishment.—For men newly under Communist control, filled with anxiety and fear for their future, probably the greatest reward for conformity to the demand for ideological participation was escaping punishment for non-conformity. The sanctions against speech that reflected former roles or former values, or passivity toward new roles and new values, were meshed so as to provide increasingly severe penalties for deviant communications behavior. Together these constituted an elaborate and efficient system for the control of speech and, to some extent, thought.

The immediate punishment for deviant communication was that of group disapproval, which the individual felt acutely. Anxiety, humiliation, terror were all associated by the informants with being instructed by a criticism group after having fallen into error. When deviant communications were exposed, they could meet only with the united disapproval of the group, since disapproving another's actions was the price of every man's safety. The presence of low-level officials representing the party and army added the threat of further punishment. The combination of sensitivity to disapproval and awareness of one's insecurity made serious criticism a dreaded punishment.

A second punishment which threatened an individual who persisted in reactionary speaking was assignment to especially hard work. Such assignments were also meted out to men judged unreliable from the outset. The level of work demanded of all personnel in the CCF made any addition unpleasant indeed. Furthermore, discriminatory work assignments placed an additional burden of speaking correctly on the individuals, for complaints were taken as additional indications of reactionary speaking and lack of progressive spirit.

> After I joined the Communist army, I was sent to a squad. In this squad, only I had been in the Nationalist army, and they ordered me to do all the hard work. If I complained about the hard labor, the Communist leader accused me again. They said, "You do not want to do the hard labor and you do not want to do something good for the army, so you are a reactionary agent." (N-22)

Beyond these relatively mild punishments lay imprisonment, deportation to forced-labor camps, and finally execution. The informants reported that relatively short periods of imprisonment were a common punishment for failure to speak correctly.

Captured Nationalist soldiers often considered execution an imminent threat. Certainly part of the explanation for this lies in the Communists' systematic effort to dramatize the penalties of non-conformity through public executions. The interviewees were unanimous in affirming that incorrect speaking did in fact bring on drastic punishments in certain situations. An interesting disparity exists, however, between the accounts of different individuals about the extent to which extreme punishments were related explicitly by Communist political officers to incorrect speaking. Some informants reported witnessing executions of individuals who were accused of no greater crime than reactionary thinking. One man reported the execution of a squad member for the contents of a dream.

> There was a soldier in my company. One night that man dreamed and cried out, and it was heard by all the soldiers in my unit, and it

was reported by one party member to his company political instructor. And the company political instructor asked that man, "Why did you cry out?" And the man told the company political instructor that he dreamed about a very big cat that bit him, so he cried. He was frightened, but the company political instructor accused him of being a Nationalist spy and shot him to death. (N-4)

The occurrence of drastic punishments for minor offenses is partly confirmed by a report (by N-22) of a man's imprisonment for talking in his sleep. Still other informants reported instances of deportation where the stated reason was incorrect speaking. However, several interviewees suggested that the Communists were reluctant to have it known that they punish men severely for crimes of speaking. They stated that in such cases the Communists invented or seized on some overt act as the reason for the punishment.

Special Pressures on Subgroups.—Certain subgroups of the CCF were subjected to special pressures. For party members and officers the loss of status was an important deterrent to passivity or disagreement. The threat of expulsion from the party was serious for those who associated party membership with security. Demotion in rank seems to have held less terror than loss of party membership. However, a number of officer informants gave evidence of a strong desire to protect their position. To this desire they ascribed the performance of such unpleasant chores as exhorting men to volunteer for battlefield heroism and to criticize friends.

Other special pressures were exerted on captured Nationalist officers and men being trained in military-political universities. These groups were subjected to more intensive thought-reform programs. Perhaps the most dreaded and most effective tool utilized in these programs was the autobiography. Its purpose was to relate ideological understanding of the connection between a man's former economic and social status and his thinking and valuing, and to explain his "turnover"—his gradual acceptance of Communist doctrine and values. The informants, like captured American fliers, described the writing of these autobiographies as a shaking experience. They had to be rewritten repeatedly; the desire to be free of rewriting an autobiography became an important motivation to "see your life as they wanted you to see it."

In writing my personal history, I would claim that "I had bourgeois habits, I felt shy about criticism, but now I will reveal my whole life because I realize there is no need for shame." I would say that I have no such thing as personal friendships any more. "That is bourgeois. Now all are working for the same cause. I have enlarged my friendship to all and to Mao Tse-tung." I denounced the old idea I had of personal liberty. "I confess now that I must realize I must always identify myself with the group. I have begun to appreciate the new society, so now I have the spirit of learning." (N-1)

PATTERNS OF ADJUSTMENT

Normally, adults cannot say how they acquired the values and orientations that are reflected in their day-to-day speaking and behaving. These unconscious premises of behavior are so taken for granted that they are rarely examined or articulated. Most adults do not remember the pressures that were exerted to secure their acceptance of and conformity to these values and orientations, nor are they aware of the reinforcing pressures that operate continuously throughout society. Conformity is largely automatic.

The informants were, of course, in no such happy situation. The new requirement to conform all speech to Communist values was explicit; so were the rules governing the specific ways this demand should be fulfilled and the pressures that enforced it. This section describes how informants adapted to the new demands for ideological participation and to the enforcing pressures that were exerted; it deals with both objective and subjective reactions. Specifically, it describes how they felt about the content of the demands, about the enforcing sanctions, and about their own reactions.

As has been shown, different individuals adjusted to the demand for ideological participation in markedly different ways. Some informants adapted smoothly and quickly prepared for themselves a future under the Communist regime. Others had more difficulty, and felt conflicts of varying intensity and consequences. Later in this section some of these different patterns of adaptation will be described and an attempt made to account for them. First, however, let us consider those features of adaptation which were shared by all or almost all informants.

Common Patterns of Adjustment

Since the informants were products of the same general culture and were confronted with the same general demands, it is not surprising that there should be common reactions and patterns of adaptation.

No Acceptable Alternatives

The situation faced by the informants was inescapable. One could neither remain indifferent to the demands of the new society nor withdraw physically from the situation in which one was confronted with the demands. In the words of one informant, "I was afraid, but what could I do? I couldn't run away—there was no place to run" (N-30). The new requirements had the full force of law, and each man had to come to terms with them. Therefore, the ways in which the interviewees perceived their situation had much in common.

All respondents saw the objective necessity of making peace with the Communists; and this necessity was perhaps reinforced by the traditional Chinese view of life as a process of compromise and adaptation to a given reality. Where many Westerners see nature and society as things that can be conquered and changed, many Chinese tend to see them as things that must be accepted and adapted to. One of the attributes of a wise man is the ability to appraise accurately the forces outside him and to work out a compromise with them which preserves his interests.

Self-Conscious Adaptation

All the informants came under Communist control as adults, with formed habits—ways of thinking and behaving. In adapting to the demand for ideological participation, therefore, they were confronted with the necessity of becoming self-conscious about everything they said and did. They could not speak spontaneously, as out of habit, since they had not been trained from infancy in the type of correct speaking required by the Communists. Consequently, another universally shared reaction to the new situation was a high degree of self-consciousness about the new demands and the relation of these demands to themselves; they also shared a detailed concept of what they must and must not do.

A man did not simply act; he thought before he acted. For this reason, his behavior may be described as rational and purposive—that is, consciously directed toward the accomplishment of a particular purpose. Although normally only a small percentage of human behavior is rational in this sense, Communist behavioral requirements could be met only through such rational behavior. The individual had to keep in the forefront of his attention what he was supposed to be like and how he was supposed to feel and to think.

Behavior had to at least appear rational in another sense. Communism required that the soldier be guided by abstract moral imperatives. One should serve the revolution, rid oneself of bourgeois habits, work for the people unselfishly. Reared in a society organized and operated in terms of subtly personal relationships, the informants did not habitually pattern their behavior on such principles. Therefore, all were confronted with the necessity for behaving in ways which, at least superficially, satisfied the requirement for giving principles precedence over personality.

Conformity

Extent of Conformity. Rapid adaptation.—Both the traditional inclinations of Chinese and the objective facts of Communist power help to account for the speed with which informants, almost without exception, conformed actively to the demand for ideological participation. A few resisted the demands originally but quickly capitulated in the face of the coercive sanctions attached to them. The following account is illustrative.

> I argued with them on the question of the proletariat and the capitalist classes. I said if a country is prosperous everybody will attain a

high level of culture and material comfort like the capitalist classes. I said what you Communists want to do is to level all the people to the level of the proletariat classes. I asked whether they wouldn't need the high level of the intellectual classes to uphold the culture and the civilization of China. All that talk got me into serious trouble. . . . I was locked up in isolation for five days. Finally, I took the usual course. They interviewed me every day. I decided it was better to say what they wanted me to say, and in time they released me. (N-10)

Few such informants had to be punished more than once, and most never had to be subjected to coercion directly and personally. Among the informants there were men profoundly alienated from the regime but there were no persistent troublemakers.[11]

The swift punishment for resistance and opposition does not fully explain the speed and completeness with which informants conformed. Some felt great anxiety and fear and had compelling objective reasons for doing so. But all of them demonstrated a striking degree of flexibility. The desire to protect oneself consistently dominated hostility and habit; no emotion was so strong as the desire to get along. Informants were alert to cues for required behavior, quick to learn the ropes, and quick to apply their knowledge. Most of them did not clash with Communist authority and suffer defeat before they began to conform; they began to conform from the first.

Deviant behavior.—The foregoing statements do not mean, of course, that conformity was perfect. But cases of non-conformity were usually brief and often impulsive. Such cases were of four main types.

Non-conformity resulting from inexperience: Unconformed speaking was most likely to occur very soon after a man came under Communist control, before he was clearly aware of what he was supposed to say and the penalty for failing to do so. Although the Communists seem to have made allowances for the learning period, mistakes did not go uncorrected. A single such mistake, however, would not normally get the soldier into serious difficulty.

Dreams and fantasies: Another type of error which led to speaking that disagreed—sometimes strongly—with the prescribed rules was a dream in which the dreamer cried out against the Communists. Such an unconscious action not only revealed his feelings but sometimes constituted as serious a ground for punishment as defiance consciously con-

[11] It is true that the respondent group necessarily excluded men who resisted very strongly, since they had probably been deported to forced labor camps or executed. It is also true that the group could not, by definition, include anyone who internalized all Communist requirements and acted upon them, since such men would never have allowed themselves to be captured; following Communist orders, they would have died in battle before permitting themselves to become prisoners of war. These reservations, however, probably do not seriously affect the general findings: It should be noted, for example, that N-10, quoted above, stated that by submitting he "took the usual course."

ceived and executed.[12] The fact that a man did not intend to speak against the Communists did not mitigate the seriousness of his crime. Neither did a misunderstanding or a slip of the tongue which might reveal negative attitudes.

Outbursts: Other instances of deviant behavior occurred when some Communist action touched the individual at such a sensitive point that he lost all caution and spoke out positively and strongly against the Communists. This type of non-conformity never occurred because of ideological provocation, but happened in response to such things as the execution of parents, failure to keep a commitment made to an individual, or refusal of a request which was extremely important to the man concerned.

This type of expressive non-conformity again illustrates the relative unimportance of abstract ideology as compared to other factors. Among the respondents, there was no instance of a soldier contradicting the Communists because of their stated views about relationships between a man and his family. One informant described being extremely pained to witness and to hear the denial of filial piety and family obligation, but he was not provoked to overt disagreement. Another described his disagreement with the Communist view of family, according to which the soldier who does not wave to his mother is lauded, but he was not led to overt disagreement. Still another described swearing loyalty to the party and silently withholding assent to the oath to renounce his family, but this part of the oath did not prevent him from becoming a party member. However, when the same individual learned that his parents had been executed, he lost his temper and denounced the Communists loudly and publicly. A similar example is provided by a Red Army hero who very quickly adapted to all requirements, rose rapidly in the party and the army, and explosively rejected party discipline when he was refused permission to remarry.

Informal communication: Most unconformed speech occurred in informal situations, which the Communists, in spite of their attempts directly to supervise all the activities and contacts of their soldiers, were not able to eliminate completely. The interviews make it evident that the rule against informal communication was from time to time evaded. "In my group I sometimes talked with other people at the risk of my neck but I couldn't help it, I had to talk. But we had to be absolutely cautious" (N-25). Another informant described his formula for feeling out the loyalties of another before approaching him to talk freely.

They split us up; we were not with our former comrades. I had no new friends. I couldn't talk with the others at all. I didn't know

---

[12] The most striking instance of this sort was reported by N-4, quoted above in the "Enforcement of Participation." Other respondents mentioned similar occurrences.

whether the others were good Communists or not and would report me. When we were fighting inside China some new boys came into the army. Some of them were schoolboys. I watched. If he worked hard, I couldn't talk. If he was sometimes lazy, he might be OK; then I would ask him about his home and so on. Then one day while we were working, I would say, "The work is hard." If he said, "Yes," then I could talk to him. If he did not, then I had to watch out. Even so, we could only talk a few minutes—for example, about the hard work, or how bad the Communists were, or about how some officer was no good, and so forth. The others who were not schoolboys never complained about the officers. I was afraid of the officers—I always smiled when they came around. I never could talk to another man unless he was a proved friend. (N-9)

The danger of unconformed speaking to other individuals is illustrated by the following.

I took up the problem [of escaping from the People's Liberation Army] with a friend by the name of Liu. Liu, also a member of the army, of middle-class background, lived nearby. I gave him the money and asked him to purchase civilian clothes. I planned to go to Nanking. I did not know that Liu was a member of the Youth Group, and he betrayed me. They gave me the works. I really became a target. (N-1)

For every informant who described somehow evading surveillance to talk freely with another, there were two or three who described this as impossible because of the Communist system of social control. Most of the respondents projected their feeling that it was impossible to speak outside prescribed limits even to their concept of marriage.

So far as I know, if the husband is a party member and wife also is a party member, then they talk about the revolution. . . . The husband always has to be very careful what he says when he talks to his wife. (N-4)

Informants generally agreed that it is very difficult to find a friend in the Communist system.

This political indoctrination produced three results. The first is mutual suspicion—you don't trust anybody anymore; two, mutual cheating of one another, even lying; and three, mutual spreading of terror regarding the party organization. You scare the others, and the others scare you about the terror of the party organization. (N-25)

Some Subjective Correlates of Conformity.—The conformity of the respondents did not, of course, await their acceptance or internalization of their new roles. As soon as a man fell under Communist control, he was faced with sanctions intended to prevent the acting out of his old system of roles and to enforce conformity to new ones. In short, the situation was so organized that learning took place in the context of behavior which already conformed to the principles being learned. Some informants lived the life of proletarians in military-political universities so that they would come to feel and think like workers and peasants.

One of the fascinating questions raised by the whole system of education and social control in Communist China is whether the rulers themselves believe that acting as if something is so makes it so. As suggested previously, the whole system of indoctrination is evidence of the rulers' desire to gain consent to and understanding of the new goals, norms, and roles. At the same time, the creation of a situation in which conformity is prerequisite to personal security means that men must act out roles they could not conceivably have yet internalized, and must affirm values with which they could not conceivably yet identify, because they have not had enough time to do so. One obvious and important consequence of these procedures is the creation of a society and social groups which objectively reflect Communist culture. The subjective consequences, however, are more in doubt.

Compartmentalization.—One psychological mechanism which may account in part for the flexibility with which informants conformed to new ways of thinking and speaking is the device of compartmentalization. Most interviewees appear to have largely insulated their experience under Communism from their previous lives and to have insulated their behavior under Communist control from their previous selves. Thus they reacted to many Communist demands (for example, the demand for affirmation of particular attitudes toward their families) as though these reactions existed apart from the remainder of their lives and attitudes. Dealing with every experience as an isolated segment helped to minimize conflicts in values, and *ipso facto* created a barrier to the total integration of the personality around the new values. The exhausting, physically insulated character of the soldier's environment probably contributed to this compartmentalization. A man who is busy all day long and exhausted at night has little opportunity to relate his current experience to his past, his specific actions to his total self.

One striking characteristic of the informants' attitudinal histories is the apparent lack of psychological need for consistency in their responses to the Communist regime from one point in time to the next. An interviewee who was attracted by Communist promises of economic reform rejected Communism because of the intolerable nature of his personal environment. Another came to hate the Communists for executing his family, after having been attracted by abstract promises of social, political, and economic reform. Still another hated them because of the experience of a public trial, joined them when he was partly persuaded of their "desire to help people" and was offered the chance for promotion, then deserted them when the opportunity arose because he "never believed them" at all (N-14). None seemed to feel a need for explaining his reactions to himself in such a way as to make them consistent.

Guilt-free conformity.—Another widely shared subjective aspect of adjustment—the guilt-free nature of the adaptation of most inform-ants—may be explained in part by compartmentalization and lack of a felt need for consistency. Their conformity to Communist demands was not inhibited by principle. Although informants who agreed with Communist values would be expected to feel no guilt in affirming their belief, the lack of guilt in men who did not believe the values they affirmed is striking. Almost without exception the informants explained and justified their behavior by the words "I had to." The possibility that this might be regarded by others as a morally inadequate justification clearly never occurred to them; in their view, superior force is a pres-sure that no conscience is expected to resist. This ability to compromise without guilt is undoubtedly another important explanation for the remarkable flexibility already commented on.

Attitudes toward political ideas.—Still another factor contributing to the informants' flexibility appears to be the attitudes they brought to their exposure to political ideas. Examination of reaction and adapta-tion to specific aspects of the demand for ideological participation confirms and casts new light upon their indifference to abstract ideas, disclosed earlier.[13] Common to almost all was a definite range of inten-sity of reaction to different aspects of the demands for conformed speech; different kinds of correct speech can be ranked from those that informants minded least to those they minded most.

First, there were propositions which informants may have found either reasonable or unreasonable but about which they had no strong feelings. In this category were doctrines of social revolution, dialectical materialism, and other such abstractions. None of the group felt strongly enough about one concept of history versus another, one con-cept of economics versus another, or for that matter, any concept of abstract morality, to resent or feel anxious about having to enunciate a different one.

Second, there were propositions at a lower level of abstraction which informants sometimes felt resentment at having to affirm—such items as "The Nationalists did not fight against the Japanese" or "No respect is owed to parents." Some informants apparently identified strongly enough with the Nationalist struggle against the Japanese or the idea of filial piety that affirming such statements created some internal conflict. Another example is one informant's resentment at the statement that all landlords became rich through exploitation of the poor. Landlords were identified in his mind with his father, who, he felt, had not exploited others but had simply worked hard. His resentment at having to agree with this item in his indoctrination contrasted markedly with

[13] See Bradbury and Kirkpatrick, Chapter 1, above.

his reaction to the Darwinian concept of human evolution "from monkeys to men" with which he said he "disagreed very much." It was clear that his response to the latter proposition was not emotional, not actively resentful.

A third category of propositions which individuals were expected to affirm carried a very strong emotional content. These were statements which referred personally and directly to the individual. Statements which necessitated confessions of personal crimes and descriptions of personal feelings and intentions were by all odds the points at which the most serious difficulties arose in the adaptation of communication behavior. It was the necessity to make such self-derogatory statements which aroused such strong emotions as anguish, hate, and desire for revenge. Here we do not mean that all individuals felt negative reactions to either of the two types of propositions embodied in this category; but where problems arose in adapting to the demand for ideological participation, the propositions in this category generally posed the greatest ones.

So much for the patterns of adaptation common to nearly all informants. Let us now consider the differences.

Variations in Adjustment

General

As the preceding sections have shown, informants displayed a variety of orientations toward the Communist rulers and life in a Communist society. At the time they were interviewed, some men were on balance; they agreed with Communist aims and methods and felt that "generally speaking, in spite of the fact that the Communists do some things which are quite unreasonable, the reasonable things outweigh the unreasonable things" (R-5). Others were alienated at some stage of their careers and tended to disapprove much of what the Communists said and did. Their general views are expressed as follows by one respondent.

> I never really believed what the Communists said, but for the sake of saving my life I had to agree with them. In my mind I was always against the Communists, but in my speaking I always agreed with them. It was very painful in that period. (N-23)

Still others simply followed where they were led, without much thought or feeling about whether they approved or disapproved, agreed or disagreed. They felt that "You just have to follow just like you have to pay taxes. There is no other way. You always have to pay your taxes" (R-6).

Neither the respondents' basic orientations toward the Communists nor their adjustment to ideological participation, however, was as simple as these statements suggest. In many cases the soldier's alienation from or identification with the regime underwent drastic changes over time. Furthermore, only rarely were the general attitude toward the regime and the reaction to every specific item of ideology wholly congruent. Men who voluntarily supported the Communists and approved their policies in general sometimes did not agree with specific ideological tenets. Similarly, even informants with the most thoroughly negative view of the regime and its ideology felt that some things the Communists said were true.

These complexities make it difficult to classify the respondents precisely, either with regard to their basic orientations or with regard to their attitude toward ideological participation. In the following sections adjustments to the demand for ideological participation are discussed under two categories reflecting certain tendencies in basic orientation: sympathetic to the Communists or unsympathetic. Since the orientation of many respondents shifted at different periods of their careers, the categories refer, not to fixed groups of respondents, but simply to two directions of basic orientation.

Sympathizers

General Assent Facilitates Conformity.—Informants with a sympathetic orientation toward the regime identified sufficiently with Communist values and goals to be willing to work for them and speak about them positively; they therefore did not feel coerced. Even recognition that there was no alternative to overt loyalty to these values and goals did not alter such soldiers' feeling that they were doing what they wanted to do in supporting these values. Conflicts between their own views and those of the party on specific items, such as family loyalty, caused no difficulty so long as the individual was required only to speak as though he agreed with the Communists.

General agreement with the Communists also made it easier for such informants to adapt to the procedures of ideological participation, especially criticism meetings. Identification with the general goals, or with the rulers, led sympathizers to feel that

> This process of confession and self-criticism increases the efficiency of the people, the group organization, and the group movement . . . and so is very good, not only for the military organization, but also in civilian life. (R-9)

Although criticism was to some extent painful to most soldiers, those who agreed were susceptible to appeals based on the values with which they agreed.

> You are a fighter of the people and you must think for the benefit of the whole nation, so you will have to admit your mistakes and you must criticize yourselves. (N-4)

The Meaning of Agreement.—The informants who sympathized with the Communists also tended to agree with the contents of Communist ideology. This does not mean that they understood and accepted the whole body of Marxism, Leninism, and Stalinism; in most cases they were ignorant of these writings. But it does mean that they thought they agreed with the ideology embodied in Communist writings and, more specifically, that they did agree with the general values and policies advocated by the Communists.

It would be a mistake to assume that men who on balance agreed with what they understood of Communist ideology were necessarily dedicated or hard-core types; only one among the informants could be so described at the time he was interviewed. He was also the only one thoroughly knowledgeable about Communist ideology and, more important, the only one who had thoroughly explored the implications of Communist culture for his own life.

> When you become a member of the Communist party, you accept not only the faith but you accept the discipline; so even if you have a different viewpoint, you must submit your viewpoint to the organization. Once you accept that, it is not so difficult to follow the directives of the party. You must accept this, for the party is acting for the general welfare of the people. (R-1)

This informant gave evidence of believing this almost literally and being psychologically prepared to accept the consequences. However, most of the sympathetic respondents unconsciously or consciously placed definite limitations on their acceptance of ideology, particularly its more concrete elements.

Reservations.—Some who agreed that one ought to be willing to accept the party's position on everything had reservations about specific items of ideology. One informant described the oath he was asked to take at the time he became a party member.

> If you wish to join the Communist party, you must sacrifice yourself and devote your life to the party and you can no longer take care of your family, your parents, your sisters, or your brothers. All your life will be devoted to the party, to the people. If you wish to join the party, you must be in tune with the regulations. (N-4)

This informant stated that he had been willing to join the party, because at that time he "believed what the Communists said very much"; however, he said that he never accepted their view about family, "about giving up his brothers, sisters, and parents." Another, a former Nationalist soldier, declared that he never believed what the Communists said about the Nationalist army, although he "believed it all about the land reform making the poor and rich the same, and that everyone would be comfortable" (N-12).

Failure to see implications.—Other informants, including party members, who agreed with the general body of ideology as they understood it did so only superficially—that is, they were willing to subscribe to it verbally, without having explored what practical meaning it might have in their lives. As has been suggested, they could hold attitudes and beliefs which conflicted with Communist ideology without being fully aware of the conflict. Thus, one of the stauncher Communist supporters expressed an attachment to his family and a desire to return home which are in fact inconsistent with Communist discipline. He was somewhat concerned about whether he would be allowed to go home when repatriated, but he had never had to face the conflict on a practical level and had rationalized it out of existence.

Changes in Basic Orientation toward the Regime.—The developmental history of informants' attitudes often included a movement from one basic orientation to another; there are numerous examples of men who moved from conformity based on agreement to conformity based on fear, and several examples of informants who ceased to agree when something made them aware of the concrete, personal implications of ideological tenets they had verbally accepted or simply ignored. The execution of parents, observation of extreme punishment and unnecessary brutality, the disappointment of expectations for professional advancement, or simply concluding that "the Communists consistently did things very differently than they said" precipitated the change of several informants from sympathizers to non-sympathizers.

Whenever this happened, the psychological problems faced by the individual became similar to those of men whose adaptation had been complicated by disagreement from the beginning. They were then confronted with the necessity of affirming goals they did not approve and demonstrating loyalty to an organization they disliked. In short, they were forced to deceive. A party member described this transition as follows.

> In the beginning when I was just a simple recruit I believed everything they said and I did everything from the bottom of my heart.
> . . . No deception was necessary. . . . But in time you find that . . .
> when the organization tries to teach the people they use deceit, and in time you learn deception yourself. (N-2)

Non-sympathizers

Problems in Adjustment Created by Non-agreement.—At the same time that men were confronted with the demand to say what the Communists want them to say, they also faced the demand to do what the Communists want them to do and even the requirement always to look very happy. Informants did not react or adapt to the demand for conformed communications in isolation from other aspects of Communist control; they reacted and adapted to the totality of the demands made upon them. However, here we will limit our attention to the demand for conformed communications and to the problems which arose in adapting to it, keeping in mind that these problems were often, if not usually, complicated or simplified by other demands.

The feelings that accompanied the realization that communications must be controlled on pain of punishment were often strong. They also led quickly to conformity. Soldiers whose conformity was based on fear reacted both to the content of ideology and to the procedures which enforced participation.

Content of ideology.—For the man who did not agree, difficulty in disciplining his communications behavior depended on how closely what he had to say impinged on his life. Abstract ideological content created few problems, but the Communist insistence on the application of general principles to everyday acts often led to significant conflict. Generally, men disliked charging themselves or groups with which they identified (for example, the Nationalist army) with crimes for which they were not responsible or giving assent to propositions they believed to be wrong. Although lip service was granted readily in most cases, instances occurred in which the demand that an informant say or write some specific thing assumed a great importance to him and increased resentment against the regime. A former Nationalist officer described such an instance as follows.

> I . . . wrote a . . . letter to my old squad members in my old unit [who were also undergoing indoctrination at the hands of the Communists]. I urged these men to accept the Communist program, so that they might benefit and work for the people. I told them I had given up everything to work and to learn under the new Communist system. The Communists used . . . [the letter] to convince my former soldiers to follow their bidding. They are diabolically clever. They destroy all personal relationships and feelings. After such an action, I could no longer reorganize my men to resist even if I tried. I am convinced the men would not respond after the letter I wrote. The loyalty that used to be between us was destroyed. . . .
>
> I knew that . . . the men . . . would not hold me strictly responsible for the letter I had written, because they too had realized that I had been forced to do what I did. Nevertheless, it broke up something between us. . . .
>
> I felt a great bitterness growing in me toward the whole system, and my desire for revenge was strengthened. . . . At the time of writing the letter, I knew there was no alternative. I must write it or perish. I became aware then of the great deception by the Communists. From that time on . . . my resolve was strengthened to fight the Communists with everything I had. (N-1)

Procedures for enforcing participation.—Although sympathizers tended to approve not only the content of ideology but also the procedures for insuring participation, non-sympathizers tended to do the reverse. To the latter, such procedures as the airing of grievances and criticism meetings were distasteful as such, quite apart from the content of their communications. In other words, whereas sympathizers tended to view such meetings as valuable and instructive, even when they led to personal embarrassment or discomfort, non-sympathizers tended to view them as one more part of the Communist effort to control their lives and reduce them to helplessness. Their failure to identify with the aims of the meetings made participation in them additionally painful, although the initial shock diminished gradually in the process of adjustment.

Overt Adjustments.—Regardless of their feelings about the content or the mechanisms of ideological participation, all informants agreed on the futility of opposition. All became extremely alert to ways and means of protecting themselves. Unsympathetic respondents quickly developed protective instincts which enabled most of them to stay out of serious trouble.

> In the first place, in actual work you must be a most aggressive worker. That is easy. When you are told to do something, you just jump right up and do it; in case there are meetings, you will be the first to voice all the slogans. The most important thing is that you learn to deceive. You become a master in deception, and even then you might make a mistake at times. If you do, the moment you discover you have made a mistake, you are the first one to admit you made a mistake. (N-2)

Overt conformity, as the above passage suggests, involves several elements. Essentially, the soldiers who were unsympathetic to Communism had to deceive their masters. A first and important way of doing this was by becoming a vigorous and uncomplaining worker. This led to the paradoxical situation in which the very process of alienation drove soldiers to devote more intense effort to their assigned tasks—a reaction whose immediate consequences were obviously favorable to the regime.

In addition, the non-sympathizers had to learn to control both their speech and their emotions. As they became more accustomed to the requirements and absorbed correct speaking from every side, the possibilities of making mistakes were diminished; conformity became less difficult.

Familiarity also led to increased skill in self-protection. In criticism meetings, for example, informants learned to speak in such a way that they avoided the more painful aspects of criticism. In short, they learned to manipulate the system to some extent—even if only by conforming or humiliating themselves further.

It is clear, however, that unsympathetic informants never mastered the process of criticism to such a degree that it no longer threatened them. Nor did confession and criticism ever become so habitual that they no longer constituted a psychological threat. These men were able to take the edge off fear chiefly by so behaving that they did not incur disapproval; only within that framework were they able to manipulate the control machinery.

Subjective Adjustments.—Inevitably, the constant effort to censor one's own speaking and the anxiety which accompanied it increased the dissident individual's general feeling of insecurity under Communist control. It became one more factor contributing to the fearful state in which many of our informants described themselves as having lived.

The impossibility of overtly expressing disagreement led to its suppression; sometimes it reappeared in fantasies, dreams, and slips of the tongue. One informant said that during the period of intensive thought reform he preserved hope by endlessly repeating to himself a fantasy. At the same time that he drove himself to extreme exhaustion in his efforts to win security through hard physical labor and through confessions that humiliated him greatly.

Also expressed in dreams was the feeling of being boxed in, threatened, without means of escape; in addition, such dreams exposed the hostility of informants to their new masters.

The confrontation with a totally new world view and the necessity of affirming it in all speaking and overt behavior made some informants miserable, fearful, and dumb and feelingless. The assault on their emotions which this entailed did not, however, result in paralyzing the individuals with conflicts too intense for them to handle. Although one informant described former Nationalist officers who lost their senses or committed suicide in intensive reindoctrination schools (N-1), this reaction seems not to have been widespread even in these schools and is not reported at all in other circumstances.

SUMMARY

By all odds the most impressive aspect of the adjustment to the demand for ideological participation is the near universality and the high degree of conformity with which that demand was met. From the perspective of much of our Western psychological theory, the respondents' ability to conform without serious psychic disturbance is somewhat surprising. They were required to control their speaking and even their facial expressions at the same time that other severe and total demands were made on them, and all in a context of punishment for non-conformity. The goals, values, and orientations they were asked to affirm and reflect in their speech were disharmonious and inconsistent with those of traditional Chinese culture and, we may therefore assume, with those embodied in the basic personalities of the informants. But neither this demand nor the combination of demands nor their contrariety to traditional culture nor the pressure applied to secure their fulfillment broke the individuals in the respondent group. They did not create the psychic disorganization which would have made the informants unable to function; they did not produce psychosis.

Nor, it should be pointed out, is there any evidence that they had any consequences which were not objectively desirable from the point of view of the Communists. As long as disagreement led to redoubled efforts to conform in order to allay suspicion, disagreement did the regime no real harm. To the contrary, more zealous efforts by individuals actually reinforced the power of the regime. If anything, criticism meetings functioned better, surveillance was conducted more meticulously, and work was performed more adequately by the man anxious for his personal security. Nor was the regime weakened ideologically through overt disagreement with its tenets and principles; only very rarely did disaffection result in non-conformed communications.

Finally, failure of personnel to identify with Communist goals, even widespread opposition to these goals and to the government, does not lessen the organizational strength of Communist armies in situations where individual soldiers see no practicable means of escape. They tend to perform the tasks expected of them with perseverance and competence regardless of their subjective feelings about the masters they serve. Except in rare instances, the urge to stay out of trouble is controlling.[14]

[14] Cf. Edward A. Shils and Morris Janowitz, "Cohesion and Disintegration in the *Wehrmacht* in World War II," 12, 280–315, and Morris Janowitz and Lt. Col. Roger Little, *Sociology and the Military Establishment,* pp. 27–49 and 77–99. This conclusion is consistent with their view of the limited role that politics and ideology play in determining cohesion and military effectiveness. See Introduction for a more detailed discussion of this point.

PART III

Socio-Political Behavior of Koreans and Chinese as Prisoners of War

: V :

THE POLITICAL BEHAVIOR OF KOREAN AND CHINESE PRISONERS OF WAR IN THE KOREAN CONFLICT: A HISTORICAL ANALYSIS

Samuel M. Meyers & William C. Bradbury

PROBLEM AND METHOD

The behavior of Chinese and North Korean prisoners of war held by the United Nations in Korea during the Korean conflict created unique custodial and administrative problems for the detaining authorities. The rioting and other camp incidents attracted world-wide attention, and the resulting publicity partly obscured the U.N. political victory inherent in the prisoners' repatriation choices.[1]

The United States Army's need for a better understanding of the factors that motivated the PW's was emphasized in the research requirement that gave rise to these studies. This section deals with some of the questions implied in the army's request.

Problem

The Behavior To Be Explained

The army was interested in understanding the unexpected elements in the prisoners' group behavior, not in individual conduct as such. There were three unprecedented forms of group activity.

During the course of their imprisonment the PW's divided into militant factions, pro-Communist and anti-Communist. These factions fought bloody, life-and-death battles for domination of their prison compounds. While squabbles between individual prisoners or between

---

[1] Of the total PW population, two-thirds of the Chinese and one-third of the North Koreans refused repatriation to their Communist-controlled countries.

small groups of prisoners of course have occurred in modern warfare, PW's have tended for the most part to live peaceably under the conditions of internment.

The Communist-led prisoners resisted U.N. custodial authority persistently, violently, and in a highly disciplined way. Again, resistance against custodial authority by prisoners of war is by no means unknown in modern warfare. Such resistance, however, has generally been sporadic and passive, and has been carried out by individuals or small, informal groups of PW's rather than by highly organized groups.

Thousands of prisoners under anti-Communist leadership addressed urgent petitions to the United Nations as soon as a truce appeared likely, begging to be allowed to remain in non-Communist territory. In the last stages of the Korean conflict, the aggressive loyalty of these PW's to the government of the Republic of Korea or of Nationalist China, as the case might be, created serious problems for the U.N. custodial authorities. Resistance to repatriation has been almost unknown in modern warfare until the very recent past.

These three novel kinds of behavior are clearly interrelated. It seemed evident that if any one of them is to be understood it must be considered in the context of the other two, and that the research must deal to a considerable extent, if not equally, with all three.

The Sequence of Development

None of these forms of prisoner behavior could have sprung into being fully developed; each must have matured over time and been affected by the changing environment. To gain an understanding of the prisoners' actions, it was necessary to examine the processes by which they developed—systematically to reconstruct the chronological sequence of developments within the PW compounds.

Focus on Political Organization

Preliminary examination revealed one ingredient which was both common to, and essential to, all the unprecedented forms of behavior—militant, disciplined, politically directed organization. Past instances of PW feuds or resistance have not involved the large-scale organization which characterized both Communist and anti-Communist groups in Korea.

The organized aspect of PW activity is usually highly visible, in contrast to more covert, subconscious aspects of motivation and behavior. For the researcher this means that organization can be effectively studied; he can examine and analyze such behavior more readily than covert or unorganized aspects.

Although Communist organization was the more urgent practical problem for the U.N. Command in Korea, this research is concerned equally with anti-Communist prisoner organization.

For early in the research it became apparent that the anti-Communist organization could be neither ignored nor studied only superficially, because the development and activities of the Communist PW organization in Korea were in part a response to the development of the anti-Communist organization and the conduct of PW's under anti-Communist leadership.

Period Covered

A preliminary survey of the available data showed that existing military publications document the behavior of the prisoners of war far more adequately for the last fifteen months of the conflict than for the first twenty-two months. Major changes were made in PW policy and administration during the summer of 1952; these changed the conditions under which the prisoners acted and at the same time substantially improved reporting. As the research progressed, it became apparent that developments in PW organization and behavior after the spring of 1952 followed a line which, given the new conditions, was predictable from what had gone before.

These facts made it evident that the major aspect of reconstructing the motivation and conditions of political organization in the compounds would be the study of the period from June, 1950, the beginning of the Korean conflict, to June, 1952. This report deals primarily with this period.

Method

Although the approach was one of historical reconstruction, the central task was to interpret the causal relations operative within the unique historical setting. The core of the problem is: Why did the prisoners of war create and use politically directed organizations within the compounds, and why did these organizations become the dominant elements in the life of the camps?

When this project was initiated, almost no systematic study had been done on the motivation of the Korean and Chinese PW's. Resources for such study were, however, limited and field conditions restricted the choice of techniques.

The researchers decided to begin their reconstruction of the conditions responsible for the growth of militant organizations in the prison compounds by discovering how the prisoners themselves perceived the sequence of events. More than a hundred PW's were interviewed. Documents written by prisoners, and transcripts of army interviews with prisoners were obtained.

To permit the cross-checking of information from various perspectives, the researchers also interviewed U.S. military personnel who held key positions in the camp administration, and utilized existing army documents relating to camp administration and prisoner behavior. U.S. press coverage of events in the prison compounds comprised a final source of data.

Analysis

The analysis on which this report is based had two principal parts:

To reconstruct, for each compound and enclosure on which data had been collected, the sequence of reported events with respect to the development of political organizations (for example, shifts in prisoner motivation, group formation, U.N. administrative decisions, transfers of personnel, conflicts between leaders).

To identify conditions and processes and PW feelings, wishes, and values that were found in more than one compound and that affected the development of organization.

Chronological Reconstruction.—For some compounds only the most fragmentary information could be collected; for others an almost bewildering variety of data was available. For most compounds there were important gaps as well as important bodies of information.

These compound stories were supplemented with two other types of information. First, the much better-known story of combat trends and related political developments, including the vicissitudes of the armistice negotiations, was placed alongside the compound histories as a major point of reference.[2] (The PW's had indicated the importance of these developments as a stimulus and condition of their conduct.) Second, information on the development of various forms of communication between groups in different compounds was assembled and related to the events in the compounds. (In part, the compounds were isolated, local communities of men—but only in part. Systematic study of the development of communication and concerted action among them was essential to the process of reconstruction.)

Identification of Common Conditions and Motives.—Along with specific historical information, a considerable number of accounts by both PW's and U.N. personnel contained general statements, asserted to apply either to PW behavior generally over a period of time or to numerous compounds at a given time. These statements provided the first hypotheses in the search for common conditions and motives. Many of them stood up when tested against the ordered data; others did not.

The first hypotheses examined were those which asserted a connection between factors in the camp environment and the developments in numerous compounds. Physical conditions of internment, changing U.N. administrative policies, the progress of the fighting and the truce talks—many elements under these headings were examined, and an effort was made to trace their influence, not only on the perceptions reported by PW's, but on organizational developments.

Next, the ways in which characteristics of the populations of the several compounds affected their organizational behavior were exam-

---

[2] See Appendix B for a general chronology of the Korean conflict.

ined. It became apparent that groups of North Korean officers, North Korean enlisted men, South Koreans, and Chinese reacted differently to the experience of internment; at the same time, important threads of similarity appeared.

At this point a hypothetical pattern of the development, through various stages, of political organization in a PW compound could be constructed. This pattern was then tested against the actual sequence of events in particular compounds and was refined and elaborated. New hypotheses concerning influential factors emerged, and these in turn were tested against the remainder of the historical data.

It now became possible to make maximum use of items which previously were only isolated fragments of data. Compound A and Compound B, for example, were alike in composition and in the timing and patterns by which formal Communist and anti-Communist groupings had developed. For A, the analysts had detailed information on the motives and actions of the PW leaders, but only fragments on rank-and-file attitudes and conduct; for B, they had the reverse. Since by this time a large number of the major factors influencing PW behavior had been identified, with two such similar compounds the analysts could attempt to test, for example, the hypothesis that the pattern known to exist in B with respect to rank-and-file motivation was duplicated in A.

In these ways both the phenomena and the generalizations of the study were filled out. Although significant gaps remained in the data, the variety of the data and the number of separate compound communities provided protection against serious error in generalization.

THE PRISONER POPULATION: ITS GROWTH AND ADMINISTRATION

Under what circumstances did the PW's come into the hands of the U.N. Command? What was the setting of combat and international negotiation in which the struggle for control of the PW camps developed? What were the principal objectives of the U.N. Command in administering the PW's?

Growth of the Prisoner Population

Throughout the first two months of the fighting in the summer of 1950, the South Korean army and U.S. units were falling back and taking few prisoners. Meanwhile, the advancing North Korean army was impressing into its combat units and labor battalions tens of thousands of captured South Korean soldiers and civilians of military age.

When American forces attacked at Inchon in September, 1950, however, almost the whole North Korean army was cut off from its bases and lines of retreat, and prisoners of war began to be registered by the U.N. Command in great numbers: 104,000 in October alone, an additional 20,000 in the next two months. More than 90 per cent of the eventual total of 150,000 Korean prisoners were in U.N. hands by the end of 1950, and 97 per cent by July, 1951, when truce talks began. (See Figure 1.) [3]

Eleven Chinese PW's were registered as early as October, 1950, before Chinese units were committed in battle. The number of Chinese PW's did not begin to mount substantially, however, until the Communists launched their abortive "Fifth Phase" offensive the following spring. In April, May, and June alone, 15,000 prisoners were taken. Of the eventual total of 21,000 Chinese captives, 85 per cent had been taken by the time the truce talks began.

In July, 1951, at the beginning of the truce talks, the U.N. forces held 162,000 prisoners, Korean and Chinese, and by the end of the year that figure had risen to a combined total of 170,000. Through 1952 and 1953 the prisoner population did not grow significantly. The small number who died or escaped roughly balanced the trickle of deserters and captives taken in occasional flurries of ground fighting. Thus, by the time the war was a year old, the U.N. Command had taken 95 per cent of all its prisoners.

The Long Wait

Of the enemy soldiers interned in the first year of the conflict, the great majority—the Koreans—had had ample reason at time of capture to believe a U.N. victory was imminent and certain. Many of the Chinese taken during the punishing action of 1951 apparently believed their army was disintegrating. Whatever their hopes or fears, however, these men had more than two years to wait before the fighting ended.

As later sections will make clear, the progress of the truce talks profoundly influenced developments in the prison camps. Before the end of July, 1951, the negotiators agreed on an agenda. After four more difficult months, they agreed on a tentative cease-fire line and began to make progress on the question of guarantees for the security of a truce.

When discussion of the exchange of prisoners of war began, in December, 1951, the U.N. count showed 132,000 PW's eligible for repatriation. Actually the U.N. Command held 170,000 persons in its PW camps, but 38,000 of these were persons of South Korean origin who had already been screened by the South Korean government and found eligible for release as non-Communist soldiers or civilians. Their disposition was not to be negotiated with the enemy. Of the 132,000 for whom an exchange procedure had to be agreed on, about 21,000 were Chinese and the remainder Koreans. [4]

Early in January, 1952, the U.N. negotiators proposed an exchange based on the principle of free choice by the individual PW. This was immediately rejected by the Communists, and a long period of unproductive wrangling began.

[3] Also see Appendix A and Figure 2.
[4] *New York Times*, Dec. 18, 1951–Jan. 29, 1952; Public Information Office, Headquarters, U.N. Command, *Korean Chronology; Stars and Stripes*, Dec. 31, 1951.

Chronological Developments and Cumulative Total of Prisoners of War

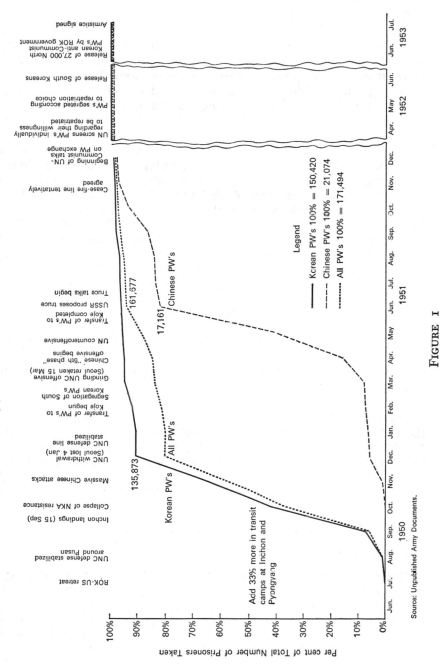

Source: Unpublished Army Documents.

FIGURE I

In March, 1952, when the PW deadlock appeared to be the only remaining major obstacle to a cease-fire, the U.N. Command undertook, with the partial acquiescence of the Communist side, to find out through interrogation how many of the PW's were determined forcibly to resist repatriation to Communist China or North Korea. Before the screening, loudspeaker broadcasts to the compounds carried Communist amnesty promises, and the U.N. Command stressed its own refusal to guarantee food, clothing, or shelter to those who refused to go home. The interrogation itself was worded in such a way as to maximize the number answering that they would consent to go home. Because of Communist-led resistance the PW's in eight large compounds could not be interrogated, but, of the tens of thousands screened in April, more than half said they would forcibly resist any effort to send them back.

The final figures, released after the Communist-controlled compounds had been broken up in June, 1952, were somewhat less unfavorable to the Communist side. Among the hundred thousand North Korean soldier captives, two-thirds consented to being returned to Communist control. Of the forty-nine thousand prisoners who had been classified as South Koreans, about one-fifth indicated willingness to be sent north. But more than two-thirds of the twenty-one thousand Chinese PW's refused to go back to mainland China and the Communists.

In May, 1952, the U.N. negotiators offered a package deal designed to compromise all the remaining major disagreements that stood in the way of a cease-fire. Among its provisions was the proposal that the PW's who had refused repatriation should be moved to a neutral zone in neutral custody and there listen to Communist "explanations" before finally committing themselves on their futures.

The negotiations remained deadlocked, however, primarily because the Chinese Communist high command continued to insist upon the forcible repatriation of all PW's. During the summer of 1952 the U.N. Command released thirty-eight thousand anti-Communist South Koreans and civilian internees to the Republic of Korea. For 132,000 PW's, however, there was another long year of waiting. Not until July, 1953, did the Communist negotiators accept substantially the U.N.'s package.

Prisoner-of-War Administration

Objectives of Administration

Like most of the other organizational and logistical burdens of the Korean conflict, that of administering the PW population fell to the U.S. Army. Although the United States had not yet ratified the 1949 Geneva Convention Relative to the Treatment of Prisoners of War,[5] American forces were in Korea as representatives of the United Nations, and it was inevitable that they would be ordered to adhere to the provisions of

[5] The 1949 Geneva Conventions for the Protection of War Victims were ratified by the United States in 1955 and came into effect in February, 1956.

the convention. Within a week of the U.N. and U.S. decision to aid South Korea, General Douglas MacArthur as U.N. Commander announced that captured enemy personnel "will be treated in accordance with the humanitarian principles applied by and recognized by civilized nations involved in armed conflict." Three weeks later he directed his field commanders that "the handling of prisoners of war will be in accordance with the 1949 Geneva Convention," and the International Committee of the Red Cross was notified to this effect.

Humanity: The Geneva Convention.—The Convention became the basis and the limiting factor for all policy decisions affecting the handling of the PW's. Through the several changes in the organizational identity and echelon of prisoner-of-war administration the provisions of the Convention remained the guide, and International Red Cross officials were constantly inspecting the camps to see that the provisions were adhered to. What kind of policy, then, did the Convention require? [6]

The agreement on prisoners of war is one of four Conventions for the Protection of War Victims drawn up in 1949. The memory of Nazi brutality was fresh at Geneva, and all the conventions are aimed primarily at the protection of the victim's physical well-being and elementary rights and dignity.

Under its provisions, prisoners of war are to be evacuated to safety in the rear at the earliest possible moment and under humane conditions. Their quarters are to be as good as those of the forces of the detaining power in the same area. Food, clothing, and sanitary measures must be such as to keep the PW's in good health. Medical facilities must be adequate and always available.

All prisoners must be "treated alike, without any adverse distinction based on race, nationality, religious belief or political opinions, or any other distinction founded on similar criteria" (Article 16).

PW's should be given deference in accordance with their rank and age and allowed to keep badges of nationality and rank. If required to work, they must be paid a fair rate and working conditions must be reasonable. They may be assigned only to certain types of work; officers may not be required to work. "While respecting the individual preferences of every prisoner, the Detaining Power shall encourage the practice of intellectual, educational, and recreational pursuits, sports and games," and provide premises and equipment (Article 38).

Every collection of PW's must have a prisoners' representative, who may communicate at will with the detaining authorities and the neutral body which ensures observance of the convention. An officer PW group is represented by the senior officer; in an enlisted group the representative is elected every six months by secret ballot. The representative may

[6] The following summary is based on Department of the Army Pamphlet No. 20–150, *Geneva Conventions of 12 August 1949 for the Protection of War Victims,* October, 1950, pp. 84–161.

appoint assistants, and all PW's must have access to him. All have the right to petition the detaining authorities and the neutral inspecting body at will concerning the conditions of captivity. By implication, furthermore, the convention grants prisoners the right to organize themselves "for mutual assistance," for it places such organization within the purview of the representative.

While PW's are subject to the regulations governing the armed forces of the detaining power, in allotting punishment for violations the detaining authorities are urged to be lenient and to take full account of the fact that the PW owes no allegiance to them.

Orders written in the language of the PW's must be posted where all can see them. Collective punishments for individual acts and collective punishments affecting food or involving corporal punishment, torture, and cruelty are prohibited. Disciplinary (administrative) punishment may not exceed thirty days' confinement. For all more serious offenses the PW must be tried by court-martial, and must have counsel and the right of appeal. The use of weapons against prisoners is to be regarded as an extreme measure to be employed only after adequate warning.

Copies of the convention must be posted so that all PW's know their rights. No prisoner may renounce his guaranteed rights.

In short, the administration of prisoners of war is conceived of by the convention—and was conceived of by American officers at the start of the Korean conflict—as a straightforward custodial task to be carried out as humanely as possible. PW's are perceived as victims of war and non-belligerents; the principal task is that of guaranteeing conditions of confinement such that prisoners can be repatriated at the close of hostilities in good physical and mental health. Clearly, the authors of the convention did not contemplate the possibility of deep political or other conflicts within the PW society, with the accompanying urgent problems for the custodial authorities.

Security.—The Geneva Convention assumes rather than includes the objective of security. The historically familiar form of the problem of security for the detaining power is, of course, the danger that PW's will escape and rejoin their comrades in arms. Through the first year of the Korean conflict, security seemed the least of the difficulties facing the U.N. custodial authorities. Later it was to become their most serious problem, but in a novel form—that of acutely embarrassing, highly organized harassment and rioting.

Civilian Information and Education.—The objectives of the Geneva Convention were not, however, the only objectives adopted by the U.N. Command in its custody of the 170,000 Korean and Chinese PW's. A program of Civil Information and Education (CIE) was also initiated in the camps, only part of which was clearly in fulfillment of the spirit of the convention's Article 38. The program was first tried during the autumn of 1950, when several hundred selected North Korean PW's headed by a colonel were given a speeded-up orientation course. This course was introduced into all the PW compounds the following summer.

The CIE program was designed "to develop . . . an understanding and appreciation of the political, social, and economic objectives of the United Nations and to assist (the prisoners) in various other ways so that they may become better citizens in their country." [7] The "various other ways" included literacy training, varied vocational training, and an extensive program of athletics, drama, art, music, and literature. These activities constituted the bulk of the CIE program, but were introduced only after the orientation course had been started.

The special and frankly political objective of the CIE program was expressed primarily in the orientation course. The purposes of this course were spelled out by the operational chief of the program in briefing American custodial officers on Koje-do:

The CI&E Program is based upon a number of long-range aims, governing all activities and procedures in the program. In general we intend to win confidence, understanding, and cooperation for the U.N. and provide the POWs with as complete a knowledge as possible of the United Nations. We mean to provide an ideologic orientation towards an orderly, responsible, progressive, peaceloving, and democratic society. We wish to promote a comprehension of, faith in, and adoption of the concepts, institutions, and practices of democracy. Specifically we would like to see these people develop a conviction that they and their people will be better off socially, politically, and economically under a democratic rather than totalitarian regime. We would also like to see develop a support of an independent, democratic, unified Korean nation.[8]

Although the majority of the prisoners were apathetic toward the orientation program, the expression of its political objectives became, as we shall see in later description of the CIE program, a major focus of conflict in the PW camps. For the present it is enough to note that this program was implemented in 1951 and that its purposes were added to, not implied by, the purposes of the Geneva Convention.

Organization for Administration

Throughout the Korean conflict, the principal unit for PW administration was the PW camp—a single command responsible for the security of all PW's within its area. Each camp was divided into a number of enclosures, each of which was in turn subdivided into several compounds. The number of compounds per enclosure varied greatly. During the period covered by this report, the enclosure was normally com-

---

[7] Letter quoted in unpublished army report.
[8] Speech by Chief, Field Operations Division, CIE, 1951.

manded by a field-grade officer, the compound by a lieutenant who had some enlisted assistants. Within the compound, the PW's were organized, for administrative purposes, into regiments (sometimes equivalent to the compound), battalions, and companies—the last usually having about 250 members each. The PW's commonly organized themselves into platoon and squad units.

Chronic Conditions Affecting Administration

Three factors which characterized the operation of the PW camps require mention here, because they strongly affected U.S. command decisions and the interaction between PW's and custodial authorities.

Shortage of Manpower.—The U.S. Army Forces in the Far East never had adequate manpower for the tasks they had to perform in the Korean conflict. Although the shortage was particularly acute in the first few months of hostilities, service functions suffered throughout the first year because of the pressure of combat requirements. PW administration seems to have had a low priority even among the service functions. Camp commanders were forced to operate with ratios of guards to prisoners far lower than those prescribed by doctrine and experience; they repeatedly reported to higher headquarters the security risks thus created.[9] It is perhaps significant, however, that they were not so conscious of a need for more administrative personnel.

Shortage of Language and Culture Skills.—The shortage of manpower was qualitative as well as quantitative. Few officers and enlisted men assigned to PW duty were trained for it; some of the latter were excessively difficult to train. For the purposes of this report, the most significant deficiency—which the PW administration shared with numerous other commands—was the lack of U.S. personnel capable of communicating with the prisoners. Of the personnel assigned to PW work, almost none could speak Korean and very few could speak either Japanese (understood by Koreans) or Chinese. Camp commanders had to depend principally on PW's and indigenous employees to interpret their orders to the prisoners and the prisoners' habits and requests to them.

The shortage of language skills was also symptomatic of a pervasive ignorance of Korean and Chinese patterns of thinking, values, and social relations; furthermore, it seriously inhibited the learning that was needed to overcome that ignorance. Lack of language and culture skills by the authorities was a major factor in the developments in the camps.

Inadequate PW Records.—During the three months following the Inchon landings, 126,000 PW's were taken. The urgency of front-line requirements and the rapid movement of the front, shortage of custo-

---

[9] For example, the Interview 0–9 (with an officer who commanded UNC POW Camp No. 1 at Pusan and Koje-do); unpublished army report.

dial personnel, and unfamiliarity with Korean names and places [10] made effective processing impossible. War crimes investigators who worked in the camps during the winter of 1950–51 had to establish their own rosters; [11] it is not known when reliable rosters were established for all compounds. Rosters were repeatedly upset by large-scale transfers, and further confused by the willingness of many PW's to be known by any number of names and by the absence of a standard method for transliterating Korean and Chinese names into English.

Furthermore, no method existed for ascertaining the identity of individual PW's; while systematic photographing and fingerprinting were begun in July, 1950, the sudden influx of thousands of PW's after the Inchon landing made it necessary for U.N. custodial personnel to divert attention from the orderly processing of prisoners to the more urgent task of feeding and housing the large PW population. For this and related reasons, systematic photographing and fingerprinting were not completed until the spring of 1953. [12]

Throughout much of the period, therefore, compound commanders could not identify prisoners reliably; PW's could switch identities or adopt aliases without fear of detection by the Americans.

The Four Phases of Prison Camp History

Apart from the general objectives and conditions governing the administration of the PW's, little can be said that applies to the whole history of the camps. That story is divided into four sharply distinct phases, and the differences among them are basic to the sections that follow.

Pusan and the Advance Camps: July to November, 1950

Construction of the first PW enclosure began in July, 1950, in Pusan. Before the Inchon landings, there were only about two thousand PW's to be accommodated in the beleaguered city. As the U.N. forces advanced northward and mopped up in the south during the fall, however, transit stockades were organized at Inchon and in the North Korean cities of Pyongyang and Wonsan, and six new enclosures were created in Pusan. At the end of October there were thirty-three thousand prisoners at Inchon and twenty-one thousand at Pyongyang in addition to the sixty-three thousand in Pusan. [13]

Physical and logistical conditions in all the camps were extremely poor. The Pyongyang camp was a group of factory or warehouse build-

---

[10] "There must have been 3,000 Kim Il Somebody-or-others in Pusan that winter," said the camp commander (Interview o–9).

[11] Interview with Captain Pak Chang Mo, an English-speaking South Korean officer. At the time of his service he held the rank of lieutenant, and he will be so identified in text descriptions of his experiences.

[12] Unpublished army POW study.

[13] Unpublished army diary.

ings, partly destroyed by U.S. bombing and surrounded by a hastily
strung barbed-wire fence. At Inchon, PW's were first housed in a prison.
Then a small tent city was constructed for the overflow, and finally a
damaged factory building was commandeered. Rations were irregular in
the advance camps and non-Oriental in all; sanitation was primitive.

Despite the improvisation, crowding, and poor supply, planning or
reorganizing prisoner-of-war administration did not appear to be necessary since it seemed unlikely that the conflict would last long. Both
PW's and captors assumed that the struggle would be over in a matter
of weeks. Then, in November, the massive Chinese attacks began. The
advance camps were evacuated and all PW's were hastily shipped to
Pusan.

Pusan: December, 1950 to Spring, 1951

The population of Camp No. 1—the Pusan enclosures—swelled from
63,000 at the end of October to about 135,000 by the end of December.
By this time there were five major enclosures and several smaller ones
scattered around the city and its outskirts. Crowding was universal, but
the extremely serious logistical problems were gradually brought under
control.

As war news filtered in to the PW's they began to realize that the war
would not be over soon, and their life began to take on a semblance of
order and organization. Here the basis was laid for the more dramatic
events that were to occur during the third phase of internment.

The United Nations Command, too, was beginning to plan for a long
struggle. The Chinese Communists had flatly rejected the U.N. General
Assembly's appeal for a cease-fire; their armies were clearly larger and
more formidable than those of North Korea had been, and the political
difficulties of the conflict had been multiplied by their intervention.
Moreover, Pusan was the principal U.N. port for both supplies and
personnel; the presence of large numbers of enemy personnel along
with tens of thousands of Korean refugees created confusion and risk
for the U.N. forces. In January, 1951, therefore, it was decided that the
prisoners should be removed from the mainland to the relative
safety—for both them and their captors—of the island of Koje, some
thirty air miles from Pusan. Only the sick, wounded, and some labor
and administrative personnel were to remain in Pusan.[14]

In the spring the South Koreans were segregated. They were to live in
an enclosure of their own on Koje-do, and they were moved to special
compounds while still on the mainland.

Koje-do: Spring, 1951, to April, 1952

Construction of the new enclosures was begun during the winter;
larger and larger PW groups were transported by boat to the new

---

[14] Unpublished army report.

locations, where they first built shelters for themselves and then built compounds for others who were to follow. By May, 1951, the great majority of the PW's had been moved to the island prison camp. Most of the Chinese PW's, now coming in from the front by the trainload, stopped in Pusan only long enough for preliminary processing or medical treatment.

Each of the Koje compounds provided far more elbow room for its inmates than had those in Pusan. At the same time, all the four huge enclosures were within relatively easy reach of headquarters. In this new Camp No. 1,[15] approximately 150,000 PW's spent a year or more. Here the factional struggles broke into the open; here appeared the mass petitions and other evidences of widespread anti-Communism which strengthened the decision of the United States to hold out against forcible repatriation; and here began the large-scale Communist harassing tactics which sometimes made Koje-do a combat and psychological warfare front as important as the quiescent one along the 38th parallel.

In response to these events, the U.N. Command adopted a series of new policies. During the winter of 1951–52 it began to place in special, segregated compounds prisoners identified as active Communist agitators in compounds controlled by non-Communists. A few months later it systematically screened the PW's to identify and segregate those who would forcibly resist repatriation.[16] At the time of screening the very large Koje compounds (some of which contained from eight thousand to ten thousand PW's) were broken up and the prisoners divided into smaller, more readily manageable units. Finally, also at the time of the screening, the command began to disperse the population widely in a series of new camps on the mainland and on other islands. At this point the prisoners were placed in camps according not only to nationality but to repatriation choice.

The Post-Screening Dispersed Camps May, 1952, to Summer, 1953

Shipment of PW's from Koje began in late April; the removal of all PW's to smaller compounds and the dispersal of camps were completed in June, after the forcible breakup of eight Communist-controlled holdout compounds. (See Figure 2.)

Communist demonstrations continued in the camps for repatriates. The thirty-eight thousand South Koreans and civilian internees were released during the summer of 1952. Then in June, 1953, before the fighting ended, some twenty-seven thousand non-repatriate North Koreans were released by their South Korean guards on the orders of the South Korean government, in an action which almost upset the signing

[15] Pusan was also still a part of Camp No. 1, but the bulk of the compounds, as well as camp headquarters, were located on Koje-do. Later the Pusan enclosures were renamed Camp No. 2.

[16] Excluded from this screening were prisoners in the eight Communist-controlled compounds, where the PW's prevented the screening personnel from entering.

Location and Type of PW Camps as of 18 August 1952

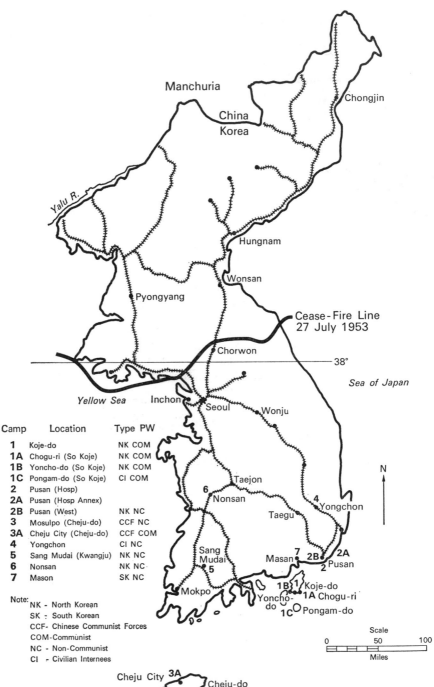

Camp	Location	Type PW
1	Koje-do	NK COM
1A	Chogu-ri (So Koje)	NK COM
1B	Yoncho-do (So Koje)	NK COM
1C	Pongam-do (So Koje)	CI COM
2	Pusan (Hosp)	
2A	Pusan (Hosp Annex)	
2B	Pusan (West)	NK NC
3	Mosulpo (Cheju-do)	CCF NC
3A	Cheju City (Cheju-do)	CCF COM
4	Yongchon	CI NC
5	Sang Mudai (Kwangju)	NK NC
6	Nonsan	NK NC
7	Mason	SK NC

Note:
NK - North Korean
SK - South Korean
CCF- Chinese Communist Forces
COM- Communist
NC - Non-Communist
CI - Civilian Internees

FIGURE 2

of the truce. In August, however, the repatriates were shipped north to exchange points, and the following month the non-repatriates were moved up to the demilitarized zone to listen to the explanations of their former Communist rulers. A few changed their minds, but the vast majority sought asylum in South Korea and Taiwan.

The events of this fourth phase contributed to the urgency of the questions this chapter seeks to answer; however, the answers are believed to lie in the conditions, moods, policies, and social evolution that characterized the first three phases of the internment experience.

THE PRISONER POPULATION:
THE MEN WHO COMPRISED IT

Who were the PW's? Of the approximately 170,000 PW's in U.N. hands in early 1952, approximately 21,000 were Chinese and the remainder Korean. The Koreans included two distinct groups—about 100,000 soldiers of the North Korean army whose homes were in North Korea, and about 49,000 persons whose homes were in South Korea.

The South Korean prisoners were of three types: soldiers who had been captured and impressed into service by the North Koreans during its initial southward advance; civilians who had been impressed into North Korean army combat or labor units; and civilians rounded up by the U.N. forces, mainly in the fighting after the Inchon landings, on suspicion of being North Korean soldiers who were trying to avoid capture by changing clothes. North and South Koreans, indistinguishable at the time of capture, were initially interned together. Not until early 1951, when hope of a quick end to the conflict faded, was action begun to segregate them, and it was the summer of 1952 before 38,000 loyal South Koreans and civilian internees were released. This group therefore constitutes part of the subject matter of this report.

What were these PW's like—for instance, in age, social background, education, military experience? The variety and urgency of the problems faced by the custodial authorities ruled out attempts to find out in detail the characteristics of their charges, and no complete census was ever made. However, a good deal of information can now be brought together from partial censuses, special-purpose surveys, and interview material.

The Koreans

Demographic Data [17]

The typical Korean PW had grown up on a small farm and regarded himself as a farmer. He was married. Under the Japanese occupation he

---

[17] These data are from the first Korean General Survey report, June 5, 1952, an element in the evaluation of the CIE program. Conducted in March, 1952, on

had received about four years of schooling. He had been in the North Korean army for less than six months.[18] He was twenty-four years old when captured in the fall of 1950.

Fewer of the North Koreans (8 per cent) than of the South Koreans (17 per cent) were illiterate. At the same time, three-fourths of the North Koreans were farmers (64 per cent) or unskilled laborers (10 per cent), whereas about one South Korean out of three was a skilled worker, student, businessman, civil servant, or professional man. About 6 per cent of the North Koreans and 2 per cent of the South Koreans were professional soldiers. Fifty-seven per cent of the North Koreans and 41 per cent of the South Koreans were married.

Such comparisons do not, however, indicate the great diversity in the group. Although almost three out of four Korean PW's had had between one and six years of schooling, about 10 per cent had never attended school at all and 6 per cent had gone beyond the Korean middle school. Although more than 90 per cent of the 150,000 were between eighteen and thirty-five years of age, about 250 had not reached their fourteenth birthday when captured, and more than 1,500 were over forty-five.

Communist Experience

North Korea was occupied by Russian troops in 1945, and the process of Communization began almost at once. According to their statements, most of the Koreans interviewed disliked the Soviet occupation, principally because of the persistent excesses of the Russian troops but also because of the disruption of traditional routines and power relations. By 1948, however, Korean cadres were exercising authority, a North Korean people's government headed by Soviet-trained personnel was set up, and the Soviet troops withdrew.

Reported reactions to the satellite Communist regime varied all the way from total identification to total rejection. Most of the population seems to have been grateful for land reform, increased industrialization, and the façade of popular participation in government, but by no means to have fully identified with either the government or the North Korean Labor (Communist) party.

South Korea was occupied by U.S. troops until 1948, and governed

---

Koje-do, this survey covered 50,761 North Koreans—about half of the total—and 42,744, or almost 90 per cent, of the South Koreans.

One South Korean and several North Korean compounds, dominated by Communists, denied admission to the census takers and were not surveyed; they account for almost all the omissions. About one-third of the North Koreans and one-fifth of the South Koreans who were surveyed chose in April, 1952, to be sent to North Korea at the close of hostilities. Pro-Communist PW's are therefore represented to some extent in the survey data. In the text, percentages given for all Korean PW's are estimated from the survey findings on the basis of a two-to-one ratio of North Koreans to South Koreans.

[18] Most were, in fact, drafted either just before or just after the attack, and were thrown into battle almost immediately. As a group, they were not trained, much less professional soldiers.

thereafter by the Republic of Korea regime headed by President Syngman Rhee. Through the occupation and until early 1950, the Communist party operated above ground and fed on a variety of discontents. Its propaganda found a sizable audience, particularly in the universities and the cities. However, most of the South Korean PW's held by the U.N. Command had known Communism in practice for only a few weeks or months in 1950, as the victims and instruments of the invasion forces.

We shall have occasion to refer again to the spectrum of popular attitudes toward Communism as they emerged from these years between the wars. Here it is enough to point out that whereas most of the Korean PW's entered their internment with habits of passive obedience to authority, the group included both pro-and anti-Communists who wanted to act on their feelings.

The Chinese

Demographic Data [19]

The typical Chinese PW had, like his Korean counterpart, grown up on a small farm. However, he had received no more than two years of schooling and was almost or wholly illiterate. He had served a little over a year in the Communist army before being captured in May, 1951. Before that, however, he had served in the Nationalist armies; during the Communist sweep of 1949–50 he had been surrendered as part of a Nationalist unit and impressed into the Communist forces. Unlike the typical Korean PW, he thought of himself as a soldier rather than as a farmer. Although twenty-five years old when captured by the United Nations, he was still unmarried.

Like the Koreans, the Chinese PW's were not a homogeneous mass. Although 92 per cent of them fell in the eighteen–thirty-five age range, about one per cent were under eighteen at the time of capture and a slightly smaller number were over forty-five. Most (81 per cent) had three years or less of schooling, but 2 per cent had more than ten years. Forty-nine per cent came from northern China, 36 per cent from southwestern provinces. By occupation, 85 per cent had been soldiers or

[19] Data are from the first Chinese General Survey, an element in the evaluation of the CIE program. Report: March 28, 1952. Conducted in March, 1952, on Koje-do, the survey covered 16,768 PW's in Compounds 72 and 86—that is, 81 per cent of the Chinese interned by the U.N. Command at the time. Omitted were a work compound, a segregation compound for PW's identified as Communist agitators, new PW's still interned at Pusan, and hospitalized PW's.

One month after the survey, the PW's were interrogated about their willingness to be repatriated at the close of hostilities. About 27 per cent of all Chinese PW's, but only 17 per cent of those covered in this survey, declared themselves willing to be repatriated. Thus, the survey clearly under-represented PW's who were pro-Communist or pro-repatriation. We believe, however, that the results with respect to demographic variables can be generalized to the whole Chinese PW population with a high degree of probability.

farmers; almost 5 per cent had been students or professional men. Although nearly 20 per cent had seen less than a year of service in the Communist forces, one per cent had been in the People's Liberation Army for over five years.

Experience under Communism [20]

The extent and character of the exposure of the Chinese PW's to Communism varied a great deal more than those of the North Koreans. Almost two-thirds had been Nationalist soldiers, captured in the late stages of the civil war, given special reindoctrination ranging in length from a few weeks to a year, and then maneuvered into "volunteering" for the Communist army. Hundreds, however, were farm boys whose home areas had been overrun by the Communists between 1946 and 1949, whose families had benefited or suffered in the land reform movement, and who had "volunteered" only a few months before their capture by the U.N. forces. A few, as university students during the civil war, had been impressed by Communist propaganda and had voluntarily undergone systematic thought reform in order to make themselves eligible for official positions in the new order. Most of these had been disappointed to find themselves assigned by the party to military service. Other PW's had lived in areas where Communist guerillas were operating as early as 1940; voluntarily or otherwise, they had joined the guerillas and were now hardened veterans.

A substantial minority of these PW's—probably about one in four—were members of the Chinese Communist party. This did not, however, mean that they were dedicated Communists. On the contrary, although conformity to Communist demands was almost uniformly high, a very large proportion of the prisoners appear to have strongly disliked the party and government. The Communist cadres had systematically distrusted, closely watched, and discriminated against large groups among them: those who had served in the Nationalist forces for a long time or as officers, those who were sons of formerly well-to-do families, and the highly educated. The practical effects of these experiences will become apparent in the sections to follow.

Feelings toward Internment

The expectations with which the men began their captivity was another factor in the background of events in the PW camps. At the start, the majority appear to have shared the feeling of these two:

> I thought I would be killed, because I had been instructed for a long time before that the prisoners are killed.[21]

[20] For further development of the statements made in this section and relevant case material, see Bradbury and Kirkpatrick, Chapter 1, above.
[21] Interview KN-19.

> In the People's Army we were told that if we were captured by South Korean troops we would be killed immediately, so that is what I expected.[22]

The intensity of this fear is demonstrated by incidents like the following, which occurred in the PW hospital enclosure in Pusan.

> During the early operation of the hospital it became evident that the human waste must be disposed of by burial. Twenty PW laborers were assigned to the detail and marched outside . . . of the hospital guarded by two medical soldiers armed with carbines. During the course of the digging the prisoners were very quiet and solemn, exchanging a few little remarks and working very slowly and methodically. It was such a slow process that the NCO in charge was inclined to give up in disgust. After about four days of labor a 10×10×10 hole was finally completed. The detail was preparing to start another hole when a sanitary truck drove up and emptied its load.
>
> The reaction of the prisoners was unusual; several laughed hysterically and rolled on the ground. Others laughed loudly and pounded each other on the back. The prisoners had thought all along they were digging their own graves and would be executed, as they had been told by their leaders. Needless to say, the same detail dug the same size hole in one day instead of four thereafter.[23]

Although many Communist soldiers were skeptical about the propaganda that they would be killed, most did expect to be beaten and treated like animals. For example,

> I believed that I would be beaten up . . . if I became a POW. Although our company commander told us that we would be killed if we fell into their [U.N.] hands, I did not believe it because [as a Chinese Nationalist soldier] I had experience that POW's were not killed. But I believed that we would be beaten up, as they said that the imperialists used to beat the people and because, when I was in the Nationalist army, even though we did not kill the POW's we did beat them.[24]

A good many, despite these anxieties, had taken the chance of trusting the U.N. propaganda leaflets and come over on their own. The great majority, however, especially among the untrained, disorganized North Koreans, seem to have surrendered because the strain of combat was unbearable or because whole units found that they had no means of continuing their resistance. In any case, it seems likely that most of the newly captured prisoners were relieved and delighted when they found themselves whole and cared for by their captors:

[22] Interview quoted from unpublished army document.
[23] Unpublished army document.
[24] Unpublished army document.

> [When I fled to the U.N. side,] I drew a deep breath and murmured to myself, "So, I am alive." . . . Everybody seemed to be relieved from fear and threats and to enjoy their fate. After our daily work it was quite common for us to rest on our beds and talk with each other about how each of us had succeeded in escaping from the battlefield.[25]

On the other hand, the thousands of former South Korean soldiers who had been impressed by the North Koreans, the numerous South Korean civilians interned as a result of mistaken identity, and the uncertain number of anti-Communist defectors from the enemy forces were shocked to find themselves in prisoner-of-war enclosures. One interviewee (KN-33),[26] for example, had worked with the South Korean security police, rounding up remnants of the North Korean army, and was formally appointed to the South Korean national police. When the U.N. forces retreated under Chinese attacks, he accompanied them. At a check point set up to prevent infiltration, however, he was disarmed and made prisoner.

The pathetic petition [27] of a group of twelve North Koreans illustrates another consequence of the rapid movement of the front, and the need for rear-area security in an army that has had extensive experience with guerilla activity and that cannot communicate with the people it meets.

> [We were political prisoners of the North Korean regime, incarcerated in a cave. On 1950 15, October] we escaped from the cave, taking advantage of the opportunity that all the prisoner guards dispersed trying to escape from a U.N. forces air attack, which was done fortunately nearby. At that time we saw that U.N. forces, including the Korean Defense Army, were marching bravely toward the north; all the houses in every village hoisted the true Korean flags. On the way returning home, we cried loudly, "Republic of Korea forever! Hurrah for the U.N. forces!", welcoming the U.N. forces until our breasts broke. But alas! We were . . . made prisoners of war, suspected of being those remnants of defeated troops, who were plenty at the time.

A North Korean interviewee gave still another reason why, in his opinion, he should never have been interned. He claimed to have deserted from the Communist forces and said:

> I didn't expect to be a PW, because the North Korean Army is a puppet army. The South Korean Army had sovereignty to control all

[25] "Essays by Prisoners of War." Essay No. 1.
[26] From unpublished army document.
[27] Petition submitted to Commander of U.N. Command PW Camp No. 6 on November 27, 1952. We do not contend that this statement or any other of its kind made by PW's is true. Like the PW authorities, we have no means of checking the accuracy of such statements. The point here is simply that incidents of this kind did occur and that thousands of PW's felt, justifiably or not, that they had been interned by mistake or because "the Americans did not care about the people." U.S. combat officers in Korea uniformly agree that such incidents occurred and could not have been avoided in the circumstances.

of Korea. I expected to be judged by the South Korean government since I am anti-Communist. (KN-21)

Others, especially among the Chinese, felt that because they had defected and helped the U.N. forces materially they should receive preferential treatment. For example:

> I had been preparing for this [surrender] all along. When I walked across, it was the South Korean troops that took me. They interviewed me briefly and asked me about the activities along the front. . . . I had maps and everything, and they brought me to the Eighth Army Command. They interviewed me there. . . . I was very familiar with [the area in which they were fighting] . . . and described it in detail. Walking over with military maps, guns, and knowledge of the movement is quite different than being captured on the battlefield. I expected that I would be treated differently. I never expected I would be enclosed behind barbed wire. (CN-31)

Among the South Koreans, the sense of unjust imprisonment was strong. As the errors to which they attributed their plight were not remedied and their internment dragged on into its second year, this feeling became, as will be shown, a dominant factor in their organized behavior.

Whatever their feelings about internment, however, the PW's were remarkably docile and cooperative in the first stages of their captivity.

ON THE MAINLAND: CONDITIONS
OF INTERNMENT

The First Period: Pusan and the Advance Camps, Autumn, 1950

During the massive encirclement and advance of U.N. forces in the autumn of 1950, PW's were rounded up in great numbers. A South Korean army officer recalled seeing "thousands of PW's" in Pyongyang who "were frozen and in great hunger, for they had just been made PW's. A man could not look at them face to face because they were miserable beasts, looking dull and withered." [28] Accounts of the treatment of prisoners on and near the front are fragmentary. An absolute minimum of personnel could be assigned to PW duty, and techniques of handling PW's were necessarily primitive. [29]

Conditions were similarly poor at all the major collecting points and transit camps. Logistical support was erratic and inadequate. Because of the language barrier, orders were given by gross gestures and shoves more often than in words. Individual American soldiers, exasperated by

[28] Pak Chang Mo.
[29] A U.S. colonel reported that he was once in command of a very small unit which had twenty-five thousand prisoners in its charge. He laid a strand of barbed wire around the mass of prisoners, and assigned seven men to guard posts around the fence with orders to shoot to kill any PW who touched the wire.

failures of communication and often frightened by the masses of Koreans in their charge—although at this point the latter were passive and docile—sometimes used more physical violence than necessary.

The following is an autobiographical account of a highly educated Korean prisoner's experience in the fall of 1950. Although no account can be considered typical, this one is confirmed on principal points by many others. It may serve as a sample because it incorporates a variety of significant elements in the experience.

[After our capture,] we walked along the main street of Pyongyang, capital of North Korea. We could see nothing on the street but a few sentries. . . . [then] several barracks surrounded with barbed wire were seen silhouetted against the starry sky. The lines were proceeding forward and [were] absorbed in the ghastly-looking barracks. It was my turn. I walked a step inside [the door] and leaped up when I got a blow on my back with something hard.

"Hubba-Hubba!" It sounded like a screaming of a wild bird.

Many times I stumbled. The barrack was apparently a barn. On the bottom I found raw rice about three inches thick. There I spent two days in the darkness, eating the rice grain by grain in the way sparrows do. The rice provided us not only food but also warmth. The air was filled with a stinking smell, for all the men in the barn urinated and stooled in every corner.

Two days later, the door opened and a GI came in. Everybody kept themselves aloof from him. It was a really dramatic scene. Sunlight shone straight through a big hole in the wall which had been shattered, I suppose by air attack. And at the sunlit spot he was standing with a stick in his hand. He flourished the stick in the air and shouted something. I thought I had seen such a scene in some movie in the past, the title of which might be *A Ship-Load of Slaves.* I heard someone whisper: "I can see the nature in him with which they treated slaves for centuries."

We all went out of the barn and got a handful of cooked wheat in the hollow of our hands. I devoured it. No food ever tasted so delicious. . . . Though the quantity . . . was barely [sufficient] to keep our lives on, I would say the problem of eating was solved compared with the first two foodless days.

Severest of all was the coldness at night. To spend the long winter night without any heating apparatus was unendurable torture for us. The majority of PW's in the barn were wearing summer clothes because they had exchanged their warm, thick army clothes for light ones when they deserted their [North Korean units]. . . .

Another physical pain was want of drinking water. . . . Once a day, a water car came and filled two jars. . . . And a thousand PW's rushed for it and drew water with their hands. Nobody had any container or bowl. Somebody had a remnant of a beef can; in that barn the can was a lot of property. Anyhow, muscular strength was the essential thing in [getting] water to drink.

Men were walking about the barrack in search of food. Cigarettes were currency. We could get clothes, food, water, and anything . . . in the barn for cigarettes. There were many [small] groups, and if a man got a piece of cigarette it was handed around among twenty or more men. They inhaled all the smoke, never puffed, because smoking was forbidden.

This was the life in the barrack. Presently we had an opportunity to go out of this enclosure. Early in the morning, a GI came and took some PW's out. And when they returned, we were told that they worked at the airfield. They said: "We ate to our heart's content."

One of my fellows said: "In the midst of working I discovered a trash can full of empty cans and boxes. I found half-eaten remnants of butter, cheese, and bread in it." And he gave me scraps of bread.

Then at night, smoke was rising up from several spots where [various PW's had] started fires and were parching the cereals they had got. The owner of each fire watched it and took a certain per cent of commission [from those who used it]. This job was really nice. But it was accompanied by some danger in case of being discovered by a South Korean guard [because fires were strictly forbidden]. Thus life was gradually improving and getting interesting.

[Then we were transferred to Inchon.] In this camp, 250 men were [immediately] put in each squad tent. However small Oriental men may be, it is beyond our imagination to put 250 men in a squad tent. And the coldness was penetrating through our bones. We spent the first night in continual fighting; the men in the [center area of the tent] had to step on the shoulders of others to get out.

Next morning before sunrise we lined up. It was the breakfast time. All were amazed at seeing their breakfast: bowlfuls of white rice! And there was picklings, too. We never expected such good treatment. It was too much food to hold in the hollow of [one's] hands. I took off my hat and dusted off the DDT which had been sprayed the night before [and put the food in there].

By these facts you can easily surmise the life in Inchon. We got . . . clothes . . . too. . . .[30]

Pusan, Winter, 1950–51

Conditions in Camp No. 1 at Pusan were essentially similar to those in the advance camps through the autumn of 1950. The number of enclosures was expanded rapidly as internees were shipped down from

[30] "What It Means to Be a Korean PW." This document by an anonymous North Korean prisoner of war was written while he was working as a member of the permanent PW detail at the 64th Field Hospital, on Koje-do. It was prepared at the request of a U.S. medical corpsman stationed there, and turned over to HumRRO by the latter. The author's crude English has been edited only enough to make his meaning clear to American readers. This document is cited hereafter by title only.

the advance camps; food supplies were somewhat more adequate and regular, but crowding was sometimes even more intense than that reported at Pyongyang and Inchon.

PW life was largely unorganized during this period. Frequent movement, extreme crowding, anxiety over supply, and total dependence on the day-to-day actions of U.S. custodial authorities kept it so. In these circumstances the role of sheer muscular strength and ingenuity in the pursuit of personal interests was inevitably great. None of the PW informants mentioned any politically tinged organization among the prisoners during this time.

Basic to the conduct of both U.N. and prisoner personnel during this period was the expectation that it would soon be over. Korean PW's recalled, for example:

> As we had survived the war, we naturally looked for the earlier end of the war. We believed that our fatherland could be unified within several months and that our eventual release would follow the end of the war.[31]

> The PW's overcame their uneasiness in hopes of being released soon. As the U.N. forces moved rapidly north, we believed the war would soon be over. Also, we believed that we would be released after a thorough screening. It was said that on Christmas day all . . . PW's would be released.[32]

After the hasty closing of the advance camps in November and December, some 135,000 Korean PW's lived through the winter and into the spring in Pusan. Information on conditions during this period is somewhat more adequate than it is for the preceding period.

Physical Arrangement

Five major enclosures were scattered about the city and its outskirts. At one time the hospital enclosure alone contained more than ten thousand PW's suffering from combat wounds, frostbite, and contagious or infectious diseases. In addition to the five large locations, small compounds were built in the port area to house labor details.

The several enclosures differed widely in size, and their populations ranged from only a few thousand to over thirty thousand. Each enclosure was subdivided into from five to ten compounds. Each compound was surrounded by a single-strand eight- to ten-foot barbed-wire fence, with machine-gun towers outside the fences at intervals averaging five hundred yards.

The average population of a compound was approximately two thousand men. The prisoners lived in squad tents, which housed an average

[31] "Essays by Prisoners of War." Essay No. 1.
[32] From a document prepared by anti-Communist Korean prisoner-of-war leaders on Koje-do in June, 1952.

of 120 PW's each—many times the number they were intended for. The compounds themselves were too small for the numbers crowded into them, offering little or, more often, no space for recreation or for individual or small-group privacy. The crowding aggravated the mud and dirt which were already everywhere.

U.N. Forces

Administrative and guard personnel were still few in number. One of the officers who commanded Camp No. 1 during this period reported that work details of from three thousand to five thousand PW's were frequently sent out with groups of 125 prisoners per guard—several times the established norm (Interview 0–9). Official complaints and requests for additional qualified guard personnel were chronic. South Korean army units assigned to guard duty were considered unsatisfactory; [33] they were poorly trained and equipped and their morale was low.

Although supply deficiencies still occurred frequently, compared to the South Korean soldiers and civilians outside the fences the PW's were rich in certain items of much-wanted American equipment, clothing, and even foods. Black-market barter through the fences grew up quickly and became common; [34] individual American guards are said to have participated in some instances. [35]

Training programs were begun for the U.S. soldiers assigned to the camps. At first, training was done principally on the job, with a weekly instruction period of about two hours conducted by the enclosure commander. [36] Not until August, 1951, were training requirements specified by Headquarters, 60th General Depot—under which the PW camps were administered at this time—to bring the replacements up to minimum standards. [37]

Logistical Problems

Food.—Many—perhaps most—of the PW's had come into U.N. custody undernourished and suffering from exposure. The irregularity and shortage of food in the transit camps had not improved their situation; now the Pusan administration faced a similar problem. In January, 1951, medical officers reported that 50 per cent of the PW's at Pusan

[33] Unpublished army report.

[34] Pak Chang Mo.

[35] Reports of black-market activities of guards came from a number of sources—from Captain Pak, from PW's, and from U.S. Army personnel.

[36] Unpublished army reports.

[37] The program was to include two hours of study of the Geneva Convention, one hour each on the administration of prisoners of war and the duties of PW guards, and twenty-eight hours of on-the-job training. During the period of on-the-job training no operational responsibilities were to be given to the trainee. His primary duty was to observe assigned U.S. personnel working with prisoners. Unpublished army report.

were suffering from malnutrition, and there were numerous cases of dysentery and tuberculosis and other respiratory diseases. Much illness was attributed to inadequate preparation and service of the PW rations, duties handled by the prisoners themselves.[38]

In contrast to the earlier situation, the difficulty at Pusan was more the kind than the quantity of food. The Western-style rations given to prisoners at first not only were disliked but appeared to aggravate the already serious problem of dysentery.[39] In January, 1951, an Oriental ration was approved and authorized for issue. Still, although medical officers insisted that the new ration had all the necessary nutritive elements and sufficient caloric content, the prisoners were unsatisfied; the food struck many of them as flat and tasteless because the normal Korean diet includes large quantities of strong condiments.

While supply procedures were constantly being improved and regularized, shortages of particular food items developed repeatedly because of leakage at various points between procurement and consumption. For example, within the compound the amount of cooked food produced did not always correspond to the amount that should have been produced from the original bags of rice. This occurred at a time when the prisoners were running their own kitchens and distributing the food themselves. At other times food was distributed by the PW's "on the basis of physique or politics," and some went hungry. Both of these problems were brought under control by putting an American MP, badly needed for guard duty, in charge of each compound kitchen to check on the food preparation, by initiating chow lines, and by having the soldier inspect the line closely to ensure equitable distribution.[40]

Sanitation.—In the Pusan compounds, enforcing sanitary standards—even those regarded as minimal in the U.S. armed forces—proved extremely difficult.[41] Sanitation with respect to food was particularly irksome for the PW's at first. Earthenware bowls with wooden chopsticks were issued initially, but breakage was high and PW's began to be observed eating from cut squares of ponchos. Often cooked food was measured out quite literally by hand. To the other duties of the mess sergeants was added that of enforcing elementary rules of sanitation. Metal Japanese army messkits were obtained and issued, and all prisoners were required to dip their trays in hot water.[42]

Another series of sanitation problems arose out of the hasty construction and extremely crowded conditions of the Pusan compounds. The compounds were very dirty, and medical officers expressed grave anxiety lest an epidemic break out. Keeping the men free from lice was a

[38] Unpublished army report.
[39] *Ibid.*
[40] Interview o–9.
[41] Unpublished army report.
[42] Interview o–9.

vexing problem; the Korean louse seemed almost immune to DDT under these conditions.[43]

Periodic serious outbreaks of dysentery were a consequence of, among other things, these deficiencies of sanitation. As the war progressed, however, the prisoners were educated in the importance of sanitation as a health measure, and with their cooperation these problems were gradually brought under control.[44]

Other problems.—The extreme crowding of the squad tents was gradually reduced as the winter proceeded. Other logistical problems, such as shortages of clothing or bedding material, developed from time to time, but most of these were only temporary.

The custodial authorities were acutely aware of the logistical deficiencies and acted resolutely to minimize them. Although by U.S. standards the PW's were not well fed or adequately equipped, from January, 1951, they were relatively well off by their own standards and exceedingly so in comparison with both the nearby civilian population and the South Korean soldiers who performed guard duty around the compounds. This seems to have been a source of strength for anti-Communist PW's in these early days, as well as a source of conflict between PW's and South Korean guards.

Utilization of PW's

Utilization of the PW's was restricted largely to manual labor details. They were used most extensively to construct facilities for their own internment, first at Pusan and then on Koje-do. In building the Koje compounds, huge work details were employed. Groups of prisoners were also used to unload ships and store goods in warehouses, to dig graves, and on engineering projects—roads, ditches, and clean-up campaigns. The PW's made stoves, sleeping mats, and furniture for their own use. Finally, of course, they performed all the housekeeping chores connected with the operation of their compounds, such as cooking, kitchen police, and sanitation details.

The actual number of prisoners assigned to work details at any one time depended on the demand for their services. During the construction of the camps thousands were employed at a time, but when the construction was completed there was relatively little for the prisoners

---

[43] *Ibid.* The search for an effective insecticide led eventually, in May, 1951, to the U.S. Department of Agriculture.

[44] See, for example, "History of Compound 65," July 2, 1952. This is a history of one of the compounds on Koje-do written by the PW's and edited by army personnel. In late 1951 or early 1952 a section of the internal compound police force was detailed specifically to enforce rules of sanitation (p. 28); discussions were held frequently about problems of sanitary education (p. 45); special teams were organized to inspect laundries, latrines, and kitchens; all kitchen personnel were inspected twice a month, and those found to be germ carriers were forced to resign their jobs (p. 104). Similar activities were generally carried on by other compounds as well in the post-Pusan period.

to do. The comparative idleness of the PW's on Koje-do—where they had only occasional opportunities for useful large-scale labor—may have played a significant part in the turning inward of their interests and social organization.

Records

The conditions under which prisoners poured into Pusan and were interned there compounded the difficulty of developing records. No reliable method of keeping track of individual PW's existed at any time in the Pusan phase.[45]

During the winter of 1950–51 the status of the South Korean prisoners became an active policy issue. South Korean government teams went through all the compounds and processed these prisoners for release, but the U.N. command then ordered that they be reclassified and placed in segregated compounds while the policy issue was being resolved. The lack of positive means of identification (especially the lack of either fingerprints or photographs) made reclassification exceedingly difficult and resulted in numerous errors. Since the training of American administrative personnel was inadequate to ensure the use of any single system for transliterating Korean names, even the making and checking of rosters created additional confusion.[46] As things worked out, only the PW's themselves could identify one another at this time.

Meeting the Problem of Communication

For a variety of reasons, U.S. camp commanders were unwilling to make extensive use of South Korean army personnel in the administration of the compounds. This placed the burden of communicating with the prisoners directly on Americans. To compensate for the deficiency in language skills, maximum use was made of PW personnel who knew even a smattering of English. An official position of interpreter was created in each compound. Knowledge of English was, indeed, the most valuable asset for any PW who desired appointment to an official position within the camp. English-speaking PW's often exercised considerable power within the Pusan compounds.

The PW authorities also sought and hired English-speaking Korean and Chinese civilians. Although critically few throughout the Pusan period, these employees were utilized from the beginning as interpreters, translators, interrogators, and clerks, and in many other tasks in which cross-cultural communication, either written or oral, was indispensable.

Administrative Organization within the Compounds

To facilitate administrative control, the camp command organized the compounds into regiments, battalions, and companies. An average

[45] Interview o–9.
[46] *Ibid.*

of 250 men comprised a company. The details of organization varied among compounds. One might have four battalions and one regiment, while another contained a total of three regiments; substantial variation in the size of companies was also common. Within the company, the prisoners themselves informally organized platoons.[47]

Each of these units was commanded by a PW, with the PW who was compound commander at the top of the hierarchy. The compound commander was appointed by the American officer in charge of the compound. No specific qualifications existed for the post; however, the appointee generally spoke some English and was intelligent, well educated, and actively cooperative with the American authorities. He served principally as an intermediary between the camp authorities and the prisoners, transmitting orders, arranging for work details, and performing other tasks as directed. To assist him in this work he was authorized a small staff, the members of which he normally selected with the consent of the American in charge.

No formal rules existed in the Pusan period for selecting subordinate unit commanders among the prisoners; formal elections were held for the first time on Koje-do. The subordinate unit commanders emerged from the mass of PW's, either by demonstrating some leadership ability in solving day-to-day problems of group life, by forcing their way into prominence and power by brute force, or by being chosen by the PW commander. Though all of them had to be acceptable to the American in charge, in some cases, even in this early period, they were selected by the PW compound commander and served subject to his pleasure.

A number of other positions within the compound were created by the camp authorities. Prisoners were appointed to jobs in supply, the kitchen, and the dispensary. These posts too, because of the privileges they carried, became significant in the prisoners' struggles for power.

In addition to this formal organization, quasi-official police forces were developed within the compounds. No clear evidence is available to indicate that the U.N. Command ever formally sanctioned these forces, but it knew of their existence and, in effect, utilized them for a considerable period. It is reasonable to suppose that the shortage of U.N. guard personnel and the huge populations of the compounds made some system of internal policing mandatory.

The principal duties of the compound police were to maintain order and enforce sanitary regulations. In addition, they escorted common prisoners on such routine details as transporting supplies to the compound and removing "honey buckets." The structure of the police organization, recruitment, and training were handled by the PW's; only the chief was appointed by the American in charge of the compound. The chief appointed or approved the appointment of policemen.[48]

[47] Interview with Captain Pak.
[48] Interview with Captain Pak.

Organized initially to maintain order, the PW police were to become the principal instrument by which incipient political organizations gained and consolidated their control over the compounds.

Compliance with the Geneva Convention

Most of what has been said in this chapter points up a strenuous effort by the custodial authorities to keep the prisoners secure, safe, and healthy. Elementary physical problems of sanitation, diet, crowding, and the like occupied most of the attention of the enclosure administrators throughout the Pusan period. And while many of these problems were solved by the end of the winter, others would not be solved without new and more spacious enclosures, necessarily in a different locale.

In February, 1951, a board of officers was appointed to investigate escapes, incidents of violence, and PW complaints in the camps. As a result of this board's action, copies of the Geneva Convention were for the first time reproduced in the Korean language and posted in all compounds, and a PW censorship section was established so that mail might be safely sent and received by the prisoners. Other provisions—for example, those calling for adequate recreational facilities—were not regularly observed until after the Pusan period.

The U.N. Command never designated a body of law under which the prisoners could be tried for serious misconduct.

Impact of Basic Conditions on the Prisoners

The anonymous PW who was quoted at length on conditions of life in the advance transit camps has written also about the hasty movement of PW's to Pusan after the Chinese breakthrough and about conditions there through the winter of 1950–51. His account illustrates the difficulties arising from the sudden mass influx of prisoners, and the hardships suffered by the prisoners themselves. At the same time it suggests some of the ways in which conditions in Pusan affected social relations among the PW's.

As the . . . war was getting worse for the United Nations, we left Inchon [in December]. It was the last evacuation ship. . . . If any cameraman had filmed what had happened during this voyage of thirty-eight hours from Inchon to Pusan, even Satan would be indignant at seeing it. . . . In a cargo ship the tonnage of which was estimated at 3,000 tons at the most, 4,500 PW's were shipped. The cause of death of over half of the dead was being trampled down under feet.

When two-thirds of the PW's [had been] put in the ship, the room of the ship was jammed with people. GI guards pushed them . . . [further in], but they found it of no use and they stabbed the men around them with jackknives. . . . I heard the piercing voice of the first prey. He fell on his face. Innumerable people stepped on him.

People found a nice place on his body to sit on. Brutality governed all. I could hear nothing in the clamor. . . .

They lifted the lid on the deck on the second day. How delicious the air was! Air! Air! A few faces looked in. And a bucket came down full of rice. Again fighting started. Then a few buckets of water came down, too. But it only satisfied those people just under the lid. Though I was hungry and thirsty, I never wished rice or a drink of water, because easing nature follows eating and drinking inevitably.

That afternoon two empty oil drums came down. It was a so-called honey bucket. Two drums for 4,500 men! [But] people abstained from going to the honey bucket. The first reason came from being deprived of the place already occupied. The second was as follows: It was too risky to get to the drum. The place was so crowded that they couldn't make for the drum. The only way left for them was to jump on the shoulders [of other PW's]. If they were caught they were beaten black and blue. . . .

In Pusan our PW camp was located by the road which extends to Seoul. The enclosure consisted of six compounds, and each compound of several companies. The organization was just like that of [the] army. Each compound was separated by barbed wire. In each squad tent (we call it a platoon) ninety to one hundred PW's were admitted.

At five o'clock [in the morning, the] mobilization chief of the company would run into each tent and shout: "Come out in five minutes with a bowl!" This is the start of the day.

We line up in five files. At seven o'clock we go to work. GI's were waiting in front of a gate, and requested how many guys they want. Then gate sergeant counted the PW's and gave them. This was the routine way. In the beginning of life in Pusan, our work was to set up a new compound for the new companions coming. We dug innumerable holes to erect poles which were used [to string the fence] to confine us.

Most of the guards were Negroes. They were generous in treating us. As all the PW's were severely undernourished, even walking was . . . hard work for them. They were watching for the chance and if they got it, they handed over their clothes or other commodities and got food or salt. At that time we were given only rice [as rations]. If the guard turned around, they pretended working. The places we were digging holes had been radish fields before. And there remained some radishes which had been left at the time of harvest because they were too small in size. People engaged in hunting those radishes. Once they were discovered in the hunting by a Negro guard, but he did no harm to them. He only showed his teeth.

This work of erecting poles took several days to finish. After that we went to a railway station and worked in the lumber yard.

This work began at eight o'clock and finished at seven o'clock. One day it rained from the morning. We thought we would have holiday. But the voice of the mobilization chief was heard as usual. In the rain without a raincoat we spent the day. We were not allowed to sit down even for a moment. A few GI's were walking around the yard with sticks in their hands. Behind the pile of lumber, people used to take a rest and they had a watchman. If the watchman wanted to tell them the GI was approaching, he said, "Air attack!" and all the men ran away. The yard was a playground of hide and seek. When night came, our clothes were wringing wet. We shuffled to our compound. There a handful of sodden supper was waiting for us. From the exhaustion of a day's work and hunger we lay on our sides soon after supper.

Through all the life in Pusan I couldn't lie on my back with my legs stretched even at night, as the tent was too much crowded. When we got up next morning, the clothes were almost dried. Now, I wonder how it was that I could get along without any disease at that time. . . . In a word, life in Pusan was the period of ordeal of hunger.

Now let this be enough. I mentioned the violence of GI's too much. But here is a man whose activity will never be blotted out from our memory. I don't know him by name. If you ask any PW's about this man, they will reply, "Oh, you mean Red! Who [else] on the earth can act like him?"

He was in charge of the mess hall. People who belonged to his mess hall were given a half the quantity of other mess halls. And they got a lot of kicks, punches, and all dirty words instead. One day just after inspection, a PW was searching for food in a trash can and was discovered by the inspector. The inspector asked why. He replied, "I get more nourishment with this trash than with my officially given meal." Next day we got twice as much as the usual quantity.[49]

ON THE MAINLAND: COMPOUND ORGANIZATION

The political organizations which eventually dominated events on Koje Island had their roots on the mainland in 1950 and early 1951. The experiences in Pusan predisposed the PW's to act in certain ways, and the development of disciplined pro-Communist and anti-Communist organizations was one result of these predispositions. The development of the groupings which were the forerunners of the militant political organizations will be described in this section.

Reactions to the U.N. Command

Throughout the first nine months or more of the conflict, the PW's remained notably docile in their relations with their captors. Almost without exception, they were extremely cooperative. New captives will-

[49] "What It Means to Be a Korean PW."

ingly provided information of substantial military value or assisted U.N. patrols in rooting our guerillas; many spoke by public-address system urging their former comrades to surrender.

At least one train load of Chinese PW's arrived in Taegu from the front without guards.[50] In the PW camps, as has been pointed out, huge labor details were repeatedly sent out with so few guards that escape would have been easy for many. Yet both escapes and complaints about heavy labor were few in these early months.

Both the cooperativeness and the docility of the PW's were symptoms of their tendency to ingratiate themselves with their captors—an apparently typical reaction of Orientals when confronted with a new center of power.[51] In such circumstances Orientals generally try to come to terms with those in power by conforming to their demands. This ingratiation may lead not only to the giving of information, but on occasion to the invention of it when one lacks the information the captor seems to want. Another manifestation may be extreme modification of speech and overt conduct, when that seems to be desired by the new master.[52]

It would be a mistake, however, to underestimate the significance of this ingratiation; a number of studies strongly suggest that it was not mere superficial opportunism.[53] At the time that the great bulk of PW's were captured, the hitherto impressive power system of their Communist masters appeared to be crumbling in the face of superior U.N. strength; the invincible revolution was being destroyed. Many of them certainly hoped to find a new source of order and direction. Furthermore, when the Oriental transfers his obedience, he hopes to be able eventually to give genuine allegiance to his new superiors. He proves his sincerity by giving everything that the new ruler asks, hoping that this will lead to a stable relationship of mutual good faith and reciprocity which protects his own needs and interests at the same time that it serves those of the ruler.

Thus, it seems highly likely that the great majority of the PW's served

[50] Unpublished Army Operation Log.

[51] See, for example, Chapters I & II above. See also Lucian W. Pye, *Comments on the Political Behavior of Overseas Chinese* and Ruth Bunzel and John H. Weakland, *An Anthropological Approach to Chinese Communism* (hectographed). Little or no comparable literature on the Korean people exists, but the research data on both the Korean PW's and the Communist regime in North Korea indicate that these generalizations apply to them as well.

[52] This tendency is illustrated by the behavior of three hundred Korean PW's interviewed in the autumn of 1950, shortly after capture, for an army-sponsored research project. Viewed in the light of subsequent events, the distribution of replies to some of the questions strongly suggests that these men were attempting to curry favor by "speaking correctly" in accordance with the captors' standards. For example, 91 per cent said they did not believe that Russia would help North Korea; 93 per cent said that living conditions in North Korea had not improved since 1945; 96 per cent denied flatly that the North Korean government had helped the common people; and 97 per cent said they wanted to achieve a united Korea with the help of the United Nations.

[53] See, for example, above, Pye, *Comments;* unpublished military studies.

the purposes of the U.N. Command not only out of a desire for immediate good treatment but in hopes of establishing good relations and a sort of bargain that would be mutually advantageous. In retrospect, it is apparent that the U.N. Command did not understand this alien moral logic. As a consequence, the custodial authorities adopted neither of the alternative policies that would have been appropriate: they did not exploit prisoner expectations systematically for U.N. Command military and political purposes, at the same time living up to the ruler's obligations under the oriental code; and they did not seek to clarify the situation—to explain the U.N. concept of the PW as a non-combatant and disabuse the PW's of their unrealistic expectations.

In considering the social organization of the PW's within the mainland compounds, it is necessary to treat the Korean and the Chinese internees separately. Although later the behavior of the two groups became comparable, the situations they faced initially differed in important respects.

Organization in Korean Compounds

Beginnings [54]

Through the fall of 1950 and well into the winter, life in the compounds was largely disorganized. To provide oneself with even the necessities of life under the rigorous conditions of the early months required muscle or the utmost ingenuity. Later accounts suggest that most Korean PW's looked back on the first months at Pyongyang, Inchon, and Pusan as a period of every man for himself and on the camps themselves as lawless and terrible places.

Spontaneous social organization began early. The PW's clustered in little groups, sometimes simply on the basis of proximity of sleeping spaces, sometimes on the basis of the locality from which they had come, sometimes on the basis of having been captured and processed together. They talked cautiously at first, avoiding anything that would suggest political preferences. In these small gatherings leaders appeared, typically on the basis of physical strength or of serving as negotiator in dealing with other prisoner groups.

These spontaneous beginnings were, however, far from the level of social organization required to keep the life of the compounds on an even keel under conditions of general scarcity. For a variety of reasons the establishment of a hierarchy based on rank in the North Korean army was either impossible or undesirable. The great hiatus of organization was filled from above, through the establishment of a military chain of command by the camp authorities. In addition, the custodial authorities tacitly approved the formation of prisoner police organizations.

[54] Much of the generalization in this section is derived from the interviews with Captain Pak and is wholly compatible with scattered suggestive material in the PW interviews.

The compound commander, as mentioned earlier, was appointed by the Americans in charge. His immediate staff consisted of men, chosen from those who thrust themselves forward, who were acceptable to the U.N. commander and compound sergeant. Subordinate leaders were selected in turn by the compound commander and his staff, but at the platoon and squad levels these were normally individuals who had already appeared as leaders in the spontaneous, grass-roots social processes. Informal representative processes and authoritarian ones merged. And, once selected, the leaders rather quickly developed the informal understandings among themselves that were needed for their operations as an organized group directing the mass.

South Korean Domination

During this period North and South Koreans were interned together. Almost from the beginning, the more important positions of leadership within the compound organizations were held by South Koreans who had been impressed into the North Korean army during its advance in the summer of 1950. While North Koreans were not excluded from leadership positions, they occupied only subordinate staff and subunit commands.

There are a number of clues as to how the South Koreans were able to dominate the compounds even though they were outnumbered two to one by Northerners. Probably more South Koreans than North Koreans spoke English; they may have been more uniformly cooperative, and hence more likely to be acceptable to U.N. camp authorities. Most important, however, the masses of prisoners fully expected the U.N. forces to win the war and were professing sympathy for the cause of South Korea.[55] The South Koreans not only felt that they had been interned by mistake but believed that as South Koreans they were entitled to leadership positions.[56] It is fair to assume that U.N. compound commanders and South Korean guards gave them preferential treatment,[57] and North Koreans may have believed the Southerners could protect them more effectively. Certainly the Northerners were relatively passive during this period.

Rewards of Office.—The leadership positions brought not only prestige but valuable material rewards as well; there was spirited competition for them. For one thing, the leaders received more and better food than rank-and-file PW's, partly because they were allowed a fourth meal for working at night, and also because they or their personal followers worked in the kitchen and distributed the food. They received better clothing, principally because through their followers they controlled the supplies,[58] and for the same reason they were able to barter effectively

---

[55] Interview with Captain Pak. See also footnote 52, above.
[56] *Koje-do in Complication*, p. 9.
[57] Interview KR-25.
[58] Hong Ji Hule.

with civilians and South Korean guards. They were never asked to come out of the compounds for work details,[59] and they were accorded considerable deference by the rank and file. Indeed, "the prisoners dreamed of nothing but becoming a leader or *hancho*." [60]

Characteristics of South Korean Leadership.—How did the South Korean leaders rule their little principalities? In considering this question, two periods divided approximately by New Year's Day, 1951, must be sharply distinguished.

Concentration on material interests.—During the initial period, when supply shortages were intense and the situation uncertain, the leaders commonly seem to have been concerned principally with enhancing their own material welfare. Political considerations as such appear to have played a secondary role.

It was assumed by the PW's as well as by the custodial authorities that the leaders' sentiments were anti-Communist (although some of them later turned out to be or became pro-Communists). Throughout the compounds the atmosphere was distinctly anti-Communist, but the tone was rather subdued; anti-Communism apparently was so generally taken for granted that specific organization or active demonstration did not seem to be called for. Few if any skirmishes of a political nature occurred during this period, and the leaders made no attempt to indoctrinate or otherwise control, manipulate, or mobilize masses of prisoners in the name of any principles or long-range purposes.

The typical leader appeared, indeed, to be singularly uninterested in the rank-and-file prisoners; only the challenge of a rival clique could stir him into furious negotiation or into organizing for violence. These early organizations which ran the affairs of the compounds were highly personal machines of a traditional Oriental type, concerned principally with obtaining such spoils as their power permitted. According to Captain Pak, few of the leaders were highly educated, and a good many of them were "Big Shoulders" and former gangsters or outlaws who knew how to exploit a relatively disorganized collection of men.[61] Only occasionally, however, did the leaders' appropriation of food and other supplies during this period become so blatant as to arouse the active indignation of the rest of the prisoners.

Within the compounds the PW police were the principal instrument of control. In fact, the chief of police was commonly the most powerful man in the compound.[62] While the police enforced order and discipline, the significant questions here are: What kind of order? Whose discipline? The fact that the policemen were handpicked by the chief suggests that the police commonly constituted private armies. Clearly they

---

[59] Captain Pak.

[60] *Ibid.*

[61] This view is supported by some of the interview data; none of the data contradict it.

[62] Interview with Captain Pak.

were considered the elite of the prisoners. They usually had their own tents and manufactured and wore brassards on their arms. They arrested PW's on their own, placed them in improvised jails within the compounds, interrogated them, and beat recalcitrant individuals in accordance with tradition.[63]

The custodial authorities were too few in number to keep close track of what was going on. As their mission required, they were concerned about the security and order of the compounds, and on occasion they intervened to stop police violence. It seems unlikely, however, that they were fully aware of the extent to which the functions of the police centered in preserving the power of the *hanchoes*.

Actions directed against Communists by PW leaders.—The second phase in the rule by the South Korean prisoners began in January, 1951. At that time the U.N. dispatched investigation teams to the camps at Pusan to determine whether any PW's had committed acts which, under the definitions developed after World War II, might be considered war crimes.

At Enclosure 3, Lieutenant Pak Chang Mo, as a South Korean officer assigned to the U.N. War Crimes Section, developed a network of informants within each of the compounds in order to simplify the identification of suspects.[64] This network operated through the intra-compound police. Whereas the police force had been only an above-ground operation, it now added an underground section. Carefully selected prisoners with anti-Communist backgrounds were spotted through the compounds, to observe, listen, and report the names of persons suspected of having committed war crimes.

For the first time, it began to appear to the South Korean prisoner leaders that the camp authorities were interested in distinguishing sheep from goats and in punishing the guilty. The leaders responded with enthusiasm, if not with discrimination. Instead of simply turning the names over to Lieutenant Pak, they instituted preliminary interrogations of suspected war criminals, whom they beat in the process. Furthermore, on their own initiative they added to the lists turned over to the War Crimes Section the names of men who had been party members or, especially, who had held responsible political posts, either in the North Korean army or as civilians, and demanded that these men also be removed from the compounds.

Lieutenant Pak tried repeatedly to persuade his American superior to see what could be done about the party members and politicians, but to no effect. The custodial authorities were willing to remove North Korean

[63] Interview with Captain Pak. Supported also by numerous prisoner interviews.
[64] We have no exact information on the extent to which the situation in Enclosure 3 and Lieutenant Pak's activities were duplicated elsewhere. PW's interned in other enclosures reported events which suggest a pattern similar in kind but less systematic than that in Enclosure 3; Pak's account indicates that similar but less effective efforts to identify war crimes suspects were made in other enclosures.

officers posing as enlisted men, since regulations called for interning officers separately, but even in these cases there were often delays.[65] About other PW's identified as Communists, the camp command— which was officially concerned only with segregating suspected war criminals and, in the framework of the Geneva Convention, administering the camps in a nonpolitical, humane way—could do nothing.

In Lieutenant Pak's eyes and those of the PW's, the Americans were just indifferent. This indifference was incomprehensible to the Korean PW's, as the following account indicates.

> One day a North Korean PW was somewhat seriously beaten up by the South Korean PW police. This immediately attracted the attention of the camp authorities. The authorities did not try to find out the reason why the man should be treated like that; instead, they transferred the chief of police out of the compound. This caused a big sensation among the South Korean *hanchoes,* because the police chief was a great [i.e., important and powerful] man. Without him the morale of the rest would certainly become low. One of the South Korean *hanchoes* remarked: "I do not know what the American people are fighting for. We should cooperate with each other to pick up the Communists in the compounds, but the camp authority doesn't even help us." As a matter of fact, the North Korean who was beaten up was a North Korean cultural officer who was seen to be instigating the rest of the PW's.[66]

Pro-Communist and anti-Communist PW's alike had fully expected the U.N. Command to deal with Communist prisoners. But when it did not do so, the prisoners therefore began to take matters into their own hands.[67] They continued to round up, beat, and torture war crimes suspects and Communists alike. Lieutenant Pak's sympathies were with the anti-Communist PW's; he believed that the Communists must be adequately dealt with, and he in effect cooperated with the PW's. On receipt of a list of suspects, he had the PW's who were named sent to his interrogation tent, where they were "interrogated" and soundly thrashed. Then they were sent back to their compounds, obviously the worse for wear. It is highly significant that Communist PW's later described this reign of terror as instigated and carried through under U.N. Command auspices.

Aside from the tracking down of Communists by the South Korean leadership, the research staff found little evidence of anti-Communist political activity in the compounds during the first months of 1951; nor

[65] Lt. Pak.
[66] *Ibid.*
[67] "The camp authorities and American agencies were so entirely indifferent . . . that the anti-Communist PW's were impelled to establish and maintain power over Communists." *Ibid.*

did they find much evidence of official U.N. interest in such activity per se.

Within the prison compounds there was general acquiescence in the activities of the PW leadership; pro-Communists kept quiet. The mass of the prisoners, North and South Koreans alike, seldom took part and tried to stay out of trouble.

Other Bases of Social Organization

Throughout the Pusan period the only actively power-oriented groups within the prison compounds were those centering in aggressive South Korean organizers. Other informal groupings—based on religious affiliation, educational level and old school ties, army experience, and local and personal bonds—did develop. Most of these informal groups were simple, face-to-face cliques with elementary mutual-assistance functions; they were seldom concerned with compound politics, although they produced some squad- and platoon-level leaders.

Christians.—Christian groups did tend to be more extensively organized and sometimes became nuclei for anti-Communist activity. The Christians in Enclosure 3, for example, had a relatively formal, enclosure-wide organization. Their group included, not only an over-all head and officers for recruitment and administration, but also a chief of instruction whose principal duty was to explain the difference between democracy and Communism.[68]

Some of the activities of this group were *sub rosa.* An American missionary not only ministered to the religious needs of the prisoners but also sought to use them as a source of anti-Communist information. About forty of these Christians became informants, gathering information on the activities of suspected Communists and turning it over to camp authorities.[69] As far as can be determined, these activities were carried on independently of the formal leadership of the several compounds. The group never made a bid for compound or enclosure leadership.

Communist Nuclei.—No source available to the research team describes any pro-Communist groups or Communist organizing activity in the PW compounds prior to January, 1951. If there were any stirrings during this period, they must have been exceedingly cautious, tentative, and small-scale; at the time most of the PW's were captured, the U.N. forces were winning the war, and it was expected that the U.N. would unify Korea on a democratic basis. With the entry of the Chinese Communists and the deep withdrawal of the U.N. troops, however, the outcome once more became doubtful.[70] Another, and more immediate,

[68] Interview KN-17.
[69] *Ibid.*
[70] Numerous PW interviews reflect or explicitly state this change of expectations in the compounds.

stimulus was the beginning of organized activity by the anti-Communists—such as the reign of terror in the compounds in Enclosure 3—which seemed to call for defensive measures.[71]

Surreptitiously and on the level of small, informal groups, Communists began to cluster together. Before the PW's were moved to Koje-do in the spring there appears to have been a well-organized Communist group in Enclosure 2,[72] and attempts had been made to organize a cell in Enclosure 5.[73] Informants in Enclosure 3 advised the War Crimes Section that there was increasing Communist activity in one of the compounds and that some of the men previously identified as Communists were moving into leadership positions. In general, however, South Korean control was still firm.

Power Vacuum [74]

The segregation of the South Korean PW's in the spring of 1951, prior to the move from Pusan, left a major organization and power vacuum in the North Korean compounds. At least three kinds of PW's stood ready to fill the gap: North Korean anti-Communists who had played subordinate leadership roles in the period of South Korean dominance; other North Koreans, politically uncommitted but eager for the rewards of power; and Communists.

In most compounds the departing South Koreans named members of the first group as their successors. But these men lacked an important basis for authority that their predecessors had had—they were not identified in the minds of the masses of PW's with the capturing and detaining authority. Moreover, there was no organized popular support for their rule. Although the South Koreans had built up personal machines with an anti-Communist cast, they had no mass "parties" or movements which could choose or legitimate their successors.

The Communists, on the other hand, were forming their organization among the rank and file. At this time they were not agitating large masses or even calling themselves Communists. They concentrated their efforts on two steps: forming a secure network among the party members within a compound, and working within relatively small groups of prisoners to push forward leaders who would do their bidding. North Korean medical-officer PW's who visited compound dispensaries daily and returned at night to the officers' compound constituted a channel of communication for some pro-Communist groups. On the whole, how-

[71] Captain Pak.
[72] Interview with Hong Ji Hule.
[73] Interview KN-17.
[74] Much of this section is derived from the written and oral accounts of Captain Pak. Since his experience in Pusan centered in Enclosure 3, the generalizations made here reflect principally trends in the several compounds of that very large enclosure. The account given here is, however, wholly compatible with interview statements made by PW's from other enclosures and with the scattered information contained in U.N. Command Reports on the period.

ever, it seems clear that at this time the individual compounds were the principal focuses of party activity.

As the intra-compound party networks grew, their coordination of the activities of individuals in different groups greatly enhanced Communist ability to influence the naming of leaders on higher levels, for the great mass of the PW's were still tied together only in little cliques and in the formal military-type organization. At this stage, however, Communists were still hampered by the need to disguise their activity.

Aspirants of the remaining type—politically uncommitted individuals and cliques—seem to have operated at this time in traditional fashion. The role of sheer muscle was by now much smaller than it had been, but the material rewards of office were, if anything, more evident. If previously PW's "dreamed of nothing but becoming a *hancho*," it now developed that those with will and ingenuity had a chance to make their dreams come true. The PW who could speak for a group could hope to exact a price for cooperating with the official PW hierarchy.

The mass of PW's sensed these new anti-Communist, pro-Communist, and neutral stirrings and the resultant competition for leadership positions. Just as they had previously acquiesced in the dominance of the South Koreans and tried to stay out of trouble, they now behaved cautiously, waiting to see which way the wind would blow. The North Korean anti-Communist leaders who had inherited formal leadership from the departing South Koreans soon began to experience difficulty in getting their orders carried out. Lists of Communists and war criminals prepared for the War Crimes Section carried fewer and fewer names.

Watching their informant networks melt away, the Koreans in the War Crimes Section were quick to investigate. They discovered that Communists and persons whose rivals called them Communists were moving into leadership positions, and that North Korean anti-Communist leaders and rank-and-file PW's alike were becoming anxious and cautious. Since leaders put forward by the Communists cooperated fully with the custodial authority and did not reveal themselves as Communist stooges, compound sergeants and U.S. officers did not realize what was happening. Since the Communists did not sponsor known Communists—and since, indeed, some non-Communist North Koreans may unknowingly have received Communist support—it is doubtful that most prisoners had more than a suspicion that Communist organizations as such were beginning to function.[75]

The length of the period that intervened between the transfer of the South Koreans and the shipment of North Koreans to Koje-do varied from one compound to the next. In some it was only a few days, in others several weeks. The longer it lasted, the more uncomfortable

[75] Thus, KN-3 and other interviewees reported that they were surprised to find evidence of well-organized Communist groups when they moved into the new compounds on Koje-do.

became the position of the North Korean anti-Communist leaders. Their ability to get their orders carried out at lower echelons in the compound declined; some of them reported to Korean war crimes investigators that they were being "tailed" wherever they went. Rumors flew among them that the Communists were conducting secret "people's courts" at night and condemning such leaders to death, and more than one found himself deposed and without protection as new leaders moved in.

Korean war crimes investigators shared these leaders' fear for their lives. On at least one occasion they removed a dozen alleged Communist leaders from a compound and beat them severely for two days before sending them back, in order to make it clear that violence against anti-Communists would not be tolerated. The Korean war crimes teams were, however, the only outside help on which PW's who had committed themselves to an anti-Communist position could rely.

The political flux which began with the removal of the South Koreans was further developed by the movement to Koje-do; organized groups of all kinds were broken up by the reshuffling involved in assigning PW's to the new compounds. At any rate, it was in a mood of radical uncertainty and renewed tension that the PW's moved into the Koje-do enclosures between February and June, 1951.

Organization of the Chinese Compound [76]

The Initial Period

It will be recalled that the first eleven Chinese were captured or surrendered in October, 1950, with two hundred more added in November; the total continued to grow slowly until the U.N. counteroffensives in the spring of 1951 brought an influx of Chinese prisoners.

Among the first hundred Chinese PW's was Fu. Fu had come from poor peasant stock and had little schooling; he was a big man, blunt, straightforward, and forceful. A former Nationalist NCO who had been captured by Communist forces during the civil war, he remained staunchly pro-Nationalist throughout his two years of Communist service. At the first opportunity he deserted and surrendered to the U.N. forces, hoping to join one of the Nationalist units he had been told were fighting on the U.N. side.[77] Arriving in Pusan late in November, he was placed in Enclosure 5 with about sixty other Chinese, and immediately made efforts to organize anti-Communist sentiment to oppose repatriation. He told the prisoners, "We have suffered much under the cruel control of the Communists and now we have a chance to get out of their control, so we must make up our mind that we are never going back to Red China and suffer more from the Communists" (CN-22). He was

---

[76] The principal sources drawn on for this section are long interviews with CN-24, CN-22, and a few other early Chinese captives (including CF-2), and additional interviews with these men conducted by military personnel.

[77] For a more detailed picture of Fu, see Chapter 1, above.

able to persuade about ten of his fellows to commit themselves to his position. These few formed a very close relationship; they probably formed the nucleus of the more formal anti-Communist organization that was created somewhat later.

In December the Chinese PW's were transferred to an enclosure at Tongnae. Here they found themselves in compounds dominated by Koreans; they had no independent status. Indeed, they felt that they were persecuted by the Koreans—and they were probably right. Their food was worse than that eaten by the Koreans and of insufficient quantity; they were bullied by what they called the "Korean Communists." They felt that the South Korean guards also treated them harshly, requiring them to salute smartly or be struck, and to keep their rice bowls clean or have them smashed. They were not allowed to enter their quarters during daylight hours, and at night were required to go to the latrine in groups of at least five.[78]

Since none of the Chinese prisoners spoke English, they could not complain to the camp authorities and were wholly at the mercy of the Koreans. Within a few weeks, however, an English-speaking PW named Yu appeared in the camp. Fu questioned him closely about his political background and satisfied himself that Yu's family had been closely tied to the Nationalist regime and that Yu himself hated the Communists. Fu's group then sent the new prisoner to petition American officers for a separate Chinese unit. The negotiations were successful.

After the Chinese had their own sub-compound, Fu urged his fellows to make themselves a disciplined unit. In accordance with his suggestion, each of the three Chinese tents constituted itself a platoon and elected a leader. Fu was the logical choice for company commander but he refused, urging his fellows to name Yu, who could speak English. At a meeting of the entire group of Chinese PW's, he announced that Yu had been selected; rank-and-file agreement was given by a show of hands. So it was that the first Chinese PW's, being few and acutely conscious of the need to look well in the eyes of their custodians, formed a definite organization of their own under anti-Communist auspices.

Ching's Leadership

On the following day some sixty more Chinese prisoners arrived in the compound. Among them—and already their leader—was Ching, who was destined to become the principal Chinese anti-Communist PW leader. Ching had been a Nationalist officer, and had been in one of the last Nationalist units overrun by the Communists on Hainan Island in May, 1950. He had lived under Communist control for only seven months; at the first opportune moment he had deserted his unit and surrendered to the U.N. forces.

Takeover.—Ching was a natural leader and in addition had the

[78] Interviews CN-22, CN-24, and CF-2.

prestige of Nationalist officer rank and recency of capture by the Communists. Within a short time he had become the unofficial leader of all the Chinese incarcerated at Tongnae. How he actually assumed the leadership is not clearly spelled out, but he says:

> To understand this [how I became leader] you have to know how a leader understands other people. I found out that practically all of the Chinese PW's were former Nationalist soldiers and officers. I went among them and [spoke to them individually, asking:] "Do you want to go to Formosa?" They would say, "Yes." Then I would say, "Well, let us then keep this as a secret objective between us." In this way I became their confidant. They would all come to me with their troubles. (CN-24)

Ching proceeded to modify the existing organization by creating a "security committee," which seems to have corresponded closely to the intra-compound police developed in the Korean compounds. The committee was made up of six groups, with a nucleus of trusted men in each.

Even after moving to their own sub-compound, the Chinese still were not entirely free of Korean rule. They were not allowed out of their sub-compound and were dependent upon the North Koreans for food, which consequently was insufficient. Furthermore, they were afraid of the North Koreans, whom they regarded as mostly Communists.

At Ching's instigation the Chinese prisoners refused to submit to the North Koreans any longer, fought them, threw them out, and were left alone to manage their own affairs.

Gradual Expansion.—In February, 1951, this group of Chinese prisoners, now totaling about four hundred, was transferred back to one of the principal Pusan enclosures, where a Chinese compound was set up. Ching was elected compound commander and became formal leader of the Chinese. He retained this leadership—though later there were as many as three Chinese PW compounds—throughout the period of captivity. He personally appointed all subordinate leaders, on the basis of anti-Communist sentiment, but doubtless also on the basis of personal loyalty to him.

In effect Ching had now created, with the sanction of the U.N. authorities, an organization with a definite political as well as a personal cast. Since the number of Chinese PW's increased but gradually through the early spring of 1951, he was able to maintain control without difficulty, screening new PW's as they made their appearance. According to Ching, newcomers were classified in the following manner.

> You have to study how they were taken prisoner, how they were captured—whether they surrendered, whether they were captured, and whether they gave assistance to the U.N. after their capture. . . . When a man is first approached . . . by some older PW's, he is apprehensive. It is necessary at first to cultivate his friendship . . .

to get his agreement to minor questions. You give him good food, you ask him if he likes the food, and you set up a convenient and livable situation for him. You continue to cultivate him in this way more and more, talking about material things and the life of the camp. And gradually you begin to talk of other subjects. You ask: "You have been from the front? How is the fighting at the front? How is it going? Have a lot of people been killed?" I think this is a key question, because if they say, "Well, many are bound to get killed," then they are Communists. If they say, "Many are killed, and this is very bad," then they are probably non-Communists. Also they are probably non-Communists if they say, "I don't care if they kill them all, all of those Communists." In later conversations you ask them, "What are you going to do here?" Maybe he will say, "It is all right to go back to the Communists in China." That means that he is a Communist. Others will say, "It is all right to stay with the U.N." This is a wavering element; it has to be worked on. Some say outright they will never go back; these are non-Communists. The next question is to ask if they wish to go to Formosa. You see, there are many questions like this that we have developed so that we can actually tell whether or not a man speaks like a Communist or like an anti-Communist. (CN-24)

If as a result of this screening the prisoner was judged to be anti-Communist, he was accepted into Ching's organization. If he was considered to be pro-Communist or wavering, efforts were made to "educate" him. The methods employed in the "education" of such PW's have also been described by Ching.

I would ask them: "The Communists claim that you joined the Communist army as honorable volunteers. Tell me now, where is the honor? What did you get out of it?" Then I would explain to them other actions and deceptions that had been worked on them by the Communists. I would tell them freely about my own experience with the Communists. The process of conversion is a long and tedious one. One must talk to me like this all the time, just keep talking and get others to talk to them. One must treat them nicely, be friendly and kindly at first. One must not challenge or provoke them. These men are so used to the Communist methods that if you apply these same methods it tends to work very well. I would point out to them, for example, that they are fed better in the PW camps than they were in the Communist army. I pointed out, therefore, how the Communists lied about PW treatment. I also pointed out how the North Koreans, who were to help us as supply people, gave us worse treatment as PW's than the U.N. people did. (CN-24)

If education failed, the Communist elements within the compound were kept under close surveillance by the security committee.

During this early period, when there was much uncertainty and the PW's were comparatively unorganized, Ching probably did use the predominantly persuasive methods he described. As time went on and his power became solidified, however, he began to use increasingly coercive measures and to assume the privileges of a warlord or bandit chieftain.[79] At any rate, he was regarded by Americans throughout the period of internment as the most effective and consistently cooperative of the Chinese PW leaders. And, whatever may be said of his personal characteristics and methods, Ching was a shrewd leader and organizer in the traditional Chinese mold. As a result, when he and his fellow prisoners were shipped to Koje Island in May, 1951, as the first Chinese contingent, he was already in firm control of 3,400 prisoners. Furthermore, his organization was solidly committed to an anti-Communist position, and at least implicitly against repatriation.

KOJE-DO: CONDITIONS OF INTERNMENT

By the end of June, 1951, more than 146,000 PW's were housed in the new compounds on the island of Koje. What were the conditions of internment which colored the development of their political activity in this third phase of the PW story?

Physical Layout

Twenty-eight compounds were constructed, distributed among four enclosures, which were numbered 6, 7, 8, and 9 to avoid confusion with the five in Pusan. Each compound was designed to house 4,500 men,[80] but most of them actually contained many more. The average per compound after a year of operation, when the Koje-do population had been stabilized, was about six thousand; the two Chinese compounds contained over eight thousand prisoners each. The individual compounds on Koje-do, however, were as large as the enclosures in Pusan; consequently, sufficient room for recreational activities was generally available. Overpopulation did not at first appear to be a serious problem, although later it was greatly to intensify the problem of control.

The compounds in Enclosures 7 and 8 were close to each other and to native villages; some compounds were separated by no more than a narrow roadway, and in some instances existing villages were directly beside the wire fences surrounding the compounds. As it turned out, not only were the members of different compounds able to communicate freely with each other, but groups in one compound were able to exercise control over other compounds. Messages and news moved easily between the PW's and the outside world, and the black market flourished.

[79] Of this, more will be said below.
[80] Unpublished army report.

U.N. Administration

Guard Force

The guard force was a continuing problem until fairly late in the conflict. Although training for guards was increased on Koje-do, the problem of procuring adequate numbers was not so quickly resolved. As late as September, 1951, the ratio of PW's to U.S. guards was 188 to 1.

When South Korean guard personnel were counted the ratio was 33 to 1, but this was still 65 per cent above the recommended ratio of 20 to 1.[81] Moreover, use of the South Korean units for guard duty had serious disadvantages; the units had been hastily organized and had little training and poor equipment. Their morale was low, since prisoners received better rations, clothing, and even shelter.[82] The South Korean guards were not trusted for difficult assignments.

Recommendations by military officials for improving the guard situation resulted in some changes,[83] but it was not until May, 1952, that drastic improvement occurred.

Administrative Procedures

Administrative procedures were generally unsatisfactory throughout 1951; not until 1952 did they approach accepted standards. Some of the deficiencies could not be corrected by the authorities with the resources at their disposal; others resulted from their concept of their mission and from their limited understanding of prisoner behavior.

The extent to which administrative practices fell short of the ideal is vividly suggested by the corrective measures ordered after an inspection of the Koje Island camp by the commanding general, Eighth Army, in September, 1951. Camp authorities were ordered:

> To establish procedures for proper supervision and control of visitors, ensure their search prior to entering PW compounds, and require positive proof of relationship to prisoner.
>
> To prohibit contact between civilians and prisoners and to post signs in the Korean language forbidding loitering, using cameras, and bartering with prisoners.
>
> To give proper instruction in methods of guarding PW's to guards of labor details and to utilize sufficient guards.
>
> Properly to instruct enclosure guards in their duties during alerts, this instruction to include use of weapons and methods of quelling PW riots and disturbances.
>
> To take positive measures to prevent South Korean guards from assisting prisoners to escape.

[81] Unpublished army reports.
[82] Unpublished army POW study.
[83] Unpublished army reports.

To improve records so that identity and whereabouts of prisoners would be known at all times.[84]

Although the logistical problems discussed earlier had become much less serious, they continued to plague the camp authorities; the always vexing problem of inadequate Oriental language skills remained unsolved.

Civil Information and Education Program

Formal instruction under the Civil Information and Education (CIE) program was begun with the 7,500 prisoners in Compound 63 on June 1; in the weeks that followed, the program was introduced into all compounds.[85]

The instructional plan for the heart of the program—the orientation course—included both formal classroom work and informal instruction. Classes were scheduled for thirty weeks, to be devoted to six topics in sequence: background of the war, democracy and totalitarianism, lives of people in nations of the free world, Korea and the world, reconstruction of Korea, and developing leadership and skills in group action. The following themes, emphasized in the unit on democracy and totalitarianism, afford examples of the more specific subject matter: what is democracy?; civil liberties and freedom—under democracy and under totalitarianism; behind the Iron Curtain in North Korea.[86] All PW's and civilian internees were required to attend these classes.

The informal aspect of the orientation program reached into many phases of the prisoners' lives. Radio programs and recordings were broadcast into the compounds three times a day. Censored materials in the form of books, pamphlets, and newspapers were furnished to the prisoners through libraries and information centers; in addition, periodic exhibits and displays were provided.

Independent of the orientation program, a major effort was made to educate illiterates. This was probably the most difficult problem which confronted the instructional staff. Not until the end of 1951 were Korean and Chinese language primers prepared, first and second readers ready, and the orientation lecture series rewritten in the simplest terms for those who had completed the basic reading and writing courses.[87]

The over-all plan of CIE also provided for a vocational-training program. Each prisoner was to be given an opportunity to spend a minimum of four hours each week learning some practical skill, such as carpentry, tailoring, or shoemaking. One phase of the program was the construction of permanent-type housing. Some effort was also devoted

---

[84] *Ibid.*
[85] *Chronology of PW Events.*
[86] The program for Chinese PW's differed in detail but not in essential outline.
[87] Unpublished army document.

to acquainting the prisoners with new practices in agriculture, and some demonstrations were conducted; however, the limited land area available for such work severely restricted this aspect of the program.

Finally, CIE formulated a comprehensive recreational program, with time allocated to athletics, plays, hobbies, art, music, and literature.

To carry on a program of this sort required a sizable staff. Since the CIE section was a military organization, its over-all planning and daily operation were under military control. However, it employed numerous American civilian specialists as educational psychologists, statisticians, and the like. In addition, about 2,500 prisoners served on the CIE staff in various capacities—teaching, leading dramatic groups, directing athletic activities, and assisting in the vocational program.

As the program developed, the PW teachers were replaced by qualified Korean civilians; however, a sizable number of prisoners continued to participate in the administration of the program. Finally, some Korean military personnel attached to the United States forces (KATUSA) were assigned to teach, monitor, and assist in the program. This group was recruited in the last quarter of 1951, when both PW and civilian teachers were being threatened by prisoner elements hostile to the CIE program; it was hoped that the Korean military personnel could put a stop to the intimidation.

The arrival of large numbers of Chinese prisoners presented an additional language problem to CIE, as it did to the camp command. Eventually, twenty-three Chinese were hired in Formosa, by agreement with the Nationalist government. In general the Chinese teachers were high-caliber men, but their mere presence in the compounds stimulated pro-Nationalist, anti-repatriation sentiment among the PW's. There is considerable scattered evidence that, both in the classrooms and outside, some of the Chinese teachers functioned, in effect if not by intent, as agents of the Chinese Nationalist government.

The CIE section was an independent unit, superimposed upon the camp command, with its own pipeline to the high command; it operated independently of the camp command in carrying out its assigned mission. Evidence now available indicates that mutual understanding between custodial officers and CIE personnel was never great; as the months passed and the orientation program became a major focus of unrest in the PW compounds, conflict between custodial and educational objectives became chronic.

Mood of the Prisoners

Adjusting to Extended Internment

When the prisoners were sent to Koje-do, they realized that the war would not soon be over and that the date of their release could no longer be predicted. The majority resigned themselves to their fate,[88]

[88] Unpublished Korean PW document.

and set about making their life more livable. In the bleak surroundings of the prison camp, they engaged in athletic contests and art contests, developed drama groups, engaged in various handicraft activities, and tried to prepare themselves in various ways for the day when they would return home. Some of the feelings which underlay their attempt to make the best of their situation are expressed in this excerpt from a document prepared by some of the prisoners.

> We, being captives, became very sensitive; naturally, we were apt to be more pessimistic than optimistic. As the days passed, we became more and more sentimental. We suffered from homesickness. We wasted our lives and wandered in an abyss of agony. Especially because we were exiled to this solitary, seagirt island of Koje, even the grass and the trees made us think ourselves unhappy and forlorn. On the other hand, we came to understand the real value of life, and naturally we became eager to start our new life. We had to console ourselves and make ourselves happier, conquering pessimism and despair. To do so, we realized, we had to do everything spontaneously and voluntarily.[89]

Intensification of Group Activity

While most PW's attempted to find simple pleasures and to prepare themselves for their release, some concentrated their efforts on gaining prestige and power. One informant stated:

> To be sure, from the time we came to Koje Island, we received sufficient clothing and food. This fact spurred the PW's on to a more fierce competition for responsible positions. By that time we felt our prisoners' life would continue indefinitely, like a wandering traveler without any destination. As we had nothing except the prolongation of our precarious life, the PW's united more strongly in group activities. . . . I would like to mention at this point what the so-called group activity in the compound was. It was the activity of group organization whereby each group competed with the others in order to gain hegemony in the compound, and thus to enjoy power, sufficient food, and relatively better living, even within the much restricted compound life. Such groups were many in number. Of course, I joined in a group too as soon as I was brought into the compound, and occupied the kitchen. Another group, to which I did not belong, occupied the administration department. The situation being such, each group was feuding with the others within the same barbed-wire compound, and conflicts among the groups became a daily occurrence. On the other hand, the rest of the PW's—some seven thousand—remained as bystanders and merely worked as laborers.[90]

[89] "History of Compound 65," p. 70.
[90] "Essays by Prisoners of War," Essay No. 1.

This intensification of group rivalry was a consequence of the social fluidity created by the movement from Pusan. Apart from the leadership vacuum created by the segregation of the South Koreans, old groups of PW's had been physically split up in the move; new ties and hierarchies had to be evolved, and a variety of politically oriented and self-interested groups were vying to shape the new pyramid of power.

Effect of the Truce Talks

With the opening of truce talks in July, 1951, the activity of the prisoners took a new and inescapably political turn. Now again there was hope of release. But, where formerly clearcut victory had been anticipated for one side or the other, now a military stalemate formed the basis for the talks. From this time on, repatriation clearly meant return to Communist control.

All of the prisoners' anxiety about their future now centered in the success of the talks and the character of the armistice that might be agreed upon. Those who, for whatever reasons, wanted to avoid repatriation had to take actions that would increase their chances of not being sent back to face Communist judgment. The struggle between pro- and anti-Communist elements was no longer merely a conflict over which should oppress the other in the compounds; the importance of prison camp spoils also receded in the presence of these new, larger stakes. Group activity took on an increasingly political cast, political struggles became increasingly intense, and the proportion of PW's involved in the struggles increased.

Typical Power Shifts

From spring, 1951, to the time of the official screening of PW's with respect to their repatriation choices in April, 1952, feuding and bickering were constant as various groups of prisoners sought to gain control over the compounds. Control often shifted back and forth, sometimes in a series of bloody battles. In the eight compounds where Communists finally gained thorough control, U.N. authority was repeatedly defied in the spring of 1952. Short case histories of a few compounds will indi-cate the nature of the shifts of power and suggest some of the tactics and motives of the prisoners, and so will serve as an introduction to the analytical discussion in the next three sections.

Compound 86

Compound 86 was one of the two major Chinese compounds on Koje-do. Most of its inmates were men captured in the Fifth Phase Offensive of the Chinese Communist Forces during May and June, 1951. When the first group of prisoners, some twelve hundred strong, were placed in the compound, the dominant single group was a loose Szechwan provincial organization. This group reflected the area from which a large minority of the PW's had come, but had no definite political aims.

A few weeks later, six thousand more PW's arrived. Among these was a sizable group of Communists, who immediately engaged in organizing activity designed to give them control. The Szechwan group, holding most of the formal control positions, continued to be dominant, however, and tried to avoid or eliminate all activity relating to Communism while operating the compound in simple accordance with the Geneva Convention.

In July, Fu (mentioned above in connection with the first group of Chinese captured by the U.N.) arrived at the compound with about five hundred men.[91] He had instructions from Ching to bring the compound under pro-Nationalist control, and immediately began to organize anti-Communist activity.

Thus, three relatively well-organized factions were operating in the compound. For about three months factional disputes and disturbances were common; the identity of the PW compound commander changed repeatedly. Little by little, however, the Szechwan group lost its identity as its members were enticed into the more militant Communist and anti-Communist factions. The continuing disputes caused some concern among the camp authorities; Fu's group informed them that only segregation of the PW's according to political belief would eliminate the strife.

Events continued in this fashion until the evening of October 9, 1951, when the anti-Communist faction met to formulate plans for raising the Nationalist flag on October 10, the principal Nationalist counterpart of the Fourth of July. When word was received that the Communist faction had learned of the plan and was mobilizing to do battle, the meeting was adjourned and the pro-Nationalist group sought out the Communists. There ensued a furious battle, which was stopped short of a decision only by the intervention of U.N. troops.

After the compound had quieted, the anti-Communists sought out all the Communist leaders, arrested them, and placed them in confinement. The next morning the arrested men were removed from the compound by U.N. military police. The Nationalist flag flew over the compound on October 10 as scheduled, and the compound was safely in anti-Communist hands.

The few Communists who remained were now easily controlled by the dominant group, and the compound entered a phase of comparative tranquility which did not end even when the PW's were screened for

[91] How Fu and his men got into Compound 86 is a minor mystery. Ching says he sent Fu from Compound 72. The U.N. may have decided to transfer five hundred men to even up the numbers in the two compounds, or in the hope of getting 86 organized as smoothly as Ching had organized 72. It is even possible that Fu, who had been away from the PW camps for a few weeks, was put in charge of a new group of PW's and assigned to 86 without any plan of any kind.

their repatriation choices. In December more than six thousand PW's in Compound 86 signed a petition to the U.N. command asking to be sent to Formosa; in April, 1952, fewer than 20 per cent voted to accept repatriation. The compounds of non-repatriate Chinese made up on Cheju Island from the former inmates of 86 were among the best disciplined throughout the remainder of the conflict.

Compound 85

In North Korean Compound 85, neither Communists nor anti-Communists were able to gain the upper hand through the spring and summer of 1951; men of both factions held administrative positions. Contrary to the usual practice, the leader of the Communist organization is said to have proclaimed himself a Communist and to have operated openly.

Almost constant feuding marked the period from July to September, 1951. Then, one night in mid-September

> Suddenly, at midnight, the singing of the Kim Il Sung song arose. In the darkness someone called out, "The staff members [office holders] have sucked the blood of the PW's." [This was the beginning of] the big riot made by the Communists. Its purpose was to murder the anti Communists. . . . They caught the staff members and beat them to death with barbed wire or poles. (KN-3)

Seventeen "reactionaries" were killed and their bodies hidden. The next morning Communists appeared in all of the administrative positions and assumed control of the compound; even the chief of the PW staff assisting in the CIE program was now a Communist appointee.

The leader of the anti-Communist organization, however, had managed to escape from the compound during the fight. He told his story to the U.N. authorities, and three days later U.N. troops entered the compound and dug up the bodies of the dead. With the assistance of the leader and other anti-Communists, U.N. authorities picked out Communist leaders who had taken part in the riot. Several hundred alleged Communists were finally segregated and transferred to other compounds. With the core of Communist leadership gone, control shifted to anti-Communists.

The anti-Communists controlled the compound until March, 1952. Although they continued to have periodic trouble with dissident elements they were able to hold their own, assisted by two more mass removals of alleged Communists. However, they became corrupt. They appropriated supplies intended for the prisoners and sold them in the black market at fabulous profits; they were harsh in their treatment of PW's who objected to their rule or their techniques. In January a group of PW's petitioned the camp command to remove the leaders, explicitly warning that a fight like that in September was brewing. Then PW's from other compounds, of unknown political allegiance but alleged by some to be Communists, were transferred into 85. They participated in dissident political activity.

Finally, early in March, 1952, the camp command, perhaps in response to another petition, removed seven top anti-Communist leaders. In less than a month the compound was under iron-clad Communist control. Compound 85 was one of the eight which, in April, refused admittance to U.N. personnel who had been detailed to ascertain the prisoners' repatriation choices. These compounds were not brought under effective U.N. control until June, when the forcible break-up of Compound 76 made it evident to the others that the U.N. was prepared to use force, if necessary, to move the PW's to smaller compounds.

Compound 78

Compound 78 housed North Koreans. Spoils were the principal interest of most of the groups involved in the jockeying for power which began as soon as the PW's moved in, but a Communist group, of a much more political cast, was organizing secretly. By July, 1951, this group had succeeded in capturing the major leadership posts. The compound leaders did not take an openly Communist position and cooperated effectively with U.N. authority. They appeared to be relatively strong not only within the compound but in their relations with the American compound sergeant.

In his official capacity Lieutenant Pak managed to place ten anti-Communist informants in the compound. By September the informants had ascertained the existence of an underground Communist organization and were able to identify the key leaders as well as numerous other members. Without official approval, Pak thereupon attempted to shift control of Compound 78 by transferring fourteen Communist leaders to another compound and substituting trusted anti-Communists in key posts.

One of the top Communist leaders, however, was out of the compound on detail when this coup occurred, and on his return quickly realized what had happened. The anti-Communists would have silenced him but for his close friendship with the American compound sergeant,[92] to whom he immediately complained of the arbitrary purge. The sergeant carried the complaint to the enclosure commander as his own. At the same time, large groups of PW's in adjacent Communist-controlled compounds conducted demonstrations, objecting to the removal of the leaders in 78 as a violation of the Geneva Convention. Moreover, this occurred only a few days after a series of Communist-led

---

[92] According to Captain Pak, "several PW's witnessed that Communist PW's bribed" the sergeant with "gold rings and money." However, essentially similar cases of politically naive behavior by custodial personnel could be cited in which bribery was certainly not present.

demonstrations against the issuance of red PW uniforms,[93] and the situation in the enclosure was touchy.

Under these conditions the enclosure commander personally intervened and, after an investigation which involved discussions with Communist prisoner representatives, he ordered the reinstatement of the fourteen deposed Communist leaders. Compound 78 reverted to Communist control, and within a month four known anti-Communists had been killed. Ultimately 78 became one of the militant core of Communist compounds; like 85, it refused to submit to forcible screening, and was brought under control only in June, 1952.

Compound 83

Compound 83 was one of the first compounds on Koje Island to be filled with North Korean PW's. Almost immediately the Communists sought to control it through a covert organization, and by July they had succeeded. Their nominees held the major administrative posts and they controlled the compound police. Under this regime the situation of PW's who had been active anti-Communists was difficult and dangerous. They felt that both the South Korean government and the U.N. had forsaken them and that they had no resources for an effective struggle against the Communists.

Lieutenant Pak, however, was prepared to help them. Late in July there were rumblings of trouble in the compound, and Pak persuaded the compound sergeant to appoint as chief of police a PW with whom he had worked closely in Pusan and whom he knew to be a convinced anti-Communist and an effective organizer. The new chief gradually replaced all the policemen with his own men.

In addition to serving as informants for the war crimes investigation, the police supplied Lieutenant Pak with lists of major figures in the covert Communist organization. Later—probably in September—they uncovered a plot to stage a breakout from the compound and to assassinate the anti-Communist leaders. This information was immediately turned over to the camp authorities, who removed the alleged plotters, including the key Communist leaders, from the compound.

With the Communist leaders out of the way, the anti-Communist faction exercised full control. Although covert Communists sometimes attempted to cause trouble, they were not a matter of serious concern; the anti-Communist leaders either persuaded the U.N. authorities to remove them or subdued them by force. Compound 83 remained firmly

[93] In July, 1951, the U.N. Command issued red-dyed, short-trouser uniforms to the prisoners, presumably to facilitate identification and so ease security problems as well as reduce black-market activity. The most basic of several PW objections to the uniforms was the fact that under the Japanese occupation of Korea, only convicted criminals had worn such clothing (interview with Captain Pak and other PW interviews). This association seems not to have been known to the custodial authorities. If it was known, its power as a grievance among prisoners who already felt humiliated by their status was seriously underestimated.

anti-Communist and became the pacemaker for a series of similar power shifts in other compounds.

THE STRUGGLES FOR CONTROL AND
INITIAL CONSOLIDATION OF POWER

The Problem

The most striking feature of the Koje period, and that which most clearly differentiated it from other periods of PW internment, was the continuing factional struggle for control of the compounds.

Gaining control had a definite meaning. A faction was in control when it could command obedience without active challenge from competing leadership groups. Each competing faction had to aim for one or more of the following: power, in the form of punitive force sufficient to compel obedience; a genuine identity of interest with the masses, so that support would be spontaneous; and mass acceptance of the group's claim to be the legitimate, proper source of decision in the compound.

Whether a faction's approach was primarily coercive, democratic, or authoritarian, effective exercise of control entailed monopolizing the key administrative positions in the formal U.N.-created compound organization. As long as even one battalion was dominated by a rival group, those who held the compound posts could not feel wholly safe; if a rival faction still controlled the compound police, they were in serious danger. Control of supply provided a valuable sanction and source of persuasion.

The struggles for control became increasingly polarized as the months passed, with nonpolitical groups tending to be absorbed into or overshadowed by pro- and anti-Communist factions. The establishment of control was never sudden or spontaneous; it depended on the use of definite techniques and the meeting of definite conditions. Once a faction had control, it could manipulate, coerce, or persuade the mass to engage in a wide variety of conforming behavior. This mass behavior, whether it involved rioting against the U.N. or refusal to accept repatriation, had great significance for the U.N. Command.

Initial Formation of Political Organizations

The creation of an informal group, based upon common interests and existing outside the formal military structure within the compounds, was vital to the success of any faction. One or more such groups were to be found in every compound. Their membership was usually small when compared to the total prisoner population; at an early stage they might have as few as five or as many as a hundred members in a compound of several thousand. These members were likely to be leaders or potential leaders, to possess above-average intelligence, and to be familiar with organizational tactics. The evidence of this study indicates that the leaders at a later, more advanced stage were generally men who had joined early and been consistently active.

Some groups were loosely knit, others more systematically organized. They were formed and met in secret, particularly at first, in order to prevent detection by the camp authority, which had forbidden such organizations, and to forestall disruptive action by rival factions. Most pro-Communist groups were, of course, more formally organized because the core of party men had been schooled in the use and techniques of organization as a weapon of control. They also had to operate more covertly.[94]

Anti-Communist groups often tried to model their organization on that of the Communists, particularly as they faced the problem of defending their power against Communist counterefforts. At first the Korean anti-Communists were content to develop local, single-compound organizations, whereas from the beginning the Communists aimed at developing an organization that would embrace all compounds.[95]

Tactics for Acquiring a Foothold

Agitation

Once formed, an organization tried to recruit new members and enlist the support of the masses of prisoners.

Communist Agitation.—Communist agitation was directed much more to immediate issues and problems of prison life than to general ideological or policy questions. A staunchly anti-Communist North Korean PW who was a platoon leader in Compound 77 through the spring of 1951 told why, in his opinion, "the Communists had so much success on Koje-do." He described his compound in Pusan as having been dominated by South Koreans who kept Communists terrorized and under control. In March, 1951, his group was moved to Koje. There

> The staff members [holders of administrative positions] of the compound in Pusan were scattered apart. [In Compound 77] . . . the Communists—I think they were Communists—began to say that the staff we had in Pusan had beaten our friends, had squeezed our food, etc. They said, "We need men who will take care of us and who will request of the detaining authorities enough food for us." [Actually] . . . the leaders had the same food at the same time and the same place as everyone else, but the Communists utilized the PW complaints about food. . . .
>
> Still the compound was under the control of the anti-Communists. During that period the Communists slowly raised their heads among

---

[94] The organizational structure employed by the Communist PW's and the related techniques for maintaining secrecy and internal security are described in various unpublished army reports.

[95] Interview KR-4.

the PW's. When a Communist was beaten, the Communists would . . . say: "In the civilized twentieth century no beatings should occur. That was a thing that only occurred before 1945, under the Japanese." [Furthermore] at that time we had very hard outdoor details—building roads, breaking up stones for the roads, etc. When the PW's were lazy the American or South Korean guards might beat one of them. A PW who had been beaten would . . . tell about it in a loud voice.

Day by day, they [the Communists] collected party members, and men who complained a lot about the detaining power, and men who sympathized with those who complained—and they organized these men into a group. . . . We tried, but we couldn't stop the Communists . . . instigating the mass. Also, the work details were very hard. The staff members of the anti-Communist compounds told the PW's, "We have to cooperate with the detaining authority and be faithful to the orders we have been given." But the work details got tougher day by day.

One day most of the PW's in the compound complained [as a group] to the staff members about the hard work, but it continued. The Communists said that the staff members were not trying to improve our life. "With the staff we have now, nothing will be improved. Let us make a change." Therefore, there was a distance between the masses and the staff members [i.e., the masses felt that the officeholders were only feathering their own nests and were unconcerned about the rank and file].

When they [the Communists] had a certain number, they rushed into the battalion headquarters in the battalion I was in and beat up the [PW] battalion commander. Right after that, the whole compound became Communist. Then the Communists instigated the whole mass against the authorities, and their main complaint was food. And then they propagandized for Communism and the Communists. I lost my job as platoon leader at that time.

If there had been South Korean guards, as in Pusan, I think the compound would not have turned Communist. The U.S. was too ignorant about the situation in the compound, and the U.S. officers didn't care. (KN-4)

In several cases, crude abuse of power by non-Communist leaders provided propaganda material for the Communists. This description of the situation in Compound 85 provides a good illustration.

From the riot [of September, 1951] to February, 1952, we cleaned out the Communists three times—three hundred Communists. . . . But it is a very regrettable fact that the staff members [leaders] made many mistakes. They failed in carrying out the work. What they did was a good example of what the Communists propagated. For example . . . the staff members exploited their fellow PW's, beat down many PW's, which the Communists had said they did. This was not fair treatment. . . . From January to March, 1952, some PW's transferred to our compound. They were Communists. . . . They, joined together, made a petition to the detaining power that beating was too severe, that freedom could not be maintained under these staff members. . . . At that time, almost all the PW's believed it. (KN-3)

Compound 76 was another major center of resistance to U.N. authority in 1952. The Communist leaders there refused to allow the inmates to be screened for repatriation in April, and kidnapped and held the commanding general for days in May. They ignored repeated orders to move out of the compound and finally, in June, offered violent resistance to the troops sent to bring the prisoners out.

Some light is shed on the development of Communist control in 76 by the story of the compound commander, who was appointed during the summer of 1951. This North Korean enlisted man—Mo—was probably not a fluent or long-time professional Communist but a rank-and-file party member. He had been rewarded by the Communist authorities as a highly productive factory worker. Capable of keeping secrets though not schooled in the fine points of political intrigue, he was an excellent front man for the Communists. At the same time, there is no reason to doubt that his story of how he gained popular support contains at least some truth.

Before I assumed that post I hated very much the staff members [officeholders] and those PW's who had good clothes and nice food compared with the others. I said: "If I get that position, I will divide equally. All the PW's will get the same food and there will be no differences." From the time I assumed my post I was respected by all and supported completely because I treated them equally concerning food and clothing. The detaining power did not say anything about the staff members having . . . [better] food . . . [than the others] and so on, but they did have it. I cleaned that up. (KR-19)

Agitation by the Communists did not slacken after they achieved administrative control. For example, when the U.N. Command issued red-dyed, short-trouser uniforms to the prisoners in the summer of 1951, the Communists were quick to exploit the general resentment in the compounds where they were organized and active.[96] While most of the prisoners put on the red uniforms, with some grumbling, the Communist leaders in compounds 76, 77, and 78 urged the PW's to resist. The inmates turned out in towels, raincoats, ponchos, or underclothing, and in some cases naked. Obviously organized and under competent leadership, they massed, sang Communist songs, and threw stones at the compound guards. Three prisoners were killed and four wounded

[96] See footnote 93.

before the demonstration was brought under control and the uniforms withdrawn.[97]

Although objection was inevitable and, from the prisoners' point of view, justified, the organized resistance in these three compounds shows how the Communists, already dominant but seeking to strengthen their hold, exploited the issue to prove to the rank and file that their leadership was based on and devoted to prisoner interests, and that those interests could be furthered better by active resistance than by verbal complaints.

This organized protest was one of the first overt evidences of Communist influence in these compounds. More important, however, its effectiveness greatly strengthened the Communist organization there.

Other grievances used or created by Communist leaders to persuade the rank and file to identify with them as protecting PW interests included issuance of bad food by prisoner cooks,[98] brutal interrogation methods employed by interrogators of the War Crimes Section,[99] misappropriation of supplies by prisoner leaders,[100] beatings administered by U.N. guards,[101] the alleged use of PW hospital patients as medical guinea pigs,[102] and anti-Communist propaganda which "insulted leaders of North Korea." [103]

The skepticism and pessimism of South Korean PW's who had hoped in vain to be released were also exploited to maximum advantage.[104] In fact, the disappointment of South Korean PW's at not being released early in 1951—as they had been led to expect—was probably the principal underlying factor which enabled Communists and disillusioned non-Communists to agitate effectively for North Korea in the South Korean compounds of Enclosure 6. The power of this source of disaffection from South Korea contributed to the violence and arbitrariness with which loyal pro-South Korean elites ruled most of the South Korean compounds; this in turn added to the disaffection of a minority of their subjects.

Prisoner ignorance about the actual causes of the military stalemate constituted still another exploitable factor; it enabled the Communists to make claims about the victories of the Red armies, with a good chance of being believed.[105] After the truce talks got well under way, the repatriation issue also became a major focal point of prisoner discussion. As we shall see, however, the Communists treated this in a very special way.

[97] Unpublished army documents.
[98] Captain Pak.
[99] *Ibid.;* Interview KR-28.
[100] Interview KR-28; petition by PW's in Compound 85, January 10, 1952.
[101] Interview with Captain Pak; Interview KN-4.
[102] Letter from Captain Pak August 13, 1954.
[103] Interviews KR-26, KR-4, KN-20; interview with Captain Pak.
[104] Letter from Captain Pak August 13, 1954.
[105] *Ibid.*

Anti-Communist Agitation.—Some anti-Communist cliques had, of course, been established in Pusan, particularly as a by-product of the clean-up of Communists sparked by the war crimes investigation. Although many of these groups were more interested in exploiting their connections with U.N. authorities than they were in agitating the masses of PW's and acquiring power based on mass support, it is clear that most of them engaged in some form of propaganda and agitation.

The agitative slogans of the anti-Communist groups tended to be drawn, particularly at first, from the experience of Communist rule prior to capture rather than from prison life. The Communists were in a position to monopolize identification with popular complaints against the U.N. administration; also, since the Communists did not usually operate openly—that is, as Communists—in the early months at Koje, the anti-Communists could not point to definite abuses during this period.

As part of an attack on general issues of national policy and on the prisoners' pre-capture experiences, Ching, the anti-Communist Chinese leader, went among the PW's arguing that they had been deceived into joining the army, and that the Communists had lied to them about the treatment they would receive as prisoners. The principal slogans used by anti-Communist Chinese also reflected concern with the general issues of national revolution: "Anti-Communism—resist Russia," "Down with the Chu-Mao treacherous bandits and man-eating devils." "Every day that the Communists are not eliminated, the people will have no peace."

Specific issues initially used by Korean anti-Communists in popular agitation are not clear. In the winter and spring of 1951–52, however, the question of forcible repatriation gave all anti-Communists a specific issue which they used to the hilt. As we shall see, when repatriation became an issue in the truce negotiations, anti-Communist leaders who had been lackadaisical about popular support found themselves driven to large-scale agitation in order to make a maximally impressive case for their views to the U.N. authorities.

Moving into Key Administrative Positions

While the development of interest groups and their agitational campaigns were important, occupying the major positions in the formal administrative structure of the compound was essential to the success of an organization. At the top levels, this depended on the active support or the approval of the U.N. custodial authorities.

Ingratiation.—Although the bases for U.N. appointment of PW's to key positions, or for acceptance of those who claimed them, are not clear and surely were not uniform, certain qualifications worked in favor of an aspirant. Some knowledge of English was a prime consideration in selecting prisoners for jobs that involved working with the custodial personnel. The ability of the prospective candidate to get orders carried out by the PW's, as well as his ability to maintain order within his jurisdiction, was another major factor. The political affiliation or attitude of an aspirant seems seldom to have been inquired into by the custodial authorities, particularly through the critical summer and early fall of 1951. Furthermore, appointment procedures during this period were largely casual.

In these circumstances, competing groups sought to ingratiate themselves with U.N. personnel, either to promote and influence new appointments or to prevent the discharge of members already in key positions. The cases of Compounds 78 and 83, described in the preceding section, illustrate both techniques. Similarly, anti-Communists in Compound 82 persuaded U.N. authorities to remove pro-Communist officeholders by presenting evidence that the latter planned a riot against U.N. authority. Later, this became a favorite device for getting rid of opposition groups.

Discrediting Existing Leadership.—A person or group seeking power would seek to discredit the existing compound elite in the eyes of both the rank-and-file prisoners and the U.N. custodial authorities. To discredit a compound commander, compound police officer, or compound spokesman with the authorities, it had to be shown that he was unable to get his orders carried out. To discredit him with the rank and file, the prestige that grew out of his apparent power had to be undermined.

The case against a leadership group might be made to the U.N. authorities either directly or indirectly. Anti-Communists sought out or manufactured evidence that their opponents were planning murders within the compound or riots against U.N. authority. If the evidence was at all convincing, the custodial officers could be counted on to remove the alleged troublemakers. Communists also used evidence of violence as a lever to get U.N. action against anti-Communist leaders.

Communist organizations were particularly skillful at using rank-and-file sentiment in undermining opposition leaders in the eyes of the authorities. Where they had succeeded in undermining the prestige and power of a leader, they saw to it that U.N. orders were not carried out, so that the custodial authorities had to look for new spokesmen and commanders. Agitation, particularly the argument that the leaders were not representing the immediate interests of the plain PW's, was the first step. Then meetings would be rigged at which a target leader would be criticized in the presence of his followers for various forms of misconduct. If the aspirant group was strong enough to refuse to obey orders without fear of punishment, it would use this means of proving the impotence of the target. If the aspirants could intimidate a target by close surveillance or actually beat him, he was ready to be overthrown or used as a front man. Alternatively, if an excuse could be made to get the U.N. authorities to pull him out of the compound for questioning, or criticize him in the presence of others, his devaluation in the eyes of the rank and file would be complete.

Seizure.—In several instances, a faction simply wrested the administrative positions from its principal rivals by force. Cases of this kind in Compounds 77, 85, and 86 have been described; similar events occurred in others. Such seizure was possibly only to the extent that the custodial authorities were indifferent to events inside the compound, or believed they could not control these events, or were pleased by the outcome. Although the anti-Communist victory in Compound 86 was achieved in direct defiance of U.N. orders, the compound authorities did not reverse it. On the other hand, the Communist seizure of power in 85 was nullified by subsequent removal of the leaders. In 77 and some other compounds, however, the authorities either did nothing when Communist power was established or reinforced it by physical seizure and restraint of non-Communist jobholders.

Variations in Clarity of Purpose and Organizational Skill.—Informed observers of the Koje scene hold that through the summer of 1951, during the initial months the prisoners spent in the new Koje compounds, Communist-controlled groups dominated most of the prison compounds.[106] While ingratiation with U.N. personnel doubtless played a significant part in this early seizure of control, clarity of purpose and skill in organizational techniques were even more important. At this time Communist groups could not operate openly as such; they functioned through front men and front groups, using this screen to establish individual Communists or puppets in key spots. In some compounds, the Communists were able to establish such complete control that eventually they could foment disciplined, compound-wide rebellion against U.N. authority, even at the cost of numerous PW lives. In others, they were interrupted in mid-course by the counteractivity of equally shrewd anti-Communist groups and either forced into the open prematurely or disorganized.

Election to office was a formal route through which members of a faction could conceivably gain control of the administrative structure. However, formal election did not become a common practice in the compounds until the late autumn of 1951, and by that time the pattern of party-type organization and extra-administrative discipline had been set. Almost invariably, compound elections merely registered the power structure which already existed.

Initial Consolidation of Power

Filling Lower-Level Jobs

It was generally understood that U.N. approval of a group of top-level PW "officials" gave the latter the right to fill the lower positions with their own men. Their problem was to find enough reliable men to perform these jobs without creating new, independent nuclei of power.

[106] Captain Pak; Interview o–13; "History of Compound 65."

It has been pointed out how the appointed chief of police in Compound 83 built a new police force loyal to him. Similarly, a non-repatriate PW recalls how the Communists consolidated their control in Compound 77.

> In Pusan, I didn't know . . . which side had power, but about a month after I was transferred to Compound 77 I knew that the Communists controlled that compound. I belonged to the 4th Battalion, where the battalion leader and almost all the section leaders were anti-Communist. I was sure that about 70 per cent of the men in the 4th Battalion were anti-Communist, but as the compound was controlled by the Communists they started to kick out all the anti-Communists from positions of power [in the several battalions]. . . . At this time I worked as a company clerk and I too was kicked out of my job and became an ordinary PW. . . .
>
> Always they tried to make some excuse to kick out the anti-Communists. For example, they always watched us. If we did something wrong, they had a discussion group and criticized us in front of all the other people.
>
> They had a guard [compound police] company which was . . . authorized by the U.N. authorities. As the guard was organized by the Communist PW's, they had control over the situation. If some company leader or battalion leader did something wrong and was known as anti-Communist, the guard company would . . . beat him and they gave his position to some other man. I was not beaten by them, but one of the company leaders, a dear friend of mine, was beaten . . . all night. . . .
>
> They had some Labor party organization underground, and they had guards who dispatched men to watch in each section or tent. They could check everyone's background and personal history. They could separate the real Communists from anti-Communists. Then when they selected leaders, they selected only the real Communists. . . . (KN-10)

Wrecking the Opposition

In addition to placing its members or puppets in the key positions, a group that wished to be sure of its power had to wreck the rival organization in order to be certain of maintaining control.

Use of Police Power.—Disruption of the opposing group was principally a task for the compound police and other disciplinary organs. By systematic espionage and surveillance, raiding opposition cell meetings, beating, incarceration, and killing, the police were able to render impotent the organized opposition,[107] and neither Communist nor anti-Communist groups hesitated to use these methods.

As a matter of policy, the Communists normally made the compound police into a mere law-and-order force, using their own covert organs for

[107] "Interviews With 24 Korean PW Leaders," Interview KN-5; Captain Pak.

the control of political criminals. In Communist-controlled compounds men would simply disappear without a trace—and the ruling group gained additional power from this unknown terror.

Removal of Dissident Elements.—Communist groups assuming power in the compounds tended to try to control all PW's rather than allow or encourage the removal of their opponents. Successful anti-Communists, on the other hand, tended to welcome any opportunity to get physically rid of Communist agitators.

Throughout the spring and summer of 1951, in order to persuade U.S. authorities to transfer dissident elements to other compounds, compound leaders had to provide evidence that the opposition PW's were planning to riot against U.N. authority or to engineer a mass escape; this was the only kind of threat that would galvanize the authorities into action. Lieutenant Pak's abortive effort to remove Communist leaders from Compound 78 might have succeeded had he been able to present evidence of this kind. It is not beyond the bounds of possibility, therefore, that non-Communist groups sometimes manufactured such evidence in order to achieve their ends.

As conflict became more frequent in the compounds, the custodial authorities adopted an informal policy of transferring troublemakers—that is, unsuccessful aspirants for power—from one compound to another. While the authorities paid little or no attention, at least initially, to political allegiances in determining who should be removed or where they should be sent, this transfer policy did make it easier for successful PW leadership groups to wreck their opponents' organizations.

Removal of actual or potential troublemakers by U.N. personnel helped various anti-Communist groups to gain and maintain control of compounds. The case of Compound 85, however—where as late as March, 1952, the removal of a group of anti-Communist leaders, perhaps as the result of a prisoner petition, enabled Communists to assume full control—should serve to remind the reader that the policy of segregating troublemakers was nonpolitical and could be carried out on occasion with pure, if disastrous, impartiality.

MOTIVES AND STIMULI FOR INDIVIDUAL COMMITMENT

We have now explored the major social processes and conditions involved in the power struggles in the compounds prior to the repatriation screening. One further social process—that by which the power of the rulers was finally consolidated and used with maximum effectiveness—remains to be described, and will be taken up in the next section. First, however, let us consider why individual prisoners became active participants, since it appears that motives in the 1952 struggles and in the consolidation stage differed significantly from those which impelled the original activists in 1951.

Why, then, did PW's initiate political organizations or join them before they had achieved firm control? Why did prisoners come to perceive their problems as requiring them to choose between a Communist and an anti-Communist orientation? Why did they become militant and desperate?

It is important to repeat here that until a ruling clique had fully consolidated its power only a relatively small minority of the prisoners of war were politically active and identified with one group or another. In the earliest struggles, the activists were a tiny minority. As the struggle for power moved forward and conditions changed, these men were joined by others. However, even at the height of the struggles in those compounds where conflict was most intense and prolonged, there is no evidence that even 25 per cent of the inmates played active parts. Yet the outcome of these minority struggles committed and compelled the behavior of the great inert mass of prisoners.

Conditions and motives differed in detail from one compound to the next and from one moment to the next. We, therefore, have examined the sequence of events in a number of compounds and attempted to extract those developments which, in the view of the PW's themselves, most acutely affected their lives and their futures.

These general sources of personal commitment will be discussed under three headings. First, to what extent did pre-capture attitudes and orientations affect political choices in the prison camps? Second, what part did the motives of personal safety and aggrandizement play? And third, how did U.N. policies and practices, both within the camps and in the armistice negotiations, stimulate and channel the political energies of the prisoners?

Pre-Capture Attitudes toward Political Authority

Attitudes toward Communist Authority

It has been pointed out that at time of capture, the attitudes of the prisoners toward political authority in general and Communist authority in particular varied greatly. A few illustrations will suggest the importance of pre-capture experiences on both sides of the political fence.

Hard-Core Anti-Communists.—Among the men who initiated anti-Communist activity in the compounds, a disproportionately large number came from backgrounds with high prestige and authority in the pre-Communist social orders of Korea and China. Precisely because of these backgrounds, they had suffered discrimination at the hands of Communist authority.[108]

For example, Pak Chang (KN-10), a minor anti-Communist leader from his earliest days on Koje-do, had been a clerk in Japanese-occupied

---

[108] See, for example, data on class origins and personal histories in "Interviews With 24 Korean PW Leaders," and information on Chinese anti-Communist PW leaders cited earlier.

Korea and had inherited some land. The Soviet occupation forces abolished the Japanese organization he worked for, his land was confiscated under land reform, and he was reduced to earning his living as a peddler. He helped form a sports association which was in reality a clandestine anti-Communist organization and which became suspect; the members were kept under close surveillance. Pak concluded that his future in North Korea was bleak; he "suffered, and hoped for an opportunity to leave the country." Drafted in 1950, he surrendered to U.N. forces as soon as he had a chance.

Some young men of similar background had tried to cooperate with the Communists but had found themselves discriminated against nonetheless. Wang Tsun-ming, who became a major anti-Communist leader among the Chinese PW's, was the son of a landlord and county official and himself a Nationalist army officer. Captured by the Communists, he felt at first that they were not so bad after all and resolved to make the best of his situation. The rigors of thought reform, the necessity to break publicly all his old ties, and the persistent suspicion with which he was regarded, however, soon hardened Wang against the Communists. After deserting to the U.N. he immediately made it apparent that he was violently anti-Communist.[109]

Not all anti-Communist PW leaders were representatives of social classes which the Communists had set out to destroy. Fu, the first active anti-Communist agitator among the Chinese PW's in Pusan, came from a poor family, but grew to distrust and dislike the Communists during his ten years of Nationalist army service. Captured by the Communists, he complied with their demands only far enough to avoid serious punishment; unlike many other Nationalist soldiers, he was not won over by his reindoctrination. Assigned to a Red Army unit, he was given all the hardest work and was jailed twice—once for attempting desertion, once for expressing reactionary opinions. A physically powerful and blunt-spoken man, Fu apparently lacked the ability of most Chinese to dissemble and adjust to outward necessities; the longer he lived under Communist authority, the more he hated it.

Similarly, Sun (KN-4), an early anti-Communist platoon leader in Pusan and in Compound 77, was the poorly educated son of a North Korean middle farmer. Some members of his family were Christians, however, and he reacted negatively to Communist propaganda and control from the first. As early as 1946, he was fired from his job as a factory truck driver for not attending the weekly political meeting and was drafted into the army. As a soldier, Sun attempted to desert and never gave enthusiastic assent to Communist ideas. Consequently, although the army expanded greatly and most early recruits won leadership posts, he rose no higher than private first class.

Anti-Communist sentiment as such was a significant factor among at

---

[109] For additional detail, see Chapter 3, above.

least some of the prisoner leaders at an early stage. It will be recalled that some of the Pusan compound leaders spontaneously asked Lieutenant Pak to accept and act on lists of hard-core Communists and that, when Pak failed to persuade his American superiors to take action, the PW leaders resorted to torture in order to wring false confessions to war crimes out of Communist PW's so that the authorities would remove them. This action by these leaders was, therefore, not a means of ingratiation with the U.N. authorities but a means of revenge and political prudence based on hatred of Communists as such. The men who took the initiative in organizing the Chinese PW's did so from the beginning on a more or less explicitly anti-Communist basis. All leaders who took such early actions were marked and committed by them; having begun so, they had to continue to try to subdue or convert their Communist fellow prisoners.

Generally speaking, the evidence available to the authors suggests that, at the time of their capture by the U.N., a larger proportion of the Chinese than of the Korean PW's were animated by vigorously anti-Communist feelings. This difference seems to have been not so much a function of different class origins as of different experience with Communist authority.

In any case, the available evidence indicates that, of the PW leaders who entered actively into the struggles for control and ran risks for their position, only a minority were animated principally and from the beginning by strong anti-Communist convictions.

Hard-Core Communists.—Several of the principal Communist leaders were long-time, professional party officials. Sang,[110] the chief of these, posed as a rank-and-file enlisted PW under the name of Mun. First in Pusan and then in Compound 77 on Koje-do, he gradually but systematically built up a disciplined underground party organization. He consolidated his control of 77 during the summer of 1951, and 76, 77, and 78 became a coordinated trio during the autumn. Communist organizations in other compounds became subordinated to his headquarters during the same period, and by the spring of 1952 those compounds under Communist control were pursuing a common strategy. Sang's headquarters continued to be the center of Communist planning and action even after the breakup of the original Koje compounds, until Sang himself was picked up and segregated in October, 1952.

Why did other Communist leaders, physically independent, submit to this man's orders, and why did he pursue such an aggressive policy against the U.N. detaining authorities? He was in fact the highest-ranking Communist among the PW's. He was one of some thirty Soviet citizens of Korean ancestry who had come into North Korea with the Soviet occupation forces in 1945. Already a party member and political official, he played an active part in the occupation and then became one

[110] Interview KR-4.

of the principal figures in the North Korean Labor (Communist) party, vice-chairman but real chief of the party in an important province. Interviews revealed him as a man to whom Bolshevik principles were second nature; he was not a fluent ideologist or debater but a practical administrator and political intriguer in the service of the party, almost literally incapable of thinking in any but Leninist terms. He recognized early that the war would be prolonged and in the most systematic manner set about building a covert, conspiratorial organization on established Leninist lines. Its success as well as his personal prestige contributed heavily to its expansion.

Colonel Chul (KR-9) and Hung (KR-6), both leaders in Compound 66, had fought the Japanese as members of Communist guerilla units in Manchuria and had been party officials in North Korea; Hung was sent into South Korea on an espionage mission; Myong (KR-7) had become a Communist while a university student in Japan and had subsequently been a member of the staff of the party's central committee in Pyongyang; he was recognized as a major leader among the officer PW's.

Ro (KR-20) was a South Korean who became an underground Communist while a military student under the U.S. military government. He was commissioned in the South Korean army and then caught and jailed as a Communist agent in 1948. In prison he learned to use the hospital as a message center—a bit of knowledge that was put to use on Koje-do. Released from prison by the North Korean army in June, 1950, Ro was immediately commissioned a captain in that army. He became a battalion commander in Compound 66. Kwan (KR-11), another South Korean, had become a Communist while in Japan during the 1930's and as a Communist courier had been jailed by the Japanese in 1944. He became the PW compound representative in Compound 95.

Other front men in the Communist organization were newer recruits and more genuine members of the working class. One of these, Mo (KR-19), has already been referred to.[111] Another was Won Sung (KR-36), who joined the party in 1946 and was rewarded like Mo; he became PW spokesman for Compound 77.

Parenthetically, it should be noted that a man's background had no effect upon his assignment as a PW; in fact the information acquired on these men during processing did not follow them into the camps. Rank-and-file PW's in the camps knew more about the personal histories of certain Communist leaders than did the custodial authorities.

A survey of available data suggests strongly that only a minority of the captured Communist (or Labor) party members were highly motivated by pro-Communist convictions and loyalties dating from pre-capture experiences in organizing PW's or initiating action in the camps.[112] Among the Chinese prisoners in particular, party membership

[111] See "Communist Agitation," above.

[112] Membership in the party-controlled Youth Corps, almost compulsory for North Korean males aged sixteen–twenty-eight, was of no predictive value. See, for ex-

prior to capture had almost no predictive value with respect to a man's camp behavior; several PW's who became high-level leaders in the anti-Communist organization had been party members.[113] North Korean officers, the majority of whom were party members, were somewhat more predictably pro-Communist.[114] As in the case of the anti-Communists, however, only a minority of the PW leaders in pro-Communist compounds can be said to have been motivated principally and from the start by Communist convictions.

The Predisposed and the Neutrals.—Most of the prisoners seem to have regarded politics as outside their sphere of action, and political struggles as facts of life to which one must adjust but which one could scarcely influence. At least in this sense, many of the PW's cannot properly be said to have held any strong political preferences.

Some of those who were initially passive, however, were mobilized fairly easily by skillful leaders. Lee, born and reared in North Korea but a resident of Seoul since shortly before the liberation, is a case in point. As a university student in Seoul in the years leading up to the North Korean invasion, he was alienated by his belief that

> The government . . . neglected their own people. There was much terror and police action. . . . On May 10, 1948, we had the first big election in South Korea. Terror was used on all sides by the government. The government mobilized youth groups at election places. If men refused to vote for the right people, they were beaten up. . . . I saw goon squads all around with sticks at election time. . . . Each man seemed only to want to check off his vote for a name he had heard about and then get away from the polling place as fast as he could because there was an atmosphere of terror all around there.
>
> Most of the youth of South Korea belonged to Rhee's party. All parties used youth organizations. They were organized in schools.
>
> The Rhee government put terrorists in the schools, not to study, but to keep surveillance on all other students. . . . Terrorists came

---

ample, the interviews with KN-3, -5, -8, -23, -26, all of whom became non-repatriates, and KR-8, -30, -38, -40, who were passive, rank-and-file PW's. KR-20 and KR-44 were party members, but did not play active roles in the prison camps.

[113] Ten of the forty non-repatriate Chinese PW's interviewed for this research were members of the CCP: CN-2, -4, -5, -7, -8, -10, -14, -16, -30, -31. A sample study of non-repatriate Communist cadres indicates that 39 per cent of them (12 per cent of the entire non-repatriate group) were members of the CCP itself. (Alan S. Whiting, "The New Chinese Communist," *World Politics,* 7 [July, 1955], 592–606.)

[114] The North Korean officers' compound, 66, became Communist-controlled at an early date, and apparently without any overt struggle. This fact is not, however, an adequate index of the effects of pre-capture experiences with political authority upon the personal convictions and loyalties of individual company-grade officers. Normal military discipline would weld the officers into an effective organization. If the highest-ranking officers and a minority of the lower-ranking officers were dedicated Communists, their organizational weapons would effectuate full control, and the compound would thereafter present a wholly united front to the U.N. authorities—as, indeed, it did.

into the classroom. . . . There was no freedom to study or discuss political ideas or share opinions about politics. Anyone talking about politics would be sure to be regarded as a Communist. These terrorists were ignorant, strong-arm boys, not interested in discussing politics. They were just interested in beating people up. . . . I was beaten up [for refusing to sign a statement exonerating students who had been arrested for the murder of a professor]. (KR-25)

According to his statement, Lee's yearning for national unity and constructive action led him to volunteer gladly for the North Korean army in 1950. His military experience was too brief to disillusion him. Then, as an inmate of a South Korean civilian internee compound, he witnessed more anti-Communist terror both in Pusan and on Koje-do. As a result, he was readily recruited for the Communist organization as soon as he had an opportunity to choose.

Tai (KN-3) is a man of somewhat similar temperament and social origin whose experience predisposed him toward the anti-Communist side. As a young school teacher in North Korea, he had resented the misbehavior of Russian occupation troops and distrusted Communist propaganda. Eventually, however, he realized how completely his career as a teacher depended on the Labor party's approval. He joined the Youth League and later applied for party membership, but was turned down, presumably because his family background made him a poor risk. As a PW, he was actively interested in the CIE program, became a PW teacher, and used the information and interpretation the program presented as a basis for reassessing his own pre-capture experience. He became a convinced and intelligent democrat, and participated in the counsels of the anti-Communist PW's in Compound 85.

In some cases, strong political preferences had no effect on PW behavior because of the overriding desire to play safe. In most, the view of political authority as part of one's fate was a major factor inhibiting even the formation of definite preferences, let alone the playing of an active role. And, of course, many prisoners' experiences had been so nearly neutral, or they felt so uncertain about the nature of the alternatives, that they were not swayed significantly in either a pro- or an anti-Communist direction.

General Orientations toward Authority [115]

The behavior of the great bulk of the PW's was influenced much more by certain traditional modes of response to authority and new situations than by attitudes toward specific political movements and values.

Authoritarian Order.—In the first place, the Korean and Chinese soldiers were thoroughly habituated to a system in which authority has

[115] This section summarizes material on Korean and Chinese culture contained in existing studies, so far as it is consistent with the data of the present study. Chapter 1, above; Pye, *Comments;* Bunzel and Weakland, *Anthropological Approach.*

traditionally been exercised without regular accountability to the ruled. The idea of a society in which the individual has a wide area of free choice with respect to his alliances and his path of life is absent. Also absent is the concept of effective, regular popular control over the wielder of power. Traditionally, the Chinese or Korean has expected to live under rules and orders imposed from above.

Adaptation to Circumstances.—The traditional Chinese view, shared in large part by the Koreans, is that the individual cannot hope to influence the pattern of authority; he can only hope to improve his own situation by adapting to it. Deeply ingrained by centuries of experience, the pattern of rank-and-file behavior is one of passivity and resignation in the face of any evident power—and also in the face of the periodic struggles between rival elites.

Short-Range Calculation.—This orientation to power or authority gives rise to a tendency to act in an expediential way, to calculate the consequences of an act so as to ensure maximum personal benefit. In addition, most Chinese and Koreans tend to think and act in terms of the immediate situation, rather than to consider the possible long-range effects. This is partly a function of the fatalism just referred to. Because much of the environment is uncontrollable, it is useless to plan ahead too far to achieve one's goals. It is partly a function too of intellectual limitations; the poorly educated individual is less likely to be able to estimate the forces at work, and correspondingly more likely to remain passive.

Personal Bargaining.—Although obedience is ingrained, with it goes the expectation that the ruler will recognize cooperation and grant favors in return. The Oriental assumes that he can make bargains with the representatives of power, trading his active assistance for personal security and small privileges. The failure of the Communists to follow this traditional pattern was a major source of alienation for Chinese soldiers who came under their control during the civil war.[116] The same factor was a source of deep misunderstanding between the U.N. custodial authorities and the PW's.

Impact on PW Behavior.—All of these ingrained modes of response to authority are evident in the behavior of the PW's in Korea, particularly the rank-and-file. The initial marked docility and cooperativeness of the Korean PW's can be attributed in large part to the powerful position of the U.N. forces at the time they were captured. It was obviously realistic to seek to come to terms with the captor, in the hope that, having done so, one would be in a position to petition or bargain with his representatives for personal safety or privilege.[117] Even the hard-core Communist prisoners were influenced by their traditional expediential orientation; Bolshevik doctrine, like tradition, dictated ex-

116 See Chapter 1, above.
117 Interview with Captain Pak.

treme caution during this period, but there is no evidence that they sought even to reestablish party communication, let alone to organize into political groups.

On the other hand, after the Chinese Communist Forces entered the war and the U.N. armies were forced to withdraw, the situation again became ambiguous and the great mass of PW's became cautious and watchful. The power vacuum that resulted when the South Korean PW's were segregated in Pusan stimulated the development of new elites. Under changed conditions the Communists began to reestablish lines of communication and to set up a disciplined party organization in the compounds.

We believe that the traditional orientation toward authority affected every phase of the struggle for power and the developing relations between the PW's and their custodians.

Self-Aggrandizement and Self-Protection

Material and Prestige Rewards of Office

Much of the earliest organization in the Korean compounds had been simply the result of strong-arm tactics employed by rivals for the highly prized staff positions. Later as well, personal material gain was an important motivation in some nonpolitical leadership cliques. Over time, however, the relative importance of plunder as a motive for organization declined markedly. Not only did exploitation of the PW's give rise to counterorganization, but the activities of those who sought power progressively polarized around the Communist issue.

Putting a Stop to Exploitation

Leadership groups varied greatly in the skill with which they exploited the masses of PW's. Both Communist and non-Communist leaders, when they had control, systematically diverted compound supplies for the use of their organizations; they either used them directly or bartered them through the barbed wire for the goods they needed to carry out their plans. For the most part, however, the Communists seem to have managed their appropriations without the majority of the prisoners becoming aware of what they were doing, and they did not use the goods for personal enrichment. Non-Communist leaders, on the other hand, especially in Pusan and in the first months on Koje-do, sometimes diverted food, clothing, and even prisoners' personal possessions openly and by strong-arm methods, or in such a way that their personal enrichment became evident to the rank and file.

Patent corruption of this kind was a major factor in the formation of opposition organizations and in the decisions of PW's to affiliate with them. The significance of corruption in North Korean Compound 85 has already been mentioned; the following excerpts from a petition submitted by inmates of that compound as late as January, 1952, suggest not only the extent of the inequities but—more important for the present purpose—the feelings of the PW's affected.

> The monsters [PW leaders] made a quantity of money by selling clothing, blankets, shoes and other material which was supplied to distribute to all PW's. And so they supplied only two [thirds] or one third of these articles to PW's. They will use the money after their releasing outside.
>
> Here is another fact, that is, they . . . [forcibly] gathered many blankets from PW's and they bought watches, fountain pens with these . . . blankets. . . . As a result, about two thirds of all PW's have only one blanket. . . .
>
> 1. Having plundered and sold about twenty blankets which should be distributed for common PW's, they drank whiskey on spokesman's birthday.
>
> 2. . . . they sold about two hundred jackets (for summer) to South Korean guards outside fence and drank whiskey.
>
> 3. On the pleas of celebration of Christmas, last year, they forced much money, about 720,000 won, from PW's and bought four wrist watches made in the U.S.A. . . . which were given to [the PW] commander, vice-regimental commander.
>
> 4. Regimental 1st Battalion leading member plundered much cigarettes from PW's. The cigarettes should be given to PW's, but they did not give to PW's, but sold and bought wrist watch.
>
> 5. At 4th Battalion, after leading member compelled 15 blankets from PW's, they sold and got wrist watch for 4th Battalion chief monitor [police chief]. . . .
>
> 10. Here we could find the reason why we PW's would not express our thankness for U.N. good will and would hate some of leading members. On account of . . . these kind of leading member all PW's hate these men . . . and try to raise a riot and kill these kind of men. These kinds of men only make PW's Communist and raise a riot. To hide their guilt, they speak as if all the PW's are Communists and they would expose Communists. Not all of us are Communists. We are captured to live, don't want to die.[118]

The custodial authorities did not respond to this petition. We shall see shortly how, when the issue of corruption was combined with that of brutality, a Communist group was able to take control of Compound 85.

Among the Chinese somewhat similar abuses of power occurred without producing a comparable reaction. Although Ching became an absolute monarch in his compound and demanded all the appropriate privileges, the study uncovered no evidence of organized resistance to his rule, except from acknowledged Communists, during the Koje period.

[118] Petition submitted on January 10, 1952.

Putting a Stop to Brutality

Brutality was widely employed by both factions. The Communist organizations, however, seem for the most part to have used violence for definite purposes and as part of their over-all plan of total control. Anti-Communists, on the other hand, often adopted violence emotionally, out of fear or a desire for revenge but without an accompanying propaganda strategy, so that they gave many PW's the impression that they were more cruel, even sadistic.

Thus one of the principal complaints of PW's with Communist leanings— and, we believe, a genuine spur inducing them to organize even under conditions of terror—was the brutality of anti-Communist compound police.

Generally speaking, brutality was most evident in the anti-Communist South Korean compounds, many of which continued to be controlled by strong-arm men. When the PW's were screened in 1952, approximately 20 per cent of the South Koreans declared their desire to be sent to North Korea. We believe that the behavior of certain anti-Communist leaders contributed significantly to the size of this proportion.[119]

For example, Min, a South Korean engineering student, hated his forced service in the North Korean army but was decisively alienated from his former loyalties by his experience in South Korean compounds 64 and 84. He described the robbery, brutality, and anti-Communist terror of the compound administration and the effects on PW attitudes.

Q. When did you make up your mind that you preferred North Korea?

A. In August, 1951, I made up my mind that [if given the opportunity] I would be a repatriate for North Korea.

The anti-Communist leaders ignored the fact that the lot of all PW's was the same and should be shared equally.

The American authorities seemed to ignore what was going on. If they knew, I feel that was very immoral on their part. . . .

More and more of the PW's complained that they did not like this corruption on the part of the leaders. The exploited groups of PW's got more and more powerful. Some of the [battalions and companies within the compound] tried to revolt against the leaders and drive out the anti-Communists in order to establish just control over the compound. Sometimes they succeeded; they . . . seized control, beating and killing the bad managers. The Communist groups assisted in this drive to seize control in order to punish the guilty managers. . . .

[119] Numerous interviews with South Korean PW's (e.g., KR-25 and KR-42) indicate that anti-Communist leaders' exploitation, strong-arm methods, and brutal oppression of Communists constituted a major source of alienation. In Compound 71, made up largely of troublemakers and splinter groups transferred out of other South Korean compounds, 30 per cent of the inmates voted, when screened, to go to North Korea.

When I first got to be a PW in the compounds, I did not notice any political separation between the men, but when the anti-Communist leaders started to oppress the PW's the PW's revolted. At first the PW's had no political thought in mind; they were just against the bad managers. But then [in the spring of 1952] the Communist leaders gained control of the revolt, and the Communist leaders attracted the PW's because they set up a fair system. . . . (KR-28)

Compared with the South Koreans, North Korean non-Communist leaders were generally less sure of their power, more cautious about identifying themselves with a political ideology, and more moderate in their methods. Nonetheless, plunder and brutality were significant sources of alienation from the leadership and of counterorganization in these compounds too. The very fact that power was somewhat less thoroughly centralized in most North Korean compounds made it easier for pro-Communist elements to organize and agitate, and the behavior of the leaders gave them a specific non-ideological issue.

A North Korean PW who was active in CIE described how corruption and brutality that went unchecked by the camp authorities induced not only rank-and-file PW's but certain compound leaders to change their political allegiance, and how as a result Communists were eventually able to gain control. The following passage relates specifically to Compound 85.

Among the petitioners [i.e., PW's in 85 who exploited the serious grievances of rank-and-file prisoners against the elite and petitioned the U.N. command to have elite members removed] was Sung, the vice-chairman of the Korean Young Men's Anti-Communist Association. Therefore, the detaining authority believed this petition, and . . . [soon] seven of the most important staff members of the Anti-Communist Association . . . were transferred to another compound. Afterward, it became clear that Sung was a Communist. But at that time, almost all the PW's believed what he said.

Q. Was Sung a Communist all the time, or do you think he became one because of the corruption in the compound?

A. I believe he became one when he watched the corruption of the staff members. He had had a narrow escape from death at the hands of the Communists [i.e., Communist PW's in the September 17 riot].

He was not only vice-chairman but chief of the compound police. As such, he had helped the anti-Communist administration very greatly; for example, by picking up officers who tried to disguise themselves as enlisted men, picking up war criminals, etc. As far as I know about his personal history, he became a Communist [party member] in North Korea, not by his will, but in order to get along. Then, some time later, he sold his party card to a merchant and came to South Korea.

[After the removal of the seven top leaders and their replacement by Communists and pro-Communist puppets in March, 1952] gradually the whole compound became Communist. Day by day, all the PW's recognized that the former staff members had been too brutal, and really hated them, and liked the new staff. (KN-3)

Compound 85 became one of the eight which forcibly resisted being screened, demonstrated violently against the United Nations, and had to be broken up under threat of force in June.

Brutality was not, of course, a monopoly of the anti-Communists. For example, PW's interviewed in July, 1952, had escaped only a few days earlier after months of coercion in Communist-controlled compounds; their stories are full of torture and terror. Nevertheless, the Communists in general gave the prisoners less impression of cruelty than did the anti-Communists.

Thus the South Korean engineering student quoted above described Communist violence as purposive and minimal in contrast to the vengeful brutality of the anti-Communist leaders.

The Communist leaders attracted the PW's because they set up a fair system. . . . Each small group of PW's had a spokesman, and meetings were held regularly and problems were discussed. The hard straits of the prisoners were corrected by setting up a new policy; the Communists set up legislative, administrative and judicial systems, and this all helped to create good order in the compound. More and more of the prisoners were attracted to the Communists because of this; it converted many to Communism.

There were still many anti-Communists in the compound, but these were punished by the People's Court. Charges were brought against them and [at first] many were killed. [However,] after . . . control was . . . [firmly in the hands of] the Communist leaders, they did not do anything more to the anti-Communist PW's unless we noticed that they were trying to overthrow the Communist leadership or to report the Communist leaders to [the American] S-2. We simply set up a security system so that the anti-Communists did not bring harm to the Communist organization or leadership. (KR-28)

Where violence was frequently used, counteractivity was exceedingly difficult, but victims and observers alike were predisposed to take action as soon as an opportunity presented itself.

The CIE Program as a Source of Commitment

Clearly, the introduction of the CIE program early in the summer of 1951 contributed significantly to the intensification and polarization of political conflict; it served as a catalyst in the already disturbed PW compounds. However, the fact that it was introduced almost simultaneously with the opening of the armistice negotiations prevents any final judgment of its over-all influence. The program triggered off vigorous activity by both pro- and anti-Communist factions, and stimulated numbers of prisoners to ally themselves publicly with one group or the other.

As was shown earlier, a major aim of the program was to orient prisoners toward an orderly, responsible, progressive, peace-loving, and democratic society. Particularly in the first several months, the instructional materials were openly anti-Communist.[120]

Anti-CIE Activity and Commitment

Almost immediately, Communist elements in the compounds objected to the content of the program. Sang, leader of the Korean Communist organization on Koje-do, later had this to say about CIE:

> Actually, CIE was conducted . . . to make PW's think the North Korean system is bad. The CIE hurt the North Korean policy. The CIE program was useless. As far as I am concerned, political education cannot be conducted [in PW camps]. . . . What actually happened was that the United Nations introduced things that were not facts about North Korea. . . . When a PW attempted to ask a question about the differences between Communism and democracy in favor of Communism, he was caught by the PW police and sometimes taken out of the compound and interrogated by the U.S. security section. No man was allowed to ask questions properly. I want to emphasize the point that the CIE program was not a success at all. Rather the PW's found that the U.N. authorities attempted to make propaganda out of the CIE program. So the PW's came to hate it, hate it and also the U.N. authorities.[121]

> We decided to have our own [program of] education. . . . Each [of the three compounds that my organization controlled] had a certain organization to organize the PW's, so that all might be repatriated with their own ideas unchanged. (KR-4)

The importance the Communists attached to CIE is suggested by developments in Compound 85. According to the chief PW instructor in the compound, immediately after the riot on September 17, 1951, in which they forcibly took over full control of the compound, the Communists "said: 'CIE is the objective which we must get rid of and purge,'" and they appointed a "firm Communist" as head of the PW staff of CIE (KN-3).

[120] On March 26, 1952, CIE was forbidden by U.N. command order to use explicitly anti-Communist themes (CIE, *Third Interim Report*, May 19, 1952). The circumstances suggest that this order had a double origin—the effort of the Panmunjom negotiators to work out a prisoner-exchange formula with the Communists, and the current serious disorders in the Koje camp.

[121] There is, of course, no evidence that the bulk of the PW's hated CIE; Sang here follows the standard Communist practice of identifying the party line as the view of the masses. The study indicates that while objectors to CIE were beaten up in some anti-Communist-controlled compounds, they were seldom segregated by the U.S. for this reason.

Periodically, the Communists attempted, often successfully, to disrupt the formal orientation program. These efforts brought the Communist organization more into the open than it had been, made it evident to PW's which of their fellows were part of it, and brought the organization into direct conflict with the U.N. authorities. Only twenty-four days after the program was instituted in South Korean Compound 62, the lives of the CIE teachers were threatened. On August 3, classes were suspended in Compounds 76 and 78 because of disturbances. And three weeks later, the PW's who were serving as teachers in Compounds 76, 77, and 78 "were frightened and could not hold the respect of the students." [122] CIE activities were suspended in Compound 63 shortly thereafter, when the U.N. temporarily lost control over the compound. Similarly, until May, 1952, when all CIE activities on Koje Island were suspended, classes had to be suspended in individual compounds from time to time because of threats and disturbances.[123]

A Korean prisoner indicates the way the Communist elements in his compound sought to disparage and disrupt the CIE program.

If some were reading the books [given them by CIE personnel] they were insulted. [With the introduction of CIE, feuding between Communists and anti-Communists became more intense until, by September, 1951, the compound was becoming more and more Red-tinged.] In the Red compound, instructors still tried to continue their lectures. But the students utilized the hours of lectures not for . . . studying but for . . . demonstrating their hostile attitude. At the beginning of the lecture hours, they sang in chorus the North Korean songs (such as "March of the People's Army," etc.). The instructors finished the lectures with much disappointment. They were afraid of even discussing democracy and Communism. In this way the compound had a big movement against CIE education.

The leaders of the Communists protested to the detaining authorities about the CIE program verbally or, sometimes, by means of letters. When the instructors entered the classrooms, the students made a fool of them. Finally, the authorities left the chances for education to the students' own decision, and the program was discontinued.[124]

It seems clear that the Communists felt that they could not allow the CIE program to operate unhampered. In view of the party's emphasis on indoctrination and control of information, they must have foreseen that with the U.N. controlling the ideas available to the prisoners, such a program might endanger their objectives. Rank-and-file prisoner comments on the content of the program indicate that the Communists

[122] *Korean Chronology.*

[123] *Chronology of PW Events;* Weekly Reports, Chief, Field Operations Division, CIE, to Chief, CIE, GHQ, UNC, July, 1951–May, 1952.

[124] "CIE Program in the Compound," an essay by Kim-Uk-Sang.

overestimated its effectiveness in remolding the thinking of the prisoners. There is evidence, however, that opposition to the program provided a basis for unification, under the leadership of Sang, of independent Communist nuclei in a number of compounds.

It is important to recognize, however, that even in Compounds 76, 77, and 78, which were controlled by Sang's Communist organization continuously from the late summer or early autumn of 1951, the program continued to operate through the winter. The Communists' failure to wreck it, even where they were in control, resulted from two basic conditions. First, the camp command stood behind the program and was prepared to remove prisoner officials who allowed or encouraged disorder. Second, opposition to CIE was not an issue on which the Communists could get enthusiastic mass support; although many rank-and-file PW's were indifferent to the program, they did not regard it as an evil. Thus, in order to wreck it, the Communist organization had to be prepared for "war" against the custodial authorities, and had to have such complete internal control that the rank and file could be manipulated and coerced without fear of organized opposition. These aims were not achieved until February and March, 1952.

CIE and Anti-Communist Organization

Existing non-Communist and anti-Communist groups accepted and in general assisted the development of the CIE program—recruiting PW teachers, for example. And in certain ways, the program served to unify and strengthen them.

A Korean observer has described the situation of the anti-Communist North Korean PW's during the Pusan period as follows.

> They did not know what to say about Communism. They had no system of beliefs, no ideological phrases to describe their feelings. I guess this would have been the time to bring the CIE program into the compounds and help everybody understand . . . democracy. But when the CIE program did come in, it could not exploit the opportunity, because under the [conditions of conflict created by Communist efforts to gain control of the compounds] it was difficult to expect people to follow [in their compound organizations and behavior] the idea of democracy.[125]

Whatever the difficulties of applying democratic principles in the compounds, interviews with PW's indicate that the ideas promulgated by CIE convinced some anti-Communist PW's, in addition to providing others with part of the system of beliefs and ideological phrases they wanted. Tai, a North Korean school teacher quoted earlier, described the effect of his exposure to the program as a PW teacher.

[125] Captain Pak.

My determination took a long time—several months. I read many books from CIE and I talked with the CIE officer, Lieutenant ———. He lectured an hour a day about freedom. It was he who introduced me to the development of South Korea and the free countries. For the first time I understood that Communism is dictatorship. He explained it to me; at first I couldn't understand, but I thought about it again and again. Since I was a teacher in CIE, my opportunity [to study] was ample. . . . With his explanation I analyzed my past life under the Communists; then I compared what I heard in North Korea and what I saw in this camp. . . . [Tai's compound, 85, went Communist in March, 1952, and the PW's were unable to register their individual repatriation wishes.]

In the Communist compound I thought over and over about my past life and my future. I came to the realization of what would be good for my native country and my countrymen. I became more clear about the falsehood of Communism. [For a long time, however, Tai hesitated to act because of fear that he might be forcibly repatriated in any case or that anti-Communist PW's might refuse to accept him. Eventually, he took the bull by the horns.] . . . [in] February, 1953, [when] I was outside of the compound on a work detail . . . I wrote what I thought in the past and now and gave what I wrote to a GI. After three hours the [American] compound commander came and took me to the anti-Communist compound. (KN-3)

Effects as striking and decisive as this were, however, rare. Most of the PW's who were consciously and importantly influenced by the content of the CIE orientation program seem to have been men with some Christian background [126] or, like Tai, with higher education.

Anti-Communist PW leaders interviewed about the CIE program generally expressed disappointment in it; they wanted something more concrete and hard-hitting.[127] Apart from the special interests of these leaders, it seems likely that the teaching failed to have maximum intellectual and emotional impact because it could not break loose from its Western origins and because its ideas were presented too abstractly to fire the imaginations of poorly educated Korean and Chinese soldiers. Even so, some anti-Communist PW leaders asserted that the program influenced to some extent the prisoners' repatriation choices.

Although the content of the orientation was not of first-rate importance in creating anti-Communist sentiment or unifying and solidifying anti-Communist groups, the operation of the program committed numerous prisoners to the anti-Communist side. Those who participated in some official capacity, especially as teachers, assumed that these acts stamped them as traitors—or, at best, as unreliable elements—in the

[126] Interview KN-7.
[127] "Interviews With 24 Korean PW Leaders" and other interviews with PW's conducted by CIE personnel.

eyes of the Communists who were trying to destroy the program. Many of them consequently felt impelled to identify with anti-Communist organizations for self-protection, and so committed themselves further.[128]

The principal effect of the program upon anti-Communist organization seems to have been exerted through the civilian teachers recruited by the U.N. command from South Korea and Formosa. Speaking the prisoners' own language and sometimes adapting the prescribed materials as they saw fit, these teachers constituted a visible reminder that there were two Koreas and two Chinas.

The Korean PW's had, of course, other tangible reminders of this fact. The nearby civilian settlements, the South Korean guards who spoke their language—all served to emphasize the existence of the Republic of Korea and the fact that the struggle in which the PW's had been caught up was more than a contest between impersonal forces called Communism and the U.N. However, since the CIE teachers were inside the compounds and in direct communication with the PW's, their impact was greater. As educated men, and men who had constant access to news of the world beyond the barbed wire, they carried great prestige.

The civilian teachers were under orders not to relay current news to the PW's or to engage in political discussion outside their prescribed duties. It is unlikely, however, that they did not become involved in the life of the compounds or offer advice on prisoners' problems when asked. When repatriation became a live issue, they certainly encouraged those North Koreans who wished to remain in the south.

For the Chinese PW's on Koje-do, the twenty-three CIE teachers from Formosa were the only visible symbol of the continuing existence of a non-Communist China. The evidence is strong that some of these teachers acted as vigorous propagandists for the idea of repatriation to Formosa rather than to the Communist-held mainland; some of them probably served as *de facto* advisers to the anti-Communist PW leadership groups.

The Truce Talks: Initial Impact

The eventual effects of the truce talks upon prisoner behavior were so profound that they overshadowed everything else. This was true particularly from December, 1951, when the negotiators reached the issue of PW exchange. However, the mere opening of negotiations, accompanied as it was by a slackening of combat and a stabilization of the front, had significant repercussions in the PW camps.

Officially, current news of combat and negotiations was kept from the

[128] For example, after the anti-Communists were restored to power in Compound 85, Tai, as chief prisoner instructor, became head of the Anti-Communist Youth League Organization in CIE, with 150 members under him; and in December, 1951, he "prepared the blood petition from all PW's to the commanding general of the Far East [Command] and to the South Korean government" expressing their determination to fight Communism. (KN-3).

PW's. In fact, however, they learned a good deal of what was going on through a variety of channels—informal comments by South Korean guards, compound administrative personnel, and CIE teachers; smuggled copies of *Stars and Stripes;* conversation with civilians through the wire; and, in the North Korean officers' compound, by means of a standard-broadcast radio receiver which was effectively hidden from the authorities until the compound was broken up.[129] In addition, of course, rumors were rife. Let us, then, examine how the prisoners' perceptions of the negotiations affected their thinking and their organized behavior.

The Meaning of Military Stalemate

As has been pointed out, the conditions under which the majority of the prisoners, both Korean and Chinese, were captured led them to feel the U.N. forces were victorious; their initial docility and cooperativeness reflected this factor. Conversely, the U.N. withdrawal following the intervention of the Chinese Communist Forces provided the initial impetus for Communist PW organization.

The opening of armistice negotiations suggested to the PW's that both sides might have given up their determination to achieve decisive victory. The psychological blow was most severe for anti-Communists. Their opponents were now able to argue plausibly that the armies of China and North Korea had decisively halted the powerful American forces. In the light of the historically dominant position of the West and the rising nationalist aspirations of Korea and China, this was easily viewed as a solid victory for Communist arms and morale. Anti-Communists had to acknowledge that America lacked either the purpose or the power to subdue its adversary; in either event, the admission was damaging. In terms of its effect on the PW's, the U.S.-U.N. decision to allow the conflict to end this way was a boon to Communist propaganda, which always rests heavily on the assertion or prediction of irresistible power. It immediately stimulated Communist activity, created apprehension among declared anti-Communists, and increased the wariness of the great uncommitted mass.

The Prospect of Repatriation

The negotiations also signified to the PW's that the ordeal of imprisonment might soon be over. The inference drawn from the start of the talks was that, if agreement should be reached on the terms of an armistice, all PW's would probably be sent north to Communist control. Rumors swept through the camps as the negotiations were broken off and then resumed, as conflicts arose and were resolved.

The very possibility of being returned to Communist control was a blow to avowed anti-Communists more serious than any they had previously faced. Those who had committed acts of violence against Communist PW's or informed on major leaders could only regard themselves

---

[129] Preliminary interview with Captain Pak. Interview KN-7.

as dead men if repatriated. Even South Korean prisoners were disturbed.[130] Would the U.N., having failed to release them earlier, now allow them to be exiled to the state which had conscripted them? Would they be separated from their homes by an impassable political frontier?

For a time, the shock of these possibilities seems to have been dulled by two factors—the tendency not to look too far into the future, and the tendency to assume that the U.N. authorities, in the manner of good Oriental rulers, would take care of their friends. Yet the very fact of negotiation and even the possibility of being handed over to Communist control seemed to these prisoners to imply a measure of perfidy on the part of the authorities. Some PW's had surrendered because, among other reasons, they had read leaflets which seemed to promise political asylum. U.N. personnel had encouraged them to inform on Communist fellow prisoners, and South Korean guards had, in effect, encouraged them to oppress and even kill pro-Communists. South Korean PW's had an additional grievance: They had been led to expect release early in 1951; yet they were still held and apparently subject to whatever agreement the negotiators might reach.

For the bulk of the South Koreans, and for committed anti-Communist North Korean and Chinese PW's, therefore, the truce talks were a source of alienation from their custodians. As these prisoners perceived the situation, the Americans could not be trusted to finish the struggle against Communist aggression to which they had committed themselves; they could not be trusted to protect those prisoners whom they had instigated or permitted to carry on an anti-Communist crusade within the prison compounds; it was not even certain that they could be trusted to live up to their implied promise of political asylum.

The fact that the U.N. forces later held out against the principle of forcible repatriation, even at the cost of prolonging the bloodshed at the front, doubtless reestablished some measure of confidence and good will. By that time, however, anti-Communist prisoners had committed themselves to full reliance on their own organizations and efforts. The developments of the second half of 1951 saw the end of their willingness to depend principally upon U.S. help and encouragement.

Other PW's were, of course, encouraged and exhilarated by the prospect of early repatriation to Communist control. For the few dedicated Communists and the much larger number of prisoners who by now had become identified among their fellows as pro-Communist, the continued existence of a Communist Korea and the prospect of repatriation to it were the most hopeful news they had yet heard.

This first realistic, practical hope was, to be sure, complicated by awareness that they would probably be punished for having allowed themselves to be taken captive. Among those already committed, how-

---

[130] A petition addressed to General Ridgway by "all South Korean PW's of Compound 63" on October 27, 1951, requested reclassification and release, and added: "If we are turned over to the Communists in case of an exchange of PW's, we will protest against that to death."

ever, the principal effect of this was a resolve to struggle harder in the prison camps and win merit to offset that black mark.

The possibility of return to Communist control thus introduced a new element into the competition of rival elites for rank-and-file support. If the North Korean PW's were to be sent back to Communist control, they would probably fare less badly there if they returned under Communist discipline. The progress of the truce talks during the fall of 1951 tended to strengthen the hands of the Communist PW organizations,[131] and induced some non-Communist leaders to avoid public commitment on outside political issues.

For some months after the truce talks opened, these effects were not acutely evident, because it remained uncertain whether the armistice negotiations could lead to agreement. The talks were broken off and renewed; issues arose which appeared irreconcilable, and the oral exchanges were bitter; discussion was broken off again, moved to a new location and renewed. Until November, when a tentative line of demarcation was agreed upon, many PW's, like many persons elsewhere, could regard the negotiations less than seriously.

Nonetheless, the struggle for control in the prison compounds was intensified by the summer's developments, and the political aspect of the struggle became more prominent. Anti-Communists in several compounds petitioned the U.N. Command, opposing any settlement that would forgo the unification of Korea under non-Communist auspices.[132] In order to get the mass signatures required to make such petitions impressive, they needed control of their compounds. Similarly, Communist activity increased markedly and became more open. It was directed largely against CIE "slave education," and full control of the compounds was necessary if that program was to be effectively sabotaged. This wave of conflict reached its climax on the night of September 17, when the Communist organization engineered simultaneous coups in several compounds.

The custodial authorities were driven to initiate, at first in individual cases and then as a general policy, the practice of removing troublemakers from the compounds. This led to a temporary easing of tension and overt conflict during the autumn of 1951;[133] in almost all compounds the controlling groups consolidated their hold.

This was only a prelude, however, to the climactic organizational

---

[131] "The armistice meetings influenced [events in the PW camp] very greatly. From the start of the talks the Communists [in Compound 77, where they were in control] propagandized that all PW's are supposed to be repatriated whether they are for the Communists or not. That is the most important reason why anti-Communists turned pro-Communist." (KN-4).

[132] Letter from Chief, Field Operations Division, CIE (Koje-do), to Chief, CIE, GHQ, UNC, dated July 19, 1951.

[133] The frequency of disturbances in the compounds which the camp command reported as requiring intervention by custodial authorities declined in this period. Sang, leader of the Korean Communist PW's, described the period after the red-uniform controversy and the initial protests against CIE, "The PW's were divided into the left side and the right side, and they calmed down." (KR-4).

activity of the winter and spring of 1952. The issue of repatriation had not yet become urgent and dominant; the question of who should be repatriated had not yet found its eventual formulation.[134]

The Truce Talks: The Repatriation Issue

On November 17, 1951, the U.N. negotiators offered a plan for a truce within thirty days, and the Communist side agreed in principle. On December 8, Communist newsmen at Panmunjom asserted that agreement could be reached on PW's if the U.N. would consent to turn over all North Korean and Chinese prisoners. U.S. news reports hinted that a truce was even closer than official reports indicated.[135]

Anti-Communist Panic and Organization

These developments struck panic into avowedly anti-Communist PW's. At first, leaders approached American custodial authorities and War Crimes officers to ask for guarantees that they would not be repatriated.[136] When the answers proved unsatistfactory,[137] they sought means of consulting together and taking action on their own. With the help of Lieutenant Pak, North Korean PW leaders formed the Korean Anti-Communist Youth Association. Now for the first time, and principally in the hope of avoiding repatriation, these hitherto fiercely independent leadership cliques accepted centralized leadership and adopted a common strategy. The Association remained underground for about a month, but came out into the open to fight repatriation on 11 January.[138] At about this time, too, the South Korean prisoners' branch of the Syngman Rhee Daihan Youth Corps, formed the preceding summer in Compound 65, also came out into the open.[139]

A rash of mass petitions to the Commanding General, U.N. Command, accompanied these organizational developments. The following excerpt from a petition signed in blood by thousands of North Korean PW's suggests the desperation of the leaders who drafted these pleas.

The World War II has brought a violent government and more cruel oppressors to the North Korean people. Their sweet and deceitful

---

[134] Sang has been quoted on the motivation for his organization's opposition to CIE. While repatriation under Communist discipline was clearly in the minds of the leaders, they seem to have *assumed* at this time that general repatriation would be the outcome. As late as November 24, 1951, a petition from anti-Communist North Korean PW's in Compound 74 requested that the signers be allowed to join combat on the U.N. side, but made no mention of the repatriation issue.

[135] *New York Times*, November 16, 17, 22, December 4, 8, 11, 1951.

[136] Interview with Captain Pak; interviews with U.N. personnel.

[137] Some U.S. personnel interviewed for this research expressed certainty that individual U.S. custodial officers had given assurances to anti-Communist PW leaders, in the interest of preserving order in the compounds for which they were responsible. By December, however, the news from Panmunjom struck new panic and led to demands for more solid reassurance.

[138] Interview with Captain Pak.

[139] "History of Compound 65."

propaganda made a very little number of ignorant and stupid men blind, and it caused to make them Communists. There is no coincidence between their propaganda and practice in their forcing government. Their propaganda is not over than itself [i.e., is mere words].

As a practice they pulled all people in North Korea [into] poverty and they killed many free-loving youths who were longing for the free world. Thus they did those destroying and jealous deeds as if they were their duties. This is the fundamental rule in Communism.

Our anti-Communistic youths knew it plainly, and in spite of their tyrannical government they did not hesitate fighting against them and much of them died. We had been fighting spiritually or physically in underground or in the mountains whenever we thought it was useful for advancing on the way toward the free-living world.

In the meantime, the Communists started to invade the South Korea on 25 June 1950, and it was the last purpose of their tyrannical government. Then we were forced to come out to the battlefield, making up our minds to escape to United Nations' side when a proper occasion arrives, and just as our hopes, we were able to dash to the United Nations side raising a white flag . . .

And now we heard in the peace treaty talks . . . there will be taken place the change of prisoners of war on both sides. Hearing that, all of our anti-Communistic men are feeling uneasiness and a kind of anguish. We, all of our anti-Communistic youth, know what will happen when we . . . go back to our native towns in North Korea. No doubt it will be unhappy facts.

If we are forced to go back to North Korea . . . we are going to have suicides on the way to the North. And at the same time we make a request to Your Excellency to let us choose one of these two ways below:

(1) Execute us by shooting . . . [us] here.

(2) Let us stay in South Korea.

We offer you these two items expecting Your Excellency's suitable judgment.

Please favor those sons of Korea with Your Excellency's generous heart.[140]

Similarly, 85 per cent of the Chinese PW's in Compound 72 signed a petition listing a few grievances and asking to be allowed to go "to our free, native country, Taiwan, to join the anti-Communist, anti-U.S.S.R. tide." According to the writers, "We still remember the promise made by the Allied troops when we surrendered either to send us back to Formosa or to let us work for the Allied troops." If the U.N. sought to return them to mainland China, they said, they were resolved to "oppose it

[140] A petition prepared by the Korean prisoners of war in Compound 82 and addressed to General Ridgway, dated December 4, 1951.

bitterly, even to sacrifice our lives." Beside each of the thousands of signatures was a large drop of blood.[141]

These petitions did not necessarily represent spontaneous mass feelings; to a great extent they reflect political control by highly motivated leaders. Nonetheless, the Field Operations Division of CIE reported to Tokyo early in December that "a considerable amount of unrest is developing among the PW's. The prisoners seem to be most concerned as to what effect the cease-fire talks will have on their future. . . . Many anti-Communists are requesting that they not be repatriated to North Korea or the Chinese mainland." [142] And while this report reflects principally contacts with PW leaders, it indicates that some of the rank and file were restive as well.

In mid-December, the U.N. negotiators gave the Communists a list of 132,000 PW's held by the U.N.[143] In January some prisoners received letters from their families and in this way learned that their identity had been made known to Communist officialdom. Anxiety deepened.

Early in January, however, the U.N. delegates presented a plan by which each PW and civilian internee would be given an opportunity to choose whether he would be repatriated. The Communist side rejected this principle almost immediately, and a deadlock ensued until March, when hints were dropped that the U.N. Command was seeking a way of bypassing its principle of voluntary repatriation.[144]

On March 17, the Korean Anti-Communist Youth Association organized mass demonstrations against forcible repatriation. These began in Compounds 81, 82, and 83, then spread to seventeen other anti-Communist-controlled compounds. The crucial issue was now squarely joined on Koje-do.

Communist Response

In the meantime, Communist leaders had been quietly perfecting a multi-compound underground network. The disagreement at Panmunjom over prisoner exchange had raised an issue basic to Communist power and prestige; the organization had to fight and the apparatus went into high gear.

When Sang was interviewed and asked about his view of the repatriation issue, he first replied in non-ideological terms. As the following excerpts indicate, however, his later statements are more in line with the way in which a disciplined, hard-core Communist might be expected to perceive this question.

---

[141] Petition signed by 7,329 Chinese PW's in Compound 72, dated 5 December 1951. See also *Korean Chronology*, Part II. On December 20, 6,500 Chinese PW's in Compound 86 addressed a similar petition to U.N. Secretary General Trygve Lie (with fingerprints in blood beside the signatures). The petitioners requested a general survey of the PW's to determine who should be repatriated and who should be sent to Formosa.

[142] Report to Chief, CIE, GHQ, UNC, week ending December 7, 1951.

[143] For the rationale of this figure, see the "Prisoner Population," above.

[144] *New York Times*, January 2, 3, March 7, 1952.

I believe that the People's Army should be repatriated after the war according to the Geneva Convention, and that they should not forget about the unification of Korea. . . . They all came from their fatherland and they should be repatriated without any exception. . . .

Q. Do you think they should be made to go even if they don't want to go?

A. I would not force them to repatriate, but they came as North Koreans in the People's Army and they are supposed to go back. That is their basic duty as soldiers.

Q. I don't quite understand. Do you mean you're in favor of curing the disease even if the patient gets killed in the process?

A. That is not the same thing. . . . We have to remember that the whole army came out to work for their fatherland. They were captured as PW's. If they repatriate, they will be treated as ordinary soldiers; they will not be killed by the North Korean government. . . .

Q. I have been told that the main concern of the U.N. authorities was to prevent violence and murder; that many PW's did not want repatriation, and that the only way the United Nations could keep the PW's safe from fights was by separating them.

A. All the PW's were Communist PW's. The anti-Communists were forced to become anti-Communists. The U.N. is to blame for this because it allowed Communist PW's to become anti-Communists. The Communist PW's were citizens of the People's Republic of Korea and fought for the People's Republic of Korea. Nobody has the right to make them anti-Communist.

Q. I have met many who walked across the line in combat because they were anti-Communists. In what way were they forced to be anti-Communists?

A. I admit there were a few groups of anti-Communists at the start who, according to you, escaped from the People's Army. When they came to the PW camp, the U.N. allowed them to organize anti-Communist groups. The U.N. instigated the PW's. (KR-4)

The Communist-controlled compounds did not immediately begin demonstrations on the repatriation issue itself. The leaders seem to have assumed at first that traditional practice would be followed despite the agitation of their opponents; in this they were supported by the news that the Communist negotiators had flatly rejected the U.N. proposal for voluntary repatriation. Rather, the organization centered its attention first on tightening control of the compounds in which it was dominant, and on cancelling the influence of CIE. A CIE Field Operations Division report early in December noted that

The Communists are attempting to exert more influence in many compounds. . . . Compound monitors [compound police] showed a lack of complete control . . . in Compound 76. Students gave the shortest possible answers when asked questions. Some acted like puppets when called upon—as if someone is watching. There is no doubt of the opposing element's control in these compounds. . . . CIE PW's told civilian CIE staff members [in another compound] that the compound chief had replaced all key personnel with Communists.[145]

Compound 62, composed of South Korean civilian internees, was the first of the Communist-controlled units to shift over to a strategy of violent resistance. "Extreme unrest" forced the suspension of all CIE activities there on 22 December.[146] Then in February the U.N. Command began to screen South Korean captives individually with a view to releasing those loyal to the Republic of Korea. The effort to enter Compound 62 for this purpose, however, precipitated a major riot in which seventy-five internees and one American lost their lives.[147] This compound was not screened, and was broken up only under threat of force in June.

Overt agitation concerning repatriation was begun by North Korean Communist-controlled compounds only in mid-March, by which time Sang had achieved control of the eight compounds, including 62, which resisted screening. The "repatriation struggle," as it was later called by Communist PW "historians," appears to have taken shape in response to the anti-Communist demonstrations. Sang's account of these events throws important light on his organization's rationale and actions. Taking off from the period of relative calm in the late autumn of 1951, he says:

> Later, the right side tried to fight the left side intentionally. They made signs and placards and posters which said "Anti-Communist" and "Kick out the Communists." I thought that, according to the Geneva Convention, that should not be allowed by the authorities, so we submitted a petition to the authorities to prevent that. But it was continued.
>
> A little later we read about the repatriation in the newspaper, but I thought that all the army should be repatriated without exception. So we submitted another petition. . . . In spite of our petition opposing voluntary repatriation nothing was done. On the contrary, in the rightist compounds they hung placards and demonstrated and hung up the national flag of the Republic of Korea. [This refers to the anti-repatriation demonstrations of March 17, which originated in the group of compounds immediately adjacent to 76, 77, and 78.] . . . We submitted another petition to stop the other compounds from hanging up the South Korean flag, but it was not stopped. So we told

---

[145] Report to Chief, CIE, GHQ, UNC, week ending December 7, 1951.

[146] Report by Chief, Field Operations Division, CIE, to Chief, CIE, GHQ, UNC, week ending December 28, 1951.

[147] *Korean Chronology.* It is not known whether 62 was at this time taking its orders from Sang's organization; later, it did.

the U.N. authorities that if they didn't stop the rightist group from hanging up those flags we would hang up the flag of the People's Republic. . . . But the anti-Communists didn't take them down, so I could not help but start to put up our own propaganda posters and Communist flags in the compounds. . . . A little later on, the U.N. authorities prohibited both compounds from hanging up flags. . . . that ended the matter. . . .

Meanwhile, each compound . . . [controlled by Sang organization] made protests . . . against the screening of PW's. . . . (KR-4)

These protests led, in April, to violent demonstrations against the U.N. plan for individually screening the PW's and to forcible barring of screening personnel. They led also to mass parades, singing, and cheering on May Day, to the kidnapping of General Dodd on May 7, and to the bloody, last-ditch resistance of Compound 76 when the U.N. sought in June to break it up.

Sang described his organization as acting defensively and in response to provocation only. In part, of course, this image of Communist behavior can be dismissed as propagandistic; however, we believe that the Communist PW leaders actually did regard their actions as very largely defensive and to some extent even as legally appropriate. First, as it happened, they were in this instance defending traditional practice with respect to the disposition of prisoners of war. Second, the Marxist-Leninist principles which guided their thinking led inescapably to the judgment that U.N. personnel had instigated the PW's to act as anti-Communists and that those who opposed repatriation had been forced to become anti-Communist. And third, the Communist organization at this time controlled fewer than a third of the compounds; in most of the others a suspected Communist was not physically safe. Thus, the Communist leaders' image of themselves as struggling desperately against a highly organized tide of reaction is not merely a piece of propaganda. It helps to account, indeed, for their actions in April, May, and June, 1952, which put Koje on the front pages of newspapers all around the world.[148]

CONSOLIDATION: ORGANIZATIONAL ELABORATION AND MOBILIZATION OF THE MASS

After gaining control of a compound, a faction next faced the problem of maintaining and consolidating control, and using it with maxi-

[148] To say that the Communist leaders thought of themselves as defending right against force is not to justify them. Official Communist behavior in North Korea and China had, by creating deep disaffection in large numbers of individuals, removed the humane premise on which the traditional practice of automatic repatriation had rested. Moreover, to say that the Communists saw themselves as fighting defensively is not to say that the U.N. Command could have avoided events like those of 1952 by agreeing to send all the PW's north. Once the events of 1950 and 1951 had transpired, the PW's who opposed repatriation were at least as desperate and determined as the Communists, who demanded that all be returned.

mum effectiveness for the purposes of the ruling elite. The conditions and techniques of doing so are the principal subject of this section.

Organizational Development

After filling administrative posts with its own men and wrecking the organization of its rivals, the dominant group typically took two additional kinds of action to consolidate its power. It modified the formal administrative structure, particularly of the compound police force, and it set up a more or less covert political apparatus which could not only control the formal structure but perform additional functions not recognized or permitted by the custodial authorities.

Modification of Police Organization

Anti-Communist and Communist modification of police organizations differed in purpose as well as detail.

In anti-Communist compounds the monitor organizations became the principal arm through which the extra-administrative, often covert "party" organizations exerted their authority.

In South Korean Compound 65, for example, the compound monitors were initially organized with two departments, for administration and inspection, and two platoons of two squads each. Later, when the threat of Communist agitation became serious, the number of platoons was increased to three, each with three squads. In December, 1951, the population of the compound was reduced by the transfer of hundreds of men to other compounds, and at this time the police force was reorganized along South Korean army lines. The new force, which had about 250 members, operated directly out of the compound PW headquarters. It was organized under three staff sections (see Figure 3), with responsibilities extending over all compound affairs and prisoner behavior.

Similarly, in the North Korean compounds controlled by anti-Communists, monitors were spotted throughout the companies and platoons, and the force had its own chain of command from top to bottom. Although details of organization varied, the broadly inclusive powers of the police and their independence of the normal PW chain of command were almost uniform.

On the other hand, when Communist elites assumed power, they tended to circumscribe the powers and functions of the police force so that the administration of the compound appeared to be more permissive and less autocratic. At the same time, of course, they developed secret organs for safeguarding internal security and punishing political criminals.

Extra-Administrative Formal Organizations

Anti-Communist Groups.—In most instances the anti-Communist leadership groups were loosely and informally organized before control was established. Once in power, however, as they were joined by many

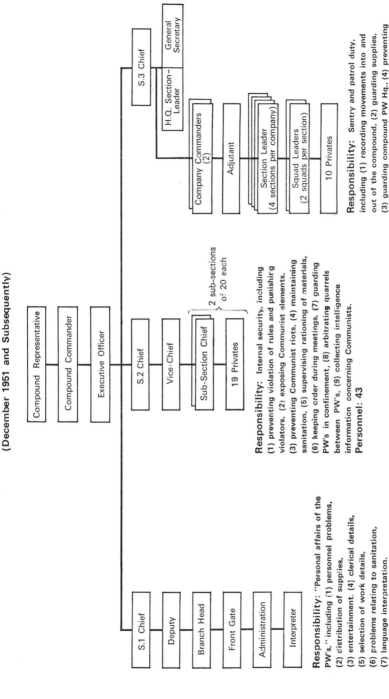

Organization of the PW Monitors of Compound 65
(December 1951 and Subsequently)

Compound Representative
Compound Commander
Executive Officer

S.1 Chief
Deputy
Branch Head
Front Gate
Administration
Interpreter

Responsibility: "Personal affairs of the PW's," including (1) personnel problems, (2) distribution of supplies, (3) entertainment. (4) clerical details, (5) selection of work details, (6) problems relating to sanitation, (7) language interpretation.
Personnel: 11

S.2 Chief
Vice-Chief
Sub-Section Chief
2 sub-sections of 20 each
19 Privates

Responsibility: Internal security, including (1) preventing violation of rules and punishing violators, (2) exposing Communist elements, (3) preventing Communist riots, (4) maintaining sanitation, (5) supervising rationing of materials, (6) keeping order during meetings, (7) guarding PW's in confinement, (8) arbitrating quarrels between PW's, (9) collecting intelligence information concerning Communists.
Personnel: 43

S.3 Chief
H.Q. Section-Leader
General Secretary

Company Commanders (2)
Adjutant
Section Leader (4 sections per company)
Squad Leaders (2 squads per section)
10 Privates

Responsibility: Sentry and patrol duty, including (1) recording movements into and out of the compound, (2) guarding supplies, (3) guarding compound PW Hq., (4) preventing escapes, (5) supervision of work-detail crews.
Personnel: 191

FIGURE 3

Adapted from material presented in "History of Compound 65."

times their original numbers, they tended to develop more formal political and ideological organizations with distinct names, explicit rules and regulations, tables of organization, procedures for the selection of officers, and methods of recruitment.

Anti-Communist and Fight against Russia Youth League.—Before the Chinese anti-Communists established control of Compound 86 in October, 1951, they were not formally organized. Immediately after subduing the Communist faction and seeing its members removed from the compound, however, the leaders organized the Anti-Communist and Fight against Russia Youth League (ACFR).

> First, the rules of the new party were worked out. The initial membership of the organization was less than a hundred individuals. The ACFR was divided into one branch for each battalion, with three cells for each branch. The anti-Communist fighters . . . were divided among the various battalions. Each member would discuss with his friends and former schoolmates the advantages of the free-world way of thinking. At the same time the party members were careful to "stay equal" with their schoolmates. . . . A candidate for membership had to have a party member introduce him and three party members to guarantee him. The application first went to the cell, where, if approved, it was forwarded to the branch. Finally, it was sent to the central organization of the ACFR. If a man was approved, he was permitted to tattoo the words "anti-Communist fight Russia" on his arm. (CN-1A)

Daihan Youth Corps.—As early as May, 1951, the anti-Communist South Koreans in Compound 65 narrowly escaped defeat at the hands of a Communist group, and concluded that only a militant organization could ward off future attacks. They organized a branch of the Daihan Youth Corps, a South Korean youth organization. By June 20 a platform and a list of functions had been formulated, but the organization was forced underground at this point by the U.N. camp authorities. In December the corps came out into the open, in defiance of U.N. regulations. Since scattered evidence indicates that other South Korean compound organizations were similar, the corps organization in 65 will be treated as illustrative.

According to the platform, members of the corps were to: drill their minds and bodies in order to become defenders of the South Korean nation; work for the unification of Korea, and purge all subversives and work for world peace. Membership rules were not explicit except for a lower age limit of eighteen; over six thousand prisoners eventually joined. For administrative purposes the corps was divided into a headquarters unit and five groups, corresponding to the five battalions in the compound. At the compound level, the top leadership had operating bureaus—training, mobilization, intelligence, culture, propaganda, inspection, and organization.

Generally speaking, the corps used and paralleled the formal administrative organization of the compound. Thus, each group leader was also a PW battalion commander. He had a staff corresponding to the compound administrative staff, except that the intelligence and inspection functions appeared only at the compound level. At the company level too, each PW commander was also a section leader in the Youth Corps. The organization of the corps in Compound 65 is shown in detail in Figure 4.

All observances of a compound-wide nature were sponsored by the corps. The CIE program was fused, so far as the PW's were concerned, with the corps program, and ultimately all the activities in the compound came under the control of the corps.[149] There is no doubt that the corps tail wagged the U.N.-created formal administration dog.

Korean Anti-Communist Youth Association.—North Korean anti-Communists also developed formal organizations similar in some respects to the Daihan Youth Corps. The first such organization pointed to by available evidence—and the one which later became the basis for the multi-compound organization of North Korean PW's who opposed repatriation—was formed in Compound 83 in August, 1951. This group, called the Korean Anti-Communist Youth Association,[150] had to operate covertly at the start because the camp authorities forbade prisoner organizations.[151]

The association's major aim was the continuance of the struggle against Communism and the unification of Korea. In pursuance of these objectives, it sought to train young people for service in the South Korean army, favored the development of mutual respect among PW's, and looked forward to assisting in the reconstruction of Korea "according to the policy of the Republic of Korea." Membership was open to young rightists who swore with blood to fight against the Communists, who could pass an investigation of their personal backgrounds, and who could secure two persons who would guarantee their loyalty.

The structure of the association is shown in Figure 5. Its activities were directed by a central committee of about a dozen members who were the *de facto* leaders of the compound; they elected one of their number chairman of the central committee, supreme leader of the party, and chief executive officer. Members of the central committee also headed each of the five major administrative sections.

The central committee appointed a branch committee of some eight or ten men in each battalion; these elected, with the approval of the

[149] "History of Compound 65," pp. 119 ff.

[150] The name has been translated variously: "Youth" sometimes becomes "Young Men's"; "Association" is translated often as "Party," "League," even "Corps."

[151] Although the new organization came out into the open in defiance of U.N. orders in January, 1952, members continued throughout the conflict to treat its organization as highly confidential information. Scattered evidence indicates that the structure resembled that described here, with the addition of a super-echelon composed of a multi-compound leading committee.

Organization of Daihan Youth Corps, Compound 65

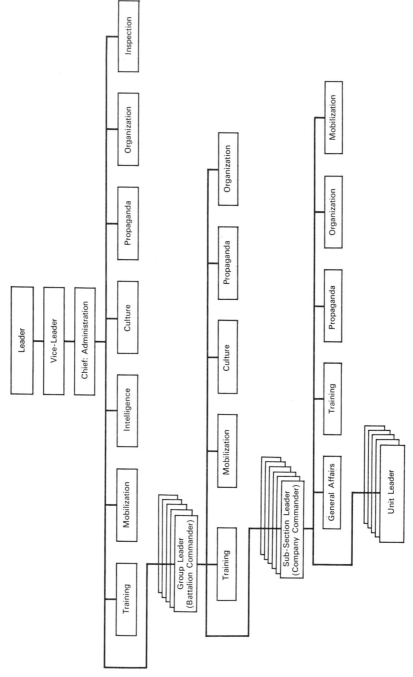

FIGURE 4

Adapted from material found in "History of Compound 65."

Organization of Korean Anti-Communist Youth Association, Compound 83, 1951

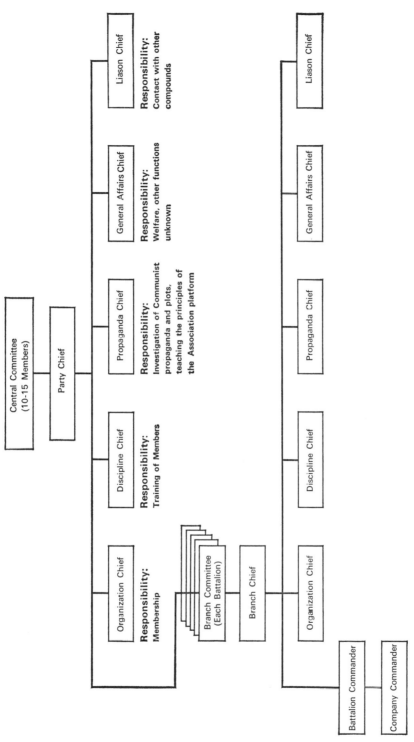

FIGURE 5

central committee, a branch leader. Staff organization was similar to that at the compound level. The branch party leader selected a battalion CO and company and platoon commanders; however, these administrative posts were not filled by members of the branch committee. Here we find the distinction between the party and the U.N.-sponsored administrative organization clearly recognized, and the latter made a subordinate front for the former. Nonetheless, it was seldom difficult for U.N. personnel to identify the real holders of power in anti-Communist compounds and sub-units.

Communist Organization.—Communist organization did not change basically during the period covered by this study. It began and ended as an underground operation conducted by experts, and its form followed established models. While some elaboration occurred over time, the very same organizational system was used in initial rallying of party members and sympathizers, in struggling for control of the compounds, and in administering compounds where power was consolidated. The basic structure and the functions of the several units have been described in detail by reports and publications of the U.N. Command.

Similarities and Differences.—Certain similarities existed between the anti-Communist and Communist PW organizations. Each was geared for quick, effective action under the command of a single person with enormous powers. Each was capable of multifaceted control of the lives of the mass of PW's. All were organizations of the sort that Westerners identify with police states; in fact, as control was consolidated, each compound tended to become a little police state.

Staff organization at each echelon tended to duplicate that at the next higher echelon; and the identity and functions of the several staff sections of both Communist and anti-Communist organizations tended to be similar. Indeed, anti-Communist leaders reported that, recognizing the effectiveness of Communist organizational techniques, they had in part deliberately copied those techniques.[152]

Very important differences remained, nonetheless—some of them reflected in organization charts, some not. In the first place, the essential form of the Communist organization was established, according to Leninist doctrine, when it was first set up, while the anti-Communists typically created formal organizations after they had seized power. Although the Communists elaborated their organization somewhat as it grew, it had a basic continuity through all the phases of the struggle for and the exercise of power. The anti-Communists, on the other hand, elaborated theirs more extensively, in response to necessity rather than on principle, and much of their organization directly paralleled the U.N.-sponsored administrative apparatus. Much of it was, therefore, in effect above ground, while almost the whole of the Communist apparatus was hidden from view.

[152] Interviews KN-10, CN-13, CN-23.

Second, the Communist system relied on a pre-existing elite organization. Only pre-capture members of the Korean Labor party could hold positions in the political apparatus; auxiliary organizations like the Youth League and Anti-American Fight League were used to reach and recruit secondary cadres. The anti-Communist groups, on the other hand, developed within the PW camps and became mass organizations in their own right. A total of six thousand inmates of Compound 65 joined the Daihan Youth Corps; membership in the Korean Anti-Communist Youth Association ranged from just over a thousand in Compound 94 to 2,600 in Compound 83; similarly large proportions of the Chinese in Compound 86 joined the Anti-Communist and Fight against Russia Youth League. While informal distinctions between inner-circle members and "plain" members existed in these organizations, the organizational basis for secrecy and central manipulation of the mass was less secure than among the Communists.

Third, the distinction between military and political lines of authority was more clearly drawn, and the supremacy of the latter more consistently implemented, in the Communist organization. For example, anti-Communist compound monitors included among their duties vital political-security functions which the Communists carefully segregated in their secret Sixth Squad. At the same time, the Communists reached the rank and file not only through the military chain of command but through auxiliary mass political organizations. They showed a far greater ability to separate functions and to organize them rationally, with a minimum of confusion and overlapping but a maximum of cross-checking on loyalty and performance from top to bottom.

Inter-Compound Relations

Communications

Communication between politically like-minded groups in different compounds, always present on Koje-do, became increasingly systematized as the months passed. Some compounds were so close together that PW's could communicate without even raising their voices. And both pro- and anti-Communist groups soon learned how to switch individuals from one compound to another while they were outside on work details, so that lengthy conferences could be held and instructions carried back to fellow prisoners.

Communication over greater distances was achieved by a variety of techniques. Anti-Communists were often able to use South Korean guards, KATUSA personnel,[153] and indigenous employees of the U.N. Command as, in effect, couriers. Although Communists had to operate more covertly, they too developed effective means of communication. In Pusan, North Korean medical officers who made the rounds of the

[153] Korean military personnel attached to U.S. units.

compounds both sparked and helped to coordinate the Communist revival. On Koje-do the 64th Field Hospital became the message center; apart from U.S. medical personnel, certain wards were wholly controlled by the Communist organization.[154]

Formation of Multi-Compound Organizations

Sang, the Korean Communist leader, aimed from the start at a unified political apparatus covering all of the compounds.[155] Evidence now available indicates that while he was able to achieve effective control of three adjacent compounds during the summer and fall of 1951, the activities of other Communist-controlled compounds were not effectively coordinated until early in 1952. Sang's liaison seems to have been inhibited principally by anti-Communist PW's; at this stage the U.N. authorities had little if any inkling of such a conspiracy.[156]

Anti-Communist leaders, on the other hand, initially aimed only to control their own compounds. Although three adjacent compounds (81, 82, and 83) were informally coordinated under the leadership of Kwan, not until the repatriation issue became urgent and leaders in many compounds grew panicky was a single organization formed. This was done without the knowledge of U.S. authorities but with the active help of Lieutenant Pak. Additional compound elites joined the organization after it was formed in December;[157] it came out into the open in January. As in the case of the Communist network, unified control became more effective after the screening and the segregation of politically hostile groups in the spring of 1952.

The Problem of Neighboring Compounds

Communication between neighboring compounds was so continuous that any major shift of control in one compound inevitably had repercussions elsewhere, and the PW's adopted techniques to maximize these effects. Something close to open warfare often developed between compounds with opposing leadership; in other instances, psychological warfare was employed.

Psychological Warfare.—The North Korean officers' compound, 66, was one of the first, most fanatic, and most openly Communist-controlled on Koje-do. Adjacent to it was an anti-Communist South Korean compound, 68. Enlisted men from 68 were frequently sent into 66 to perform work details for the officers. They reported:

> Compound 66 made every effort to overthrow Compound 68's leadership. When we were in Compound 66 on work details, they did everything possible to change our minds [presumably by persuasive

[154] Unpublished army documents. Efforts of anti-Communist PW's to clean out the Communists in the hospital during 1951 are described in Interview KN-26.
[155] Interview KR-4.
[156] Unpublished army documents.
[157] Interview with Lieutenant Pak.

arguments]. But by maintaining a continuous watch, we were able to destroy their plots. They found it impossible to gain power by force. They then began to use psychological tactics. Every night at twelve or one o'clock, they would sing Communist songs loudly. The purpose of this was to shock us psychologically. However, we resisted this by singing ourselves. We had all members of the CM [compound monitors or police] and the [anti-Communist] Student Corps at midnight, even in the dead of winter, gather in a mass singing attack upon them.[158]

Sometimes the mere fact that one compound in a group similarly controlled turned over to opposing leadership induced dissident members of the neighboring compounds to agitate and fight. For example, Lieutenant Pak "knew that, of course, it was certain" that Compounds 81 and 82, adjacent to 83, would become anti-Communist as soon as 83 was firmly in anti-Communist hands.[159] On the other hand, during the summer of 1951, Compound 65, the only compound in the sixth enclosure not dominated by Communists, provided an example and encouragement for anti-Communists in the others.[160]

Invasion.—Numerous attempts were made to send groups of PW's belonging to one faction into compounds dominated by the opposition.

Ching said that he sent Fu and a group of five hundred Chinese PW's, including two hundred militant anti-Communists, from Compound 72 to Compound 86 to end the factional squabbles and organize the latter along Nationalist lines.[161] And a group of anti-Communist Korean PW's told the following.

In December, 1951, about three hundred of the anti-Communist young men in Compound 63 organized a Forlorn Hope society named Hwa Rang. Our purpose was to liberate the fellow anti-Communists in Compound 62, which was controlled by fanatical Reds. There were five thousand PW's in Compound 62.

The Communist organization in Compound 62 was stronger . . . than it had ever been. However, the Hwa Rang group was never afraid of going there. We sent in [to the U.N.] a false statement saying we were Communists [and] asking to be transferred to Compound 62. Finally, we were allowed to do so.

The Red guards in Compound 62 never quite understood why we moved there. When the Reds began to hold inspections, our Hwa Rang troops rose up suddenly and made a sudden and mass attack upon each executive office and arrested two hundred of the leading Red members. We then put them in a temporary jail. We rapidly

[158] Korean PW history.
[159] Interview with Lieutenant Pak.
[160] "History of Compound 65"; "Interviews With 24 Korean Leaders," Interview 19.
[161] Interviews CN-24, CN-24A.

replaced them with rightists. Thus the right wing was able to assume power.

Taeguk [South Korean] flags were seen flying on the compound for the first time. Nothing happened the first night. At six o'clock [the next morning], the mess hour, when we opened the door of the jail to give the prisoners food, two hundred of the captives suddenly rushed out.

Although we were very tired, our fellow fighters fought on. However, it was too late. We were overcome by superior numbers because many hidden Communists joined the imprisoned Reds. We were compelled to pull back. Although our plot failed, the result of our activity was effective. We took a hundred anti-Communists out [of the compound] when we were pulling out.[162]

The Communists also attempted compound invasions. On one occasion about two hundred pro-Communists from Compound 61 slipped into 65 and attempted unsuccessfully to kill the compound monitors.[163]

Many so-called invasions were, however, unintended results of the camp command's policy of transferring prisoners who made trouble from one compound to another. At first, the authorities perceived no pattern in the troubles they were trying to stop and moved PW's about without regard to their political commitments. Later, it was often difficult to determine the relevant facts. Anti-Communist leaders tended to use the charge of Communist sympathies freely and loosely, and Communists as well as non-Communists who were being expelled roundly denied any such sympathies. Furthermore, successful Communist elites did not identify themselves as such or their defeated opponents as anti-Communists.[164]

Internal Control Processes

Although the question of repatriation or non-repatriation had the most vivid meaning for every PW and civilian internee, the vast majority obeyed their leaders, irrespective of the political complexion of the latter.

Laissez-faire Policies

In some instances—though not in Communist-controlled compounds—PW elites did not aim at total control over all their subordinates. Anti-Communist leaders in about half a dozen North Korean compounds were content to organize for maximum effectiveness those PW's who voluntarily joined the Youth Association and declared their

[162] Korean PW history.

[163] *Ibid.*

[164] As late as January, 1952, a group which included hard-core Communists was transferred into anti-Communist Compound 85, where they fed—and fed on—the already substantial resentment against corrupt leaders. That PW's tended to interpret these developments as opposition plots is wholly understandable.

opposition to repatriation.[165] In Compound 94, an extreme case of this kind, 98 per cent of the 1,025 Association members chose to remain in South Korea when they were screened by the U.N., while 90 per cent of the remaining 4,207 inmates consented to be sent back to North Korea.[166] "Plain" PW's in most of these compounds were not bothered so long as they kept quiet; they were not required to sign petitions or even join the public demonstrations opposing forcible repatriation; they were not systematically threatened, though in some cases they were propagandized prior to the actual screening.

In all Communist-controlled compounds as well as in the majority of those controlled by anti-Communists, however, the leaders sought to make all the PW's serve their policies and objectives. Consolidation therefore involved the elaboration of a variety of techniques for controlling the behavior of the mass of plain PW's.

Coercion and Isolation

The people's courts [167] constituted only the most obviously threatening form of control employed in Communist compounds. Continuous surveillance was the lot of PW's suspected of reactionary tendencies or sympathies. One who was transferred to a Communist-controlled compound said:

> After I was transferred, there were four Communist PW's who watched me all the time, even when I went to the latrine, or washed my face, or went to bed. I was a very tough boy, so the Communist leaders said they feared me and dispatched four men to guard me. I couldn't talk to the other prisoners. If I talked to them or to the monitors, I would be caught. (CN-19)

This kind of isolation was exceedingly effective for breaking the spirit of a deviant.[168] In addition, only trusted party members were permitted to work or stand near the compound gate; PW's under suspicion were prevented from going out of the compound even on work details or for sick call. The Communist apparatus for intimidating and isolating suspected deviants was in many cases so effective that, once power had been seized and the leaders of the organized opposition disposed of by violence, the party had little further need to rely on outright force, and the devices of intimidation and isolation were made to appear as expressions of the popular will.

The anti-Communist elites lacked this elaborate Communist apparatus for legitimating such coercion, and, as has been pointed out, their

---

[165] Compounds 81, 82, 91, 94, and 96 were generally in this category. In all but one of these compounds, over 90 per cent of the Association members rejected repatriation; in none, did as many as 40 per cent of the non-members refuse to go home.

[166] Captain Pak.

[167] See "Interviews of Korean PW's." CN-19 and other interviews contain evidence of similar procedures by Chinese Communist PW's.

[168] Interview KN-7.

compound police used the weapons of beating, torture, and murder with at least equal frequency. No PW on either side remained unaware that it was physically dangerous to oppose an entrenched leadership group.

Possessing a less elaborate and efficient apparatus for surveillance than the Communists, several anti-Communist compounds maintained special detention tents or areas for PW's suspected of Communist sympathies or other dissident views. Many anti-Communist leadership groups genuinely hoped to reform those whose thinking was misguided. Meanwhile, the subjects had to be removed from contact with their fellows in order to prevent their views from being spread. Other leaders, who preferred to have dissidents removed from the compound, were likely to find the custodial authorities deaf to their pleas, particularly in the first six to eight months of the Koje-do period, before the authorities recognized the depth and danger of political divisions in the compound. The PW's solution was often to establish their own compound jail or reeducation center.

In either case, the lot of the segregated PW's was likely to be hard. They got far more than their share of assignment to heavy work details, always under close supervision by members of the monitor force; they were subjected to lengthy indoctrination and interrogation; they were watched continuously, and punished severely even for minor infractions of discipline. Their very lives were in danger. Their situation thus constituted a practical lesson for the remainder of the plain PW's.[169]

Indoctrination

Neither side was content to employ only negative, coercive controls; both developed programs for educating both party members and "plain" PW's. Although some Chinese groups developed their own indoctrination and discussion materials, most of the anti-Communist organizations worked closely with the CIE, adapting it in part to their own purposes.

In Communist-dominated compounds, on the other hand, the leaders undertook their own program partly to offset the effects of the CIE teaching. Sang, it will be recalled, described the desire to provide "patriotic education" as one of the principal reasons for the creation of his organization.

At first, Communist indoctrination was restricted to party members and was held at night. In compounds where control was stabilized, however, an additional program was developed for the plain PW's, which became compulsory and was given for a number of hours daily. Both the party and the mass programs included both political and military subjects; the party program was more advanced on the political side and included self-teaching materials on Bolshevik history. Discussion and self- and mutual criticism were regular adjuncts of the program, especially with respect to the application of teachings in daily life

169 Interviews KR-28 and KR-44; "Interviews With 24 Korean POW Leaders."

and the development of a fighting spirit against the American imperialists.[170]

Formal indoctrination was supplemented in both political camps by calculated mass propaganda in the compound newspapers [171] and dramatic productions.

As soon as the Communist leaders succeeded in shutting out CIE and other sources of objective information, they were able to develop patently false themes in indoctrination and make them stick. For example, when the repatriation issue became acute, the Communists followed a line calculated to convince even the most ardent Communist-hater that he had better act like an enthusiastic supporter of the People's Republic. They propagandized that repatriation was inevitable. In Compound 85, where the Communists finally became dominant during the first quarter of 1952, they had to overcome the previous organized propaganda against forcible repatriation. They made their case in these terms:

At first they [the Communists] said: "I think all PW's may be repatriated." Such propaganda they carried on for some time. Then they said: "All the PW's should be repatriated." As the next stage they said: "All the PW's must be repatriated." Then finally they said: "It has been decided that all PW's must be repatriated." The development of this propaganda campaign from stage to stage took from March, to May, 1952. During that period their education and propaganda were remarkable; the mental state of almost all PW's was one of believing them. (KN-3) [172]

[170] Reports written by PW's in Compound 62 and surreptitiously handed to CIE personnel in November, 1951, told that: "Almost every day there are Communist orientation classes, character critics [self- and mutual criticism meetings], etc. held under Communist leadership. . . . They are getting worse and worse. . . ." (Memoranda from CIE Staff to Chief, Field Operations Division, CIE, and to Headquarters, POW Camp No. 1, November 29, 1951; also, translation of discussion period in Compound 62, forwarded to Chief, Field Operations Division on November 23, 1951.)

[171] Although the newspapers produced in Compounds 76, 77, and 78 during the summer and autumn of 1951 were not analyzed systematically, examination of a sequence of issues indicated a steady increase in the consistency and militance of Communist control and thinking.

[172] KN-4 has been quoted previously in similar vein. This informant had been in Communist-controlled Compound 77. Shortly after it was broken up in June, 1952, he escaped to become a non-repatriate. Then he voluntarily went back into several other Communist compounds to identify Communist leaders for the U.N. In August, 1953, shortly after the armistice had been signed, he stated it as his opinion that "by now most PW's [in the repatriate, i.e., Communist-controlled, compounds] know that they could choose South Korea and not be repatriated, but some still doubt it. Most PW's with no education believe that all are supposed to be repatriated whether they wish it or not. That is what the Communists propagandize." Similarly, KN-7, an inmate of Compound 66 and later of the officers' enclosure on Yoncho-do (Camp 1-B), defected just prior to boarding an LST for repatriation. He reported that "the Communists made propaganda to the other [officer] PW's that, even if any PW opposed repatriation, all would be forcibly repatriated in accordance with the North Korean proposals at Panmunjom, and that after repatriation many such PW's would be killed. Thus the PW's were threatened." The effectiveness of this line obviously depended on the ability of the party organization to shut out conflicting information.

Communist indoctrination also included a constant and developing review of the "history of the PW struggle." Each new series of events was interpreted to the mass of PW's in such a way as to constitute further proof of the "imperialistic slaughtering policies" and "reactionary, slanderous political intrigues" of the detaining authorities, and of the wisdom and success of Communist PW resistance.[173] A constant effort was made to create a frame of reference that would lead the PW's to perceive any new event as supporting the justice of the Communist cause. PW's were required to memorize dozens of alleged instances of American brutality and treachery.

Creating Esprit de Corps

In addition to vigorously indoctrinating the prisoners under their control, the leaders had to find ways of creating strong group solidarity, of encouraging the PW's to identify simultaneously with each other and a cause. The extent to which the prisoner leaders understood this need cannot be ascertained; in any event all of them adopted measures which performed this function.

The requirement that new members undergo initiation rites was one way of creating *esprit de corps*. North Koreans who wanted to join the Anti-Communist Youth Association were required to swear an oath and sign their names in blood before being granted the privileges of members.[174] This requirement made the act a solemn occasion, and must have indicated to the signer the overwhelming importance of what he was doing. Initiation into the Chinese Anti-Communist and Fight against Russia Youth League was signalized by the tattooing of four characters—"Anti-Communist Fight Russia"—on their arms. This tattoo marked a man as an anti-Communist almost irrevocably; it isolated him from pro-Communist elements and drove him to orient himself toward a future with the Nationalists (CN-1A).

The wearing of distinctive articles of clothing and decorations also contributed to *esprit de corps*. Anti-Communist Chinese manufactured and wore hats similar to those of the Nationalist soldiery; they also made and wore on their hats the insignia of the Kuomintang party. The Korean Anti-Communist Youth Association created a party emblem which could either be worn by members or affixed to the entrance of their quarters. North Korean Communists manufactured headgear similar to that worn by the soldiers of the North Korean army, and affixed to their hats a five-pointed red star. Likewise, hats and insignia corresponding to those of the Chinese Communist Forces were manufactured and worn by Communist-oriented Chinese.

---

[173] See Appendix C for extracts from a sample Communist history. Documents like the "History of Compound 65" indicate that the anti-Communists also used history for practical purposes, but their historical efforts tended to be for elite consumption.

[174] By-laws of the Korean Anti-Communist Youth Association, Bu Byong.

Exceedingly important to these Oriental PW's was the sense of being accepted, trusted, and protected by a group. Thus, admittance to even a few elementary secrets of an organization, or to plans before they were generally announced, was exceedingly effective in binding men to the organizations.[175]

Mass songfests, with rousing military songs and others, were a favorite device of both Koreans and Chinese, regardless of political disposition. Military drill, mass calisthenics, demonstrations, and holiday celebrations also led the men to identify emotionally with one another and their group, and tended to create a powerful, even if temporary, spirit in the rank and file as well as in the organized core.

Indoctrination, drill, and other group activities filled a serious void that had existed in the life of the prisoners. One PW, who lived as a suspect in an anti-Communist compound and then participated in a revolt which brought the Communists to power, spontaneously described as a major attraction the full day now provided for him: "Before the revolt and the Communists gained control, there was not much activity in the compounds except to eat, work on details, and sleep. Afterward, there was much more to do, and now we study and discuss a lot" (KR-28).

Similarly, an active member of the Anti-Communist Youth Association recalled that after the boredom of the first ten months of captivity, being caught up in the drive and mission of the association's work made life interesting again, even full (KN-3).

Mobilization of the Masses

Through all these procedures, the elites in many compounds were able to weld their subjects into highly disciplined instruments for their purposes. The results are apparent not only in mass signatures on petitions to the camp command and in mass demonstrations but also in the outcome of the screening for repatriation choice.

With the exception of the officers' compound, the North Korean compounds appear to have resembled one another markedly in the general composition—age range, variety of social origins and political experiences, and so on—of their populations. Yet some of these compounds refused to permit U.N. personnel to screen them, while in others more than 75 per cent of the inmates, though questioned individually in a way designed to encourage repatriation, declared their determination forcibly to resist repatriation.[176] Among North Korean compounds headed by anti-Communist leaders, the proportions of inmates who insisted on remaining in South Korea ranged from a low of 27 per cent (in Compound 94) to a high of 81 per cent (in 73 and 83).[177]

[175] KN-3, KN-7, and many other interviews. In addition, see Chapter 1, above.

[176] Compounds 73, 83, and 93. For the methods which achieved this result in Compound 93, see "Interviews with Korean POW Leaders," Interviews Nos. 2, 4, 7, 8, 10, and 12.

[177] Captain Pak.

One of the factors which markedly affected this variation—the vigor, as measured by the size, of the membership of the Korean Anti-Communist Youth Association—is suggested by Figure 6. Generally speaking, the larger the proportion of the total compound population that belonged to the association, the larger the proportion of non-members who refused to be repatriated. Since no strong reasons exist for assuming marked differences in relevant pre-capture characteristics of the rank-and-file PW's in the several compounds, it seems likely that the size and vigor of the association in each compound influenced the repatriation behavior of non-members.

Relation between Anti-Communist Youth Association Membership and Non-Member Repatriation Choice in Nine North Korean PW Compounds Controlled by Anti-Communist Elites

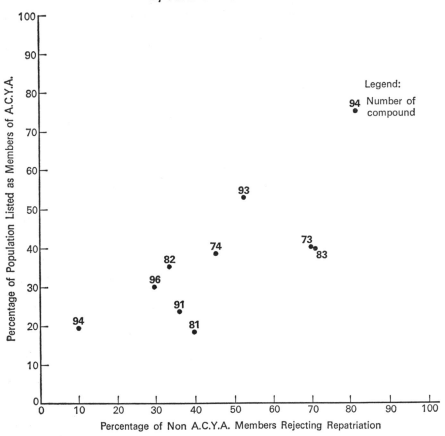

Source: Koje-do in Complication, Appendix on screening results.

FIGURE 6

The fact that the correlation is substantially short of perfect, however, indicates that other factors were at work, and some idea of these influences can be gained from study of the exceptional cases. In Compounds 82 and 83, 35 and 40 per cent, respectively, of the populations belonged to the association. But in 82, two-thirds of the non-members consented to be returned to North Korea; in 83, fewer than one-third did so. The evidence available indicates that this difference reflects largely differences in the missionary spirit of the association leaders and the amount of coercion and intimidation they brought to bear upon the screening process itself.[178]

In Compounds 81 and 94 also, almost identical proportions of the population belonged to the Association—19 and 20 per cent respectively. Yet of the non-members, 40 per cent in 81 and only 10 per cent in 94 refused to return home. The evidence in this case suggests a difference, not only in the effort put forth by association members, but also between a compound which was part of the major nucleus of North Korea anti-Communist activity (81, 82, 83) and one which was relatively isolated from that center, and a relatively old, stable compound and one which still contained a plurality of power centers.

In Chinese Compound 86, the leaders estimated that between 20 and 50 per cent of the inmates were ideologically and politically neutral.[179] However, only two months after the anti-Communist faction gained full control and forced the removal of all active Communists, 6,500 PW's—about 80 per cent of the compound population—signed a blood petition asking to be allowed to go to Formosa. In the individual screening conducted by the U.N. in April, only 16 per cent of the inmates expressed willingness to be returned to Communist control.[180] From the moment of its seizure of power, the new leadership had conducted an organizing and propaganda drive with missionary intensity.

The similar but even more complete front of unanimity which the Communist-controlled compounds were able to present to outsiders needs no description here.[181] Some previous accounts, however, have tended to overemphasize the role of mass singing and drill in fomenting demonstrations and collective defiance of authority; correspondingly, they have tended to underrate or ignore the interlocking system of positive and negative controls, including sustained indoctrination, which made possible and enforced the disciplined behavior which was observed.

[178] Interview with Lieutenant Pak.
[179] "Essays by Prisoners of War, Group II."
[180] *Demographic Study of Korean and Chinese PW's*, Hq, AFFE, 1953. In the other Chinese compound, 72, Ching had been in control since the summer of 1951. In December, 85 per cent of the compound strength signed a blood petition; and in April, 80 per cent refused to be repatriated.
[181] See Army POW study; the numerous eyewitness descriptions of Communist demonstrations and riots which appeared in U.S. newspapers and magazines in 1952 and 1953.

The continuing ability of the elites to mobilize the masses of PW's after the breakup of the Koje compounds also requires no documentation here. Field interviewers for this study, visiting the PW camps in the summer of 1953, were repeatedly struck by the very high level of discipline and overt solidarity which existed in both Communist and anti-Communist compounds. Furthermore, both sides were prepared to defy or passively resist constituted authority when their vital interests were at stake. The fact that the Communists resisted frequently and deliberately should not obscure the fact that the anti-Communists were almost equally capable of creating serious trouble when and if they considered it necessary.[182]

CONSOLIDATION AND INDIVIDUAL COMMITMENT

Having fixed in mind the social processes and control techniques which accompanied the consolidation of power in the compounds, let us consider some of the psychological correlates of consolidation. What changes were occurring, during the last months of the Koje period, in the orientation of those PW's who had participated actively in the struggles for power and who now were consolidating their gains? And what of the bulk of the PW's? Were those who joined political organizations at this stage mere opportunists? What can be said about the genuineness of the enthusiastic obedience exhibited by the plain PW's on both sides?

Modification of Elite Objectives

Alienation from the Custodial Authorities

The initial desire of both leaders and rank-and-file PW's to please the Americans had been, in the Pusan period, one source of anti-Communist activity in the compounds. As the conflicts among PW's polarized more and more around the Communist issue, however, the leaders were increasingly puzzled by what seemed to them the inconsistency of American policies. Both Communists and non-Comunists gradually perceived that, with regard to the PW's, the custodial authorities were principally concerned not with political issues as such but simply with security and the physical welfare of their charges. To a

---

[182] For example, Chinese non-repatriate PW's refused to leave Koje-do in the spring of 1952, for the move to Cheju, until they were assured that their chaplains and CIE teachers would accompany them as guarantors of their safety. Korean and Chinese non-repatriate PW's repeatedly held noisy patriotic mass demonstrations with U.N. permission or in defiance of U.N. orders throughout the last year of the conflict. Finally, Chinese and North Korean non-repatriate leaders initiated preparations to resist forcibly the U.N. effort to move them to the Demilitarized Zone for Communist "explanations" after the signing of the armistice—until the South Korean and Chinese Nationalist governments sent deputations to ask them to comply.

considerable extent, both sides learned to manipulate this situation for their own purposes.

The persistence with which the camp command on Koje-do sought to comply with the Geneva Convention created some serious problems for the Communist leaders in their struggle for power. In the first place, the non-intervention of American personnel in prisoner affairs within the compounds, coupled with custodial opposition to violence per se, handicapped opposition groups (usually Communist, as during most of the time on Koje the controlling groups in most compounds were anti-Communist). These policies made it possible for the group in control in a compound to oppress opposition groups provided they took precautions to hide their acts of violence from the camp command. The opposition, on the other hand, was handicapped in using violence as a means of seizing power; even if their coup were successful through violence, the authorities might oust them for that very reason.

Second, the predominant U.N. policy made it difficult for the Communists to develop issues with which they could incite the rank and file against the authorities. On the whole, the argument that the Americans were trying to slaughter the PW's or to "rearm them in the service of imperialism" simply did not make much sense to plain PW's during the first nine months on Koje-do. The worst that could plausibly be said to the rank and file was that the Americans were wrongly permitting certain PW's to carry on activities that were corrupt, oppressive, and brutal. It was, indeed, almost wholly on issues of compound administration that the Communists gained such popular support as they had prior to consolidating their power.

At the same time, the authorities' non-intervention in the internal life of the compounds made it easier for the Communists to form their underground network and to assume power in the compounds without appearing dangerous or even being politically identified by the authorities.

The neutrality of the U.N. custodial policies also created serious problems for the anti-Communists. In order to get pro-Communists removed from their midst, they had to discover or fabricate plans of riot or mass escape. They were forbidden public expressions of their beliefs, such as putting up South Korean or Nationalist flags, and the only channel through which they could spotlight their problems and express their feelings freely was that of formal petition. Anti-Communist leaders, who initially considered themselves on the same side as the Americans, came to feel that the Americans could not be trusted, because they never fully understood American custodial objectives and principles or the impersonal American criteria of satisfactory performance and cooperation. As they saw it, the Americans, in combining war crimes investigations and anti-Communist indoctrination with custodial emphasis on Geneva Convention principles, were pursuing objectives which appeared to be mutually contradictory, not merely different.

The restrictions imposed upon these PW's, together with their distrust, encouraged the formation of covert organizations, at the same time that U.N. non-intervention made it possible. Ever increasing proportions of the important affairs of the compounds were decided and acted on through these channels. Thus, both in attitude and in organization, the anti-Communists became progressively alienated from their custodians.

The alienation of both sides was furthered by the language barrier and the authorities' ignorance of Korean and Chinese culture. The resultant unnecessary misunderstandings and conflicts often left the PW's with a sense that the Americans were utterly indifferent to them, or even brutal.

Winning Merit with Future Rulers

The repatriation issue created the greatest single source of alienation in both camps of prisoners. This was partly due to the fact that it intensified intra-compound coercion and covert organization and because the PW's, never certain just how solidly the U.N. Command would support its principle of voluntary repatriation, tried to force the command's hand.

For the most part, however, such alienation was inherent in the nature of the repatriation issue under conditions of military stalemate. Of necessity, all organized PW efforts now centered in winning merit with the governments to which they hoped to be turned over. More than any other single factor, this dominant orientation accounts for the organized behavior of the PW's in the last weeks of the Koje period and especially through the final year of the Korean conflict. Let us examine how activists in the several PW groups perceived their situation after the screening.

Anti-Communists.—Although the anti-Communist leaders could not consider allowing themselves to be returned to Communist control, they were not at all certain how they would be received by the Chinese Nationalist or South Korean government.

Of the Chinese, almost two-thirds were former Nationalist soldiers. And however extenuating may have been the circumstances of their capture and incorporation into the Communist armies, the record showed that they had volunteered for such service. Furthermore, some had become members of the Communist party; others had "volunteered" for special training in Communist doctrine.[183] Records of the circumstances of their internment by the United Nations—whether they had sought surrender or been captured—were not available. Only evidence of expiatory and enthusiastically pro-Nationalist behavior in the prison camps could be counted on to influence their future Nationalist superiors in their favor.

[183] Chapter 1, above.

For this as well as for more immediate reasons, thousands of them submitted to being tattooed with anti-Communist slogans; the whole body of non-repatriate Chinese PW's drilled as Nationalist army units; systematic and rigidly pro-Nationalist indoctrination was carried on in addition to CIE; military discipline and instant obedience to orders became almost automatic. Prisoners who exhibited any deviation from the established norms were punished or expelled from the compounds. On Cheju Island, the custodial authorities had to create a special compound for PW's who were not safe in the non-repatriate compounds because of deviations or personal ambition but who still did not wish repatriation. A brilliant Chinese who served as a compound leader during two periods analyzed the situation as follows.

[The indoctrination presented to PW's by the anti-Communist organization] has to be negative because the people are very sensitive . . . [and] keyed up. . . . You can't explain that the Communists have done certain things well. . . . [I used to] tell them that certain things the Communists did are good, others are bad. They charged me with being sympathetic with the Communists . . . and got all the people to give me a beating. . . . Now I don't go into it so deeply. . . . After you are trained by a couple of years of Communism, anybody can put up a front. . . . The teaching has been restricted to a very narrow approach. . . . It is unavoidable; there is absolutely no other way. . . . We have to get organized for our existence, for a cause . . . The only hope is that it is temporary. . . . The [anti-Communist] organization was born out of necessity, out of the environment, and not out of the type of people. . . . After living through Communism they have been indoctrinated in one thing: blind obedience to the organization. . . . Under the present conditions if you permit yourself to be bound by using only means that are proper, then you will be committing suicide. (CN-13)

When the armistice was signed and the PW's were told of the plan to send them to a demilitarized zone to hear the Communist "explanations," the Chinese leaders talked seriously of organizing a mass refusal to go north. They accepted the official terms only when assured by Nationalist officials that the Nationalist government wanted them to do so.

Similarly, North Korean anti-Communists had by mid-1952 traveled so far on the road of treason to the government which controlled their home areas that they could not turn back. On the other hand, they had yet to establish their reliability in the eyes of South Korean officials. The struggles of 1951 and early 1952 had stamped a few leaders as unmistakably committed against Communism, but they as well as their followers now needed to create records of positive loyalty to the South Korean government.

As in the case of the Chinese, therefore, they now shifted away from obedience to American custodial authorities and toward proving their devotion to the government under which they hoped to live. Again we find a record of patriotic demonstrations, compulsory study of the South Korean constitution and propaganda, military organization and drill, highly emotional petitions to the government authorities, and rigorous disciplinary measures for dissenters. The wisdom of this behavior seemed, of course, to be confirmed when the government permitted the mass escape of twenty-seven thousand non-repatriate Korean PW's just before the armistice was signed.[184]

Even South Korean anti-Communists perceived themselves as having to live down a record of disgrace. The following oration expresses in typically florid language the attitudes found in many prisoner expressions.

The "POW" marking placed on our clothes was only paint—but how gloomy and ashamed it has made us and how often it has caused us to shed tears! We have been poor prisoners of war, doomed involuntarily to fight against our nation and our brothers. And because of our guilt we are often ridiculed by all peace-loving people of Korea and the world. . . .

Though [we were] obliged against our will to help the North Korean puppet government under circumstances of terror and darkness, it is true that [we] took up weapons against South Koreans and committed a great crime, instead of fighting on for a better future for the Republic of Korea. No fraudulent pretext whatever can justify such a crime as has kept me fearful, weighted with a sense of responsibility, and depressed. . . .

But, gentlemen, we have wakened from our evil dream! The door to a gleam of hope and bright prospects has been opened to us [by our being reclassified as civilian internees]. . . . I would like to believe that our fatherland is awaiting us in a spirit of generosity. But our greatest problem is: Do we make a resolution [of loyalty] to the fatherland, and can we sustain the qualities [that will deserve the fatherland's generosity]?

We must go further: We must make ourselves healthy in mind and strong in body. And so, with sound minds and sound bodies, I hope we shall be able to help in the [tasks of] unification [and] rehabilitation of Korea which will confront us, with our fellow-citizens, when we are released from internment. . . . We who are called by the fatherland are honored beings! Let us ahead! Dawn is breaking! [185]

[184] William L. White, *The Captives of Korea: An Unofficial White Paper*, pp. 230–32.

[185] Speech by a South Korean civilian internee, Compound 65 (forwarded by Chief, Field Operations Division, CIE, to Chief, CIE, 6 December 1951).

The pattern of efforts to win merit with the South Korean government was, therefore, repeated in the South Korean compounds, until these internees were released late in the summer of 1952.

Communists.—By Communist party standards, capture by the enemy in battle was wrong; it signified failure on the part of the captive to carry out the mission entrusted to him. The judgment of failure lay heavily on the minds of the party members:

> I think I didn't do my best, so I will not be recognized by them [North Korean government] as a successful man. . . . Of course, I will be recognized as a bad man, or by some as a traitor. . . . (KR-4)

> I think I am a coward because I was captured without dying to accomplish the duty of my country. To be captured is a shameful thing, because other comrades were killed but I am still living. (KR-39)

> I committed a crime because I could not do my duty for my nation. (KR-35)

> It is a very sorry thing to have been captured. (KR-6)

Almost all the repatriate party members interviewed for this study said they expected to be demoted, expelled from the party, or otherwise punished when they returned.[186] At the same time, their actions in the prison camps had made it impossible for them to seek sanctuary with the free Chinese or Korean governments, even if they had wished to do so. The best they could hope to do was to cancel out some small part of the disgrace they had incurred by being captured.

Many of the non-Communist PW's interviewed for this study and by CIE personnel emphasized this motive in explaining Communist activity in the compounds. A single Korean PW essay will serve as an example; the author describes what Communists said to him and his friends.

> If we simply waste the time until we are repatriated [they said], without utilizing our time as PW's for the benefit of Communism, it is obvious that we will have to face severe punishment. Therefore, first, we have to intensify our systematic struggle with the detaining side;

---

[186] The importance of this expectation as a factor leading some prisoners to reject repatriation can only be guessed at. A few (e.g., CR-9) mentioned anxiety about punishment as a factor which influenced their choice. Communist PW leaders were emphatic in denying that ordinary soldier PW's would be punished (e.g., KR-4), though they did not expect to be well received themselves. On the other hand, at one time in the winter of 1951–52, field officers of CIE urged headquarters to deemphasize the theme of Communist cruelty, on the grounds that fear of reprisals after the war as well as in the camps was paralyzing the activity of anti-Communist PW's.

second, we have to punish severely any coward-betrayer in our columns; and lastly, we have to liberate all of Koje Island. Only by doing all these things can we excuse ourselves for being captive prisoners.[187]

The disgrace of the party men was, in fact, multiplied: They had failed to win control of most of the compounds; they had failed to persuade or force fifty thousand North Korean and Chinese PW's to accept repatriation: they had been unable to force the U.N. Command to abandon its opposition to forcible repatriation; and they had not yet been able to break out of the compounds,[188] although their aggressive behavior had induced the U.N. to divert some additional combat forces for their custody.

Thus, during the last year many Communist-controlled compounds incurred serious risks and substantial loss of life in order to harass the custodial forces and to create propaganda unfavorable to the U.N. Command. This story has been told and is not a principal concern of this report. It should only be added that there was much evidence of factional disagreement between Communist leaders who urged a violent, aggressive course giving maximum support to the Communist armies and negotiators and those who pressed for legalistic moderation and cooperation with the U.N. custodial authorities on the grounds that they could serve the cause better by getting home in one piece.[189] We do not know the extent to which the authorities exploited these divisions.

Latecomers to the Organizations

We now return to the Koje period for some examination of the motives of those PW's who had not been active during the initial struggles for power. It will be recalled that only when one faction had gained firm control did large numbers of sympathizers—or opportunists—begin to identify themselves with and seek participation in the administration.

Thus, in Compound 86, skirmishing between rival Chinese elites continued for some months, and during this period anti-Communist activists found it exceedingly difficult to recruit others to their cause. No more than four hundred of the compound's eight thousand inmates were actively involved when, one night in October, 1951, the Communist group was decisively beaten in a violent clash and its leaders removed from the compound. Afterward, however, additional "anti-Communists" appeared in such numbers that recruitment was no longer

[187] A composition by Tong Park, one of a series of essays by Korean prisoners of war published by Hq, AFFE, October 19, 1953.

[188] While the Communist PW's organized and drilled as if in preparation for mass escape, and while their propaganda to the faithful emphasized the hope of escape, the research team felt that the objective of breaking out was presented to the PW's more to fire their imaginations than with any expectation that they could succeed in doing it.

[189] Interviews with officers, UNC POW Camps Nos. 1, 1-A, 1-B, 1-C; and numerous documents captured in these camps.

a problem. On the contrary, the difficulty became one of screening applicants for membership in the anti-Communist "party." [190]

Likewise, in North Korean compounds, where control was uncertain, membership in the Anti-Communist Youth Association was small. When power was consolidated, however, and especially when it appeared to the PW's that the anti-Communist faction had consistent support from the custodial authorities, the association tended to grow rapidly. The PW commander of Compound 82 explained the growth of his organization as follows.

> In March, 1951, I was moved [from Pusan] to Compound 82 on Koje-do. About two months elapsed before we got wind of a plot calling for a riot by the Communists on May 27. . . . We of course reported this to the South Korean and U.S. authorities. As a result, the ringleaders . . . were put into jail in the compound. Later 148 others who had taken an active part in the disturbance were also put in jail. Now I was made the compound leader. There were four men whom I trusted, so I appointed them to positions of authority which had previously been held by Communists.
>
> On the anniversary of the beginning of the Korean war, June 25, another left-wing organization emerged; their objectives were the same as the others. Again we turned this information over to the U.N. authorities and had the plotters locked up in jail.
>
> Seeing this process, the other right-wing men gradually joined our five-man organization.[191]

This additional personnel enabled the anti-Communist group to staff the police and mess detail with reliable men, and to place informers in all the tents in the compound to guard against any resurgence of Communist organization.[192]

By April, 1952, membership in the Anti-Communist Young Men's Association ranged from a high of 53 per cent of the prisoners in Compound 93—where control was established early and extended effectively—[193] to a low of 17 per cent in Compound 71, which contained a melange of ill-assorted PW's transferred from other compounds.[194] Variations between these extremes reflected the length and thoroughness of anti-Communist control in the several compounds as well as variations in the missionary effort put forth by the leadership.

The interviews confirm one point suggested by the foregoing—that many men with deep political feelings did not join PW political organizations until it was evidently safe to do so. The available information does not permit determination of the relative importance of mere oppor-

[190] Interviews CN-1, -1A, -22, -24.
[191] "Interviews with 24 Korean PW Leaders," Interview No. 11.
[192] *Ibid.*
[193] "Interviews with 12 Korean PW Leaders."
[194] Captain Pak.

tunism and political conviction in the growth of organization membership.

Rank-and-File Behavior

A number of pieces of evidence support the view that, in the end the vast majority of PW's were handed over to the government in whose power by that time they preferred to be. After the breakup of the Koje compounds it was possible, though risky, for PW's to climb the barbed-wire fences and to defect from either repatriate or non-repatriate compounds. Few did so. And just before they boarded ships to return home, repatriate PW's were given an additional opportunity to reject their return to Communist control. Very few did so. In those non-repatriate compounds which were rescreened just after the armistice, the great majority reaffirmed their original choices;[195] and in the Demilitarized Zone, the repatriation ratios among the small number of groups who heard Communist "explanations" averaged less than one per cent.[196]

The data, however, support a further judgment which is suggested by objective evidence—that many of the PW's were convinced only after they had come under the control of a leadership dedicated to one side or the other, and that they were influenced at least as much by self-interest as by any general judgment of the character of the alternative governments. Furthermore, a man's calculations of self-interest tended to be based largely on his record as a PW and what he thought it would mean to the officials who might judge him. The longer he had lived in a Communist or anti-Communist compound, the less likely he was to feel that he could ever be accepted by the other side.

Although a comparatively small factor in their personal decisions, the indoctrination seems to have had considerable effect upon such thinking as the rank-and-file PW's did about larger political issues. When interviewed in 1953, they tended to interpret large events, trends, and movements principally in terms of the official lines laid down by their leaders. This did not, however, seem to impair their willingness to talk about contrary events which they had witnessed or participated in.

In the final analysis, it is impossible to judge how many of the rank-and-file PW's were spontaneously pro-Communist or anti-Communist in sentiment, or how intensely they felt about it. Inextrica-

[195] Compound 1-H on Koje-do, composed of Koreans who had defected from Communist-controlled compounds during the period July, 1952–July, 1953, was rescreened in August, 1953. Although these six hundred PW's were isolated from other anti-Communist prisoners and were watching thousands of repatriate PW's board ship for home, 89 per cent refused repatriation.

[196] Of 3,200 PW's interviewed by Communist "explainers" in the Demilitarized Zone, fewer than 150 chose to be repatriated; the circumstances were such that reprisals, by anti-Communists, against those who chose to repatriate were out of the question. Of the approximately nineteen thousand other non-repatriate PW's who were in the DMZ but did not hear Communist "explanations," about three hundred applied to the Indian custodial forces for repatriation.

bly mixed with the Communist issue as they faced it was the question of when and how one would be released from prison and whether one would be able to rejoin one's family and neighbors. Furthermore, as we have seen, freedom of choice in the Western sense, involving a fair chance to hear the arguments and choose on the evidence without fear of punishment for choosing wrongly, was available to few of the prisoners, and to those only for short periods of time.

The evidence of this study does support the belief that spontaneous anti-Communist sentiment was significantly more widespread and intense among the Chinese—and probably also among the South Koreans—than among the North Koreans. In spite of the fact that Communists organized and agitated in all compounds as far as they were able, South Korean Compound 62 was the only Chinese or South Korean compound in which they were able to consolidate control. This was true despite the existence of serious sources of popular disaffection from anti-Communist rule. Strong-arm rule and corruption continued widespread in South Korean compounds from the Pusan period throughout, and the repeated disappointment of hope for release on the part of the South Koreans produced a great deal of bitterness. In Chinese Compound 72, Ching exercised a personal monarchy over eight thousand PW's, exacting subservience and personal privileges and indulging in personal violence on a scale not reported in any other compound.[197] The Chinese PW's finally deposed Ching, but not until they were aboard ship being transported from Korea to Formosa—that is, after the period of common peril in which unity was indispensable. The contrast between this outcome and that in Compound 85 (reported piecemeal in preceding chapters) is instructive.

Finally, the great bulk of evidence favors the judgment that conformity resulting from fear or manipulation was considerably more pronounced in Communist than in anti-Communist compounds. This was partly a function of differences of intent, partly a function of differences in organizational efficiency.

The leaders in several anti-Communist compounds made little or no attempt to compel dissenters, preferring to encourage or try to force their transfer. Furthermore, all anti-Communist-controlled compounds submitted to individual screening without protest, and even in Compound 83, where extreme pressures had been used just prior to the screening, more than one in four of the plain PW's declared themselves willing to go back to North Korea. Opportunities for PW's to plead their cases directly to the custodial authorities were greater than among the Communists.

The Communist-controlled compounds, on the other hand, refused to

[197] Memorandum, Subject: "Observations Made of the Tyrannical Type of 'Leadership' That Existed in Enclosure No. 1, Cheju-do," dated October 28, 1953; Statement, Subject: "Cruelty of a PW Leader," CIE files. American soldiers gave Ching the nickname Little Caesar.

submit to screening and gave an appearance of absolute unanimity against the U.N. Command. Yet when these compounds were broken up in June, 1952, approximately a thousand PW's broke ranks and fled to the protection of the U.N. forces, although this action involved imminent risk of being killed either by Communist PW's or by U.N. personnel who might mistake their intent.[198] The relatively few PW's who defected from Communist compounds after the Koje period uniformly reported a regime of highly efficient intimidation against dissenters.[199]

Finally, documents captured in Communist-controlled compounds during the last months of the Korean conflict show that the leaders still found it necessary to lie to and manipulate the masses of PW's, and even the bulk of the party members, in order to get disciplined action against the custodial authorities. For example, a directive intercepted by U.S. authorities on Koje-do in June, 1953, just prior to the signing of the armistice, gave detailed instructions for "countermeasures" against the "plans" of the U.N. forces "to slaughter the PW's on a large scale." It ordered the formation of anti-chemical squads, medical squads, song and slogan leaders, and so on; indicated how the custodial and guard forces were to be provoked by shouting, singing, and finally by stone throwing; and how the fight was to be carried on and expanded. Then

> When a fierce fight is developed, the enemy's armed troops will start to trespass into one compound or another. In such a case, the neighboring compound will strongly encourage the compound where enemy troops are trying to trespass, and the [latter] compound will mobilize the nucleus company and convert the fight into an armed fight with bloodshed, and upon dying at the gate will shout a war cry. . . . By such bloodshed, the American Imperialists will be recognized as the murderers on the international stage. . . .
>
> For a successful execution of this decision, the respective compound committees will call the members and will make a new written decision in their meetings and distribute it to all party members. *The written decision of the compound which is distributed to the lower organizations will not include the phrase "blocking up the main gate with blood and force of arms."* Different words will be substituted therefor.[200]

The research as a whole has made it evident that the proportions of prisoners who were repatriated in 1953 cannot be regarded as a measure of the relative strength of spontaneous pro- and anti-Communist sentiment. The considerations just advanced suggest that these proportions particularly overstate the extent of pro-Communist sentiment

[198] *Korean Chronology;* "Interviews with Korean PW's" consists of interviews with prisoners who escaped from Communist control at this time.

[199] KN-3, -4, -7, -12, -15, CN-17, -19, and other interviews with post-screening defectors. For a case study of the battery of Communist controls, see Appendix D.

[200] Documents captured in UNC POW Camp No. 1, June–July, 1953—Directive of 20–22 June, 1953. Emphasis added.

among Korean captives. All of the approximately fifty thousand PW's who could not be screened individually, and who were subjected also to the long-term, subtle effects of Communist control, were Koreans.

SUMMARY AND CONCLUSIONS

Problem

The unprecedented behavior of the Chinese and Korean PW's held by the U.N. during the Korean conflict took three forms, each of which created special difficulties for the U.N. Command and for the U.S. Army, the custodial authority:

Formation of disciplined factions among PW's.—Following the first nine months of hostilities, during which the PW's were remarkably docile, rival factions began a year-long period of strife in which the order of the prison compounds was disturbed repeatedly. Hundreds of PW's died in the disorders.

Widespread rejection of repatriation.—More than two-thirds of the Chinese prisoners and more than one-third of the North Koreans declared themselves irrevocably opposed to being repatriated to Communist control. Because the U.N. Command committed itself to support their right to refuse to return, the signing of an armistice was delayed for eighteen months.

Organized resistance to U.N. authority.—During the period of armistice negotiation, demonstrations by PW's, particularly those in Communist-controlled compounds, embarrassed and hampered the army and the U.N. Command.

These developments accounted directly or indirectly for thousands of U.S. casualties and for the diversion of needed manpower from combat.

All of these considerations led the headquarters, Army Forces Far East, to request social science research on the motivation of these Oriental PW's. The aspect of the research described in the present report was designed in answer to the army's interest in the behavior of groups, not the conduct of individuals as such, and in the conduct of these captives in the prison camps rather than as combat soldiers.[201]

This phase of the research is focused on the formation of disciplined, widespread, politically directed organizations by the prisoners. This factor of organization played a crucial role in the actions, both pro- and anti-Communist, of the PW's in Korea.

Research Method

More than a hundred intensive interviews were conducted with prisoners by a field team. Data were also obtained from documents written or furnished by PW's, transcripts of PW interviews conducted by army

[201] Certain factors affecting the motivation of Chinese Communist soldiers in the Korean hostilities are dealt with in the report on another aspect of the research. See Chapter 1, above.

personnel, interviews with U.S. and Republic of Korea (ROK) military personnel who held key positions in the camp administration, army documents on camp administration and prisoner behavior, and accounts of events in the compounds published in the United States.

The analysis involved:

A chronological reconstruction of events in the prison compounds, particularly in terms of the effects of these events on organizational developments (e.g., group formation, U.N. administrative decisions, conflicts between PW leaders, shifts in PW motivation in response to external or internal developments).[202] Because the events of the last year of the conflict have been analyzed elsewhere [203] and because the pattern for these events was set in the original Pusan and Koje PW camps, the analysis dealt almost wholly with the period from the start of hostilities to June, 1952.

Identification of conditions and social processes, and PW feelings, wishes, and values, found in more than one compound and affecting the development of organizations.

Findings and Conclusions

The Influence of Custodial Policies

Non-intervention in Compound Affairs.—Throughout the Korean War, U.N. custodial officers adhered to the spirit, and, insofar as possible, to the letter, of the 1949 Geneva Convention Relative to the Treatment of Prisoners of War, which gives primary emphasis to the rights of prisoners of war rather than to the custodial problem.

The convention, however, was drafted to cope with traditional, national wars and the administration of a politically homogeneous PW population. It did not conceive the possibility of deep political conflict among prisoners or offer guidance to custodial authorities confronted with a bitterly divided PW population. To the contrary, it implicitly counseled a policy of non-intervention in prisoner organizations.

Custodial authorities, however, intervened in the internal affairs of the compounds even less than might have been done under the conditions of the convention. The major reasons were:

The linguistic and cultural differences between custodial personnel and PW's, which inhibited understanding and communication.

An acute shortage of custodial personnel, particularly during the first two years, which limited the amount of supervision that could be exercised.

---

[202] Figure 1 above indicates graphically the growth of the PW population and the major events of the Korean conflict which affected PW behavior. A detailed chronology of the conflict appears in Appendix B.

[203] Unpublished army document.

For administrative purposes, the authorities grouped the prisoners into companies and battalions within the compounds and transmitted their orders through PW spokesmen of their choice.

Custodial Policies as a Factor in Compound Organization and Violence.—The policy of non-intervention in compound affairs by the authorities had these effects:

It enabled cliques of prisoners to rob and terrorize fellow PW's and this, in turn, stimulated the development of counter-organizations for self-protection.

It facilitated the growth of underground prisoner organizations and illicit techniques of control.

It deprived the camp command of the eyes and ears through which they would have learned what was going on in the compounds.

The restraints on violent action among the PW's were insufficient, both because of the general policy of custodial non-intervention and because the U.N. Command failed to designate a body of law under which PW's could be tried for serious misconduct. In a sense, these conditions added up to a *de facto* violation of the Geneva Convention. Disciplinary and judicial powers were regularly exercised by the dominant prisoner organizations in direct contravention of Article 96 of the convention. This was the principal kernel of truth underlying the Communist PW charge that the U.N. Command systematically violated the convention and had a policy of "butchery."

When the authorities did intervene in compound struggles between rival political factions, they did so principally to prevent or stop violence, irrespective of its origin. Such impartiality helped anti-Communists on some occasions, Communists on others. As it happened, the anti-Communists probably benefited more frequently, but the failure of the authorities to see below the surface of the conflicts introduced an element of unpredictability into the PW struggles for power.

The authorities seldom achieved a high level of mutual confidence, even with law-abiding anti-Communist PW leaders. As a result, many disagreements could be resolved only through imposing repressive sanctions. This situation stemmed from: the linguistic barrier; the general cultural barrier (in particular, the authorities never recognized the need to explain that U.N. rules were impersonal and did not permit recognizing "friends" and negotiating personal bargains in the Oriental manner); the failure of the authorities to make clear the consistency of their policy with respect to intervention in prisoner affairs; the impression of contempt for the PW's, and for Orientals generally, which many custodial personnel created.

Effect of Two Exceptions to Policy of Non-intervention.—There were two major exceptions to the general practice of non-intervention through June, 1952—the war crimes investigations and the Civil Information and Education program.[204] Each of these operations stimulated individual PW's to commit themselves to an anti-Communist position, encouraged such individuals to organize, and assisted anti-Communist groups. The activities in turn stimulated Communist counter-organization designed to neutralize their effects.

War crimes investigators and CIE personnel learned a good deal about significant events in the compounds. However, the fact that both programs were independent of the camp command tended to keep this knowledge from reaching the custodial authorities except in a diluted or distorted form.

Custodial Control.—Control was, on the whole, effectively reestablished during the last year of the conflict, within the terms of the Geneva Convention, through the following custodial policies.

Segregation of pro-Communists from anti-Communists, and of PW's identified as subversive leaders from other pro-Communists.[205]
Construction of small, adequately separated compounds.
A considerable increase in guard forces.
Operation of "tight prisons" in the repatriate camps.

However, periodic outbreaks of violence against the authorities persisted to the end; at this stage the root of the trouble could have been removed only by a huge and ruthless interrogation-identification effort.

Importance of U.S.-U.N. Stand against Forcible Repatriation.—By December, 1951, when the question of repatriation became of vital concern to the PW's, anti-Communists were in control in about two-thirds of the compounds of Koje-do. From the desperation of these men when it appeared that the U.N. Command might try to send them north, it must be concluded that if the U.N. Command had not stood firm against forcible repatriation, then and later, the custodial authorities would have faced even more serious trouble with the PW's. The evidence suggests that adoption of a policy of forcible repatriation would have resulted in more intra-compound violence, more riots against constituted authority, and more bloodshed than the eight Communist-controlled compounds were able to create.

Although it opposed forcible repatriation, the U.N. Command failed to create conditions under which the individual PW could make an uncoerced, unintimidated, informed choice. In the months that preceded the repatriation screening in April, 1952, PW's in most com-

[204] The CIE program set up for the prisoners by the U.N. Command had as its principal component an orientation course designed to acquaint the PW's with the political, social, and economic objectives of the U.N. The program also included literacy training, vocational training, and an extensive program of athletics, drama, art, music, and literature.

[205] Almost all that is known about the Communist PW organization is set forth in the eight Special Reports issued by UNC POW Camp No. 1 between September, 1952, and April, 1953. During this period the location of the central Communist headquarters was inferred and high-level Communist leaders were identified and segregated.

pounds, Communist and anti-Communist alike, were freely exploited by the controlling groups to serve their political purposes.

Prisoner Political Behavior

Initial Formation of Groups.—At the same time that custodial authorities were organizing the prisoners into companies and battalions for administration of the compounds, spontaneous organization was beginning among the PW's. Leaders emerged from small groups, either by mutual consent or by strong-arm tactics. During early internment, before North and South Korean prisoners were separated,[206] the principal prisoner leaders were South Koreans and the political atmosphere in the compounds was distinctly anti-Communist. Hard-core Communists began to organize when it became apparent that the Communist armies were not irrevocably beaten.

Motivating Factors in Early Group Activity.—Although anti-Communist sympathies dating from pre-capture experiences were among the factors motivating those who competed for power during the first year, the desire of individuals to ingratiate themselves with the captor power, which the PW's believed would be victorious, and to gain special privileges was at least equally important. The South Korean leaders and their North Korean supporters used their staff positions to divert supplies for their own use and to oppress Communist PW's. The segregation of the South Koreans early in 1951 created a power vacuum among the remaining prisoners and ushered in the period of struggle for control of the compounds.

Hard-core Communists organized with the objective of achieving full control over the prison compounds, for self-protection and to be prepared for such action as events might require. No evidence available to this study indicates that at the outset they planned or hoped to engineer mass escapes or to systematically harass the U.N. authorities.

Organizational Growth and Shifts in Prisoner Motivation.—Some PW's drawn into groups in the struggles for power had strong political preferences dating from before their capture, but their participation was brought about by events in the camps. Many joined to further specific short-run interests, without being aware of how their action committed them. Only afterward did such PW's realize that their personal safety now depended on continuing to work for the victory of the faction they had assisted. Both factions gained strength in this way, but the Communists were particularly adept at gaining supporters by exploiting immediate grievances inherent in the prison situation.

Other PW's committed themselves after experience convinced them that a particular group deserved support. The CIE program established

---

[206] In the first two months of the fighting, the North Korean army had impressed thousands of captured South Korean soldiers and civilians of military age. When captured by U.N. forces, such men were, in the absence of effective identification procedures, interned with others of the North Korean units of which they were members at time of capture by the U.N. The South Koreans were placed in segregated compounds in the spring of 1951.

by the U.N. Command and the coercive methods used by Communist PW leaders contributed to anti-Communist sentiment; the corruption and brutality of some non-Communist leaders created support for their opposition.

The Role of Various Factors in PW Organization and Resistance. The repatriation issue.—The U.N. and U.S. stand against forcible repatriation became the principal target of Communist activity and the principal reason for the Communist organization's overt conflict with constituted authority. However, the mass of PW's did not regard free choice on repatriation as an evil; so Communist groups could not enlist mass support by agitating on this issue.

Anti-Communist PW's were made desperate by the opening of negotiations for prisoner exchange in December, 1951. Active leaders apparently had assumed that they would be "taken care of" by the U.N. authorities. The possibility of being returned to Communist control drove them to coordinated underground organization and the use of more ruthless means in seizing and consolidating power in the compounds, in order to mobilize larger numbers of PW's for their political programs.

By the time U.N. negotiators proposed free choice on repatriation and Communist negotiators rejected it (January, 1952), power had been consolidated by either Communist or anti-Communist factions in nearly all the compounds on Koje-do. In the months that preceded the U.N. screening (April, 1952), the great majority of PW's were subjected to sustained, one-sided indoctrination and social pressure. Differences among compounds in the direction and intensity of these influences were reflected in the proportions of PW's in the various compounds who rejected repatriation, and in the identity of the eight compounds which forcibly resisted screening.

Subsequent developments tended to reinforce the repatriation choices of rank-and-file PW's. Having publicly refused or accepted repatriation, the PW had reason to believe that the government of his nationality which he was thus opposing would now regard him as a traitor. More important, in the new, segregated prison camps he was under the control of a totalitarian PW organization which mobilized him for demonstrations of loyalty to the chosen government. The great majority appear to have been carried along and in considerable measure convinced that they had chosen rightly.

The motive of winning merit with a government of their own nationality—a traditional Chinese and Korean orientation toward political authority—also became a factor. Both repatriate and non-repatriate PW leaders were concerned principally with the reactions of the governments of their own nationality, and defied U.N. custodial authority when their vital interests were at stake.

The CIE program.—Another focal point of Communist opposition to authority was the CIE orientation course, which was introduced into the compounds almost simultaneously with the opening of the armistice negotiations and had a more immediate effect on prisoner organization. Again, however, most of the PW's did not regard the CIE program as an evil; so the Communists could not make use of this issue in attracting mass support.

Ideology.—Ideology was not significant in determining the behavior of the great majority of PW's during the struggle for power.

Although top-level Communist leaders—a small minority of the prison population—thought and felt as disciplined Marxists, as a matter of practical necessity their propaganda concealed its doctrinal base. Only after they fully controlled a compound did they attempt to indoctrinate the rank and file with a frankly Marxist-Leninist perspective on events. However, during the final sixteen months repatriate prisoners were influenced increasingly; most of them probably eventually believed that Communist demonstrations and defiance of custodial authority were justifiable protests against "imperialist brutality."

Anti-Communist activists did not have, initially, any single pattern of thinking or set of concepts that can properly be called an ideology. Although many were opposed to Communism, they were guided mainly by traditional concepts of authority and their notion of what the situation required. Only a minority who were highly educated or were Christians seem to have been markedly influenced by liberal-democratic ideology as such.

Communist organizational techniques.—The effective techniques of Communist organization were an element of major importance; they enabled the few convinced Communists to exert an influence out of all proportion to their numbers. They were able to mobilize as "volunteer fighters" for their political purposes thousands of PW's who, under conditions of really free choice, would not have resisted the CIE program, the principle of voluntary repatriation, or the normal exercise of U.N. custodial authority.

Anti-Communist PW's, aware of Communist efficiency in this respect, adopted essentially similar methods. By so doing, they contributed further to destroying the conditions of free choice for the mass of prisoners. Forced to fight fire with fire, the anti-Communist leaders saw no alternative, even though some expressed revulsion at the coercion, violence, and deception.

The existence of two Chinas and two Koreas.—Prisoner behavior was deeply affected by the fact that two Chinas and two Koreas were in existence. This meant that a prisoner could refuse to return to Communist control without having to give up his nationality and cultural community. Fewer prisoners would have resisted forcible repatriation had this alternative not existed.

Many of the PW's who had deserted in the hope of joining Nationalist or South Korean units continued to act in furtherance of their loyalties even after they were interned. Non-Communist prisoners were further stimulated to identify with the Republic of Korea or Nationalist China by the physical presence of citizens of those countries around the prison compounds.

The fact that one Korea and one China were Communist while their opposite numbers were anti-Communist induced PW's to espouse political positions even if only to show where their loyalties lay. After the U.N. screening and the breakup of the original Koje camp (spring, 1952), the dominant prisoner organizations were oriented not to the United States or the U.N. but to the Korean or Chinese government of their choice. Their behavior was predicated on judgments about what these governments wanted them to do, not on obedience or disobedience to constituted authority as such.

Two-way communication with the outside.—We believe that, through indigenous CIE and guard personnel, anti-Communist PW organizations were able to communicate with the South Korean and Chinese Nationalist governments at least as effectively as the North Korean Communists could communicate with theirs.[207] Directives from these governments almost certainly affected details of organized PW activity.

We also believe, however, that such communication did not substantially change the course of political organization and conflict and the relations with the detaining authorities. The basic orientations and loyalties of the PW leaders existed and were expressed in political organization before external communication was established.

Incarceration phenomena.—Prison life per se, and the attitudes and modes of organization bred by it, apparently played only a secondary role in the prison-camp developments.

It is true that many South Korean PW's became hostile toward the American custodial authorities when their hopes for early release were raised and then dashed. Grievances common among inmates of penal institutions, such as tasteless food, arbitrary regulations, monotony, and instances of cruelty by custodial personnel, were a constant irritant. These conditions were subject to exploitation. Moreover, experienced underground organizers made full use of the loose prison conditions existing on Koje throughout 1951.

On the other hand, unlike civil prisoners, the PW's were not initially united by hostility toward their jailers. While the cultural and linguistic barrier seriously impeded mutual comprehension and communication, it is not comparable to the attitudinal estrangement between the inmates and the custodians in a civil prison. The principal PW disturbances were not explosions of pent-up fury and frustration stemming from captivity but collective actions planned by highly disciplined men for objectives which far transcended the prison situation itself. To create these mass disturbances, the Communist leaders had to incite their men, not merely channel and organize existing discontents.

[207] From an unpublished army documented study of the efforts of Communist leaders in North Korea to communicate with Communist PW's, and vice versa.

Appendixes

: A :

TABULAR DATA

TABLE 1

REGION OF ORIGIN OF RESPONDENTS AND CHINESE PW's, AND REGIONAL DISTRIBUTION OF CHINESE POPULATION, 1953

REGION	RESPONDENTS [a]		CHINESE PW's [b]		CHINESE POPULATION [c]	
	No.	%	No.	%	No. (Millions)	%
Northeast	7	18	1,866	11.1	41.7	7.2
North	17	44	5,165	30.8	154.0	26.4
Northwest	2	5	1,178	7.0	41.5	7.1
Central	4	10	1,855	11.1	108.1	18.6
Southeast	3	8	681	4.1	83.5	14.3
Southwest	6	15	6,004	35.8	153.8	26.4
Other	0	..	19	0.1	0.0	..
Total	39	100	16,768	100.0	582.6	100.0

[a] Four were excluded for lack of information.
[b] Unpublished army document.
[c] Unpublished army document.

TABLE 2

SOCIAL CLASS OF PARENTAL FAMILY
(Respondents)

Class Level of Father	Non-Repatriates	Repatriates	Total [a]
Landlord [b]	10	1	11
Urban capitalist	5	0	5
Government official, army officer [c]	2	0	2
Rich farmer [d]	5	0	5
Middle farmer [e]	5	4	9
Poor farmer	2	3	5
Small shop owner	2	0	2
Total [a]	31	8	39

[a] Three non-repatriates and one repatriate were excluded because of lack of information.
[b] Three fathers also held governmental posts prior to the Communist take-over. Two were county officials, the third a magistrate in the Manchukuo government.
[c] One father was a white-collar employee of the Nationalist government Salt Bureau; the other was an officer in the Nationalist army.
[d] One father was also head of the local village militia.
[e] One father was a small-town official prior to the Communist take-over.

TABLE 3

EDUCATION [a]

(Respondents and Chinese PW's)

Years of Schooling Completed	Respondents [b]		Chinese PW's [c]	
	No.	%	No.	%
None	2	5	7,512	44.8
3 or less	14	35	6,103	36.4
4–6	6	15	2,071	12.4
7–9	5	12	748	4.5
10 and over	13	33	334	2.0
Total	40	100.0	16,768	100.1

[a] Formal schooling, including village schools if attendance was regular.
[b] Three were excluded because of lack of information.
[c] Unpublished army document.

TABLE 4

OCCUPATIONS JUST BEFORE ENTRY INTO COMMUNIST WORLD

(Respondents)

Occupation	Non-Repatriates	Repatriates	Total
Soldier, anti-Communist force	21	1	22
Student	5	3	8
University or normal school	(3)	(0)	(3)
Lower schools	(2)	(3)	(5)
Non-manual worker	5	3	8
Official [a]	(2)		(2)
Teacher		(1)	(1)
Office worker	(1)		(1)
Peddler, "merchant"	(2)	(2)	(4)
Manual worker	2	2	4
Farmer	(1)	(2)	(3)
Fisherman	(1)		(1)
Minor living at home	1		1
Total	34	9	43

[a] One was village mayor, one chief of police.

TABLE 5

PRE-COMMUNIST MILITARY SERVICE
(*Respondents*)

Military Service [a]	Non-Repatriates	Repatriates	Total
Forces			
Nationalist army only	15	1	16
Local militia and Nationalist army	2	0	2
Manchukuo army and Nationalist army	2	0	2
Local militia only	1	0	1
Local militia and provincial warlord army	1	0	1
None	13	8	21
TOTAL	34	9	43
Years of service			
None	13	8	21
Less than 1	1	1	2
1–2.9	3	0	3
3–4.9	5	0	5
5–6.9	2	0	2
7–9.9	3	0	3
10 and over	3	0	3
TOTAL [b]	30	9	39

[a] Highest rank achieved by 17 respondents with pre-Communist military service: field-grade officer, 1; company-grade officer, 6; noncommissioned officer, 7; private, 3. Information on rank was not available for five men with previous service.

[b] Four non-repatriates who had pre-Communist military service were excluded for lack of information on length of service.

TABLE 6

NATIONAL MILITARY SERVICE
(*Respondents and Chinese PW's*)

NATIONALIST SERVICE	NON-REPATRIATE PW's				REPATRIATE PW's			
	Respondents		Whole Population [a]		Respondents		Bulk of Population [b]	
	No.	%	No.	%	No.	%	No.	%
Some	19	56	9,549	66.7	1	11	1,936	59.3
None	15	44	4,776	33.3	8	89	1,311	40.7
Total	34	100	14,325	100.0	9	100	3,247	100.0

[a] Unpublished document.
[b] Based on a survey conducted in Korea, June, 1952, by an official of the State Department.

TABLE 7

ENTRY INTO COMMUNIST WORLD
(*Respondents*)

	Non-Repatriates	Repatriates	Total
Age at time of entry			
14–19	4	6	10
20–22	10	0	10
23–25	10	2	12
26–30	6	1	7
31–35	4	1	5
TOTAL [a,b]	34	10	44
Date of entry			
Before 1945	3	2	5
1945–46	5	2	7
1947–48	10	4	14
1949	15	2	17
1950	2	0	2
TOTAL [b]	35	10	45
Nature of contact			
Prisoner of war	21	1	22
Home area occupied	11	6	17
Joined Communist forces voluntarily	1	3	4
Detained by guerillas while traveling, and required to join Communist forces	2	0	2
TOTAL [b]	35	10	45

[a] One non-repatriate was excluded because of lack of information.
[b] One non-repatriate and one repatriate who came under Communist control on two separate occasions were counted twice.

TABLE 8

YEARS LIVED UNDER COMMUNIST CONTROL
(*Respondents*)

Number of Years	Non-Repatriates	Repatriates	Total [a]
Less than 2	9	0	9
2–3.9	11	1	12
4–6.9	10	3	13
7–9.9	2	3	5
10 and over	2	1	3
Total [a]	34	8	42

[a] One repatriate was excluded because of lack of information.

TABLE 9

MEAN TIME IN VARIOUS STATUSES UNDER COMMUNIST CONTROL
(Respondents)

	TIME IN MONTHS		
STATUS	Non-Repatriates (N = 33)	Repatriates (N = 8)	Total [a] (N = 41)
As a civilian	2.9	22.2	6.6
Being indoctrinated under military auspices preparatory to regular military service	2.8	0.4	2.3
In the Communist military forces	38.5	56.9	42.0
Total [a]	44.2	79.5	50.9

[a] One repatriate and one non-repatriate were excluded because of lack of information.

TABLE 10

LENGTH OF SERVICE IN CHINESE COMMUNIST MILITARY FORCES [a]
(Respondents and Chinese PW's)

PERIOD (MONTHS)	NON-REPATRIATE PW's				REPATRIATE PW's			
	Respondents [b]		Bulk of Population [c]		Respondents [d]		Survey Population [c]	
	No.	%	No.	%	No.	%	No.	%
12 or fewer	4	12	7,522	54.3	2	25	312	10.7
13–24	7	21	3,925	28.3	1	12	1,561	53.7
25–36	7	21	1,741	12.6	0	—	781	26.8
37–60	9	28	574	4.1	2	25	209	7.2
61 or more	6	18	97	0.7	3	38	46	1.6
Total	33	100	13,859	100.0	8	100	2,909	100.0

[a] Includes time spent by new inductees and prisoners in special indoctrination centers under military auspices.

[b] One non-repatriate was excluded. He was captured by the U.N. as a fisherman from Manchuria, and had no military service in the Chinese Communist Forces.

[c] Unpublished army document.

[d] One repatriate was excluded because of lack of information.

TABLE 11

HIGHEST RANK ACHIEVED IN COMMUNIST FORCES
(*Respondents*)

Rank	Non-Repatriates	Repatriates	Total [a]
General officers	0	1 [b]	1
Regimental- and battalion-level officers	4 [c]	1	5
Company-level officers	6 [d]	0	6
Platoon-level officers	6	1	7
Noncommissioned officers	4	1	5
Privates ("warriors")	12	4	16
Total [a]	32	8	40

[a] One non-repatriate and one repatriate for whom information is not available, and one non-repatriate civilian internee were excluded.

[b] Divisional political commissar.

[c] Includes one battalion political officer.

[d] Includes three company-grade political officers, one company-grade cultural officer.

TABLE 12

*LENGTH OF SERVICE IN COMMUNIST FORCES,
RANK, AND PARTY MEMBERSHIP*
(*Respondents* [a])

RANK AND PARTY MEMBERSHIP	LENGTH OF SERVICE IN CCF (*Months*)				
	0–18	19–36	37–60	61 and over	Total
Highest rank achieved					
Battalion or higher level officer	0	0	1	5	6
Company-level officer	1	0	2	3	6
Platoon leaders or equivalent	1	2	4	0	7
Lower-echelon leaders	2	1	1	1	5
Privates	9	4	3	0	16
Party membership					
Members	0	0	5	8	13
Non-members	13	7	6	1	27
Total	13	7	11	9	40

[a] Respondents for whom information is lacking on any variable were excluded.

TABLE 13

EDUCATION AND PRE-COMMUNIST BACKGROUND, STATUS
IN COMMUNIST FORCES, AND PARTY MEMBERSHIP
(*Respondents* [a])

BACKGROUND	STATUS [b] IN CCF			PARTY MEMBERSHIP		
	Officer	Enlisted	Total	Members	Non-Members	Total
Education						
3 years or less	7	7	14	6	9	15
4–9 years	3	9	12	3	9	12
10 years or more	9	4	13	4	9	13
Total	19	20	39	13	27	40
Status of parental family						
Landlord or rich farmer	6	10	16	4	12	16
Urban capitalist, official, army officer	5	2	7	3	4	7
All others	6	9	15	6	10	16
Total	17	21	38	13	26	39

[a] Respondents for whom information is lacking on any variable were excluded.
[b] "Officer" is here defined to include platoon leaders and higher-echelon personnel, "enlisted" to include assistant platoon leaders and lower-echelon personnel.

TABLE 14

PRE-COMMUNIST MILITARY SERVICE, STATUS IN
COMMUNIST FORCES, AND PARTY MEMBERSHIP
(*Respondents* [a])

PRE-COMMUNIST SERVICE	STATUS [b] IN CCF			PARTY MEMBERSHIP		
	Officer	Enlisted	Total	Members	Non-Members	Total
Length						
No service	12	7	19	7	14	21
Less than 5 years	5	5	10	4	6	10
5 years or more	0	7	7	1	7	8
Total	17	19	36	12	27	39
Status [c]						
No service	12	7	19	7	14	21
Enlisted	3	7	10	4	6	10
Officer	0	7	7	0	7	7
Total	15	21	36	11	27	38

[a] Respondents for whom information is lacking on any variable were excluded.
[b] "Officer" is here defined to include platoon leaders and higher-echelon personnel, "enlisted" to include assistant platoon leaders and lower-echelon personnel.
[c] "Officer" is here defined to include second lieutenants and above, "enlisted" to include master sergeants and below.

TABLE 15

PRE-COMMUNIST BACKGROUND AND LENGTH
OF SERVICE IN COMMUNIST FORCES
(*Respondents*)

	LENGTH OF SERVICE IN CCF		
PRE-COMMUNIST BACKGROUND	Less Than 3 Years	3 Years or More	Total
Status of parental family			
Landlord or rich farmer	11	5	16
Urban capitalist, official,			
army officer	3	4	7
All others	6	10	16
Education			
3 years or less	5	9	14
4–9 years	7	5	12
10 years or more	8	5	13
Military service			
None	9	10	19
Less than 5 years	4	6	10
5 years or more	6	2	8
Military status			
No service	9	10	19
Enlisted	5	5	10
Officer	7	0	7

TABLE 16

DATE OF CAPTURE OR SURRENDER
(*Respondents and Chinese PW's*)

DATE	RESPONDENTS [a]		CHINESE PW's	
	No.	%	No.[b]	%
Before March, 1951	5	12	1,672	7.9
April–June, 1951	14	32	15,489	73.5
July–December, 1951	5	12	3,404	16.2
1952	12	28	509	2.4
1953	7	16		
Total	43	100	21,074	100.0

[a] Includes three for whom period of capture was inferred from related information in interview.

[b] Office of the Provost Marshal General, Department of the Army. They indicate dates of internment in "permanent" PW camps, about two weeks later than dates of surrender or capture at the front. The total figure is slightly larger than the number held at the close of hostilities, because of deaths, escapes, etc.

TABLE 17

MARITAL STATUS AND AGE DISTRIBUTION
(Respondents and Chinese PW's)

STATUS AND AGE	RESPONDENTS		CHINESE PW's [a]	
	No.	%	No.	%
Marital status				
Single	13	42	10,911	65.1
Married	12	39	4,672	27.9
Divorced, separated, or widowed	6	19	1,185	7.0
Total	31 [b]	100	16,768	100.0
Age (as of March, 1952)				
Under 26	15	36	7,910	47.2
26–30	15	36	7,577	45.2
31–35	8	19		
36–45	4	9	1,168	7.0
Over 45	0	—	113	0.6
Total	42 [c]	100	16,768	100.0

[a] Unpublished army document.
[b] Twelve were excluded because of lack of information.
[c] One was excluded because of lack of information.

TABLE 18

REPATRIATION CHOICES AND PW ORGANIZATION AFFILIATIONS
(Respondents)

Status	No.	Interview Identification Symbols
Repatriate		
Always repatriate		
Lived continuously more than four months in Communist-controlled compounds....................	3	R-2, -4, -5
New PW's captured during period April–July, 1953................	3	R-3, -6, -8
Lived in segregated status [a]........	2	R-1, -7
Initially non-repatriate, changed to repatriate.......................	1	R-9
Non-repatriate		
Always non-repatriate		
Lived continuously more than four months in anti-Communist con-trolled compounds..............	23	N-1, -2, -3, -4, -9, -10, -13, -14, -18, -21, -22, -23, -24, -25, -26, -27, -28, -29, -30, -31, F-4, -5, -6
Rejected by anti-Communist organi-zation and living in segregated compounds....................	7	N-5, -6, -7, -8, -11, -12, -16
New PW's captured during period April–July, 1953................	1	N-20
Initially repatriate, changed to non-repatriate, living in segregated com-pounds.........................	3	N-15, -17, -19
Total..........................	43	

[a] General officer in CCF and his aide.

: B :

CHRONOLOGY OF THE KOREAN WAR, 1950-53

1950

June 25: Beginning of hostilities, with North Koreans crossing the 38th Parallel to invade South Korea.

June 27: President Truman orders U.S. air and naval forces to help South Korea repel the North Korean invaders.

June 28: Seoul, South Korean capital, abandoned to invaders.

June 30: President Truman authorizes General Douglas MacArthur, Supreme Commander for the Allied Powers, in Japan, to send ground forces to Korea.

July 2: First U.S. Army combat units—elements of 24th Infantry Division—land in Korea from Japan and move north to contact the enemy.

July 5: U.S. Army troops fight first engagement in Korea.

July 7: U.N. Security Council authorizes use of U.N. flag in Korea.

July 8: General MacArthur named Commander in Chief, United Nations command; first elements of U.S. 25th Infantry Division reach Korea from Japan.

July 10: U.S. tanks in first action; first Red atrocities reported.

July 13: U.S. troops fall back across Kum River near Taejon; Lieutenant General Walton H. Walker takes command of U.S. forces in Korea.

July 18: U.S. 1st Cavalry Division arrives in Korea from Japan.

July 20: Communications center of Taejon lost to enemy; Major General William F. Dean reported missing.

July 24: Reds in western Korea push to southern coast and attack toward Pusan; General Headquarters, U.N. Command, established in Tokyo.

July 31–August 2: First reinforcements land direct from the United States (2d Infantry Division and 1st Marine Brigade); U.S. troops withdraw from Chinju.

August 3: U.S. troops fall back to Naktong River line; Reds thrust to within forty miles of Pusan.

August 7: U.S. forces launch strong counteroffensive toward Chinju, west of Pusan.

Based on a chronology prepared by Captain R. J. Loesch, Artillery, assigned to Public Information Division, Department of the Army, at the time the chronology was written; supplementary information from the Office of the Chief of Military History, Department of the Army.

August 29: First troops from other members of the U.N.—the 27th British Brigade from Hong Kong—arrive in Korea.

August 31: Communists rush Naktong River defenses in tremendous force and breach U.N. positions at several points.

September 15: U.S. X Corps (1st Marine Division and 7th Infantry Division) lands at Inchon and attacks inland.

September 16: After six weeks behind the Pusan perimeter, Eighth Army jumps off in all-out offensive.

September 26: Seoul liberated by X Corps; Eighth Army Task Force joins up with Inchon invasion south of Suwon, linking the two forces across South Korea from Inchon to Pusan.

September 30: U.N. forces regain nearly all territory south of 37th Parallel.

October 1: South Korean 3d Division pushes across 38th Parallel and speeds up east coast.

October 7: U.N. General Assembly votes for restoration of peace and security throughout Korea, giving tacit approval to entry into North Korea by U.N. military forces.

October 9: U.S. 1st Cavalry Division crosses 38th Parallel.

October 10: South Korean Capitol and 3d Divisions capture port of Wonsan.

October 19: Pyongyang, North Korean capital, taken by U.N. forces.

October 20: U.S. 187th Parachute Infantry Regimental Combat Team jumps at Sukchon and Sunchon, twenty-five miles north of Pyongyang.

October 26: South Korean 6th Division reaches Yalu River at Chosan; U.N. forces capture first Chinese Communist soldiers; U.S. 1st Marine Division lands at Wonsan, and U.S. 7th Infantry Division lands at Iwon.

November 1: U.N. pilots opposed for first time by speedy Russian-built MIG-15 jet fighters.

November 2: U.S. 1st Cavalry Division suffers severe casualties when hit by Chinese Communists at Unsan.

November 3: U.N. Civil Assistance Command (UNCACK) established to supervise civil assistance and economic aid in Korea; Chinese Communist Forces begin major fall campaign.

November 12: U.S. 3d Infantry Division arrives in Korea.

November 21: U.S. 7th Infantry Division occupies Hyesanjin on banks of the Yalu River (most northerly point to be reached by American forces).

November 24: U.N. forces launch "end-of-war" offensive; South Korean troops enter Chongjin, sixty miles from Siberian border.

November 25: Communists launch violent counteroffensive, beginning in mountains surrounding central Korean town of Tokchon and striking two days later in the Chosin Reservoir area, forcing U.N. troops to begin withdrawal.

December 5: U.N. forces abandon North Korean capital.

December 9: Special relief force makes contact with marine and army units withdrawing from the Chosin Reservoir area.

December 11: U.N. forces begin evacuation of Hungnam, Songjim, and Wonsan.

December 24: Last of 105,000 troops evacuated from Hungnam beachhead safely aboard ship.

December 26: Lt. General Matthew B. Ridgway arrives to take command of all U.N. ground forces in Korea, succeeding General Walker, who was killed in a Jeep accident on December 23.

1951

January 1: Communists (seven Chinese Communist armies and two North Korean corps) launch general offensive, penetrating deeply toward Seoul and the rail and road center of Wonju.

January 3: Seoul abandoned for second time by U.N. forces; port of Inchon abandoned and destroyed by U.N. forces.

January 7: Communist forces attack Wonju; U.N. forces abandon the town.

January 25: U.N. retakes offensive to wage war of maneuver.

February 5: "Operation Round-up" launched against North Korean forces south of Hongchon.

February 13: U.S. 2d Division's 23d Infantry and attached French battalion surrounded by three Chinese Communist divisions at Chipyong-ni.

February 21: "Operation Killer" launched to annihilate enemy forces and reestablish U.N. line east of Wonju.

March 7: "Operation Ripper" launched by U.N. forces.

March 15: Seoul retaken by U.N. forces, changing hands for the fourth time.

March 23: U.S. 187th Regimental Combat Team jumps at Munsan in attempt to cut off enemy forces south of Han River.

April 11: General MacArthur relieved of all his commands in Far East by President Truman.

April 12: General Ridgway replaces General MacArthur as Supreme Commander for the Allied Powers.

April 14: General James A. Van Fleet replaces General Ridgway as Commander of the Eighth Army.

April 22: Three Chinese Communist armies launch spring counteroffensive.

April 29: Red counteroffensive comes to abrupt halt after carrying to outskirts of Seoul in west, and forty miles south of 38th Parallel in central Korea.

May 3: U.N. forces launch a limited-objective attack to regain former positions and reestablish contact with enemy.

May 16: Enemy launches second spring offensive with approximately twenty-one divisions across seventy-five-mile front.

May 19: U.N. forces halt enemy drive on western front and launch savage counterattack.

May 21: U.N. forces halt enemy drive on eastern front and counterattack.

June 24: Jacob Malik, Russia's U.N. representative, advocates cease-fire in radio speech.

June 30: General Ridgway proposes meeting to discuss armistice; suggests Danish hospital ship in Wonsan harbor as site.

July 10: First meeting between U.N. and North Korean–Chinese delegations held at Kaesong.

July 26: After tenth meeting, the two delegations announce agreement on five-point order of business.

August 15: Far East Air Forces start "Operation Strangle," an interdiction campaign against railroad tracks, bridges, and highway traffic.

August 23: Communists suspend armistice negotiations, after charging that U.N. aircraft had attacked Kaesong.

August 31: U.N. forces open drive against northern portion of Punchbowl area, securing their objectives on September 18.

October 25: Armistice talks resumed at Panmunjom as delegates meet for 27th plenary session.

November 12: General Ridgway orders Eighth Army to cease offensive operations and to begin an active defense of its front.

November 27: Plenary session agenda item number two—military demarcation line—ratified by both sides.

December 2: "Operation Rat-Killer" launched against guerillas in Chirisan mountain area.

December 5: U.S. 45th Infantry Division reaches Korea.

December 18: Both sides exchange prisoner lists. United Nations holds 132,474 Red prisoners. Communist list contains 11,559 names.

1952

January 11: U.S. 40th Infantry Division reaches Korea.

January 24: Korean truce negotiations stalemated.

February 16: U.S. warships start second year of shelling and blockade of Wonsan.

March 20: Agreement on ports of entry, through which men and supplies would move to and from Korea during truce, reached by U.N. and Communist delegates.

May 7: Brigadier General Francis T. Dodd, commander of U.N. Prisoner-of-War Camp Number One on Koje-do, is seized and held for seventy-eight hours by Communist prisoners.

May 12: General Mark W. Clark takes over from General Ridgway as Supreme Commander.

June 10: "Operation Break-up," resettlement of Koje Island prisoners in five hundred-inmate stockades, is completed.

June 23: Large-scale U.N. air attack knocks out 90 per cent of North Korea's power supply.

July 10: Korean truce talks enter second year (101st plenary session of armistice negotiations).

August 14: Prisoner-of-War Command established.

August 29: The Fifth Air Force carries out the largest raid of the Korean War on Pyongyang, North Korean capital.

October 6: Enemy troops, estimated at from ten thousand to fifteen thousand, launch largest Red attack of year northwest of Chorwon.

October 8: Truce teams agree to indefinite recess.

October 15: Large U.S. amphibious force fakes invasion and conducts training exercise off northeast Korea below Wonsan.

1953

January 25: "Operation Smack" starts on west-central front.

February 11: General Van Fleet turns over command of Eighth Army to Lieutenant General Maxwell D. Taylor.

April 6: U.N. and Reds open talks on exchange of sick and wounded prisoners.

April 11: Agreement reached on prisoner exchange—605 U.N. troops for 6,030 Reds.

April 20–May 3: Period of prisoner exchange, Operation "Little Switch."

April 26: Communists complete return of 684 sick and injured U.N. prisoners. The exchange consists of 471 South Koreans, 149 Americans, 32 Britons, 15 Turks, 6 Colombians, 5 Australians, 2 Canadians, 1 Netherlander, 1 Filipino, 1 South African, and 1 Greek.

May 3: First round of sick and wounded exchange completed in Panmunjom when U.N. finishes turning back 5,194 North Korean and 1,030 Chinese soldiers and 446 North Korean civilians.

May 7: Red negotiators concede that the war prisoners unwilling to return to Communist control may be placed in neutral custody.

May 14: Deadlock develops in truce negotiations over plans for handling prisoners who object to returning to North Korea.

May 16: Truce talks recessed.

May 24: Allied warships enter Wonsan harbor, bombard port.

May 25: A new U.N. armistice plan on PW's submitted to Reds.

May 27: U.S. Fifth Air Force reports fifty-one Red MIG-15 jets downed since May 1 at cost of only one U.S. Sabre jet.

May 29: Chinese strike at 25th Division outposts in one of the heaviest blows of the year.

June 8: U.N. and Red delegates sign an agreement on PW's. Vigorous opposition voiced by President Syngman Rhee and South Korean government.

June 11: Attacks by Chinese Reds renewed against South Korean II Corps.

June 18: South Koreans release twenty-seven thousand North Korean anti-Red PW's rather than turn them over to a custodial commission as specified in the proposed truce agreement.

June 20: Truce negotiations suspended.

June 25: Communist troops attack South Korean positions on east-central front; anti-armistice demonstrations staged in Seoul by South Koreans.

June 30: Sabre jets score biggest one-day kill of the war by shooting down fifteen MIG-15's over North Korea.

July 13–20: Last major battle of the Korean War; Chinese Reds open major attack, driving South Korean units from a sixty square mile area to flatten out the U.N.'s Kumsong River bulge.

July 16: U.N. troops begin counterattack on east-central front in Kumhwa-Kumsong area; Red truce delegates request a recess after being warned either to sign an armistice soon or break off the talks.

July 27: Armistice agreement signed at Panmunjom at 10 A.M., the war ending twelve hours later.

: C :

COMMUNIST "HISTORY" OF THE
"MARCH 18 POLITICAL STRUGGLE"

The following is excerpted from a lengthy document captured by a U.N. search party at Camp 1-A (Choguri, on Koje Island) in July 1953.[1] The captured document is itself only part of a much longer one covering more events. Its central points are presented here as a statement by Communists, after the fact, of the rationale for the crucial acts in which their resistance to U.N. authority shifted from passive to aggressive, and as a sample of the intellectual diet on which PW's in Communist-controlled compounds lived throughout the last fifteen months of the Korean conflict.

Parts of the document have been omitted in order to reduce its repetitiveness.

II. *The character, aim, direction, and course of the March 18 political struggle against the unlawful voluntary repatriation.*

    1. *Character:*
        a. It is a struggle of justice against the political intrigue of the unlawful voluntary repatriation and the inhuman butchery policy of the U.S. imperialists toward the PW's.
        b. It is a rightful struggle for the PW's to return to the fatherland.
    2. *Aim:*
        a. To expose, denounce, and frustrate the rearmament of the PW's and the political intrigue of voluntary repatriation of the U.S. imperialists, for the maintenance of the people's democratic system.
        b. To ensure freedom and human rights in accordance with the international laws and regulations, by disclosing the true facts about the unlawful and inhuman slaughter policy of the U.S. imperialists toward the PW's; to give political support to the comrades fighting against bloody massacre and threat of the U.S. imperialists by stopping the forced demonstration for voluntary repatriation [2] and by furnishing the Communist side at the armistice talk with essential means to expose the falsehood and deception of the U.S. imperialists' political intrigue.
        c. To give support to the fighting Korean people and partisans.

[1] Captured Document D-1-1-A-69, Communist Instructional Material, obtained July 15, 1953, in Enclosure 2, Camp 1-A.
[2] The demonstrations being conducted in anti-Communist compounds.

　　　　d. To contribute to the victory of peace-loving peoples of the world and receive support from them.

　　　　e. To disclose the inhuman political system of the U.S. imperialists and inflict on them a crushing defeat in political morality.

　　3. *Direction:*

　　　　a. To organize and carry out the masses' political struggle by holding a rally against unlawful voluntary repatriation in each compound.

　　　　b. To organize and carry out the masses' demonstration to frustrate the forced demonstration supporting unlawful voluntary repatriation.

　　　　c. To strengthen the struggle individually or collectively to expose and denounce the slaughter policy of the U.S. imperialists.

　　4. *Course:*

　　　　a. To adopt a written protest to be sent to commanders of USFEC and the Koje Island, and to the International Red Cross, a written petition to Marshal Kim Il Sung, and a message to Stalin and Premier Mao at the mass meeting.

　　　　b. To hoist the flags of the [North Korean Peoples'] Republic, the Soviet Union, and the Communist China in each compound, and hold a demonstration with the portraits of Kim, Stalin, and Mao, placards and slogans.

　　　　c. To post banners around compounds and continue to expose and denounce unlawfulness of the U.S. imperialists.

　　　　d. To continue to file a written protest by each individual and inflict a crushing defeat upon the U.S. imperialists in political morality. . . .

III.　*March 18 uprising.*

　　1.　The political struggle of the North Korean and the Chinese PW's against voluntary repatriation, which was caused mainly by the demonstration supporting unlawful voluntary repatriation, begun on March 13 at the instigation of the U.S. imperialists, started at 5:15 P.M. on March [18?] with Compounds 76 and 78 as the center along with the hoisting of the Republic's flag and a chorus of the national anthem. The comrades of Compounds 95, 85, 92 and 62 followed. . . .

　　2.　At the mass meeting held on the morning of March 19. . . .

　　3.　Contents of a written protest to be sent to Ridgway. . . .

　　4.　The masses' demonstration continued until March 20, in which the PW's shouted slogans with portraits, placards, and hand-flags in their hands. The slogans were:

　　　　a. Immediately suspend the political intrigue of unlawful voluntary repatriation.

　　　　b. Immediately cease to threaten, intimidate, and menace the PW's.

　　　　c. Immediately stop the forced demonstration supporting unlawful voluntary repatriation.

　　　　d. Ensure human rights and freedom to the PW's in accordance with the international laws and regulations.

　　　　e. Abolish the slavish CIE education.

　　　　f. Immediately suspend the PW's alienation policy.

　　　　g. Immediately stop the PW's rearmament policy.

　　　　h. North Korean and Chinese PW's! Don't betray your fatherland and the people to the last!

5. The U.S. imperialists, bewildered with the March 18 uprising, issued an order in the name of Dodd on March 20 prohibiting the hoisting of any national flag as well as slogan and placard. The demonstration supporting unlawful voluntary repatriation was suspended. The slavish CIE education was abolished, and the flags of South Korea, the U.N., the U.S. and Chiang Kai-shek disappeared in some compounds.

6. Evading an answer to the PW's, the U.S. imperialists, with an effort to alleviate and stamp out our struggle of justice, carried out an economic blockade of all the compounds from May 19 until May 28 by reducing food and stopping cigarette ration. However, this attempt ended in a complete failure and the U.S. imperialists suffered a serious defeat politically and morally.

7. Dodd, head of the U.S. imperialistic murderers, implored us to remove the flags of the Republic, the Soviet Union, and the Communist China, as well as placards and slogans, which were made by our efforts, and they also attempted to stamp out our struggle by intimidatory or conciliatory measures. But the attempt was frustrated with our stubborn struggle.

IV. *Significance of the March 18 political struggle against unlawful voluntary repatriation.*

1. *The results of the struggle.*

a. The sporadic political struggle developed into an extensive, unified political struggle against inhumanity and unlawfulness of the U.S. imperialists.

b. The true nature of the political intrigue of unlawful voluntary repatriation was exposed and denounced, the demonstration supporting unlawful voluntary repatriation failed and the inhumanity of the U.S. political system was disclosed.

c. The slavish CIE education was abolished.

d. The political and ideological support was given to the comrades groaning under the oppression of the reactionary terrorists.

e. Direct and material support was given to the Communist side at the truce talk to expose and denounce the intrigue of unlawful voluntary repatriation, and the falseness and deception of the U.S. imperialists.

f. This struggle served as a great political encouragement to the fighting Korean people and the entire peace-loving peoples.

g. Political support was given to the inhabitants around the compounds [3] and at the same time the PW's won sympathy from them. . . .

.   .   .   .

3. *Conclusion.*

The March 18 political struggle developed into a new stage. It has been proved both by the bloody 170 years history and by the PW-slaughter policy of the U.S. imperialists that the U.S. imperialists pay no regard to dignity and morality for the achievement of their political ambitions and that such cannibal slaughter policy as seen in the ancient dark ages has resulted from the true nature of the U.S. imperialism.

We have learned from our bitter experiences that to submit to the PW policy of the U.S. imperialists is the road to the war slavery and cannon-

[3] Natives of Koje-do whose villages were directly adjacent to the camp.

fodder, and that to fight against it is the only road to victory and liberation.

It has been proved that the PWs' struggle against voluntary repatriation of the U.S. imperialists crushed down the aggressive power and inflicted a crushing defeat upon the U.S. imperialists politically and morally, with patriotism, having no fear of death and blood, and with a firm unity for struggle, and that a victory is gained by a strong fighting spirit for the fatherland, the people and the premier, and only through struggle.

.   .   .   .

Chapter III. *The May 7 political struggle for the detention of Dodd.*

A.   *Undisguised brutalities of the U.S. imperialists.*

The U.S. imperialists, who suffered a crushing defeat politically and morally in the North Korean and Chinese PWs' March 18 political struggle against unlawful vountary repatriation, continued a wholesale slaughter and the rearmament of the PW's, slandering the political system of the people's Republic and becoming frantic with an attempt to justify voluntary repatriation.

1.   Immediately after the March 18 political struggle, the U.S. imperialists carried out an economic blockade of all the compounds by reducing food and cigarette ration in an effort to stamp out our struggle of justice.

a. From April 21, the U.S. imperialists committed such cannibal brutalities as to stop cigarette ration completely and reduce food by half to Compounds Nos. 76, 77, and 78.[4]

b. On March 28, the U.S. imperialists stopped cigarette ration to the Compound No. 95, and carried out an economic blockade of the said compound from April 2 to 14.

c. . . . (Illegible)

d. The U.S. imperialists reduced or stopped the medical supplies to the dispensaries in all the compounds, and completely shut down the medical facilities.

2.   The slaughter of the PW's was continued openly in the daytime by the U.S. imperialistic murderers.

a. On March 30, '52, Comrade Choe Chi Kook was shot to death.

b. In Compound No. 78, Comrade Lee Sung Paek was shot to death on April 24, '52. . . . .

.   .   .   .

f. A wholesale slaughter took place in every compound on the Koje Island from March to April '52.

3.   The U.S. imperialistic murderers continuously increased military power around the compounds.

B.   *The U.S. imperialists continued the efforts to rationalize and justify unlawful voluntary repatriation.*

1.   In order to conceal a wholesale slaughter of the PW's, the U.S. imperialists made another vicious plan of the so-called "forced alienation" and fabricated "non-repatriation PW's" by force and bloodshed.[5]

---

[4] These compounds had in fact refused to allow U.S. personnel to enter their gates.

[5] This refers to the screening in which about fifty thousand North Korean and Chinese PW's declared their determination forcibly to resist repatriation.

2. Brigadier General Dodd, commander of the Koje-do PW Camp, announced that individual interviews would be carried out by April 5, '52. The murderer, Dodd, concealed and deceived the bloody nature of the forced interviews with falseness, deception, and flowery words. On April 5, Dodd issued a statement and at the same time called up all the spokesmen for each compound and forced them to undergo the forced interviews with threats, intimidation, and menace. The forced interviews were carried out from April 9 in each compound. Compounds Nos. 71, 72, 73, 74, 81, 82, 83, 84, 91, 93, 94, and 96 turned into a sea of blood.

3. The U.S. imperialistic murderers moved from the Koje Island to the main land some 20,000 "non-repatriate PW's" [6] whom they classified by force.

4. On Koje Island remained the comrades of Compounds Nos. 76, 77, 78, 85, 92, 95, 62, and 66 whom they could not classify even by force.

5. The true nature of the political intrigue of the U.S. imperialists was revealed in such bloody forced classification. . . .

C. *The continued March 18 political struggle against unlawful voluntary repatriation developed into the struggle against the forced classification of the PW's by the U.S. imperialists.*

The patriotic North Korean and Chinese PW's launched out in each compound a struggle to disclose and frustrate the crafty political intrigue of the bloody forced classification. . . .

1. Slogans for the struggle: . . . .

2. The U.S. imperialists could not succeed in carrying out the forced interviews on the comrades of Compounds Nos. 76, 77, 78, 85, 92, 95, 62, 66, and their plot was frustrated by the general boycotting struggle of the PW's.

A great political support was given, with the continued hoisting of the flags of the Republic, the Soviet Union, and Communist China, and the shouting of slogans, to the patriotic PW's of the compounds where the forced interviews were carried out.

3. The U.S. imperialists plotted to carry out the forced classification in the democratic compounds by bloody means.

On April 10, the U.S. imperialists made a challenge to Compound No. 95 by shooting the PW's willfully, and around 6 P.M. on the same day two platoons of the U.S. hired army and one platoon of the puppet army,[7] who were fully armed, intruded into the compound under the direct command of Dodd. When they started firing machine guns blindly, comrades of Compound No. 95 made a counterattack with the clubs and stones prepared in advance, killed 13 persons and wounded 35 of the intruders, thus completely repulsing the enemy and frustrating their crafty political intrigue. In this incident 14 of our comrades were shot to death and some 70 were wounded by the enemy's machine-gun fire. . . .

4. On the true state of "the forced classification."

Before the forced interview was carried out, the U.S. imperialists sneaked into compounds spies and 100 daggers. . . . (illegible)

April 10, the PW's who wanted to be repatriated were slaughtered.

The engineer battalion, by directive of the 94th MPs, supplied the ill-

---

[6] Actual figure: Almost ninety thousand (approximately thirty-five thousand North Koreans, fifteen thousand Chinese, thirty-nine thousand South Koreans).
[7] The South Korean army.

natured PW's with 100 clubs, 200 daggers (supplied special agents with 200 daggers and 100 clubs), dug 74 holes for the purpose of burying dead bodies of the PW's, establishing electric torture rooms in each compound.

250 PW's who wanted to be repatriated were massacred. . . . [illegible]

Before the forced interviews, the U.S. imperialists sneaked into the 81st brigade two cases of daggers, one pistol and one hundred flash light batteries. . . .

D. *Significance of the struggle for the detention of Dodd.*

1. The political intrigue of unlawful voluntary repatriation of the U.S. imperialists was disclosed in writing.

2. The political system of the people's democracy, fabricated by the U.S. imperialists, was disclosed and denounced.

3. Our struggle has changed into a struggle for peace. . . .

: D :

IMPACT OF COMMUNIST CONTROL
TECHNIQUES ON A DISSIDENT PW

The several techniques employed by Communist PW elites to ensure conformity and belief have been described in the body of this report and in other documents; their cumulative impact upon an individual prisoner of war is suggested by the following account. Kim Shik Won, a young North Korean from a Christian family, was frozen out of a series of jobs under the Communists after 1945. When the "Fatherland Liberation War" came, however, he was drafted and commissioned because of his experience as aide to a physician-surgeon. Captured by U.N. forces, he was placed in Compound 66, the North Korean officers' compound on Koje-do, which from its inception was solidly Communist-dominated. When the Koje compounds were broken up, the officers were transferred to the nearby island of Yoncho-do. There Kim lived for a year, until he was able to defect immediately prior to boarding ship for repatriation.

The following account of Kim's experience in U.N. Compound PW camps is distilled from the body of a series of searching interviews with him (KN-7). He was first interviewed within an hour of his defection from Communist control; after a lapse of several days, the interrogation was resumed for the equivalent of three full days. Neither the interviewer nor the anti-Communist PW's who received Kim found reason to doubt his story.

They tried to change my mind and convert me to Communism. . . . There was an educational hour, and we had to study political science and military science. In political science, we had to learn the history of the Communist party of the Soviet Union and then learn all "the criminal acts of the American imperialists" and then "the history of the PW fight." In military science, we had to learn all the military regulations of the North Korean army. . . . According to the "history of the criminal acts of the American imperialists," twenty-seven thousand PW's have been killed by the imperialists since October, 1950; the method is that they have been frozen, starved, killed by disease and by medical experimentation. . . . The PW's were not properly supplied with food and clothing and hence got sick. Also, sometimes . . . the U.S. authorities issued the wrong medicine. . . .

They tried to lead us into real Communism—to Marx, Lenin, etc. They taught us the history of human life from ancient times up to the Russian Revolution, and the struggle between the bourgeoisie and the proletariat; that our government is for the people and . . . is run by the people's will.

Sometimes they had a lecture for all the PW's, but those who were weak in Communist spirit . . . those who were not willing to cooperate with them . . . were specially educated . . . taught individually. I was one such. . . .

After mastering these subjects, everybody was supposed to put these principles into practice. If you did not do so, you were marked as a man who violated regulations. After the political lessons the individual PW's were supposed to go out to the crowd of PW's and make a speech about what they had learned. On the day after learning a particular lesson each PW was examined by the Communists, and he must answer each question correctly or he was treated as a person who was not earnest. . . . The PW's are supposed to model themselves after the Russian Communist party efforts—for example, fighting against reactionaries and capitalists not only in the compound but in the "Fatherland Liberation War" as well. . . .

Almost every day they held [self- and mutual] criticism meetings in the compound. They discussed how to defeat capitalism and to improve their ways. . . .

Those who could speak English or had a good educational background were not trusted [because this meant that] they must have been wealthy in most cases. Also, they don't trust anyone who has any kind of religion. Once I was scolded by them because I had been a Christian. . . .

The Communist leaders collected personal histories from all the PW's, not once but frequently. Then they matched the first one with the second, the third, etc. If a man gave the same information in each one, the party leaders looked into him and found other PW's with the same home town, or the same army unit, or who had been friends of his in the past either as a PW or in North Korea. . . . They conducted secret investigations on the background of the PW, and found out whether he was a capitalist in the past or was born a capitalist, and whether he was a reactionary or an earnest Communist. . . . They asked the other PW how the man in question acted, and he had to answer. The answers had to be consistent with the answers given in the first man's personal histories. . . . [If a man wrote differing personal histories] the Communist leaders did not bother him; they pretended to know nothing about it, but they blacklisted him. . . .

The Communists always made propaganda to all the PW's that all PW's had already committed a crime by being captured—including the Communists. Therefore, they said, the PW's would be punished, and must be punished, by the North Korean government. In addition, they said, if a PW neglected his duty in the camp and acted against the North Korean Army, he would be more heavily punished. . . . They propagandized that even if some PW's opposed repatriation, all would in fact be repatriated in accordance with the North Korean proposal at Panmunjom, and that after repatriation many PW's would be killed. Thus the PW's were threatened. . . .

[As for me] they never trusted me, never permitted me to learn about the secrets of the organization. . . . There were several organizations in the compound to resist the U.N. personnel and make demonstrations against U.N. authority. [I was distrusted because] in the planning of these I only followed;

I did not assist in the planning. . . . Another reason was that I did not obey the orders of the battalion headquarters. . . . [For example] the leaders often put out orders to have a week for strengthening military courtesy and military regulations. In such periods the PW's were supposed to respect and bow down to the leaders as much as possible and observe strictly the internal regulations. If anyone didn't, he would be marked by the others.

Also, those who read the books supplied by the International Red Cross representatives were blacklisted. I read [them] and was told by the Communists to reflect on my behavior and thinking. . . . Those who read such books were told that their minds were corrupt, [although] the Communist staff members themselves read them. . . . One day I got a Red Cross book about the life of the farmer in the U.S. . . . I said, "According to this book, America is the most advanced country, a good place for poor people." Immediately one PW called me into another room and asked, "What did you say?" I told him, and he said: "You are entirely mistaken, and, frankly, you lack respect for Russia. That means you haven't studied hard about Russia." [They always said that] Russia is the most advanced country politically, and the most mighty military force, on the foundation of Stalin's military science. [There follow numerous illustrations of the further claim that Russia is the most advanced country economically.] . . . I let them talk, listened, and let it all come out the other ear. . . .

I don't remember anything in particular [that I believed], but I thought it might be true. They kept on trying. . . . I was very happy to read such books, very grateful for them. They were very helpful in making up my mind. . . . In North Korea, I could not compare things; I could read only one side. Since being captured, I could read about the other side, and by that I have found that what they said was false. . . . I thought about the philosophy of Marxism, and I saw with my own eyes and read that what the Communists said was false. . . .

[I was marked as weak in Communist spirit and given special instruction because, one day] when a group of PW's were talking together (and watching) nearby American tractors and trucks, I said, "U.S. tractors and trucks are very convenient for our life." Then the PW instructor said, "Yes, I think so, but what you have to know is that in Russia and North Korea they have better machines than that". . . .

As long as we were in Koje, I was suspected, but the Communists couldn't find any definite information about me. But when we were moved to Yoncho-do [in spring, 1952] there were other PW's from the same home town, and they found out I was a Christian and had owned land . . . and that my cousin had come down to South Korea. . . . My name was put on the blacklist to be reported to North Korea for lack of patriotism. . . .

[In addition to special instruction for those who were distrusted, the Communists] had their own courts, in the platoon and in the company, and they tried those of us who were born capitalist or were reactionaries and punished us. . . . They held a people's court for me, they selected a judge, and they convicted me. . . . They made me [criticize myself publicly]. Anyone who refused to reflect upon himself in the court was killed later without the knowledge of anyone. . . .

The method of fighting the reactionary . . . to isolate him from other PW's. . . . I was isolated on Koje-do, but not completely. When we came to

Yoncho-do I was completely isolated. [On Koje-do] I had a chance to talk to PW's like the others but I was never told about important matters. On Yoncho-do none would talk to me at all. . . . The other PW's do not talk to such a reactionary [as I was], and do not give any information except very common knowledge such as what he is supposed to do each day to keep order in the compound. . . . When they had political or military classes, sometimes I was sick, but they forced me to attend by pulling at my clothes. . . . [A man who is treated this way] will come to hate the Communists. . . . I was not treated as a human being, and I did as I pleased without obeying orders. All I wanted to do was get out of the compound. . . . I felt that I was going crazy. Since I was isolated I was disappointed. [Because of the Communist propaganda about punishment and] because I had been blacklisted as a reactionary, I worried about my future after repatriation. . . .

[However,] the Communists try to prevent anybody from surrendering [to the U.N. authorities] so as to prevent the disclosure of secrets. Each sub-squad of three men is headed by one who must report constantly to the squad leader on the other two. If the sub-squad leader suspects anyone as a reactionary they don't give him a chance to go out of the compound, even on work details, and they keep their eyes on him. . . . There is also an independent platoon called the security platoon . . . directly under the battalion commander. Its mission is to guard the staff members; it consists of strong, most trustworthy party members. [It also watches] the movements and activities of the other PW's while they are on duty and reports on them if anyone sleeps or neglects his watch against the enemy [i.e., against U.N. search parties or other movements]. . . . From the time we came to Yoncho-do [more than a year ago] I have been trying to find a chance to get out, but I had no chance because the Communists would not let anyone except those who were trusted even go near the gate. Only they could talk to U.S. personnel at the gate, receive tools, etc. When I fell sick they wouldn't let me go to the dispensary. . . . I might have done it by speaking to the American personnel at the head-court, but I couldn't speak English. I might have spoken to the KATUSA's [Korean military personnel attached to U.S. units] but I was afraid the other PW's would be able to kill me if I did; I couldn't find a good opportunity.

Bibliography

BIBLIOGRAPHY

Almond, Gabriel A., *et al. The Appeals of Communism.* Princeton: Princeton University Press, 1954.

Barnett, A. Doak. *Hsueh Hsi: Weapon of Ideological Revolution in China.* American Universities Field Staff, March 5, 1954.

Bauer, Alice H. *A Guide for the Interviewing of Soviet Escapees.* (Project on the Soviet Social System.) Cambridge, Mass.: Russian Research Center, Harvard University, April, 1953.

Bauer, Raymond A. *The Developmental History of the Political Attitude of Individuals toward the Soviet Regime.* (Project on the Soviet Social System.) Cambridge, Mass.: Russian Research Center, Harvard University, March 31, 1952.

———. *The Social Psychology of Loyalty to and Disaffection from the Soviet Regime.* (Project on the Soviet Social System.) Cambridge, Mass.: Russian Research Center, Harvard University, October, 1954.

Belden, Jack. *China Shakes the World.* New York: Harper, 1949.

Benben, John S. "Education of Prisoners of War on Koje Island, Korea," *Educational Record* (April, 1955): 157–73.

Biderman, Albert D. *March to Calumny.* New York: Macmillan, 1963.

———. "The Image of Brainwashing," *The Public Opinion Quarterly,* 26 (Winter, 1962): 547–63.

Blumer, Herbert. "Collective Behavior," *New Outline of the Principles of Sociology,* ed. Alfred McClung Lee. New York: Barnes and Noble, 1946, 199–221.

Brandt, C., Schwartz, B., and Fairbank, J. K. *A Documentary History of Chinese Communism.* Cambridge, Mass.: Harvard University Press, 1952.

Bunzel, R., and Weakland, J. H. *An Anthropological Approach to Chinese Communism* (mimeo.). (Research on Contemporary Cultures.) New York: Columbia University, April, 1952.

Burchette, W., and Winnington, A. *Koje Unscreened.* Peking: By the Authors, Box 545, April, 1953.

Center for International Studies. *Chinese Communist Police System.* Cambridge, Mass.: Massachusetts Institute of Technology, 1955.

Compton, Boyd, trans. *Mao's China: Party Reform Documents, 1942–1944.* Seattle: University of Washington Press, 1952.

Creel, Herrlee, G. *Chinese Thought from Confucius to Mao Tse-tung.* Chicago: University of Chicago Press, 1953.

Fairbank, John K. *The United States and China.* Cambridge, Mass.: Harvard University Press, 1948.

Friedrich, Carl J., ed. *Totalitarianism*. Cambridge, Mass.: Harvard University Press, 1954.

Gourlay, Walter E. *The Chinese Communist Cadre: Key to Political Control*. Cambridge, Mass.: Russian Research Center, Harvard University, 1952.

Harris, Frank J. *Training the Combat Rifleman in the Chinese Communist Forces and North Korean Army*. ORO-T-52 (FEC). Chevy Chase, Md.: Operations Research Office, The Johns Hopkins University, 1954.

Hansen, Kenneth K. *Heroes Behind Barbed Wires*. Princeton, N.J.: D. Van Nostrand, 1957.

Hsu, Francis L. K. *Under the Ancestors' Shadow*. New York: Columbia University Press, 1948.

———. *Americans and Chinese: Two Ways of Life*. New York: Henry Schuman, 1953.

Hu, Hsien Chin. "The Chinese Concepts of 'Face,'" *American Anthropologist* 46 (1944): 45–64.

Hunter, Edward. *Brain Washing in Red China*. New York: Vanguard Press, 1951.

———. *Brainwashing: The Story of the Men Who Defied It*. New York: Farrar, Straus, 1956.

Inkeles, Alex. *Public Opinion in Soviet Russia*. Cambridge, Mass.: Harvard University Press, 1950.

Janowitz, Morris, and Little, Roger. *Sociology and the Military Establishment*. New York: Russell Sage Foundation, 1965.

Kendall, Willmoore, trans. and ed. *A Communist Party in Action*, by A. Rossi, pseud. New Haven: Yale University Press, 1949.

Kierman, Frank A. *The Chinese Intelligentsia and the Communists*. Cambridge, Mass.: Center for International Studies, Massachusetts Institute of of Technology, 1954.

Kluckhohn, C., and Murray, H. A., eds. *Personality in Nature, Society and Culture*, 2d ed. New York: Alfred A. Knopf, 1953.

Lazarfeld, F., and Rosenberg, M., eds. *The Language of Social Research: A Reader in the Methodology of Social Research*. Glencoe, Ill.: The Free Press, 1955.

Levy, Marion J. *The Family Revolution in Modern China*. Cambridge, Mass.: Harvard University Press, 1949.

Lifton, Robert J. *Thought Reform and the Psychology of Totalism*. New York: W. W. Norton, 1961.

Lindsay, Michael. *Notes on Educational Policy in Communist China*. New York: Institute of Pacific Relations, 1950.

Lieu Shaw-tong. *Out of Red China*. Boston: Little, Brown, 1953.

Liu Shao-chi. *How to be a Good Communist*. New York: New Century Publishers, 1952.

Mao Tse-tung. *Selected Works*, vol. I. London: Lawrence & Wishart, 1954.

Marx, Karl. *The Eighteenth Brumaire of Louis Bonaparte*. New York: International Publishers, 1964.

Mead, M., and Metraux, R. *The Study of Culture at a Distance*. Chicago: University of Chicago Press, 1953.

Meerloo, Joost A. M. "The Crime of Menticide," *American Journal of Psychiatry* 107 (1951): 594–98.

————. "Pavlovian Strategy as a Weapon of Menticide," *American Journal of Psychiatry* 110 (1954): 809–13.

Milosz, Czeslaw. *The Captive Mind*. New York: Alfred A. Knopf, 1953.

Parsons, Talcott. *The Social System*. Glencoe, Ill.: The Free Press, 1951.

Parsons, Talcott, and Shils, E. A., eds. *Toward a General Theory of Action*. Cambridge, Mass.: Harvard University Press, 1951.

Pye, Lucian W. *Some Observations on the Political Behavior of Overseas Chinese*. Cambridge, Mass.: Center for International Studies, Massachusetts Institute of Technology, 1954.

Rigg, Robert L. *Red China's Fighting Hordes*. Harrisburg, Pa.: Military Service Publishing Company, 1951.

Rostow, W. W. *A Comparison of Russian and Chinese Societies Under Communism*. Cambridge, Mass.: Center for International Studies, Massachusetts Institute of Technology, 1954.

Rostow, W. W., et al. *The Prospects for Chinese Communist Society*. Cambridge, Mass.: Center for International Studies, Massachusetts Institute of Technology, 1954.

————. "Russia and China Under Communism," *World Politics* 7 (July, 1955): 592–606.

Rowe, David N., et al., eds. *China: An Area Manual*, vols. I and II. ORO-T-229 Chevy Chase, Md.: Operations Research Office, The Johns Hopkins University, 1954 and 1955.

Schwartz, Benjamin I. *Chinese Communism and the Rise of Mao*. Cambridge, Mass.: Harvard University Press, 1952.

Segal, Julius. "Factors Related to the Collaboration and Resistance Behavior of U.S. Army PW's in Korea." *HumRRO Technical Report No. 33*. Washington: Human Resources Research Office, George Washington University, 1956.

Selznick, Philip. *The Organizational Weapon*. New York: McGraw-Hill, 1952.

Shils, E., and Janowitz, M. "Cohesion and Disintegration in the *Wehrmacht* in World War II," *Public Opinion Quarterly* 12 (Summer, 1948): 280–315.

U.S. Department of the Army. *Comments Concerning a Report by the Red Cross Society of China Entitled "Report of the Investigation of Medical Atrocities and Malpractices Committed by U.S. Armed Forces in Korea on Sick and Wounded Chinese People—Volunteer Prisoners of War."* Washington: Office of the Surgeon General, 1954.

U.S. Department of the Army. "Communist Interrogation, Indoctrination and Exploitation of Prisoners of War." *Pamphlet no. 30–101*. Washington: Government Printing Office, May, 1956.

U.S. Department of the Army. "Geneva Conventions of 12 August 1949 for the Protection of War Victims." *Pamphlet no. 20–150*. Washington: Government Printing Office, October, 1950.

Walker, Richard L. *China Under Communism: The First Five Years*. New Haven: Yale University Press, 1955.

Weber, Max. *The Religion of China*. Glencoe, Ill.: The Free Press, 1951.

White, William L. *The Captives of Korea: An Unofficial White Paper*. New York: Charles Scribner's Sons, 1957.

Whiting, Allen S. "The New Chinese Communist," *World Politics* 4 (July, 1955): 595–606.

Winfield, Gerald F. *China: The Land and the People.* New York: William Sloane Associates, 1948.

Yang, C. K. *A Chinese Village and Its Early Change under Communism.* Cambridge, Mass.: Center for International Studies, Massachusetts Institute of Technology, 1954.

———. *The Chinese Family in the Communist Revolution.* Cambridge, Mass.: Center for International Studies, Massachusetts Institute of Technology, 1954.

Yang, Martin. *A Chinese Village.* New York: Columbia University Press, 1948.

Index

INDEX

Adjustment: pre-communist background, effect of, 25, 26; patterns of, 192–99; variation in, 199–204

Advancement, criteria for, 99–100

Agitation: communist examples of, 267, 268, 269; susceptibility of PW's to, 269, 279; anti-communist examples of, 271. *See also* Prisoner of war organizations

Alienation, from Chinese communists: reasons for, 38, 47–48, 52, 54, 55. *See also* Attitudes, political, determinants of

—from U.N. custodial authorities, reasons for, 320–22

Analysis of data: difficulty in, xxv; methodological questions raised in, xxv–xxvi; far eastern consultants used in, xxvi; getting the most out of data, 15–17; chronological reconstruction, 212. *See also* Methods

Army, Chinese communist: soldier reactions to authority in, 3; soldier motivations in, 3, 4; characteristic life in, 4; soldier identifications in, 4; close surveillance in, 36; restrictions on marriage in, 37; strict discipline in, 37; reasons for joining, 40; literacy and educational classes in, 40; criticism in, 41; gaining merit in, 42; volunteers for Korea in, 42; control mechanisms in, 47; propaganda for Korean entry of, 52–53, 155; force in soldier behavior in, 110; soldier definitions in, 110; military instructions in Korea in, 156; creation of fighting spirit in, 157. *See also* Indoctrination; Control techniques

Attitudes, toward Chinese communists: loyalty, 40; positive nature of, 42–44; nature of, 53

—political, determinants of: pressure for high conformity, 60–61; personal safety and career advancement, 61, 73–75; discrimination, 62; family safety and status, 62, 79–80, 91; pur-

posefulness of communists, 72; demotion, 75; the unreliables, 76–78; public executions and beatings, 89, 90; unreasonable sanctions, 89–91 *passim*; censorship of mail, 91; marriage and sexual restrictions, 92, 154; sincerity of communists, 93; deception of communists, 94, 95, 96, 97; summary of, 101–4; fear, 141; work exploitation, 147; indoctrination, 148

—pre-capture: of hard-core anti-communists, 276–78; of hard-core communists, 278–279; toward communist ideology, 279–80; of neutrals, 280–81; toward authority, 281–82

—traditional, to authority, Chinese, xxvii–xxviii, 93, 110–11, 243, 282–83

Behavior, determinants of, distinguishing features of, 5

Careers, under Chinese communism: successful nature of, 34; illustrations of, 35–55

Civil information and education program: political objectives of, 218, 219; attitude of PW's toward, 219; characteristics of, 258–59; relation to U.N. camp command, 259; staff of, 259; communist PW objections to, 288; disruptive attempts by communist PW's of, 289; reactions by non- and anti-communist PW's to, 290–91; effects of on anti-communist PW organizations, 292; effects of civilian teachers on PW's, 292

Communism, Chinese: goals of, 45, 57, 59–60, 160; party membership requirements, 46; party secret meetings, 149–50

Conformity: through fear, 49; extent of, 99, 185, 193, 194; in discussion groups, 182, 183; reasons for, 185–86; subjective correlates of, 197–99; distinction between conformity and loyalty, 100

Contact with communism: through communist propaganda, 26–27; as volun-